Other Asias

Other Asias

Gayatri Chakravorty Spivak

BLACKWELL PUBLISHING
350 Main Street, Malden, MA 02148-5020, USA
9600 Garsington Road, Oxford OX4 2DQ, UK
550 Swanston Street, Carlton, Victoria 3053, Australia

First published 2008 by Blackwell Publishing Ltd

1   2008

Library of Congress Cataloging-in-Publication Data

Spivak, Gayatri Chakravorty.
  Other Asias / by Gayatri Chakravorty Spivak.
      p. cm.
  Includes bibliographical references and index.
  ISBN 978-1-4051-0206-3 (hardcover : alk. paper)—ISBN 978-1-4051-0207-0 (pbk. : alk. paper)
1. Asia—Politics and government. 2. Asia—Civilization. I. Title.
  DS35.S69 2007
  950.4'29—dc22

                                        2007009670

A catalogue record for this title is available from the British Library.

Set in 11.5/13.5pt Dante
by SPi Publisher Services, Pondicherry, India
Printed and bound in Singapore
by Fabulous Printers Pte Ltd.

The publisher's policy is to use permanent paper from mills that operate a sustainable forestry policy, and which has been manufactured from pulp processed using acid-free and elementary chlorine-free practices. Furthermore, the publisher ensures that the text paper and cover board used have met acceptable environmental accreditation standards.

For further information on
Blackwell Publishing, visit our website at
www.blackwellpublishing.com

To all my students, everywhere
Those who cannot yet judge this are my silent judges

Contents

Acknowledgments

The following chapters are revised versions of essays previously published by the author and we are grateful to the publishers for permission to use the material:

Chapter 1: "Righting Wrongs" from *Human Rights, Human Wrongs: Oxford Amnesty Lectures* edited by Nicholas Owen (Oxford: Oxford University Press, 2003), pp. 168–227.

Chapter 2: "Responsibility" from *boundary* 2 21:3 (Fall 1994), pp. 19–64. Published by Duke University Press.

Chapter 4: "Foucault and Najibullah" from *Lyrical Symbols and Narrative Transformations: Essays in Honour of Ralph Freedman* edited by Kathy Komar and Ross Shidler (Columbia, SC: Camden House, 1998), pp. 218–35.

Chapter 5: "Megacity" from *Grey Room* 1 (Fall 2000), pp. 8–25. Published by MIT Press.

Chapter 6: "Moving Devi" from *Cultural Critique* 47 (Winter 2001), pp. 120–63. Published by University of Minnesota Press.

Foreword[1]

"Liberal arts professors tend to be arrested young people."
                                                            Stephen Metcalf

Literary criticism in general has become more interested in globalization in the twenty-first century. Because of my sustained interest in
checking out generalizations by seeking entry into subaltern spheres,
I was not fully satisfied with the general cultural arguments about
postmodernism. And now I find myself, for similar reasons, equally
uneasy about the received ideas about culture and globalization.
Indeed, I had been uneasy about this for some time. Earlier I had called
the problem "electronification of the stock exchanges."[2] In these essays
the dissatisfaction is with the easy postnationalism that is supposed to
have come into being with globalization. The solution pondered (not
proposed outright, for such things are practical and situational) is "critical
regionalism." It helps me that Comparative Literature was regionalist
even in its first disciplinary impulses.

The chapters in this book were written before the events of
September 11, 2001. It is clear now

> that the main theatre of the War on Terror is Asia. The whole of Asia
> from West Asia to North East Asia has become the theatre of the war.
> It started in Central Asia with immediate consequences for South Asia.
> Already in January 2002, President Bush included North Korea in the
> "axis of evil." Soon after, the "second front" was officially opened in the
> Philippines in South East Asia.[3] ... In West Asia, also called the Middle
> East, the ongoing wars against Palestine and Iraq were intensified and
> declared to be part of the War on Terror. March 20, 2003 marked the US
> "strike on Iraq" for occupation.[4]

As I prepare the final draft, there is the enterprise of news management
over aid to the tsunami of 2004, legitimizing the war by its apparent

reversal. India has refused foreign aid. Indonesia wants international troops unarmed, however benevolent. Asia news.[5]

The fiftieth anniversary of the first Bandung conference on Asian–African cooperation, organized this time by South Africa, has rekindled hope of a new regionalism. Yet the forces against regionalism are strong.

> Asia in the twenty-first century presents a forbidding picture to the United States in terms of her national security interests. A rapidly threatening China, a resurgent Russia and an extremely hostile and violent Muslim world confronts [sic] the United States. Military flashpoints that are confronting or likely to confront the United States can be listed as Iraq, Iran, Afghanistan, Pakistan and the rapidly rising military power of China, aimed at expelling US military presence in East Asia. Taiwan would emerge as the pretext and the flashpoint.[6]

The signing of the nuclear accord between the United States and India can be seen as an effort to separate India from the possibility of Asian regionalism.[7]

This book, however, is not a polemic against or discussion of the events cited above. I have kept it as it is in the conviction that now more than ever it is important for us not to let the plurality of Asia be selectively studied according to the directions of US foreign policy. First and foremost, the texts offered here provide exercise for imagining pluralized Asias, preparing for an "other" principle of study – that will toughen the polemic when it arises in response to specific situations. That I believe is the role of the humanities, the empowerment of an informed imagination, a modest but difficult task.

I would like to distinguish my position from the pan-Asianism that we have known since the nineteenth century in figures such as Shinpei Goto, Sun Yat Sen, and Rabindranath Tagore.[8] My position is not competitive with other continents.[9] The pluralized Asia I am thinking of not only respects, but attempts to know the differences within Asia as imaginatively as possible. My field is not policy studies. It is comparative literature. I go toward accessing the other through deep language learning in the collectivity of the classroom. I believe that, paradoxically enough, learning to know our differences keeps leading toward all those words that policy studies conjure with: peace, justice, the rights of humanity. Keeps leading, and not inevitably. It is a persistent effort at training the imagination, a task at which we have failed through the progressive rationalization of education all over the world.

In order not only to destabilize capitalism, but to turn capital toward the social, the electorate must be trained in the habits and rituals of democracy. Not once and for all but persistently, forever. One never closes the schools. The lead piece in the book, "Righting Wrongs," delivered at the Oxford chapter of Amnesty International in 2002, discusses the nature of such training. It is a way to keep alive a spirit that might not just want to be "like America, with culture thrown in." Humble as it is, it is the description of the making of another Asia, if you like. The debate between Michael Doyle and Jack Snyder, my colleagues, as to whether we can build a community of democracies worldwide, or whether sudden democratization leads to war, is put within an international frame if one realizes that there can be no democracy if the largest sector of the electorate has no intuition of the public sphere and its relationship to constitutionality.[10] War and peace come after; and no elections can ever be considered fair without this.

It seems unquestionable that sustainable change takes place if change in the human mind supplements institutional change. This conviction itself supplements the other, that institutional change (always in the broadest sense) brings change of mind – epistemic change. Both views seem right. It is only when the latter is projected by rather pre-critical notions of the mental theater and these projections begin to affect policy in a large-scale way that both familiarity with ceaseless subalternization and the lessons learned in the classroom begin to assert themselves. If there are significant epistemic changes underfoot, we "read" the apparent change, often consolidated by the desire of the dominant to have it so. These changes may be described as the "pre-emergent" that Raymond Williams signaled so long ago.[11] The student of the socius must learn to track them, and having tracked them, write them in such a way that the readers of the indefinite future, unencumbered by our specific topicalities, may inhabit them, follow them. It is in this responsibility of writing that thought may become a textual blank for others to suture that makes the confident diagnoses of changes in the "structures of feeling" accompanying globalization banal.[12]

Even if such diagnoses were correct, they describe the effects of institutional change as event. It seems necessary to insist on the distinction between event and task. The ethico-political task of the humanities has always been rearrangement of desires. It must be repeated that the task of the rearrangement of desires engages the imagination of teacher and student – in a pedagogic situation. Any theory of the imagination which uses the English word "imagination" is no doubt linked in some way with the eighteenth- and nineteenth-century German theories. Our effort, however, is to reduce and rarefy this definition to a vulgar minimum – the ability to think absent things. The careful reader will immediately notice that this is almost indistinguishable from thought itself, in its lowest common denominator. That is indeed where pedagogy of the humanities sort starts in its efforts to rearrange desires. If the idea of the imagination thickens into a more literary vehicle – the literary being the terrain where the ability to think absent things has free reign – that does not necessarily mean that the specific rearrangement of desires that may be on the agenda has been successfully accomplished. This is the first constraint. Humanities teaching simply exercises the imagination, makes it ready for such rearrangement.

When the student receives substantive instruction in other matters – history, politics, economics and business, anthropology and cultural studies, science and technology – in school or out, one hopes that an active and robust imagination cannot not engender possibilities that are not necessarily contained in their dominant versions, radical or conservative. I say again and again, there is no guarantee for this. Yet collectivities are not formed without this, change does not stick. This is the second constraint upon the task. To dismiss this as individualistic is tragically shortsighted. And to read literature as evidence of the author's political inclinations is to undo the special gift of the literary.[13]

There is an encompassing constraint within which all work is held. One cannot not coerce while one teaches, however at ease the teacher–class situation may be. Whatever happens, happens in spite of scrupulously intended teaching. That something will have happened is the assurance and constraint in view of which one makes the attempt for a collective rearrangement of desires.

It is the third essay, "Will postcolonialism travel?," focused on Armenia, that taught me the most. I began it with the question of postcolonialism in mind. The occasion for it was a question two former students asked in 1994. The effort to answer took me clear out of the theory of postcolonialism on the model of the history of South Asia. As I kept worrying at it, it took me into the oil route and the complicity of dominant feminism with the march of capitalist globalization.

I was simply not satisfied with the piece, unable to grasp Armenia within that problematic. One of the major problems was the lack of knowledge of Armenian. Postcoloniality cannot be engaged without at least a rudimentary sense of its idiom.[14]

But globalism can. As soon as my search encountered Armenia's positioning in the efforts of the Minsk group, the OSCE (Organization for Security and Cooperation in Europe), UNESCAP, USAID and the like, its position on the oil line, I began to see this small bit of the Caucasus differently. I began to realize how uncertain the shifting outlines of "regions" can be. The fierce nationalism of a millennially diasporic group, Christian in a sea of Islam, has been ready for "postcoloniality" for a long time, but it is very much in the global. I hope the reader will read the essay on Armenia realizing that it is a learning text.

"Righting Wrongs" is a critique of globalism as universalism. It lays out in detail the argument that I began with – engaging the imagination in pedagogy – as a requirement for generating the subject of Human Rights.

This is a general comment on what is now a finished book. What follows is a more personal glance at the writing of it.

I go back 10 years in "Responsibility." The work I describe in 2002, in the first essay, had already started, by happenstance. But I did not know how to code it yet. The best I could do was to think of it as an intellectual challenge. Can I suspend my own training and learn from people with no institutional education? How good is theory at this? I needed to ask. The language is a little forbidding in that essay, because I could not ask the question of theory without entering its protocols. The chief focus of the piece is still the World Bank, not today's broad network of the international civil society. If section one of that chapter is not to your taste, skip it.

"Foucault and Najibullah" was written in 1996 in response to the death of the last Communist president of Afghanistan. It did not seem connected to the occasional earlier piece on Armenia. Putting them together for this volume, the connections came through. I had always felt Derrida's work to be more useful for ethico-political practice than Foucault's. The combination of "Responsibility" and "Foucault and Najibullah" makes it appear. After 9/11 Afghanistan became international news. I have wanted to keep the first flavor of the piece, and revised lightly.

While I was writing these essays, the Balkans and post-Soviet scholarship in general wanted to tap me for postcolonialism, but I did not connect those invitations to diversity with what I was writing. I wrote as follows to a student group that questioned me on this new direction:

"Colonizer" and "colonized" can be fairly elastic if you define scrupulously. When an alien nation-state establishes itself as ruler, impressing its own laws and systems of education, and re-arranging the mode of production for its own economic benefit, one can use these terms, I think. The consequences of applying them to a wide array of political/geographic entities would be dire if we thought colonialism had only one model. On the other hand, if we noticed how different kinds of adventures and projects turn into something that would fit the barebones description given above, we would have a powerful analysis of the politics of progressivism, of one sort or another. How do political philosophies of social justice relate to the overdeterminations of practical politics? This venerable question would receive interesting answers if we considered the irreducibility of the colonial in a situation-specific and flexible way. Additionally, if we cast our glance at the place(s) colonized (according to the rarefied formula above), we encounter great heterogeneity. This provides us an opportunity to study the politics of cultural and epistemic transformation.

The problem with applying these terms to the area you cover would be merely to follow the three most powerful models of colonial discourse theory currently available, belonging to the Middle East, South Asia and Latin America. These refer to colonial adventures undertaken by single nations as exploration and conquest nourished by mercantile capitalism – followed by the expanding market needs of industrial capital. By contrast, your area displaced the political lines of old multi-ethnic imperial formations, Ottoman, Habsburg, Russian. The Eastern edge pushes into terrain that would be even further from the single-nation model. Another great difference is the presence of an articulated ideal – versions of "scientific socialism" – which gave a seemingly greater specificity to the epistemic change. Although the single-nation model was almost invariably accompanied by explicit or implicit "civilizing missions," they did not dictate the political and economic structure of the colonial state directly.

When we look at these differences we realize that using the colonizer–colonized model creatively in your area will enhance existing colonial discourse and postcolonial studies as well as provide you with an interesting model.

Historically, it has always been the powerful who have spoken or been spoken of. I don't know enough about the area under study to go into detail here but, as a feminist and a subalternist, I am used to looking at the pores of elite texts to tease out excluded itineraries. As we move eastwards, the nature of the texts changes. Here, my disciplinary commitments kick in. I want us to use the literary imagination to read sagas and chronicles. As for the postcolonial material, I always go in search of the gendered subaltern. I spoke with women from inner Asia 10 years ago, and to folks from former Soviet Armenia more recently. They spoke of the difficulty of communication with their mothers – and for sure their grandmothers – because Russian gets in the way. (This linguistic barrier crosses the gender line: it was to penetrate this barrier that Najibullah, the last Communist president of Afghanistan, was translating *The Great Game* into Pashto when he died.)[15] The fracturing of gender is somewhat different from the nationalist insistence on native-language politics in the "new" nations bordering on the Russian Federation. However one approaches this, it seems to me a fertile field for real language-based Comparative Literature, much more like Cultural Studies than the older model of East European Comp. Lit. – where the discipline began. Colonial discourse and postcolonial studies have not been good with languages. The areas you study can certainly turn this around. I have long said that history should join hands with literary criticism in search of the ethical as it interrupts the epistemological. Your field can offer spectacular opportunities for such interdisciplinary work.[16]

Reading "Other Asias" assembled, I realized that Armenia and Afghanistan had already led me into this expansion. In both cases, I had been at pains to show how they could not fit the discursive axiomatics of the already-existing postcolonial model. None of these diversifications had much interest in feminism. And it was the collaboration of dominant feminism with the new imperialism that connected this new position with my criticism of the old postcolonialism in *A Critique of Postcolonial Reason*.[17] This appears most strongly in the conclusion to chapter 3.

I had never been persuaded by Latin-American competition for postcolonialism. On the contrary, *The Lettered City* and *The Decline and Fall of the Lettered City* had convinced me that the histories of imperialism in South Asia and Latin America were too close to compete.[18] The history of colonialism in Africa also fits the earlier existing postcolonial model. The case of the Asia-Pacific was, however, significantly different. At my own university, my East Asianist colleague Charles Armstrong wanted no part of postcolonial theory. Yet Wu Hung's work in metropolitan China seemed to me to be an important bit of postcolonialist work.[19] Liao Ping-hui was claiming postcolonial writing for Taiwan. I gathered as much of this debate as I could for an encyclopedia entry.[20] More and more, it seemed to me that the expanding versions of postcolonial theory would have to "pluralize" Asia, rather than singularize it so that it was nothing but one's own region. And that intuition of Asian plurality is prefigured in "Our Asias," the last piece in this book.

In "Our Asias," *I* am called to speak as an "Asian" in the heart of the Asia-Pacific. I suggested there that we should not think of our own corner as exemplary of our continent, that we might try to pluralize our continent. This would be the thinking of "other Asias" from above, from the university. I was writing the Amnesty piece "Righting Wrongs" while I was in Hong Kong. I was beginning to understand that "other" is not simply a matter of imaginative geography but also of discontinuous epistemes. The largest sector of the Asian electorate of the future occupies another epistemic space from the readers of "Our Asias." That other understanding of another Asia is at the conclusion of the lead piece. Who knows if the democratic structure of the state will become more regional in the coming generations? The ongoing effort to build another Asia – not necessarily in the image of the current dominant (a "selfsame," "proper," "authentic" Asia) – can belong to that future.

In 1997, I was beginning to understand the preparation of another Asia as a setting to work. I asked the question of "Responsibility" again, but now in the context of the city. Will theory work in the understanding of the megacity? As I insist now, arguments about megacities, based usually on body count, invoke built space as a signifier of a transformed episteme.[21] The episteme itself is constructed by the critics metonymically, who take the cyber mind to stand for the whole world. This metonymic postmodern subject, master of information command, and inhabitant of virtuality, makes no room for the intuition of the transcendental. This brings me to another point, which I will approach circuitously, by way of a word on the discursive style of this book.

All my teaching life I have soldiered against mere specialism. In the hands of great scholars, creative specialism can be instructive. But mere specialism, which is the lot of most scholars, is often restrictive, exclusivist, keeping itself comfortable in the indefinitely iterated conviction that the essence of knowledge is knowledge about knowledge. Like Kant's mere reason, its method is calculation, and its substitute for responsibility – *die Verantwortlichkeit* – in the robust general sense is accountability – *die Zurechnungsfähigkeit* – in the narrow sense of institutionally acknowledgeable competence.[22] This competence, according to a minimal understanding of disciplinary method, is all that the mere specialist teaches his or her student.

I think it is particularly unfortunate when teachers in the humanities refuse to live in the world and continue to contribute to their trivialization by insisting on giving their students "literary skills" alone, whatever that might mean.

Over against such restrictive specialism, there is a generalism that tries to make connections, assembling ad hoc scholarship as an aid to thinking. This problem-solving model is more like the strategy of paramedical primary health care – where the fieldworkers learn about a disease from volunteer doctors when they encounter it – than like the assured competence of qualified medical practitioners.[23]

The problem with mere generalism is ignorant speculation. What one wants is supplementation from "volunteer doctors." The root sense of "doctor" is teacher, after all. Thus my generalist work looks forward to an understanding judgment from the specialists rather than a rejection based on a minimal definition of disciplinary method equated with access to acceptable knowledge.

The essays that follow may qualify for an earlier mode of generalism. In the fifties, when I was an undergraduate at Presidency College, Kolkata, Charles Lamb's *Essays of Elia* was one of the set texts for the English Honors baccalaureate at Calcutta University.[24] Through this whimsical and instructive book I was introduced to the familiar essay. The essays in the book you hold in your hand are familiar essays, I think. The writer's life-details are always shadowily present, because the familiar essay is neither autobiography nor impartial analysis, though it courts both. It is certainly not disinterested. Indeed, the line of its interest is what makes it worth reading.

What has been my interest? Going over these occasional essays, I would say I have tried to negotiate my reluctant positioning in US academic postcolonialism without falling into identitarianism. It is because of this position, I think, that I have strained to imagine "Asia" – for I cannot construct my birthplace Bengal into the authentic contender for the cat seat of the West or Europe figured broadly. This detail, a matter of political taste, commands *Other Asias*.

As I sat revising in Honolulu, this seemed to me a good move. "Asia" is not a place, yet the name is laden with history and cultural politics. It cannot produce a naturalized homogeneous "identity." The name "Pacific" has the same salutary absence of a naturalized homogeneous identity that can be immediately connected to it. It can therefore serve to set limits to mere identitarianism in any one of the politico-geographical entities, "from Taiwan to New Zealand," with Hawaii, the Marquesas, and the Easter Islands on its eastern edge, as "Asia" can contain ours.[25] It is not insignificant that the "Asia-Pacific," claiming all of "Asia," jumps over the Pacific.

There is no specialist scholarship in this book. The familiar essay relies on what used to be called general knowledge. In the case of Armenia I struggled against my own sanctioned ignorance. I am not sure that I have been able to put together a convincing suggestion, but the risk seemed worth taking. In the case of "Moving Devi" it is a lot of unconnected bits that float up at the thought of the Great Goddess. Afghanistan, Bangladesh, and the name of "Asia" lie somewhere in between. The lesson of Armenia is the lesson that Asia is about to break anew along the line of Eurasia, so that its othering may come to have a different meaning. I am just learning to grapple with Turkey. Yet Japan had seemed to break away from Asia at a certain point. The vanishing present remains the focus of work such as this.

It is this last characteristic of the familiar essay – an unscholarly yet scrupulous inquiry – that seems most troubling to specialist readers. I am helpless here. I did not set out to write a specialist's book, but simply a "postcolonial" book that would be an example against identitarianism.

No particular word needs to be said about the pervasive feminism of this book. All my writing is marked by this.

As you will see, my book is full of hope.

Yet, I have also been cautious. Speaking directly to traditional healers in South Africa (University of the Free State, March, 2004), I said precisely that they must not accept statements that indigenous knowledge is "science," and gave them the Indian example of how it can lead to violence.

I say this because "Moving Devi," read inattentively, may seem too "religious." As I understand it, it is an example of the effort to de-transcendentalize the sacred, to move it toward imagination, away from belief, in which the secular humanities must forever engage. If a charge of obscurity is brought against it, I accept. I was called to speak as an Indian hyphenated with the United States, and this is what emerged. In it I attempt to think like an Indian-American doing identitarian cultural studies. It certainly gives the lie to the metonymic hypertextual subject of the megacity, and takes into account Manuel Castells's suggestion that identitarianism, feminist among others, manages its crisis.[26] I construct myself as a counterexample that will not allow the clichés of hybridity to work. I expect my usual detractors will make their usual detractions. Nothing I do or say will please them.[27]

Following a longstanding trend in my work and thought, describing the de-transcendentalization of alterity, "Moving Devi" sees the object of religious belief not as reference but as the permissible narratives that constitute material culture. By contrast, Sayyid Qutb's *In the Shade of the Qur'an* presents sacred text as reference.[28]

Thus, "Moving Devi" may be read within the context of de-transcendentalizing religion as *maya* or fiction; rather than confronting religion with the stern command of one version of the European Enlightenment: privatize; especially since dominant culturalism sees religion as a public bond of identity that never confronts the question of belief.[29] The essay can also be read in celebration of women – rural women, destitute widows – who do not necessarily swell the rank of the Hindu nationalists. As for the depredations of referential socialism, my work on socialist ethics has been thirty one years in the making. I still do not know if I can write it as the world changes – but let me end with promise of future work. For now: rearrange the desires of the largest sector of the future electorate, break postcolonialism into pluralized (Eur)Asias, train the metropolitan imagination to de-transcendentalize the transcendental – your move.

I have not been able to think Israel into Asia. I said to Matti Peled in 1984 that Asia had two absurdities at its two ends: Israel and Japan.[30] Japan has stepped into the Asia-Pacific for me. Israel sticks like a thorn in the side of other Asias.

There is no China here.[31] One certainly hopes for an alliance between China and India, but that regionalism is on quite another register, on the terrain of the fantasmatic level playing field. The old arguments about the social productivity of capital and the new disappointments about economic growth have play here. But that is precisely the register whose claims are unconvincing when subalternity is engaged and recalled. For me, this painstaking effort has just begun in China. On a more superficial level as well, China is changing so radically, specifically with a view to its language(s), that to think of it as writable as an "other Asia" is beyond me. I cannot yet know what the opening of the frontier at Nathu La Pass in July, 2006 will bring. The event is rich in historical textuality. Here upon this impenetrable terrain – the "natural border" of the high Himalayas – it is not without significance that the words mean "listening ear." *Critical* regionalism!

The Pass is part of the historic Silk Road, scene of the Great Game, played out in chapters 5 and 6. In the newspaper photographs the Indian faces, one of them female, are smiling, but the Chinese faces are grim. I hope this is just the protocol of the soldiers' uniform; perhaps the British-era fancy dress of the Indian frontier police calls for a different body language.

As I continue revising this introduction, I am on my way to Bandung where, on April 18–25, 1955, 29 states from Asia, Africa, and the Caribbean opted for a new economic policy that was finally sacrificed on the altar of nationalism. As Nigel Harris writes:

> The semantic history of politics is full of ideas that begin life as a radical indictment of the existing social order, but over the years pass neutered into the everyday lexicon.... The "Third World" is no longer seen as a political alternative and merely denotes a group of countries.[32]

What is the lesson of this? To take other Asias into the outlines of the globe, in the double bind of texture and structure.

Indeed, the lesson of Bandung can be compared to the lesson I have learned in my attempt to understand postcoloniality in the context of the Southern Caucasus. My efforts bear witness to its displacement into globalization. The reinvention of Bandung, hailed by everyone in 1955 as a postcolonial effort ("in your midst are old friends I knew in London years ago, where I first became part of the movement for colonial freedom," wrote Paul Robeson at the time), is being hailed today as a call to confront the problems of globalization.[33] At this point to locate the obvious weaknesses of Anglo-US-based postcolonial theory and call for a universalism emerging out of the most "European" of the Balkans can be no more than an academic holding action, just as to dismiss post-structuralism because it "rejects science" or is confined to verbal texts or books is simply uninformed.[34]

Text means web. I was shown on the Internet a document which claims that the earthquake in Bam, Iran, on December 26, 2003, a result of overbuilding due to capitalist globalization, has nothing to do with textuality. The version I was shown ends with a picture of an anonymous victim and the caption "What textuality?"

To get an answer to this one must pay attention to what Marx started: to show the text, the web, of capital-formation and capitalism to the worker, who then could have a hand in changing it. The worker, for Marx, was most emphatically not a victim, but the agent of production. I have written in the first essay about efforts to show the subaltern child that s/he is the agent not the victim, of what is still called "democracy." A longstanding textual project, if text is understood as web, rather than printed words on a page. (A big part of this project is now destroyed, confronted by the feudalism of the old latifundia system, flourishing in the grass roots, beyond the ken of the international civil society, because they cannot wait to learn the idiom.)

This particular colleague also claims that to cite a problem in the English translation of Marx is to "privatize." He must remember that English is not the only public language on earth. We cannot learn all languages, but we can learn some. As of this writing, I have persuaded at least one Italian translator of Mahasweta Devi's fiction not to translate from my English version but to consult appropriate members of the local Bangladeshi-Italian community. Is that to privatize?

Next, a word about singularity. For me, it is the repeatable difference that beings share. In my understanding, this is an immense simplification of the solution offered by Spinoza to the problem of ethical universalism. To every invocation of singularity is attached the double bind of the call to rational universalism. The agent–subject distinction in my work is a way of marking this double bind. None of this can matter to the universalists or the specificitarians, since they are not interested in the real-worldly problems created for the ethico-political by the specificities of the mental theater, which continually stages a reasonable or consistent scenario backed up by other resources.

I place these untimely essays in your hand. If you are going to engage with them, be fair. No abuse, please. Bear with them, or lay them aside, if they manage to rattle you. I am not out to convert the world.

Chapter 1

Righting Wrongs – 2002: Accessing Democracy among the Aboriginals

Argument: Responsibility-based cultures are long delegitimized and unprepared for the public sphere; rights-based cultures are increasingly committed to corporatism in philanthropy. The former need supplementation for entry into democratic reflexes just as the latter need supplementation into the call of the other. Supplementation is needed by both sides. The Humanities can play a role. Otherwise Human Rights feed (on) class apartheid.

"Human Rights and Human Wrongs," the title of the series within which this talk was given, is asymmetrical.

The primary nominative sense of "right" cited by the Oxford English Dictionary is "justifiable claim, on legal or moral grounds, to have or obtain something, or to act in a certain way." There is no parallel usage of "wrongs," connected to an agent in the possessive case – "my wrongs" – or given to it as an object of the verb "to have" – "she has wrongs."

"Rights" entail an individual or collective. "Wrongs," however, cannot be used as a noun, except in so far as an other, as agent of injustice, is involved. The verb "to wrong" is more common than the noun, and indeed the noun probably gets its enclitic meaning by back-formation from the verb.

The word "rights" in the title acquires verbal meaning by its contiguity with the word "wrongs." The verb "to right" cannot be used intransitively on this level of abstraction. It can only be used with the unusual noun "wrong": "to right a wrong," or "to right wrongs." Our title thus makes visible that "Human Rights" is not only about having or claiming a right or a set of rights, it is also about righting wrongs, about being the dispenser of these rights. The idea of Human Rights, in other words, may carry within itself the agenda of a kind of social Darwinism – the

fittest must shoulder the burden of righting the wrongs of the unfit –
and the possibility of an alibi.[1] Only a "kind of" social Darwinism, of
course. Just as "the white man's burden," undertaking to civilize and
develop, was only "a kind of" oppression. It would be silly to footnote
the scholarship that has gone to show that the latter may have been an
alibi for economic, military, and political intervention. It is on that model
that I am using the concept-metaphor of the alibi in these introductory
paragraphs.

Having arrived here, the usual thing is to complain about the
Eurocentrism of Human Rights. I have no such intention. I am of
course troubled by the use of Human Rights as an alibi for interventions of various sorts. But its so-called European provenance is for me
in the same category as the "enabling violation" of the production of
the colonial subject.[2] One cannot write off the righting of wrongs. The
enablement must be used even as the violation is re-negotiated.

Colonialism was committed to the education of a certain class. It
was interested in the seemingly permanent operation of an altered
normality. Paradoxically, Human Rights and "development" today
cannot claim this self-empowerment that high colonialism could. Yet,
it is some of the best products of high colonialism, descendants of the
colonial middle class, who become human rights advocates in the
countries of the South. I will explain through an analogy.

"Doctors Without Frontiers" – I find this translation (of *Médicins
Sans Frontières*) more accurate than the received "Doctors Without
Borders" – dispense healing all over the world, traveling to solve health
problems as they arise. They cannot be involved in the repetitive work
of primary health care, which requires changes in the habit of what
seems normal living: permanent operation of an altered normality.
They cannot learn all the local languages, dialects, and idioms of the
places where they provide help. They use local interpreters. It is as if, in
the field of class-formation through education, colonialism and the
attendant territorial imperialism had combined these two imperatives –
clinic and primary health care – by training the interpreters themselves
into imperfect yet creative imitations of the doctors. The class thus
formed – both (pseudo)doctor and interpreter, as it were – was the
colonial subject.

The end of the Second World War inaugurated the postcolonial
dispensation.

It was the U.N. Special Committee on Decolonization ... that in 1965
asked the Commission [on Human Rights, created in 1946] to process

the petitions that the Committee was receiving about human rights violations in southern Africa. ... [Until the mid-1960s, p]articularly for the
new African and Asian members, the priority was [white] racism and
[against it] self-determination from colonial rule [, in other words,
decolonization]. Later, their enthusiasm for the new procedures waned
as the protection of civil and political [human] rights [in the new nation]
emerged as the priority consideration and many of them became the
targets [since they, as the new masters, were the guilty party] for the
Commission's new mandate.[3]

For the eighteenth-century Declaration of the Rights of Man and of
Citizens by the National Assembly of France the "nation is essentially
the source of sovereignty; nor can any individual, or any body of men,
be entitled to any authority which is not expressly derived from it."[4]
One hundred and fifty years later, for better or for worse, the human
rights aspect of postcoloniality has turned out to be the breaking of
the new nations, in the name of their breaking-in into the international
community of nations.[5] This is a narrative of international maneuvering. Risse, Ropp, and Sikkink's recent book, *The Power of Human Rights*,
takes the narrative further. In addition to the dominant states, they
argue, since 1993 it is the transnational agencies, plus non-governmental organizations (NGOs), that subdue the state.[6]

Nevertheless, it is still disingenuous to call Human Rights Eurocentric.
This is not only because, in the global South, the domestic human
rights workers are, by and large, the descendants of the colonial subject, often culturally positioned against Eurocentrism. It is also because,
internationally, the role of the new diasporic is strong, and the diasporic
in the metropolis stands for "diversity," "against Eurocentrism." Thus
the work of righting wrongs is shared above a class line that to some
extent and unevenly cuts across race and the North–South divide.[7] I say
"to some extent and unevenly" because, to be located in the Euro-US
still makes a difference. In the United Nations itself, "the main human
rights monitoring function [has been] allocated to the OSCE
[Organization for Security and Cooperation in Europe]."[8] The presuppositions of Risse, Ropp, and Sikkink's book also make this clear. The
subtitle – "international norms and domestic change" – is telling. In
keeping with this, the authors' idea of the motor of Human Rights is
"pressure" on the state "from above" – international – and "from
below" – domestic. (It is useful for this locationist privilege that most
NGOs of the global South survive on Northern aid.) Here is a typical
example, as it happens about the Philippines: "'Human rights' have
gained prescriptive status independent of political interests. ... [We]

doubt that habitualization or institutionalization at the state level have proceeded sufficiently to render pressure from societal actors futile."⁹

This is pressure "from below," of course. Behind these "societal actors" and the state is "international normative pressure." I will go on to suggest that, unless "education" is thought differently from "consciousness-raising" about "the human rights norm" and "rising literacy expand[ing] the individual's media exposure," "sufficient habitualization or institutionalization" will never arrive, and this will continue to provide justification for international control.

Thinking about education and the diaspora, Edward W. Said wrote that "the American University generally [is] for its academic staff and many of its students the last remaining utopia."¹⁰ The philosopher Richard Rorty as well as Lee Kuan Yew, the former Prime Minister of Singapore, – who supported "detention without trial ... [as] Confucianist," – share this view of the utopianism of the Euro-US university. I quote Rorty, but I invite you to read Premier Lee's *From Third World to First: The Singapore Story, 1965–2000* to savor their accord: "Producing generations of nice, tolerant, well-off, secure, other-respecting students of [the American] sort in all parts of the world is just what is needed – indeed all that is needed – to achieve an Enlightenment utopia. The more youngsters like that we can raise, the stronger and more global our human rights culture will become."¹¹

If one wishes to make this restricted utopianism, which extends to great universities everywhere, available for global social justice, one must unmoor it from its elite safe harbors, supported by the power of the dominant nation's civil polity, and be interested in a kind of education for the largest sector of the future electorate in the global South – the children of the rural poor – that would go beyond literacy and numeracy and find a home in an expanded definition of a "Humanities to come."

Education in the Humanities attempts to be an *uncoercive* rearrangement of desires.¹² If you are not persuaded by this simple description, nothing I say about the Humanities will move you. This is the burden of the second section of this essay. It is this simple but difficult practice that is outlined there. It is only when we interest ourselves in this new kind of education for the children of the rural poor in the global South that the inevitability of unremitting pressure as the primum mobile of Human Rights will be questioned. If one engages in such empowerment at the lowest level, it is in the hope that the need for international/domestic-elite pressure on the state will not remain primary forever. We cannot necessarily expect the old colonial subject transformed into the new domestic middle class urban radical, defined as "below" by Risse, Ropp, and Sikkink and by metropolitan Human Rights in general, to engage in the attempt I will go on to describe. Although physically based in the South, and therefore presumably far from the utopian university, this class is generally also out of touch with the mindset – a combination of episteme and ethical discourse – of the rural poor below the NGO level. To be able to present a project that will draw aid from the North, for example, to understand and state a problem intelligibly and persuasively for the taste of the North, is itself proof of a sort of epistemic discontinuity with the ill-educated rural poor.[13] (And the sort of education we are thinking of is not to make the rural poor capable of drafting NGO grant proposals!) It is this discontinuity, not skin color or national identity crudely understood, that undergirds the question of who always rights and who is perennially wronged.[14]

I have been suggesting, then, that "human rights culture" runs on unremitting Northern-ideological pressure, even when it is from the South; that there is a real epistemic discontinuity between the Southern human rights advocates and those whom they protect.[15] In order to shift this layered discontinuity, however slightly, we must focus on the quality and end of education, at both ends; the Southern elite is often educated in Western or Western-style institutions. We must focus on both ends – both on Said/Rorty's utopia and on the schools of the rural poor in the global South.

I will argue this by way of a historical and theoretical digression.

As long as the claim to natural or inalienable Human Rights – rights that all human beings possess because they are human by nature – was reactive to the historical alienation in "Europe" as such – the French *ancien régime* or the German Third Reich – the problem of relating "natural" to "civil" rights was on the agenda. Since its use by the Commission on Decolonization in the sixties, its thorough politicization in the nineties, when the nation-states of the South, and perhaps the nation-state form itself needed to be broken in the face of the restructuring demands of globalization; and its final inclusion of the postcolonial subject in the form of the metropolitan diasporic, that particular problem – of relating "natural" to "civil" rights – was quietly forgotten. What has been forgotten, in other words, is that the question of nature must be begged (assumed when it needs to be demonstrated), in order to use it historically.[16]

The urgency of the political calculus obliges Thomas Paine to reduce the shadow of this immense European debate – between justice and law, between natural and civil rights (*jura*), at least as old as classical antiquity – to a "difference." The structural asymmetry of the difference – between mental theater and state structure – remains noticeable:

> His natural rights are the foundation of all his civil rights. But in order to pursue this distinction with more precision, it will be necessary to mark the different qualities of natural and civil rights. ... Every civil right has for its foundation, some natural right pre-existing in the individual, but to the enjoyment of which his individual power is not, in all cases, sufficiently competent.[17]

The context of the *second* Declaration brings us close to our present. To situate it historically within the thematic of the begged question at the origin, I refer the reader to Jacques Derrida's treatment of how Walter Benjamin attempts to contain this in his 1921 essay "Critique of Violence," dealing precisely with the relationship between natural and positive law and legitimate and illegitimate violence.[18] Benjamin's consideration of the binary opposition between legitimate and illegitimate violence as it relates to the originary violence that establishes authority can be placed on the chain of displacements from Hobbes's consideration of the binary opposition between the state of nature and the law of nature, with the former split by what George Shelton sees as the difference between the fictive and its representation as the real (see note 22).

I will mention Ernst Bloch's *Natural Law and Human Dignity* (1961) here to give a sense of a text at the other end of the Third Reich.[19] The sixties will witness the internationalization of Human Rights. The Benjamin/Bloch texts represent the European lineaments that brought forth the second Declaration.

Bloch faces the problem of the "natural" by historicizing it. He gives an account of the ways in which the European tradition has finessed the begged question of nature. His heroes are the Stoics – especially Epicurus – and Marx. Marx contains the potential of setting free the question of nature as freedom: "[a] Marxism that was what it was supposed to be would be a radical penal theory, indeed the most radical and at the same time most amiable: It kills the social mother of injustice." I cannot credit a "Marxism in its proper outlines." But I can at least suggest that in these times, when an internationalized Human Rights has forgotten to acknowledge the begged question of nature, a non-disciplinary amateur of philosophy, who has been taught the value

of philosophy as an "art of living" in the Stoic style through the
Nietzschean line of Foucault and Derrida, might want to point out that
Zeno and Epicurus were, necessarily, what would today be called
"colonial subjects," and suggest that we may attempt to supplement a
merely penal system by re-inventing the social mother of injustice as
worldwide class apartheid, and kill her, again and again, in the mode of
"to come," through the education of those who fell through colonial
subject-formation.[20]

I have not the expertise to summarize the long history of the European
debate surrounding natural/civil rights. With some hesitation I would
point at the separation/imbrication of nature and liberty in Machiavelli,
at the necessary slippage in Hobbes between social contract as natural
fiction and social contract as civil reality, at Hobbes's debate on liberty
and necessity with Bishop Bramhall.[21] George Shelton distinguishes
between a "hypothetical" and a "real" social contract in Hobbes, at a
certain point calling the former a "useful fiction."[22] New interest in
Hobbesian theology has disclosed a similar pattern in Hobbes's discussion of God as ground.[23] This is particularly interesting because Hobbes
is so widely seen as the initiator of individualism. Hobbes himself
places his discussions within debates in Roman law and I think we
should respect this chain of displacements – rather than a linear intellectual history – that leads to the rupture of the first European
Declaration of Human Rights.[24] I am arguing that such speculative
lines are not allowed to flourish within today's global human rights
activities where a crude notion of cultural difference is about as far as
grounds-talk will go. Academic research may contest this trend by
tracking rational critique and/or individualism within non-European
high cultures.[25] This is valuable work. But the usually silent victims of
pervasive rather than singular and spectacular human rights violations
are generally the rural poor. These academic efforts do not touch their
general cultures, unless it is through broad generalizations, positive
and negative. Accessing those long-delegitimized epistemes requires a
different engagement. The pedagogic effort that may bring about lasting epistemic change in the oppressed is never accurate, and must be
forever renewed. Otherwise there does not seem much point in considering the Humanities worth teaching. And, as I have already signaled,
the red thread of a defense of the humanities as an attempt at uncoercive
rearrangement of desires runs through this essay.
    Attempts at such pedagogic change need not necessarily involve
confronting the task of undoing the legacy of a specifically *colonial*

education. Other political upheavals have also divided the postcolonial or global polity into an effective class apartheid. (I expand my argument beyond postcoloniality in the narrow sense because of what I hope is the beginning of a long-term involvement with grass-roots rural education in China.) All that seems possible to surmise is that the redressing work of Human Rights must be supplemented by an education that can continue to make unstable the presupposition that the reasonable righting of wrongs is inevitably the manifest destiny of groups – unevenly class-divided, embracing North and South – that remain poised to right them; and that, among the receiving groups, wrongs will inevitably proliferate with unsurprising regularity. Consequently, the groups that are the dispensers of Human Rights must realize that, just as the natural Rights of Man were contingent upon the historical French Revolution, and the Universal Declaration upon the historical events that led to the Second World War, so also is the current emergence, of the human rights model as the global dominant, contingent upon the turbulence in the wake of the dissolution of imperial formations and global economic restructuring. The task of making visible the begged question grounding the political manipulation of a civil society forged on globally defined natural rights is just as urgent; and not simply by way of *cultural* relativism.

In disciplinary philosophy, discussion of the begged question at the origin of natural rights is not altogether absent. Alan Gewirth chooses the Rational Golden Rule as his PGC (principle of generic consistency), starting his project in the following way: "The Golden Rule is the common moral denominator of all the world's major religions."[26] From a historical point of view, one is obliged to say that none of the great religions of the world can lead to an end to violence today.[27]

Where Gewirth, whom nobody would associate with deconstruction, is important for our argument, is in his awareness of the grounding of the justification for Human Rights in a begged question.[28] He takes it as a "contradiction" to solve and finds in the transposition of "rational" for "moral" his solution.[29] "The traditional Golden Rule [Do unto others as you would have them do unto you] leaves open the question of why any person ought to act in accordance with it."[30] This is the begging of the question, because the moral cannot not be normative. According to Gewirth, a commonsensical problem can be theoretically avoided because "[i]t is not the contingent desires of agents but rather aspects of agency which cannot rationally be avoided or evaded by any agent that determine the content of the Rational

Golden Rule [because it] ... focuses on what the agent necessarily wants or values insofar as he is rational ..." It would seem to us that this begs the question of the reasonable nature of reason (accounting for the principle of reason by the principle of reason).[31] We would rather not construct the best possible theory, but acknowledge that practice always splits open the theoretical justification. In fact, Gewirth knows this. Toward the end of the essay, this curious sentence is left hanging: "*Materially,* [the] *self-contradiction* [that to deny or violate the Rational Golden Rule is to contradict oneself] is *inescapable* because ... the Rational Golden Rule [is] derived from the necessities of purposive agency" (emphasis mine). If we acknowledge the part outside of reason in the human mind then we may see the limits of reason as "white mythology" and see the contradiction as the necessary relationship between *two* discontinuous begged questions: proof that we are born free and proof that it is the other that calls us before will. Then the question: why must we follow the Golden Rule (the basis of Human Rights) finds an answer: because the other calls us. But it is never a fitting answer, it is not continuous with the question. Let us then call this a relationship, a discontinuous supplementary relationship, not a solution. Instead, Gewirth is obliged to re-code the white mythology of reason as unavoidable last instance, as an *"inherent* capab[ility] of exercising [human rights]."[32] If one enters into a sustained give-and-take with subordinate cultures attempting to address structural questions of power as well as textural questions of responsibility, one feels more and more that a Gewirth-style recoding may be something like a historical incapacity to grasp that to rationalize the question of ethics *fully* (please note that this does not mean banishing reason from ethics altogether, just giving it an honorable and instrumental place) is to transgress the intuition that ethics are a problem of relation before they are a task of knowledge. This does not gainsay the fact that, in the juridico-legal manipulation of the abstractions of contemporary politics by those who right wrongs, where a reasoned calculus is instrumentally necessary, nothing can be more welcome than Gewirth's rational justification. What we are describing is a simplified version of the aporia between ethics and politics. An aporia is disclosed only in its one-way crossing. This chapter attempts to make the reader recognize that Human Rights is such an interested crossing, a containment of the aporia in binary oppositions.[33]

A few words, then, about supplementing metropolitan education before I elaborate on the pedagogy of the subaltern. By "subaltern" I mean those removed from lines of social mobility.[34]

I will continue to insist that the problem with US education is that it teaches (corporatist) benevolence while trivializing the teaching of the Humanities.[35] The result is, at best, cultural relativism as cultural absolutism ("American-style education will do the trick"). Its undoing is best produced by way of the training of reflexes that kick in at the time of urgency, of decision and policy. However unrealistic it may seem to you, I would not remain a teacher of the Humanities if I did not believe that at the New York end – standing metonymically for the dispensing end as such – the teacher can try to rearrange desires noncoercively – as I mentioned a few pages back – through an attempt to develop in the student a habit of literary reading, even just "reading," suspending oneself into the text of the other – for which the first condition and effect is a suspension of the conviction that I am necessarily better, I am necessarily indispensable, I am necessarily the one to right wrongs, I am necessarily the end-product for which history happened, and that New York is necessarily the capital of the world. It is not a loss of will, especially since it is supplemented in its turn by the political calculus, where, as Said's, Rorty's, and Premier Lee's argument emphasizes, the possibility of being a "helper" abounds in today's triumphalist US society. A training in literary reading is a training to learn from the singular and the unverifiable. Although literature cannot speak, this species of patient reading, miming an effort to make the text respond, as it were, is a training not only in poiesis, accessing the other so well that probable action can be prefigured, but teleo-poiesis, striving for a response from the distant other, without guarantees.

I have no moral position against grading, or writing recommendation letters. But if you are attempting to train specifically in literary reading, the results are not directly ascertainable by the teaching subject, and perhaps not the taught subject either. In my experience, the "proof" comes in unexpected ways, from the other side. But the absence of such proof does not necessarily "mean" nothing has been learnt. This is why I say "no guarantees."[36] And that is also why the work of an epistemic undoing of cultural relativism as cultural absolutism can only work as a supplement to the more institutional practice, filling a responsibility-shaped gap but also adding something discontinuous. As far as Human Rights goes, this is the only prior and patient training that can leaven the quick-fix training institutes that prepare international civil society workers, including human rights advocates, with uncomplicated standards for success.[37] This is not a suggestion that all human rights workers should have institutional Humanities training. As it stands, Humanities teaching in the

United States is what I am describing only in the very rare instance. And the mode is "to come."

It is in the interest of supplementing metropolitan humanities pedagogy, rather than from the perspective of some fantasmatic cultural difference that we can say that the "developed post-capitalist structure" of today's world must "be filled with the more robust imperative to responsibility which capitalist social productivity was obliged to destroy. We must learn to re-define that lost imperative as defective for the emergence of capitalism, rather than necessarily pre-capitalist on an interested sequential evolutionary model."[38] "Re-define," not recover, in some pursuit of golden-ageism. As Rosalind Morris points out, subalterns in such societies "only refer to themselves – to those with whom marital relations are conceivable – with a term that is absolutely totalized (i.e., something like 'human' or 'people') and in absolute opposition to other groups, to such an extent that the killing of others is not punishable, and the enslavement of others is advocated or normativized."[39] This is why an intuition of the public sphere, which ideally teaches democratic co-existence, is the point of the whole exercise. We should remember that the public sphere relates to unconditional hospitality as law to justice, heterogeneously.[40]

A redefinition of the "lost imperatives," then: On the simplest terms, being defined by the call of the other – which may be a defining feature of such societies – is not conducive to the extraction and appropriation of surplus. Making room for *otium* and living in the rhythm of the eco-biome does not lead to exploration and conquest of nature. And so on. The method of a specifically literary training, a slow mind-changing process, can be used to open the imagination to such mindsets.[41]

One of the reasons international Communism failed was because Marx, an organic intellectual of the industrial revolution, could only think the claiming of rights to freedom from exploitation by way of the public use of reason recommended by the European Enlightenment. The ethical part, to want to exercise the freedom to redistribute, after the revolution, comes by way of the sort of education I am speaking of. This intuition was not historically unavailable to Marx: "circumstances are changed by men and ... the educator himself must be educated."[42] In the event, the pedagogic impulse was confined to the lesson of capital, to change the victim into an agent. The intuition that the lesson was historically determined was also not unavailable to Marx.[43] My position is thus not against class-struggle, but yet another attempt to broaden it, to include the "grounding condition" (*Grundbedingung,* see p. 54) of the continued reproduction of class apartheid in ancient and/or disenfranchised societies in modernity. If the industrial proletariat of Victorian England were expanded to include the global subaltern, there is no hope that such an agent could ever "dictate" anything through the structures of parliamentary democracy – I admit I cannot give this up – if this persistent pedagogic effort is not sustained.

(I am more than ever convinced of the need to re-imagine the lost cultural imperative to responsibility after the initial trip, mentioned above, to the lowest-level rural schools in a mountain province in China, in the company of a wonderfully enthusiastic young English teacher at the University of Science and Technology in the provincial urban center. He had never visited such schools, never thought of the possibility of restoring a failed Communism with a persistent effort to teach oneself how to access older cultural habits in practice in order to suture in, in rural education, the ethical impulse that can make social justice flourish, forever in the mode of "to come," because forever dependent upon the qualitative education of the young.[44] Yet he had already been used by the US industry in "China's ethnic minority education" scholarship, as a "grass-roots native informant," sent into "the field" with a questionnaire for 10 days' research! A perfect candidate for the domestic "below," for whom the "evils" of Communism seem to be open for correction only through the absolutist arrogance of US utopianism, coded as an interest in cultural difference.)

A desire to redistribute is not the unproblematic consequence of a well-fed society. In order to get that desire moving by the cultural imperative of education, you have to fix the possibility of putting not just "wrong" over against "right," with all the genealogical lines compressed within it; but also to suggest that another antonym of "right" is "responsibility," and further, that the possibility of such responsibility is underived from rights.[45]

I will now describe a small and humble experiment that I have tried over the last fifteen years, nearly every day at the Columbia University gym and, unhappily, the rate of experimental verification is 100 percent.

There is an approximately 5 ft × 4 ft windowless anteroom as you enter the locker area. This useless space, presumably to protect female modesty, is brightly lit. There is a light switch by the door from the main gym into the anteroom, and another by the door leading into the lockers. In other words, it is possible to turn the light off as you exit this small enclosed space. You can choose not to let it burn so brightly 24 hours for no one. Remember these are university folks, generally politically correct, interested in health, a special control group, who talk a good game about environmental responsibility. (I am drawing the example from within the cultural idiom of the group, as always.) I turn off the light in this windowless cube whenever I enter the locker and my sciatica keeps me going to the gym pretty regularly. In the last 15 years, I have never re-entered this little space and found the light off. Please draw your own conclusions.

The responsibility I speak of, then, is not necessarily the one that comes from the consciousness of superiority lodged in the self (the quote of the month at the gym on the day of revising was, characteristically: "the price of greatness is responsibility" – Winston Churchill), but one that is, to begin with, sensed before sense as a call of the other.[46]

Varieties of the Churchillian sense of "responsibility," nearly synonymous with duty, have always also been used from within the Rights camp, of course. Machiavelli and Hobbes both write on duty. The 1793 version of the Declaration of the Rights of Man already contains a section on the duties of man and of the citizen. The UN issued a Declaration of Responsibilities – little more than a reinscription of the rights as duties for their establishment – in 1997. There is a scientists' "Declaration of Duties." And so on. This is the trajectory of the idea of "responsibility" as assumed, by choice, by the group that can right wrongs. I think Amnesty International is correct in saying that the UN Declaration of Responsibilities is "no complement to human rights," and that "to *restate … rights* from the UDHR [Universal Declaration of Human Rights] *as responsibilities* the draft declaration introduces vague and ill-defined notions which can only create confusion and uncertainty."[47] Thus even a liberal vision is obliged to admit that there is no continuous line from rights to responsibilities. This notion of responsibility as the "duty of the fitter self" toward less fortunate others (rather than the predication of being-human as being called by the other, before will) is not my meaning, of course. I remain concerned, however, by one of its corollaries in global social movements. The leaders from the domestic "below," – for the subaltern an "above" – not realizing the historically established discontinuity between themselves and the subaltern, counsel self-help with great supervisory benevolence. This is important to remember because, the subalterns' obvious inability to do so without sustained supervision is seen as proof of the need for continued intervention. It is necessary to be involved in the everyday working (the "textuality") of global social movements to recognize that the seeming production of "declarations" from these supervised groups is written to dictation and is therefore no strike against class apartheid. "To claim rights is your duty," is the banal lesson that the above – whether Northern or Southern – then imparts to the below. The organization of international conferences with exceptionalist tokenization to represent the collective subaltern will is a last ditch solution, for both sides, if at all. And, sometimes, as in the case of my friend in Yunan, the unwitting native informant is rather far from the subaltern.

Within the rights camp, the history of something like responsibility-based cultural systems is generally given as part of the progress toward the development of a rights-based system in the type case of the European self.[48]

The Judaic articulation of responsibility, after the very war that produced the Universal Declaration, is set forth by Emmanuel Levinas.[49] Derrida attempted to unmoor this from the unquestioning support for the state of Israel by proposing a messianicity without messianism, although he acknowledged that he is caught in the traces of his own peculiar cultural production in stating responsibility just this way.[50] This history and its institutional discussions remain confined to the elite academy. If there is no direct line from rights to responsibility, there is certainly no direct possibility of supplementing the below from this discussion.[51]

It can seem at first glance that if the Euro-US mindset modifies itself by way of what used to be called, just yesterday, Third Way politics, providing a cover for social democracy's rightward swing, perhaps the dispensers of Human Rights would at least modify their arrogance. As George W. Bush claimed Tony Blair for his chum on Bush's visit to Britain in July 2001, I thought it was still worth examining this impulse, however briefly, so that it was not offered as a panacea. Today, with world governance on the agenda, it seems altogether more appropriate. Let us look at a few crucial suggestions from *Beyond Left and Right* by Anthony Giddens, the academic spokesperson of the Third Way.[52]

Giddens mentions the virtues of Third World poverty and therefore may seem at first glance to be recommending learning from the subaltern. Criticizing the welfare state, he quotes Charles Murray with approval: "Murray, whose work has been influenced by experiences in rural Thailand, asks the question, what's wrong with being poor (once people are above the level of subsistence poverty)? Why should there be such a general concern to combat poverty?" I hope it is clear that I have no interest in keeping the subaltern poor. To repeat, it is in view of Marx's hope to transform the subaltern – whom he understood only as the worker in his conjuncture – into an agent of the undoing of class

apartheid rather than its victim that this effort at educating the educator is undertaken.

Here are some of Giddens's "practical" suggestions: "A post-scarcity
system is … a system in which productivism no longer rules," a "new
ethics of individual and collective responsibility need[s] to be formed,"
"traditions should be understood in a non-traditional manner," a "pact
between the sexes [is] … to be achieved, within the industrialized societies and on a more global level" – that hesitation between the two
levels is kin to the asymmetry in the series title and the invasive gender-
work of the international civil society – and, best of all, "a new pact
between the affluent and the poor" is now needed. How is Professor
Giddens going to persuade global finance and world trade to jettison
the culture of economic growth? The question applies to all the passages I have quoted and more. He is of course speaking of state policy
in Europe, but his book tries to go beyond into other spaces: "The
question remains whether a lifestyle pact as suggested here for the
wealthy countries could also work when applied to the divisions
between North and South. Empirically, one certainly could not answer
this question positively with any degree of assurance. Analytically
speaking, however, one could ask, what other possibility is there?"[53]

However utopian it might seem, it now appears to me that the only
way to make these sweeping changes – there is nothing inherently
wrong with them, and of course I give Professor Giddens the benefit
of the doubt – is for those who teach in the Humanities to take seriously the necessary but impossible task to construct a collectivity
among the dispensers of bounty as well as the victims of oppression.[54]
Learning from the subaltern is, paradoxically, through teaching. In
practical terms, working across the class-culture difference (which
tends to refract efforts), trying to learn from children, and from the
behavior of ill-educated class-"inferiors" (a difficult task) the teacher
might learn to recognize, one hopes, not just a benevolently coerced
assent, but also an unexpected response. For such an education, speed,
quantity of information, and number of students reached are not
exclusive virtues. Those "virtues" are inefficient for education in the
responsibilities in the humanities, not so much a sense of being responsible *for*, but of being responsible *to*, before will. Institutionally, the
Humanities, like all disciplines, must be subject to a calculus. It is how
we earn our living. But where "living" has a larger meaning, the
humanities are without guarantees.

Speaking with reference to the Rights of Man and the Universal
Declaration, I am insisting that in the European context, it used to be

recognized that the question of nature as the ground of rights must be begged in order to use it historically. The assumption that it is natural to be angled toward the other, before will, the question of responsibility in subordinate cultures, is also a begged question. Neither can survive without the other, if it is a just world that we seem to be obliged to want. Indeed, any interest in Human Rights for others, in Human Rights and Human Wrongs, would do better if grounded in this second begged question, to redress historical balance, as it were, than in the apparent forgetting of the other one. In the beginning are two begged questions.

Surely the thought of two begged questions at the origin is no more abstract than John Rawls's interminable suppositions which, when confronted with the necessity of doing something, comes up with such platitudes as

> There will also be principles for forming and regulating federations (associations) of peoples, and standards of fairness for trade and other cooperative arrangements. There should be certain provisions for mutual assistance between peoples in times of famine and drought, and were it feasible, as it should be, provisions for ensuring that in all reasonably developed liberal societies people's basic needs are met.[55]

As we watch the erosion of the welfare state in the United States and worldwide, such platitudes seem all the more risible. The philosopher, trained in the humanities, takes the humanities for granted. He wins prizes. (Geo)politics goes another way. Effort is forgotten.

In the "real world," there is, in general, a tremendously uneven contradiction between those who beg the question of nature as rights for the self and those who beg the question of responsibility as being called by the other, before will. If we mean to place the latter – perennial victims – on the way to the social productivity of capital – as an old-fashioned Marxist I distinguish between capital and capitalism and do not say these words ironically – we need to acknowledge the need for supplementation there as well, rather than transform them willy-nilly, consolidating already existing hierarchies, exporting gender-struggle, by way of the greed for economic growth. (I have argued above that these cultures started stagnating because their cultural axiomatics were defective for capitalism. I have also argued that the socialist project can receive its ethical push not from within itself but by supplementation from such axiomatics (p. 24). I have argued that in their current decrepitude the subaltern cultures need to be known in such a way that we can suture their re-activated cultural axiomatics into the principles of the Enlightenment (p. 24). I have argued that socialism belongs to those axiomatics (p. 24). That socialism attempts to turn capital-formation into redistribution is a truism.[56] It is by this logic that supplementation into the Enlightenment is as much the possibility of being the agent of the social productivity of capital as it is of the subjectship of Human Rights. Yet, that the impulse to redistribute is based on training, and that an education without the humanities to train the imagination cannot foster the redistributive impulse, has been forgotten.

The general culture of Euro-US capitalism in globalization and economic restructuring has conspicuously destroyed the possibility of capital being redistributive and socially productive in a broad-based way. As I have mentioned above, "the burden of the fittest" – a re-territorializing of "the white man's burden" – does also touch the economic sphere. I hope I will be forgiven a brief digression into that sphere as well. I have prepared for this by describing the Nineties as a time "of the re-structuring demands of globalization." The reader is urged to concentrate on the lack of intellectual connection between the people at work in the different spheres. I cannot be more than telegraphic here, but it would be a mistake to leave untouched the great economic circuits that often remotely determine the shots in the human rights sphere. I remain among the unabashed walking wounded generalist aspirants from the sixties. Elsewhere, I have called this "transnational literacy."

As an introduction to this brief foray into the economic sphere, let us consider philosophers connecting Hobbes with global governance, an issue that bears on the administration of Human Rights in an economically re-structured post-state world.[57] The question they have asked, if the "stronger nations might reasonably believe their prospects to be better if they remain in the international state of nature, rather than accepting some international (but nonabsolute) equivalent of Hobbes's civil sovereign... despite the fact that in supporting it they run the risk, along with the weaker nations, of creating a monster that may well attempt to devour them," has no bearing on the institutive difference at the origin of the state of nature.[58]

The quotation above is from the early eighties, when the floodgates of the current phase of globalization – the financialization of the globe with the decentered centralization of world trade attendant upon the dissolution of the Soviet Union which in turn allowed a fuller flow for Information Technology – had not yet been opened. Yet the process had already begun, through the newly electronified stock exchanges combining with what was then called postfordism, enabled by computer technology and the fax machine. And Euro-US thinkers, connecting Hobbes with Human Rights, were certainly ignoring the question of the relationship between "natural" and "civil." Today, the "risk of creating a monster" may have been realized.

The relatively autonomous *economic* sphere of operations, worked by agents with competence restricted to this area, is explained for the *cultural* sector by other kinds of academic agents, restricted to the political sphere, in terms of a global governance story that started at the beginning of the postcolonial era at Bretton Woods for the world at large, as it had started for the Euro-US with the Marshall Plan. That is the remote start of Cultural Distance Studies.[59] The culturalists then weigh in by endlessly pointing out that world markets are old hat. This then feeds back into the cultural difference story or the hip global public culture story.[60] Other disciplinary areas involved in this are Social Psychology and Management. The former, as I indicate in note 16, gives us the multiculturalist cultural difference stereotypes that undergird human rights policy when it wishes to protect a "community without individualism" against a rogue state. Cultural Distance Studies in Management relate directly to the economic sphere and global finance, plotting the "joint ventures" opened up by neo-liberal economic re-structuring.[61] There is a compendious literature on how such ventures undermine the state and move toward the post-state world which becomes the object of global governance. In this brief compass, I refer the reader to note 57. The rogue state is disciplined by fear and pressure – the stick – with the promise of economic partnership – the carrot. (Between the first writing and this, Afghanistan and Iraq have given us other kinds of examples: puppet state and destruction.) My principal argument continues to be that a combination of fear and pressure, today supported by these powerful para-disciplinary formations proliferating crude theories of cultural difference, cannot bring about either lasting or real epistemic change although, accompanied by public interest litigation, they may be effective short-term weapons.

Meanwhile, the seriousness of training into the general culture is reflected by the fact that Morgan Stanley, Merrill Lynch, and other big investment companies are accessing pre-schoolers; children are training parents to manage portfolios. There is a growing library of books making it "fun" for kids to invest and giving them detailed instructions how to do so. The unquestioned assumption that to be rich is to be happy and good is developed by way of many "educational" excuses.

> Children are never too young to start grasping the fundamentals of money management. ... Even toddlers understand the concept of "mine!" In fact, it's the idea of owning something they like that sparks their interest in investing. Rest assured, you won't turn your child into a little money-grubber by feeding that interest. Through investing you're going to teach him more about responsibility, discipline, delayed gratification, and even ethics than you ever thought possible![62]

Such a training of children builds itself on the loss of the cultural habit of assuming the agency of responsibility in radical alterity. It is followed through by the relentless education into business culture in academic and on-the-job training, in management, consumer behavior, marketing, prepared for by the thousands and thousands of business schools all over the global South as well as the North, training undergraduates into business culture, making the supplementation of the responsibility-based subaltern layer by the ethics of class-culture difference altogether impossible, consolidating class apartheid.[63] It is now supplemented by the corporatization of the university. The Declaration of the Right to Development fits into such acculturation into the movements of finance capital. Third Way talk floats on this base. Culturalist support is provided on the Internet – in book digests on "market Taoism" and "Aristotle for capitalism."[64] It is provided in the sales presentations of countless telecommunication marketing conferences. It connects to the laughing and frequent exhortations to "follow the money" at women's rights meetings at the UN. We should keep all this in mind when we give Professor Giddens the benefit of the doubt.

Ethics within the corporatist calculus is also inscribed within this cultural formation. I team-taught a course in Political Science in fall, 2000. Our greatest problem was negotiating the difference between ethics as imagined from within the self-driven political calculus as "doing the right thing" and ethics as openness toward the imagined agency of the other, responsibility for and to – a difference meaningful to a tiny and generally non-activist radical enclave here and, as I will argue, part of a compromised and delegitimized conformity there.

Such a training of children is also a legitimation by reversal of our own insistence on elementary pedagogy of the rural poor. Supplementation by the sort of education I am trying to describe becomes necessary here, so that the relationship between child investors and child laborers is not simply one of righting wrongs from above. How does such supplementation work? If in New York, to stem the tide of corporatist ethics, business culture, appropriative New Age radicalism, and politically correct multiculturalism, the subterranean task is to supplement the radical responsibility-shaped hole in the education of the dispenser of rights through literary reading, and making use of the humanities, what about the education of those whose wrongs are righted?

Some assumptions must first be laid aside. The permeability of global culture must be seen as restricted. There is a lack of communication between and among the immense heterogeneity of the subaltern cultures of the world. Cultural borders are easily crossed from the superficial cultural relativism of metropolitan countries, whereas, going the other way, the so-called peripheral countries encounter bureaucratic and policed frontiers. The frontiers of subaltern cultures, which developed no generative public role, have no channels of interpenetration. Here, too, the problem is not solved in a lasting way by the inclusion of exceptional subalterns in South-based global movements with leadership drawn from the descendants of colonial subjects, even as these networks network. These figures are no longer representative of the subaltern stratum in general.

In 2000 I visited a so-called biodiversity festival where a rural and country town audience in a "least-developed country [LDC]" roared its derision at biodiversity songs from two neighboring nation-states, applauding enthusiastically instead at embarrassing imitations of Bollywood (the trade-name of the hugely international Bombay film industry) "adaptations" of moments from US MTV, unrecognizable by the audience as such, of course. The embarrassment of the activist leaders, from a colonial subject's class background, was compounded by their public exhortations, which were obeyed by the rural audience as a set of bewildering orders. The historical discontinuity leading to such events is one of the reasons why, although I generalize, my example remains singular. On the practical calculus, the problem of the singular and the universal is confronted by learning from the singularity of the singular, a way to the imagination of the public sphere, the rational representation of the universal. Confronted, not solved.

If the sense of doing for the other is not produced on call from a sense of the self as sovereign, packaged with the sense of being fittest, the alternative assumption, romantic or expedient, of an essence of subalternity as the source of such a sense, denies the depredations of history. Paulo Freire, in his celebrated *Pedagogy of the Oppressed*, written during the era of guerilla warfare in Latin America, warns us against subalternist essentialism, by reminding us that, "during the initial stages of the struggle, the oppressed ... tend themselves to become oppressors."[65] In the face of UN Human Rights policy making, we must be on guard against both positive and negative subalternist essentialism. If the self-permission for continuing to right wrongs is premised implicitly on the former – they will never be able to help themselves – the latter nourishes false hopes that will as surely be dashed and lead to the same result: an unwilling conclusion that they must always be propped up. Indeed, in the present state of the world, or perhaps always and everywhere, simply harnessing responsibility as accountability in the South, exploiting other-directedness, as it were, without the persistent training of "no guarantees," we reproduce and consolidate, what can only be called "feudalism," where a benevolent despot like Lee Kuan Yew can claim collectivity rather than individualism when expedient. In the present state of the world, it also reproduces and consolidates gender oppression, thus lending plausibility to the instant rightspeak of the gender lobby of the international civil society and Bretton Woods.

Declarations like the Bangkok NGO Declaration, entitled "Our Voice," and cataloging what "their right to self-determination" would be for "Indigenous People in general,"[66] may like many UN Declarations be an excellent tool for political maneuvering but it will not touch the entire spectrum of Asian Aboriginals, each group as culturally absolutist, generally unwittingly, as the rural audience at the biodiversity festival. In order to make the political maneuverings open to the ethical, we must think the supplementation toward which we are now moving, and not allow the presence of the Declaration to stop that movement.

When the UN offers violence or the ballot as a choice it is unrealistic because based on another kind of related mistake – unexamined universalism – the assumption that this is a real choice in all situations. It will soon lead to military intervention in the name of righting wrong, in geopolitically specific places. (This has, of course, come to pass in rather a big way.) For "democratization" is not just a code name, as it so often is in practice, for the political restructuring entailed by the transformation of (efficient through inefficient to wild) state capitalisms and their colonies to tributary economies of rationalized global financialization. If it is to involve the largest sector of the electorate in

the global South – the rural population below poverty level – it requires
the undoing of centuries of oppression, with a suturing education in
rural subaltern normality, supplementing the violent guilt and shame
trips of disaster politics.

I offer here a small but representative example:

I was handing out sweets, two a head, to villagers in Shahabad,
Birbhum. Some of the schools I describe later are located in this area.
This part of the village has no caste-Hindu inhabitants. Sweets of this
cooked traditional variety, that have to be bought from the Hindu villages, are beyond the villagers' means. There are no "candy stores" in
either type of village. Distribution of sweets is a festive gesture, but it
makes my Kolkata-bred intellectual-leftist soul slightly uneasy. I have
learnt such behavior in my decades-long apprenticeship in these areas.

A young man in his early thirties, generally considered a mover and
a shaker among this particular ethnic group – the Dhekaros, straddling
the Aboriginal-Untouchable divide – was opening the flimsy paper
boxes that swam in syrup in flimsier polythene bags, as I kept dipping
my hand in.[67] Suddenly he murmured, "Outsiders are coming in, one a
piece now." I thought the problem was numbers and changed to one,
a bit sad because there were now more children. Suddenly, the guy says
in my ear, "Give her two, she's one of ours." Shocked, I quickly turn to
him, and say, in rapid monotone Bengali, "Don't say such things in
front of children"; and then, "If I should say you're not one of ours?"
Since I'm a caste-Hindu and technically one of his oppressors.[68] This is
the seedbed of ethnic violence in its lowest common unit.[69] You can fill
in the historical narrative, raise or lower the degree of the heat of violence. Punishing Milosevic is good, human rights pressure and guilt
and shame trips on rogue states should continue, I suppose, but it is on
ground such as this that violence festers. This man is quite aware of
party politics; the CPM (Community Party Marxist) is strong here. He
certainly casts his vote regularly, perhaps even rallies voters for the
party. The two sentiments – first of ethnic group competition within a
corrupt quota system in the restructured state as resources dwindle;
and, secondly, of the intuition of a multi-party parliamentary democracy as a species of generally homosocial competitive sport with the
highest stakes available to players in the impoverished rural sector –
violence and the ballot – can co-exist in a volatile relationship, one
ready to be mobilized over the other, or even in the other's interest.
This is why the UN's choice – ballot box *or* "peacekeeping mission" – is
unrealistic. I will consider an answer by way of a digression into suturing rights thinking into the torn cultural fabric of the possibility of

"responsibility"; or, to vary the concept-metaphor, accessing an erased ethical script that, even at its best, was of course no more than something lodged within the group, always in the mode of "to come," and without any intuition of a public sphere to be shared with other groups. (I say all this so as not to be mistaken for a primitivist.)

Subordinate cultures of responsibility – a heuristic generalization as precarious as generalizations about the dominant culture – base the agency of responsibility in that outside of the self that is also in the self, half-archived and therefore not directly accessible. I use the word "subordinate" here because, as I have been arguing throughout this essay, they are the recipients of human rights bounty, which I see as "the burden of the fittest," and which, as I insist from the first page onward, has the *ambivalent* structure of enabling violation that anyone of goodwill associates with the white man's burden. I will rely on this argument for this second part of my essay, which concerns itself with the different way in to the damaged episteme.

From the anthropological point of view, groups such as the Sabars and the Dhekaros may be seen to have a "closely knit social texture." But I have been urging a different point of view through my concept-metaphor of "suturing." These groups are also in the historical present of state and civil society. (Human Rights punishes the former in the name of the Enlightenment.) I am asking readers to shift their perception from the anthropological to the historico-political and see the same knit text-ile as a torn cultural fabric in terms of its removal from the dominant loom in a historical moment. That is what it means to be a subaltern. My point so far has been that, for a long time now, these ethical intuitions have not been allowed to work except as a delegitimized form forcibly out of touch with the dominant through a history that has taken capital and empire as telos. As I have insisted, these forms are gender-compromised, and deformed by internal histories; they were, however, doubly blocked by capitalism, which specifically defined them as archaic and in effect overwrote them as deficient. What we attempt to recode, then, is the frayed traces of a script necessarily out of joint even when active and put it to use in the interest of a just society. My generalization is therefore precarious, though demonstrable if the effort I go on to describe is shared. These concept-metaphors, of suturing a torn fabric, of recoding a delegitimized cultural-formation, are crucial to the entire second half of my argument.

Subordinate cultures of responsibility, then, base the agency of responsibility in that outside of the self that is also in the self, half-archived and therefore not directly accessible. Such a sentence may seem opaque to secularists inspired by the Christian narrative who imagine ethics as internalized imperatives; they may seem silly to the ordinary language tradition which must resolutely ignore the parts of the mind not accessible to reason in order to theorize.[70] It may be useful to think of the archived exteriority, if considering unmediated knowledge, in terms of the inside of your body. The general premise of the Oxford Amnesty series *The Genetic Revolution and Human Rights*, for example, was that genes are digitalized words that are driving our bodies, our selves.[71] Yet they are inaccessible to us as objects and instruments of knowledge, in so far as we are sentient beings. (A smart reader mistook this as alterity being thoroughly interiorized. My exhortation is to try to think otherwise – that there is an other space – or script, all analogies are "false" here – in the self, which drives us.) Think also of our creative invention in the languages that we know well. The languages have histories before us and futures after us. They are outside us, in grammar books and dictionaries.[72] Yet the languages that we know and make in are also us, and in us. These are analogies for agency that is out of us but in us – and, like all analogies, imperfect, but I hope they will suffice for now. In responsibility-based subordinate cultures the volatile space of responsibility can be grasped through these analogies, perhaps. Please note, I am not suggesting that they are better, just that they are different, and this radically different pair – rights and responsibility / us and them – need to relate in the hobbled relationship of supplementation.

These are only analogies, to be found in an Oxford Amnesty series collection and in Saussure. They work in the following way: if we can grasp that all human beings are genetically written before will; and if we can grasp that all human children access a language that is "outside," as mother-tongue; then, on these structural models, we might grasp the assumption that the human being is human in answer to an "outside call." By way of these analogies, we can grasp the structure of the role of alterity at work in subordinate cultures. The word "before" in "before the will" is here used to mean logical priority as well as "in front of." The difference is historical, not essential. It is because I believe that right / responsibility can be shared by everyone in the persistent mode of "to come" that I keep insisting on supplemental pedagogy, on both sides.[73]

In its structure, the definitive predication of being-human by alterity is not with reference to an empirical outside world. Just as I cannot play with my own genes or access the entire linguisticity of my mother-tongue, so "is" the presumed alterity radical in the general sense.

Of course it bleeds into the narrow sense of "accountability to the outside world," but its anchor is in that imagined alterity that is inaccessible, often transcendentalized and formalized (as indeed is natural freedom in the rights camp).

I need not be more specific here. The subordinate subaltern is as diversified as the recipients of human rights activity. I need not make too many distinctions. For they are tied by a Universal Declaration.

Anticipating objections to this stopping short of distinction and specificities, I should perhaps say once again that, if these people became my object of investigation for disciplinary information retrieval as such, I would not be able to remain focused on the children as my teachers. There is nothing vague about this activity. Since this is the central insight of my essay, the reader will, I fear, have to take it or leave it. This is the different way of epistemic access, this the teacher's apprenticeship as suturer or invisible mender, this the secret of ongoing pedagogic supplementation. Writing this piece has almost convinced me that I was correct in thinking that this different way was too *in situ* to travel, that I should not make it part of my academic discourse. And yet there is no other news that I can bring to Amnesty International under the auspices of Human Rights.

Rewriting Levinas, Irigaray called for an ethics of sexual difference in the early eighties.[74] That mode in dominant feminist theory is now past. But the usefulness of the model does not disappear with a trend. Call the supplementation I am describing in this chapter an ethics of class-culture difference, then: relating remotely, in view of a future "to come," the dispensers of rights with the victims of wrongs.

With this proviso, let us consider an example of why we need to suture rights thinking into the torn cultural fabric of the possibility of "responsibility"; or, to vary the concept-metaphor, to attempt to access an erased ethical script that, even at its best, was of course no more than something lodged within the group, always in the mode of "to come," and without any intuition of a public sphere to be shared with other groups. I will give only the bare bones.

Activists from the institutionally educated classes of the general national culture win a state-level legal victory against police brutality over the tribals.

They try to transform this into a national-level legal awareness campaign.[75]

The ruling party supports the activists on the state level. (India is a federation of states. The national level is not involved here.) The ruling party on the local level is generally less answerable to the state

precisely because of the discontinuity from the grass roots that I have
been insisting upon all along. Indeed, this absence of redress without
remote mediation is what makes the subaltern subaltern and keeps
the indigenous elite feudal. On the local level the police of the ruling
party consistently takes revenge against what is perceived as a victory
over "their" party by taking advantage of three factors, one positive,
two negative:

1   The relatively homogeneous dominant Hindu culture at the village
    level keeps the tribal culturally isolated through prejudice.
2   As a result of this *cultural* isolation, women's independence among
    the tribals has remained relatively intact. It has not been seriously
    infected by the tradition of women's subordination within the gen-
    eral Hindu rural culture.
3   *Politically*, the general, supposedly homogeneous rural culture and
    the tribal culture *share* a lack of democratic training.[76] This is a
    result of poverty and class prejudice existing nationally. Therefore,
    votes can be bought and sold here; and electoral conflict is treated
    by rural society in general like a competitive sport where violence
    is legitimate.

Locally, since the legal victory of the metropolitan activists against
the police, the ruling party has taken advantage of these three things
by rewriting women's conflict as party politics.[77] To divide the tribal
community against itself, the police have used an incidental quarrel
among tribal women, about the theft of a bicycle, if I remember right.
One side has been encouraged to press charges against the other. The
defending faction has been wooed and won by the opposition party.
Thus a situation of violent conflict has been fabricated, where the
police have an immediate edge over every one, and since the legal
victory in remote Kolkata is there after all, police revenge takes the
form of further terror. In the absence of training in electoral democracy, the aboriginal community has accepted police terror as part of
the party spirit: this is how electoral parties fight, where "electoral" has
no intellectual justification. This is a direct consequence of the educated activists' – among whom I count myself – good hearted "from
above" effort at constitutional redress, since at the grass roots it can
only be understood as a "defeat" by police and party.

It is not that the women should be left alone to flourish in some
pristine tribality. I am also not speaking about how to stop women's
oppression! The police are rural Hindus, the Aboriginals are a small

disenfranchised group, and the situation is class-race-state power written into the caste system. Teaching is my solution, the method is pedagogic attention, to learn the weave of the torn fabric in unexpected ways, in order to suture the two, not altering gender politics from above. As for gender, I hope the parenthesis below will show why everything cannot be squeezed into this relatively short piece. I am suggesting that human rights activism should be supplemented by an education that should suture the habits of democracy on to the earlier cultural formation. I am the only person within this activist group – organized later as a tax-sheltered non-profit organization (now dissolved) – who thinks that the real effort should be to access and activate the tribals' indigenous "democratic" structures to *parliamentary* democracy by patient and sustained efforts to learn to learn from below. "Activate" is the keyword here. There is no tight cultural fabric (as opposed to group solidarity) among these disenfranchised groups after centuries of oppression and neglect. Anthropological excavation for description is not the goal here. (I remain suspicious of academic golden-ageism from the colonial subject.) I am not able to give scholarly information. Working hands-on with teachers and students over long periods of time on their own terms without thinking of producing information for my academic peers is like learning a language "to be able to produce in it freely … [and therefore] to move in it without remembering back to the language rooted and planted in [me, indeed] forgetting it."[78] As I mentioned above, I do not usually write about this activity, at all. Yet it seems necessary to make the point when asked to speak on Human Rights, because this is a typical wake of a human rights victory. The reader is invited to join in the effort itself. In the mean time I remain a consensus breaker among metropolitan activists, who feel they can know everything in a non-vague way if only they have enough information, and that not to think so is "mystical." The consensually united vanguard is never patient.

This narrative demonstrates that when the human rights commissions, local, national, or international, right state terrorism, police brutality, or gender violence in such regions, the punishing victory is won in relatively remote courts of law.

Catharine A. MacKinnon describes this well: "The loftiest legal abstracts … are born … amid the intercourse of particular groups, in the presumptive ease of the deciding classes, through the trauma of specific atrocities, at the expense of the silent and excluded, as a victory (usually compromised, often pyrrhic) for the powerless."[79] In the aftermath of victory, unless there is constant vigilance (a "pressure" that is itself a species of terror), the very forces of terror, brutality, or violence, that suffer a public defeat, often come back to divide and oppress the community even further. If the community fights back, it does so by the old rules of violence. The dispensation of justice, the righting of wrongs, the restoration of Human Rights, is reduced to a pattern of abyssal revenge and/or, at best, a spirit of litigious black-mail, *if* the group that has been helped has a strong connection to the regional human rights agencies or commissions (the dominant pres-sure groups described as "below"), which is by no means always the case. Legal awareness seminars, altogether salutary in themselves, can exacerbate the problem without the painstaking foundational peda-gogy which prepares the subject of rights from childhood and from within a disenfranchised culture of responsibility. And, if we get away from such remote areas, human rights dependency can be particularly vicious in their neo-colonial consequences if it is the state that is the agency of terror and the Euro-US that is the savior.

(Incidentally, this narrative also demonstrates that Carole Pateman's invaluable insight, "that the social contract presupposed the sexual contract," has historical variations that may not always justify the Eurocentrism that is the obvious characteristic of even *her* brilliant book.[80] On the other hand, today the history of domination and exploitation has reduced the general picture, especially for clients of human rights intervention, to a uniformity that may justify Pateman's remark: "[o]nly the postulate of natural equality prevents the original [European] social contract from being an explicit slave contract." Even so brief a hint of this historicized and uneven dialectic between past and present surely makes it clear that feminists must think of a differ-ent kind of diversified itinerary for teasing out the relationship between Human Rights and women's rights rather than cultural con-servatism, politically correct golden ageism, or ruthless-to-benevolent Eurocentrism. The suturing argument that I will elaborate below develops in the historical difference between the first two sentences of this parenthesis.)

Even if the immense labor of follow-up investigation on a case-by-case basis is streamlined in our era of telecommunication, it will not change the epistemic structure of the dysfunctional responsibility-based community, upon whom rights have been thrust from above. It will neither alleviate the reign of terror, nor undo the pattern of dependency. The recipient of human rights bounty whom I have described above, an agent of counter-terrorism and litigious blackmail at the grass roots, will continue not to resemble the ego ideal implied by the Enlightenment and the UDHR. As long as real equalization through recovering and training the long-ignored ethical imagination – not necessarily an operative script – of the rural poor and indeed, all species of sub-proletarians on their own terms – is not part of the agenda to come, s/he has no chance of becoming the subject of Human Rights as part of a collectivity, but must remain, forever, its object of benevolence. We will forever hear in the news, local to global, how these people cannot manage when they are left to manage on their own, and the new imperialism, with an at best embarrassed social Darwinist base, will get its permanent sanction.

The seventh article of the declaration of the Rights of Man and of Citizens, following eighteenth-century European radical thought, says that "[t]he law is an expression of the will of the community."[81] Among the rural poor of the global South, one may attempt, through that species of education without guarantees, to bring about a situation where the law can be imagined as the expression of a community, always to come. (Justice is another issue.) Otherwise the spirit of human rights law is completely out of their unmediated reach. The training in "literary reading" in the metropolis is here practiced, if you like, in order to produce a situation, in the mode of "to come," where it can be acknowledged that "[r]eciprocally recognized rating [to acknowledge a corresponding integrity in the other] is a condition without which no civil undertaking is possible."[82]

The supplementary method that I will go on to outline does not suggest that human rights interventions should stop. It does not even offer the impractical suggestion that the human rights activists themselves should take time to learn this method. Given the number of wrongs all the world over, those who right them must be impatient. I am making the practical suggestion for certain kinds of humanities teachers, here and there, diasporics wishing to undo the de-linking with the global South represented by impatient benevolence, second-generation colonial subjects dissatisfied by the divided postcolonial polity. (This is not to limit the readership of this essay, of course. Anyone can do what I am proposing.) Only, whoever it is must have the patience and perseverance to learn well one of the languages of the rural poor of the South. This, I hope, will set them apart from the implicit connection between world governance and the self-styled international civil society. This will also allow them to insert themselves into domestic movements for the right to education, equitable education and the like, and follow if moves are made for rearranging the mindset of children at society's ground level for an intuition of the public sphere.[83] In the field itself, the long-term goal is beyond the readership of this essay. The Secretary-General of the United Nations has said:

> Ultimately, global society will be judged on how well, or how poorly, it treats its weakest and most disadvantaged. With one-tenth of humanity living at the margin of survival, our record is not one that can be celebrated. We must change it. We must act collectively and decisively to bring about this change.[84]

Poverty and disease eradication is seen as the way to change, not the slow changing of minds of the now poor and diseased, so that whatever is eradicated by the bounty of the best can remain in place and good change, rather than mere consumerization and venality, is more assured and secure. Even in the short term however, the kind of intense activity of training I am reporting on supplements and corrects the educational initiatives of the state. The long-term hope is to affect state practice. Later in this book I will speak of re-inventing the state as structure. In the re-invented state, one hopes that the ministries of education will profit from the insights gained by what I describe in the second part of this chapter. A vain hope, perhaps, but surely worth working for.

I say above that the participant in this sort of teaching needs to learn *one* of the subaltern languages. For the purposes of the essential and possible work of righting wrongs – the political calculus – the great European languages are sufficient. But for access to the subaltern episteme to devise a suturing pedagogy, you must take into account the multiplicity of subaltern languages.

This is because the task of the educator is to learn to learn from below, the lines of conflict resolution undoubtedly available, however dormant, within the disenfranchised cultural calculus; giving up convictions of triumphalist superiority. It is because of the linguistic restriction that one is obliged to speak of just the groups one works for; but, in the hope that these words will be read by some who are interested in comparable work elsewhere, I am always pushing for generalization. The trainer of teachers will find the system dysfunctional and corrupted, mired in ritual, like a clear pond choked with scum. For its cultural axiomatics as well as its already subordinated position did not translate into the emergence of nascent capitalism. We are now teaching our children in the North, and no doubt in the North of the South, that to learn the movement of finance capital is to learn social

responsibility. It was when capitalism began to be understood as responsibility in the narrow sense (Adam Smith, if you like) and thus formed
the ideological justification for colonialism, that groups such as these
Aboriginals entered modernity as a distancing leading to gradual
atrophy.[85] Arguments for alternative modernities, however advanced,
remain confined to culture, a luxury allowed to intellectuals who take
the benefits of the public sphere, however corrupted, for granted.

This history breeds the need for activating an ethical imperative atrophied by gradual distancing from the narrative of progress – colonialism /
capitalism. This is the argument about cultural suturing, learning from
below to supplement with the possibility of the subjectship of rights.[86]

Now I go back to my broader argument – a new pedagogy. The national
education systems are pretty hopeless at this level because they are the
detritus of the postcolonial state, the colonial system turned to rote,
unproductive of felicitous colonial subjects like ourselves, at home or
abroad. This is part of what started the rotting of the cultural fabric of
which I speak. Therefore, I am not just asking that they should have
"the kind of education we have had." The need for supplementing
metropolitan education – "the kind of education we have had" – is
something I am involved in every day in my salaried work in the United
States. And when I say "rote," I am not speaking of the fact that a student might swot as a quick way to do well in an exam. I am speaking
of the scandal that, in the global South, in the schools for middle-class
children and above, the felicitous primary use of a page of language is to
understand it; but in the schools for the poor, it is to spell and memorize.

Consider the following, the vicissitudes of a local effort undertaken
in the middle of the nineteenth century.

Iswarchandra Banerjee, better known as Iswarchandra Vidyasagar, a
nineteenth-century public intellectual from rural Bengal, was 20 when
Macaulay wrote his "Minute on Indian Education." He fashioned pedagogic instruments for Sanskrit and Bengali that could, if used right (the
question of teaching, again), suture the "native" old with Macaulay's
new rather than reject the old and commence its stagnation with that
famous and horrible sentence: "A single shelf of a good European
library [is] worth the whole native literature of India and Arabia."[87]

Vidyasagar's Bengali primer is still used in state-run primary schools
in rural West Bengal.[88] It is a modernizing instrument for teaching. It
activates the structural neatness of the Sanskritic Bengali alphabet for
the teacher and the child, and undermines rote learning by encouraging
the teacher to jumble the structure in course of teaching at the same

time. The wherewithal is all there, but no one knows (how) to use it any more.[89]

The first part of the book is for the active use of the teacher. The child does not read the book yet – just listens to the teacher, and learns to read and write by reading the teacher's writing and writing as the teacher guides. Reading and writing are not soldered to the fetishized schoolbook. In very poor rural areas, with no books or newspapers anywhere, this is still a fine way to teach. (If you have been stumped a hundred times in a lot of places by both teacher and student producing some memorized bit from the textbook when asked to "write whatever comes to mind," you are convinced of this.) Halfway through the book, the child begins to read a book, and the title of that page is *prothom path*, "first reading," not "first lesson." What a thrill it must have been for the child, undoubtedly a boy, to get to that moment. Today this is impossible, because the teachers, and the teachers' teachers, indefinitely, are clueless about this book as a do-it-yourself instrument. Well-meaning education experts in the capital city, whose children are used to a different world, inspired by self-ethnographing bourgeois nationalists of a period after Vidyasagar, have transformed the teacher's pages into children's pages by way of these ill-conceived illustrations.[90]

In the rural areas this meaningless gesture has consolidated the book as an instrument for dull rote learning. The page where Vidyasagar encourages the teacher to jumble the structure is now a meaningless page routinely ignored. I could multiply examples such as this, and not in India alone. Most of the subordinate languages of the world do not have simple single-language dictionaries that rural children could use. Efforts to put together such a dictionary in Bengali failed in false promises and red tape. The habit of independence in a child's mind starts with the ability to locate meaning without a teacher. If the dictionary is put together by the kind of well-meaning experts who put together the pictures in the primer, it would be geared for the wrong audience.

The generalizable significance of this case is that, at the onset of colonialism / capitalism, when the indigenous system of teaching began to be emptied of social relevance, there had been an attempt to undo this. The discontinuity between the colonial subject and the rural poor is such that the instruments of such undoing were thoughtlessly deactivated. (This relates to the concept-metaphor of activation that I am using in this part of the essay.) As I indicate above, the metropolitan specialist has no sense of the pedagogic significance of the instruments. My discovery of the specific pattern of the primer was a revelation that

Figure 1.1   Ill-conceived illustrations.

came after eight years of involvement with using the primer. Since I do
not consolidate instruction for the teacher except in response to a felt
need, it was only then that I was letting the teacher at one school take
down hints as to how to teach the students at the lowest level. As
I continued, I realized the primer had pre-empted me at every step!
I hope the impatient reader will not take this to be just another anecdote
about poor instruction. And I hope I have made it clear by now that, in
spite of all the confusion attendant upon straying from the beaten

track, the practice of elementary pedagogy for the children of the rural poor is one of my main weapons, however humble.

The interference of the state can also be a cruel negligence. That is the point of the following story. I have included two personal details to show how caste politics, gender politics, and class politics are intertwined in the detail. These details are typical.

Each of the rural schools of which I speak has a tube well. This provides clean water for the entire group. Near two of these schools the tube well is broken. The Aboriginals could not mend it for the same reason that the metropolitan middle class cannot do these repair jobs. They are not used to it and Home Depot hasn't hit yet. (Even if it did, the Aboriginals – subalterns – would not have access to it.)

One of my fellow students in college occupies a leading position in a pertinent ministry on the state level. I renewed contact with this man after 31 years, in his office in Kolkata, to ask for tube wells. Not only did I not get tube wells after two trips separated by a year, but I heard through the rumor mill that, as a result of his boasting about my visit, his wife had disclosed in public, at a party, that she had complained to his mother about our ancient friendship!

A near relative in the next generation, whom I had not seen but briefly since he was an adolescent, held a leading administrative position on the district level. I got an appointment with him, again to beg for the tube wells. I did not get them. But he did tell me that he was in line for a fellowship at the Kennedy School. Where the infrastructure for the primary education of the poor seems negligible even in the line of official duty, boasting about one's own spectacular opportunities for higher education seems perfectly plausible: internalized axiomatics of class apartheid. I use the detail to point at a pervasive problem.

The Hindu villagers insulted a boy who went to fetch water from the tube well in the main village. At night, the oldest woman was about to go get water under cover. We sat together in her kitchen and boiled a pot of water.

The next morning, the teacher in the school could not prove that the students had learnt anything. She is a young Hindu widow from the village, who has failed her Secondary School leaving exam. As a rural Hindu, she cannot drink water touched by the Aboriginals, her students. As I kept berating her, one of these very students spoke up! (She loves the students, her not drinking water from their hands is internalized by them as normal, much less absurd than my drinking hot boiled water. On her part, going back to the village every afternoon, keeping the water-rule, which she knows I abhor, compares to

my standing in the snow for six hours to replace my stolen green card,
I later thought.)

The student spoke up to say that all but three in the school had
accompanied their parents "east," and so had not come to school for
months. Going east: migrant labor.

Just as not repairing tube wells is taken as proof of their feckless-
ness, taking their children on these journeys is seen as proof that they
don't know the value of education. These are oral tradition folks for
whom real education takes place in the bosom of the family. By what
absurd logic would they graduate instantly into a middle-class understanding of something so counter-intuitive as "the value of education"?
Such lectures produce the kind of quick-fix "legal awareness"-style lessons whose effects are at best superficial, but satisfying for the activists,
until the jerrybuilt edifice breaks down. When the community was
addressed with sympathy, with the explicit understanding that behind
this removal of the students from school lay love and responsibility,
some children were allowed to stay behind next year. When I spoke of
this way of dealing with absenteeism to the 100 so-called rural teachers
(stupid statistics) subsidized by the central government, one of the
prejudice-ridden rural Hindu unemployed who had suddenly become
a "teacher" advised me – not knowing that this elite city person knew
what she was talking about – that the extended aboriginal community
would object to the expenditure of feeding these children. Nonsense,
of course, and prejudice, not unknown in the native informant.

When I saw that the three students who had not "gone east" were
doing fine, and that a year had gone by without tube wells, I said to
them, write a letter. Another student, sitting back, looked so eager
to write that I let her come forward as well. Each one give a sentence,
I said, I will not prompt you (see figure 1.2).[91] I told them the secret of
alphabetization. They successfully alphabetized their first names. My
second visit to this man's office, the source of the prurient party gossip
in Kolkata, was to deliver the letter, in vain.

I have covered the place names because we do not want a tube well
from a remote international or national philanthropic source. The
water's getting boiled for me. They are drinking well water. We want
the children to learn about the heartlessness of administrations, without short-term resistance talk. The bounty of some US benefactor
would be the sharp end of the wedge that produces a general will for
exploitation in the subaltern.[92] *Mutatis mutandis*, I go with W. E. B.
DuBois rather than Booker T. Washington: it is more important to
develop a critical intelligence than to assure immediate material comfort.[93]

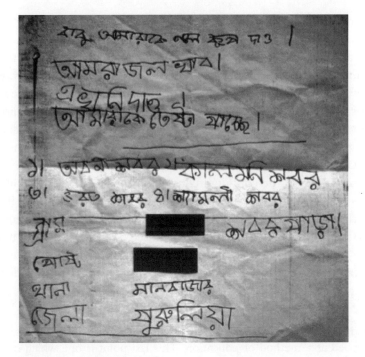

Figure 1.2 Students' letter

This may or may not bear immediate fruit. Let me repeat, yet once again, although I fear I will not convince the benevolent ethnocentrist, that I am not interested in teaching "self-help." I am interested in being a good enough humanities teacher in order to be a conduit (Wordsworth's word) between subaltern children and their subaltern teachers. That is my connection with DuBois, who writes a good deal about teacher training. (The ruling party has given the school a tube well.)

The schools have now been given over to the corporate sector by the local feudal leader because the students were beginning to question authority. No more slow training into democracy.

The teachers on this ground level at which we work tend to be the least successful products of a bad system. Our educator must learn to train teachers by attending to the children. For, just as our children are not born electronic, their children are not born delegitimized. They are not yet "least successful." It is through learning how to take children's response to teaching as our teaching text that we can hope to put ourselves in the way of "activating" democratic structures.

And it is to distinguish between "activating" and producing good descriptive information for peers (the appropriate brief for an essay such as this), that I should like to point at the difference between Melanie Klein and Jean Piaget. Attending to children, Klein's way of speaking had turned into a kind of sublime literalness, where the metaphor is as literal as "reality." In order to flesh out Freud's intuitions about children, Klein learnt her system from the children themselves. Her writings are practical guides to people who wished to "learn" that language. That too is to learn to learn from below.

By contrast, all the confident conclusions of Piaget and his collaborators in *The Moral Judgment of Children* would be messed up if the investigators had been obliged to insert themselves into and engage with the value-system the children inhabited. Piaget is too sharp not to know this. "[I]t is one thing to prove that cooperation in the play and spontaneous social life of children brings about certain moral effects," he concludes,

> and another to establish the fact that this cooperation can be universally applied as a method of education. This last point is one which only experimental education can settle. ... But the type of experiment which such research would require can only be conducted by teachers or by the combined efforts of practical workers and educational psychologists. And it is not in our power to deduce the results to which this would lead.[94]

The effort at education that I am describing – perhaps comparable to Piaget's description of "practical workers" – the teachers – and "educational psychologists" – the trainers – with the roles productively confused every step of the way – hopes against hope that a permanent sanction of the social Darwinism – "the burden of the fittest" – implicit in the human rights agenda will, perhaps, be halted if the threads of the torn cultural fabric are teased out by the uncanny patience of which the Humanities are capable at their best, for the "activation" of dormant structures. I put the quotation marks to remind ourselves that we are not talking about cause-and-effect here but an imaginative labor that opens the way to a possibility.

Indeed, this is the "humanities component," attending upon the object of investigation as other, in all labor. Here is the definitive moment of a Humanities "to come," in the service of a Human Rights, that persistently undoes the asymmetry in the title of the series by the uncoercive rearrangement of desires in terms of the teaching text described above.

The Greek poet Archilochus is supposed to have written "the fox knows many things, but the hedgehog knows one big thing." This distinction between two types of thinkers was developed by Isaiah Berlin into the idea that fox-thinkers are fascinated by the variety of things, and hedgehog-thinkers relate everything to an all-embracing system.[95]

My experience of learning from the children for the last decade and more tells me that nurturing the capacity to imagine the public sphere and the fostering of independence within chosen rule-governance is the hedgehog's definition of democracy which will best match the weave of the torn yet foxy fabric – great variety of detail – of the culture long neglected by the dominant. The trick is to train the teachers by means of such intuitions, uncoercively rearranging *their* (most often unexamined) desires for specific kinds of futures for the children. No mean trick, for these teachers have been so maimed by the very system of education we are trying to combat, and are so much within the class apartheid produced by it, that they would blindly agree and obey, while the trainer was emoting over consciousness-raising. Great tact is called for if the effort is to draw forth consent rather than obedience. In addition, the children have to be critically prepared for disingenuously offered cyber literacy if these groups get on the loop of "development."[96] The hope is that this effort with the *teachers* will translate into the teaching of these reflexes in the educational method of the children who launch *the trainer* on the path of the hedgehog. The children are the future electorate. They need to be taught the habits and reflexes of such democratic behavior. Do you see why I call this necessary and impossible? As I remarked about Humanities teaching on p. 23, you cannot gauge this one.

To suture thus the torn and weak responsibility-based system into a conception of human dignity as the enjoyment of rights one enters ritual practice transgressively, alas, as a hacker enters software. The description of ritual-hacking below may seem silly, perhaps. But put yourself on the long road where you *can* try it, and you will respect us – you will not dismiss us as "nothing but" this or that approach on paper. In so far as this hacking is like a weaving, this too is an exercise in *texere*, textil-ity, text-ing, textuality. I must continue to repeat that my emphasis is on the difficulties of this texting, the practical pedagogy of it, not in devising the most foolproof theory of it for you, my peers. Without the iterative text of doing and devising in silence, the description seems either murky or banal.

Subordinate cultural systems are creative in the invention of ritual in order to keep a certain hierarchical order functioning. With the help of the children and the community, the trainer must imagine the task of recoding the ritual-to-order habits of the earlier system with the ritual-to-order habits of parliamentary democracy, with a teaching corps whose idea of education is unfortunately produced by a terrible system. One learns active ritual as one learns manners. The best example for the readership of this book might be the "wild anthropology" of the adult metropolitan migrant, learning a dominant culture on the run, giving as little away as possible. The difference here is that we learn from the vulnerable archaic (Raymond Williams's word captures the predicament better than the anthropological "primitive"), but also without giving much away. The point is to realize that democracy also has its rituals, exaggerated or made visible, for example, when in our metropolitan life we seek to make politically correct manners "natural," a matter of reflex.

It is because this habit – of recoding ritual (always, of course, in the interest of uncoercive rearrangement of desires) for training other practitioners, rather than for production of knowledge about knowledge – has to be learned by the teacher as a reflex that I invoked the difference between Klein and Piaget. I will not be able to produce anthropologically satisfying general descriptions here because no trainer can provide satisfactory descriptions of the grammar of a language that s/he is learning painfully. This *is* the distinction I want to convey.[97] What follows must remain hortatory – an appeal to your imagination until we meet in the field of specific practice, here or there. Of course we all know, with appropriate cynicism, that this probably will not be. But a ceremonial lecture allows you to tilt at windmills, to insist that such practice is the only way that one can hope to supplement the work of human rights litigation in order to produce cultural entry into modernity.

Fine, you will say, maybe human rights interventions do not have the time to engage in this kind of patient education, but there are state-sponsored systems, NGOs, and activists engaging in educational initiatives, surely? The NGO drives count school buildings and teacher bodies. The national attempts also do so, but only at best. Activists, who care about education in the abstract and are critical of the system, talk rights, talk resistance, even talk nationalism, sometimes teach math, science – the way into modernity – or vocational skills. But instilling habits in very young minds is like writing on soft cement. Repeating slogans, even good slogans, is not the way to go, alas. It breeds fascists just as easily. UNESCO's teaching guides for Human Rights are not helpful as guides.

Some activists attempt to instill pride, in these long-disenfranchised groups, in a pseudo-historical narrative. This type of "civilizationism" is good for gesture politics and breeding leaders, but does little for the development of democratic reflexes.[98] These pseudo-histories are assimilated into the etiological mythologies of the Aboriginals without epistemic change. Given subaltern ethnic divisions, our teaching also proceeds in the conviction that, if identitarianism is generally bad news here, it is also generally bad news there.

Let me now say a very few words about the actual teaching, which is necessarily subject to restricted generalizability, because it is predicated upon confronting the specific problems of the closest general educational facility to which the teachers have had, and the students might have, access. Such generalizations can only be made within the framework of the undoing of those specific problems. One generalization seems apposite and relates to my parenthesis on Pateman on p. 41. Whatever the status of women in the old delegitimized cultural system, in today's context emphasis must always be placed on girl-children's access to that entry, without lecturing, without commanding, earning credibility, of course. Another minimally generalizable rule of thumb in this teaching I will focus on is the one that Vidyasagar, the nineteenth-century Bengali intellectual, picked up 150 years ago: undermine rote learning.

As I mentioned at the beginning of this discussion, I am not speaking of the fact that a student might swot as a quick way to do well in an exam. I'm speaking of the scandal that, in the global South, in the schools for middle-class children and above, the felicitous primary use of a page of language is to understand it; in the schools for the poor, it is to spell and memorize. This is an absolute and accepted divide, the consolidation of continuing class apartheid I referred to above. It is as a result of this that "education" is seen upon subaltern terrain as another absurdity bequeathed by powerful people and, incidentally, of no use at all to girl-children. And by the feudal authorities, any effort at remedying this is finally seen as a threat to their own power and authority.

My own teachers, when I was a student in a good middle-class Bengali medium primary school in Kolkata, explained the texts. But as I have mentioned, there is no one to explain in these rural primary schools. I walked a couple of hours to a village high school in the national system and waited an hour and a half after opening time for the rural teachers to arrive. This is one of many experiences, involving

other students of course. I begged them to take good care of the two
aboriginal young women I was sending to the school. In late afternoon, the girls returned. "Did she explain?" I asked. "No, just spelling
and reading." An absurd history lesson about "National Liberation
Struggles in Many Countries," written in incomprehensible prose. I am
going into so much detail because no urban or international radical
bothers to look at the detail of the general system as they write of
special projects – "non-formal education," "functional literacy,"
science projects here and there. Just before I left India in January 2001,
a filmmaker made an English documentary entitled something like
"A Tribe Enters the Mainstream." My last act before departure was
to make sure that the shots of my school be excised. The so-called
direct interviews are risible. How can these people give anything but
the expected answers in such situations? And yet it is from such "docu-
mentaries" that we often gather evidence. This video was later shown
at a nationwide human rights gathering in the capital city with international attendance in September, 2001. What is the generalizable significance of these embittered remarks? To emphasize the discontinuity
between the domestic "below" and the grass roots before I offer the
final report on the education of Gayatri Spivak.

My project seems to have defined itself as the most ground-level
task for the breaking of the production and continuation of class apartheid. I now understand why, in Marx's world, Marx had come down to
something as simple as the shortening of the working day as "the
grounding condition [*die Grundbedingung*]" when he was speaking of
such grand topics as the Realm of Freedom and the Realm of
Necessity.

The discovery of the practical use of the primer was an important
moment for me. Other moments would be difficult to integrate into
this; they might seem inconsequential or banal. Something that can
indeed be reported is that, since I presented a version of this chapter to
Amnesty International in February 2001, I have learnt how to communicate to the teachers and students – for whom the absurd education
system *is* education – that it is the class apartheid of the state that is
taken on in the move from rote to comprehension. I can now show
that there is no connection between this absurd education (to memorize incomprehensible chunks of prose and some verse in response to
absurd questions in order to pass examinations; to begin to forget the
memorized material instantly) and the existing cultural residue of
responsibility. (In metropolitan theoretical code, this lack of connection may be written as no sense at all that the written is a message from

a structurally absent subject, a placeholder of alterity, although the now-delegitimized local culture is programmed for responsibility as a call of the other – alterity – before will. Thus education in this area cannot activate or rely on "culture" without outside/inside effort.) For the suturing with enforced class-subalternization I had to chance upon an immediately comprehensible concept-metaphor: when there is no exercise for the imagination, no training in intellectual labor – *matha khatano* – for those who are slated for manual labor – *gatar khatano* – at best, the rich/poor divide (*barolok/chhotolok*, big people/small people) is here to stay.[99] At least one teacher said, at leave-taking, that he now understood what I wanted, in the language of obedience, alas. There is more work for the trainer down the road, uncoercive undermining of the class-habit of obedience.

Perhaps you can now imagine how hard it is to change this episteme, how untrustworthy the activists' gloat. For the solidarity tourist, it is a grand archaic sight to see rural children declaiming their lessons in unison, especially if, as in that mud-floored classroom in Yunan, six- to nine-year olds vigorously dance their bodies into ancient calligraphy. But if you step forward to work together, and engage in more than useless patter, the situation is not so romantic. Learning remains by rote.

It is a cruel irony that when the meaning of *sram* in Vidyasagar's Lesson 2 – *sram na korile lekhapora hoy na* – is explained as "labor" and the aboriginal child is asked if she or he has understood, he or she will show their assent by giving an example of manual labor. In English, the sentence would read – without labor you cannot learn to write and read – meaning intellectual labor, of course.

Produced by this class-corrupt system of education, the teachers themselves do not know how to write freely. They do not know the meaning of what they "teach," since all they have to teach, when they are doing their job correctly, is spelling and memorizing. They do not know what dictionaries are. They have themselves forgotten everything they memorized to pass out of primary school. When we train such teachers, we must, above all, let them go, leave them alone, to see if the efforts of us outsiders have been responsive enough, credible enough without any material promises. When I see rousing examples of "people's movements," I ask myself, how long would the people continue without the presence of the activist leaders? It is in the context of earning that credibility that I am reporting my access to the new concept-metaphor binary: *matha khatano/gator khatano*: class apartheid: *barolok/chhotolok*.

I am often reprimanded for writing incomprehensibly. There is no one to complain about the jargon-ridden incomprehensibility of children's text books in this subaltern world. If I want you to understand the complete opacity of that absurd history lesson about "National Liberation Struggles in Many Countries," devised by some state functionary at the Ministry of Education, for example, I would have to take most of you through an intensive Bengali lesson so that you are able to assess different levels of the language. Without venturing up to that perilous necessity, I will simply recapitulate: First, the culture of responsibility is corrupted. The effort is to learn it with patience from below and to keep trying to suture it to the imagined felicitous subject of universal Human Rights. Secondly, the education system is a corrupt ruin of the colonial model. The effort is persistently to undo it, to teach the habit of democratic civility. Thirdly, to teach these habits, with responsibility to the corrupted culture, is different from children's indoctrination into nationalism, resistance-talk, identitarianism.

I leave this essay with the sense that the material about the rural teaching is not in the acceptable mode of information retrieval. The difficulty is in the discontinuous divide between those who right wrongs and those who are wronged. I have no interest in becoming an educational researcher or a diasporic golden-ageist. I will ask my New York students what concept-metaphor served them best. (Dorah Ahmad told me this afternoon that what she liked best about my graduate teaching was the use of stories that made immediate sense!)

Here are some nice abstract seemingly fighting words:

> [G]enerative politics is by no means limited to the formal political sphere but spans a range of domains where political questions arise and must be responded to. Active trust is closely bound up with such a conception. ... No longer depending on pregiven alignments, it is more contingent, and contextual, than most earlier forms of trust relations. It does not necessarily imply equality, but it is not compatible with deference arising from traditional forms of status.[100]

If you want to attempt to bring this about – for the sake of a global justice to come – hands-on – you begin with something like what I have described in this chapter.

I am so irreligious that atheism seems a religion to me. But I now understand why fundamentalists of all kinds have succeeded best in the teaching of the poor – for the greater glory of God. One needs some sort of "licensed lunacy" (Orlando Patterson's phrase) from some transcendental Other to develop the sort of ruthless commitment that can undermine the sense that one is better than those who are being helped, that the ability to manage a complicated life support system is the same as being civilized. But I am influenced by deconstruction and for me, radical alterity cannot be named "God," in any language. Indeed, the name of "man" in "human" rights (or the name of "woman" in "women's rights are human rights") will continue to trouble me.

"Licensed lunacy in the name of the unnamable other," then. It took me this long to explain this incomprehensible phrase. Yet the efforts I have described may be the only recourse for a future to come when the reasonable righting of wrongs will not inevitably be the manifest destiny of groups that remain poised to right them; when wrongs will not proliferate with unsurprising regularity. A future around the corner.

Chapter 2

Responsibility[1] – 1992: Testing Theory in the Plains

Section I of this chapter is a reading of Derrida's *Of Spirit*. I include it here because I want to make the point that the structures of today's European benevolence may be a displacement of yesterday's – and Derrida's reading of Heidegger in the context of twentieth-century Europe provides an analysis like no other. If Derrida is not to your taste, skip this section and go on to section II.

Argument: *Of Spirit* is Derrida's consideration of Heidegger's involvement with Nazism. Derrida thinks that the trajectory of "spirit" in Heidegger's work gives us a clue. Derrida's reading shows that European thought is marked as such by the ethnocentrism that took an extreme form in Nazism. Such an extremism is possible when the best lessons of the European Enlightenment are forgotten, as they were by Heidegger. In this chapter, I examine an enlightened European activist conference to show how European benevolence is still burdened by this heritage, even when far from the extreme. I also suggest that among the non-European beneficiaries, class-difference amounts to cultural difference. I have not offered a simplified reading of *Of Spirit*. The reader is invited to read the book together with my comments.

Responsibility annuls the call to which it seeks to respond by necessarily changing it to the calculations of answerability.

What is it, then, to be responsible to a changeful thought on the question of responsibility? "[;W]hat could be the responsibility ... [toward] a consistent discourse which claimed to show that no responsibility could ever be taken without equivocation and without contradiction?"[2] To open a chapter with such a question is perhaps already to be a traitor to the ideal of academic responsibility in which one was trained. That ideal was to give an objective account of an argument with textual demonstrations, and subsequently to evaluate it, on its own terms as well as by the standards of an impartial judgment. By comparison with the imperatives of that austere responsibility, the first years of my teaching career, which began in 1965, seemed to be haunted by demands of an extreme *ir*responsibility toward the impersonality of history and augury: "Do *we* like it?" "Is that relevant to *us*?", and then, "to *me*?" seemed to be the question of the US in the sixties.

To open a chapter with the question, of responsibility to a thought, precisely of responsibility, from which a lesson of responsibility is learned, goes against the grain of both those imperatives. For it shows, first, that one is already partisan. And, secondly, it reveals that one's anxiety is for one's responsibility *to* the text, not the other way around. And yet, are there not similarities between the first two approaches outlined in the paragraph above and mine, here? For we know that the early lesson of disinterested objectivity was in fact an unacknowledged loyalty – a partisanship – to a sort of universalist humanism which dictated that one show, even if by the way and by default, that the literary or philosophical text in general is good. And as for the other, does one not, given the current demand for the justification of an interest in "deconstructive philosophical speculation" in a politically inclined female migrant, demonstrate again and again, its relevance to such inclinations and such provenance?[3]

And further, there is the necessity to be responsible to the warning to "a community of well-meaning deconstructionists, reassured and reconciled with the world in ethical certainty, good conscience, satisfaction of services rendered, and the consciousness of duty accomplished (or more heroically still, yet to be accomplished)."[4] Responsibility to the reminder that, when the philosopher – or anyone – tries and tries to explain and reveal, and the respondent tries and tries to receive the explanation and the revelation, the something that must of necessity not go through is the secret and changeable "essence" of that exchange, the event that escapes the performative conventions of the exchange. Abdicating this responsibility as "individualism" makes collectivities fragile.

Perhaps there is no answer to this question but the constant attempt "to let oneself be approached by the resistance which the thinking of responsibility may offer thought."[5] Perhaps to be responsible to the question of responsibility is not to resist what will have happened, that the reader(s) will have judged, necessarily with and in spite of standards, necessarily related and different. In this the thought of responsibility is a more affirmative formulation of what was written 30 years ago: "*thought* is ... the blank part of the text."[6] If deconstruction comes tangled with responsibility to the trace of the other, the reader(s) stand in here as the indefinite narrow trace of that radically other which cannot even (have or) be a face.

For this reader the difficult giving of permission to be approached by that which most resists thought can be reduced to a literal translation (with all the necessity and impossibility that translation calls for and by which it is called).[7] This specific "translation," in this essay, takes off from a literal understanding of statements such as the following: "[T]hese new responsibilities cannot be *purely* academic ... Between ... [the principle of reason and an-archy] ... only the staging [*mise-en-scène*] of this 'thought' can decide.... To claim to eliminate that risk by an institutional program is quite simply to erect a barricade against a future."[8]

One attempts, then, to stage the thought of responsibility in ways that are not *purely* academic. The peculiar (con)textualities of the theatres where each of these attempts is made inscribe an experience of the necessity of such translations and their impossibility. These experiences also teach how conservative it is to remain content with radical institutional programs alone.

Not being a philosopher by talent and training, I cannot philosophize the delicate ruptures involved in the brutality of these literal translations. That more profound speculation would look upon the night of non-knowledge and non-rule in which all decisions are taken, even when it is the most detailed knowledge that has been used in the staging of responsibility. (This sentence already begs the question of responsibility, assumes its nature known.) This essay may be distinguished from those more perilous watches as the quicker tempo of the eve and the morning-after of that night, the night of non-knowledge when a just decision tears time, the time of effect following just cause.[9] What the two share is the guess that "the limit of ... [the] formalization ... [of a problematic is] a sort of intermediary stage."[10]

Whatever is formalizable remains at a sort of intermediary stage. This is perhaps one way of being responsible to the thinking of responsibility. The rest cannot be *purely* formalized. Formalizing steps must be formally taken *and* experienced as limits, before the usual beginnings of a setting to work can be made. Full formalization itself must be seen not as impossible, but as an experience of the impossible, or a figure for the impossible, which may be to say the "same thing."[11]

I can formalize responsibility in the following way: It is that all action is undertaken in response to a call (or something that seems to us to resemble a call) that cannot be grasped as such. Response here involves not only "respond to" as in "*give* an answer to," but also the related situations of "answering to" as in being responsible for a name (this brings up the question of the relationship between being responsible for/to ourselves and for/to others); of being answerable for, all of which Derrida presents within the play, in French, between *répondre à* and *répondre de*. It is also, when it is possible for the other to be face-to-face, the task and lesson of attending to her response so that it can draw forth one's own. (I believe both Derrida and Luce Irigaray have seen the psychoanalytic model at its impossible purest to accede to this sense of responsibility.[12])

With this formalization of the problematic of responsibility, seen as an intermediary stage, caught between an ungraspable call and a staging, or production, this essay will offer two readings, of Derrida's *Of Spirit*, and of a conference on the World Bank's Flood Action Plan in Bangladesh.[13] My readings finally show that (the thinking of) responsibility is also (a thinking of) contamination. If one will, then, seem to have shown that deconstruction is relevant to what is called the political sphere, after all, it will be the moment to ask you to remember that such demonstrations can only happen within the intermediary stage, and to make relevant is a taming.

I   *Of Spirit: Heidegger and the Question*

Of all the texts of Derrida that I have read, this seems to me to be the one that assumes in the reader a careful and intimate reading of all the texts on method that have come before, a familiarity with a specialized vocabulary that might otherwise seem deceptively "metaphorical" or transparent. It is, therefore, a "secretive" text, both in the colloquial, and in the Derridian sense. In the first sense, because it seems to guard its own secret, it is difficult to understand. (To a careless speed-reader it will even provide confirmation of stock responses.) In the second sense, because, even though, to the responsive reader, the text wishes to reveal itself to the full, it still seems to leave the reader with questions. There is nothing authorized about the reading I offer below, and especially about the "reasons" that I submit for the secretiveness of the text. Indeed, I have not tried to pry out the secret by referring to less secretive writings by Derrida on the Heidegger question. The secrecy of the secret does not disappear with revelation. "The secret never allows itself to be captured or covered over by the relation to the other, by being-with or by any form of 'social bond'.... No *responsiveness*."[14]

One of the reasons for the "secretiveness" may be the impossibility of a fully justified position of accusation.

In one respect, *Of Spirit* traces Heidegger's seeming failure of responsibility toward his own thinking. In *Being and Time*, Heidegger had found it prudent to keep the question of the spirit open, broachable only within quotation marks, if at all.[15] Already in the opening pages of his text, Derrida suggests that in fact Heidegger's entire earlier philosophy was dependent upon a question of the spirit that was merely avoided or foreclosed. The spirit works away at the text, finally to emerge with a terrifying role, perhaps precisely because its question had been avoided. Toward the end of section V, Derrida demonstrates this with reference to the *Rectorship Address*:[16] "... suddenly, with a single blow ..., the lifting of the quotation marks marks the raising of the curtain.... [T]he entry on stage of spirit itself.... Six years later, and here we have the *Rectorship Address*" (OS 31; I take responsibility for extrapolating from this closely orchestrated prose).

Here for the first time, Derrida writes, Heidegger defines spirit. The definition is not in contradiction with *Being and Time*, for spirit still does not seem to belong to subjectivity, "*at least* in its psychical or egological form" (OS 37). We are not speaking, in other words, of the human spirit, even in the most metaphysical sense. Thus, by appealing to such a "spiritual force," unattached to the merely human, the address may "*seem* ... no longer to belong simply to the 'ideological' camp in which one appeals to obscure forces – forces which would not be spiritual but natural, biological, racial, according to an anything but spiritual interpretation of 'earth and blood' (OS 39)." But, and this is why we must proceed cautiously, *every* such gestures turns back "against its 'subject' ... [b]ecause one cannot demarcate oneself from biologism, from racism in its genetic form, one cannot be *opposed* to them except by reinscribing spirit in an oppositional determination" (OS 39). Thus one binds the philosophical a-partness of spirit by determining it into a narrow sense as that which is the opposite of biologism or genetic racism. It loses its (non)character of guarding question. Hence it no longer remains prior to – or outside of – all differences between subject and whatever is not subject. It belongs to the subject(s) who rally in its name. It becomes negotiable. It is made to take a side and thus becomes unilateral. Thus

> reinscribing spirit in an oppositional demarcation, ... once again mak[es] it a unilaterality of subjectity, even if [especially?] in its voluntarist form.

> This constraint ... reigns over the majority of discourses which, today
> and for a long time [he cannot say forever] to come, state their opposi-
> tion to racism, to totalitarianism, to nazism, to fascism, etc., and do
> this in the name of an axiomatic – for example, that of democracy or
> "human rights" – which, directly or not, comes back to this metaphys-
> ics of *subjectity* . ... The only choice is the choice between the terrify-
> ing contaminations it assigns. Even if all forms of complicity are not
> equivalent, they are *irreducible*. The question of knowing which is the
> least grave of these forms of complicity is always there – its urgency
> and its seriousness could not be over-stressed – but it will never dis-
> solve the irreducibility of this fact . ... [I]t calls more than ever, as for
> what in it remains to come after the disasters that have happened, for
> absolutely unprecedented responsibilities of "thought" and "action."
> (OS 39–40)

I have quoted this passage at such length because it should be read
carefully and slowly. No academic eager to take sides (in "thought")
cleanly without any "active" responsibility wants to acknowledge the
final and irreducible complicity between *all* unilateral binding of the
spirit in a single cause. And all sustained "activists" know that victories
are warnings, even if they are unable to articulate it philosophically,
and even if they often silence that knowledge in the interest of the
decision, in the interest of tying down the future of the "movement,"
even if, by so doing, they do nothing to keep the unexpected at bay.
Derrida attempts to undo that gap, again and again.

It is not that we must not take sides. We must continue to try to
know and make known "which is the least grave of these forms of
complicity." It is just that the decisive testing of the intellectually clear
"thought" – which can construct systemic ways and means of avoiding
logical risks through the fine-tuning of knowledge – must therefore be
in "action," the element of which is the risky night of non-knowledge.
This is a position against the vanguardism of theory, not against risk-
taking. The position is not heroic enough for armchair left liberals. But
for those of us who have seen Gandhi's *Rām-Rājya* (the kingdom of
Rāma) where, to give Gandhi the benefit of a doubt which he perhaps
did not fully deserve, Rāma was a nomination of the spirit of indigenous democracy, become the excuse for a state on the brink of a
Fascism committed to the genocide of Muslims; and seen Marx's project
of the proletarian's collective use of reason (class-consciousness),
where rationality is the nomination of the human spirit, become an
imperialism that, in postcoloniality, hankers after an underdeveloped
capitalism as an alternative to genocide; and for those of us who daily

see the covert and overt violence regularly practiced by the ideological
and systemic manipulation of rational principles such as due process,
Human Rights, and democracy – these warnings must be taken seriously. We cannot necessarily assume, however implicitly, that the
European-style invocation of spirit is uncontaminated, whereas other
invocations of spirit are by definition ignorant or fundamentalist. The
passage I have quoted is hard to understand only if the lessons of history
("the disasters that have happened") have not been heeded. Indeed,
inspirational academic heroics resist understanding here. The implacable logic of the terrifying contamination by putting the radically other
within an opposition is doing its supplementary labor in these becomings,
these happenings. A "responsible" thought describes "responsibility" –
caught in a question necessarily begged in action – as attending to the
call of that irreducible fact. This is a practical position, an elaboration
of the earlier position that, in effect, practice norms theory.[17]

As a practical academic, it is my unauthorized conviction that it is
because of this academic resistance to acknowledgement of complicity that Derrida writes this most painful text in a language that must be
learned: in other words, accessible to a reading that is responsible to
the text. (The steps of such a reading are laid out in Paul Celan's search
for Lenz embedded in "Shibboleth".)

But why is this text painful? I think because in a sense more restricted
than the general position outlined above, deconstruction cannot not
acknowledge complicity with Heidegger. Precisely because of "responsibility," Derrida cannot and indeed will not, unlike Richard Rorty,
simply separate the man from the work.[18] I have been arguing, in a
certain way, that Derrida's is "a teaching language." And indeed that is
what Derrida says of the Heidegger of the Rectorate speech:

> Here we have a teaching language.... No more than in 1933 does it
> rehabilitate the concept of spirit deconstructed in *Sein und Zeit*. But it is
> still in the name of the spirit, the spirit that guides in resolution toward
> the question, the will to know and the will to essence, that the other
> spirit, its bad double, the phantom of subjectity, turns out to be warded
> off by means of *Destruktion*. (OS 41)

I have been spelling out so far that, according to Derrida, the phantom of subjectity cannot be warded off. Indeed, that is the responsibility Heidegger gives up and thus moves relentlessly toward unilaterality.
This unilaterality has a bad trajectory because the philosophy of
Destruktion cannot be used to ward off accountability, answerability,

responsibility as *répondre de*.[19] Unilaterality can only ever be a reminder of its open-ended and irreducible risk.

You will remember that between the journal and the book-form publication of *De la grammatologie*, Derrida changed the word *déstruction* to *déconstruction*. Heidegger's case demonstrates why *Destruktion* (as task) must not be used to ward off responsibility but rather (as event) must be acknowledged as a reminder of how we are written. Unable as we are (and should be) not to take sides, Derrida must speak of the folly of "doing" deconstruction as if it were fully under our control. (This relates to the conviction that the decisive ethico-political evaluation of thought is not self-contained but rather in its setting-to-work.) In other words, paradoxically (impossibly) yet necessarily, in the setting-to-work, deconstruction may be bound to good or bad uses. This *is* the double bind of deconstruction, its peculiar humility, responsibility, and strength; its acknowledgement of radical contamination. It can be undertaken by someone who has learnt it to work with it, against the grain of the merely philosophical, acknowledging responsibility toward its history. Even "knowing" it is not enough, just as knowing the rules of a card game does not mean that you have learnt to play it well. Deconstruction is caught between the high rollers of the establishment who, without the patience or the training to read the material carefully, congratulate themselves on having discovered its lack of moral muscle; and the "defenders": those who claim it learnedly for philosophy, disowning its dependence on the un-philosophical or diagnosing the latter as simply literature; and those who do "correct politics" with it.[20]

But Nazism is a consequence that requires a careful reckoning of the lesson of deconstruction; not a denunciation that will please academics, but also not a defense that will endorse the two different kinds of defenders. It is in this position that Derrida writes for those who will read with care. We must not forget that the object of his investigation is still a speech that is given at a university, and the point of his critique is that *Destruktion* cannot be used to ward off the dangers of the necessarily unilateral subject. Before we pursue the critique further, it might therefore be pertinent to quote another statement of it in a speech given by Derrida himself at Columbia University, where he spoke of the responsibility of the academic in a modern university, necessarily imbricated with the structures of a post-industrial managerial society: "One can doubtless decenter the subject, as is easily said, without retesting the bond between, on the one hand, responsibility, and, on the other, freedom of subjective consciousness or purity of intentionality."[21]

Heidegger, in using *Destruktion* as if he could control it, bypasses this challenge with murderous consequences. The armchair deconstructor, decentering his or her subject at will, "denies the [prior] axiomatics *en bloc* and keeps it going as a survivor, with minor adjustments *de rigueur* and daily compromises lacking in rigor. So coping, so operating at top speed, one accounts and becomes accountable for nothing: not for what happens, not for the reasons to continue assuming responsibilities without a concept."[22] How would it be if a fully deconstructive or *destruktiv* text could be produced? Its surface would be "given over to ... an animal machine ... a figure of evil" (OS 134). Let us pursue this enigmatic pronouncement.

In "L'animal que donc je suis (à suivre)," Derrida elaborates his meditation upon "*the* animal."[23] He cites there the very footnote that we were discussing in the original version of this chapter, published in 1994 (p. 289). Derrida suggests that the "animal-machine is something that the Christian tradition operates in order to keep the autobiography-confession line working" (p. 272). In a note to this note, Derrida suggests further that the responseless-ness of the *Zusage* ("language of 'before' the question") of the late Heidegger would make it amenable to the "animal" (who by definition cannot respond) and thus deprive the related tradition – "from Descartes to Heidegger, from Kant to Levinas and to Lacan" – of its "fundamental sales pitch [*argumentaire*]" (p. 289n). I am always delighted when I, on a cruder register, am fair to (*suis juste avec*) a Derridian move (to be distinguished from attempting to imitate the way he writes). In the present essay, distinguishing the largely fish-eating Muslims of Bangladesh from the sacrificial Abrahamic tradition (see p. 82), I was perhaps acknowledging, altogether crudely and before the letter, the heterogeneity of *the* animal, that Derrida marks with the word "animot" in the 1999 essay, delivered at Cerisy in 1998? I do not yet know how to read the *agnicayana* (fire-assembling) account in the ninth and tenth chapters of the *Satapathabrāhmana*, where the animals (*prajā* should rather be translated "creatures" here, literally) escape the creator as the master of the creatures or *prajāpati* himself, who then makes man, measure, bricks and much else, and coaxing co-operation with the animals, now named as "horsy," – generically? – "the *ashvins* [those who have horses] have now become everything," the text says repeatedly.[24] This account is only one etiology of sacrificial practice in a polytheist heteropraxy and thus additionally non-continuous with the Abrahamic.

In the section that follows the passages we have been reading, Derrida reads Heidegger as the latter names the animal, and exposes a humanist teleology for Heidegger's "deconstruction of ontology" (OS 57).[25]

Let us focus on the comment on that most Heideggerian/Derridian gesture, the "sous rature."[26] It might be thought of as a gesture of warding off – keeping a thing visible but crossed out, to avoid universalizing or monumentalizing it. As we have been reading it, this gesture can only be used (indeed must be performed in deconstruction as task in view of deconstruction as event) in the form of a warning of an irreducibility outside of intentional control, rather than a controlled gesture of saving oneself from the worst consequences of that irreducibility; as in Heidegger's implicit reliance upon *Destruktion* in the Rectorate address.[27] The gesture in Heidegger's *Zur Seinsfrage* seems not inconsonant with this:

> Heidegger proposes to write the word Being under a line of erasure in the form of a cross (*kreuzweise Durchstreichung*). This cross did not represent either a negative sign or even a sign at all, but it was supposed to recall the *Geviert*, the fourfold, precisely, as "the play of the world"... [which] – recalled in this way by an erasing of "Being" – [allows the decipherment of] the becoming-world of the world... It means in this case that one cannot derive or think the world starting from anything else but it. But look at this other proposition of crossing-through (*Durchstreichung*) from twenty-five years earlier.... (OS 52)

and we flashback to the animal. I will attempt the daunting task of summarizing Derrida's itinerary.

Derrida deduces a certain "anthropomorphic or even humanist teleology" in the thinking of *Dasein* in view of the difference between "the animal's privation [*Entbehrung*] from *Dasein*'s privation [*Privation*] in comprehension of the world" (OS 55, 54). The animal "lack[s] access to the entity as such ... as if ... the Being of the entity ... were crossed out in advance, but with an absolute crossing-out, that of privation" (OS 53). This is not the philosophical crossing-out that the philosopher must practice to "recall" that *Dasein* cannot get behind the world worlding. It is a "crossing-through of the crossing-through" (or being-crossed-through) (OS 56).

Further, "the animal can be after a prey, it can calculate, hesitate, follow or try out a track, but it cannot properly question.... [I]t can use things, even instrumentalize them, but it cannot gain access to a *tekhnè*" (OS 57). Thus, in terms of the question and of technology, *Dasein*'s definitive predications, "it is always a matter of marking an absolute limit" between *Dasein* and the animal (OS 54).

Yet "the lizard" (Heidegger's example) does have "a relationship with the sun – and with the stone [Heidegger's example of the non-living], which itself has none" (OS 52). Derrida extends the set or *ensemble* that predicates the animal: "we should now have to say of spirit what one says of the world for the animal: the animal is poor in spirit [*Geistarm* as it is *Weltarm*, as it were], it has spirit but does not have spirit and this not-having is a mode of its being-able-to-have spirit" (OS 55).

It is important that the animal is off-limits to the Heideggerian deconstruction of ontology. Heidegger can only mention, not use "the animal crossing-through"; or rather, his philosophy is used by it, although he implies a negative "hierarchization and evaluation" by using "the words 'poverty' and 'lack' [*Entbehrung*]" about the animal: "What is signaled by this animal crossing-through, if we can call it that? Or rather, what is signaled by the word 'crossing-through' which we write a propos of the animal 'world' and which ought, in its logic, to overtake all words from the moment they say something about the world?"(OS 54) For the animal has some relationship with the world, and yet the animal is absolutely marked off from *Dasein*. Therefore, every inauguration of the world by *Dasein* is struck through by the inaccessible animal. Heidegger's philosophy "responds" against its grain to the animal by the formalizable logic of contamination – not just a threat, but a compromise:

> Can one not say, then, that the whole deconstruction of ontology, as it is begun in *Sein und Zeit* and insofar as it unseats, as it were, the Cartesian-Hegelian *spiritus* in the existential analytic, is here threatened in its order, in its implementation, its conceptual apparatus, by what is called, so obscurely still, the animal? Compromised, rather, by a *thesis* on animality *in general*, for which any example would do the job.... These difficulties – such at least is the proposition I submit for discussion – ... bring the consequences of a serious mortgaging [*hypothèque*, the word for a large mortgage loan taken out, for instance to finance the purchase of a house] to weigh upon the whole of his thought. (OS 57)

This is an indictment, and Derrida stands behind it: "such ... is the proposition I submit ..." It may be remembered that the discussion of correct politics began with the impossibility of avoiding the unilaterality of subjectity. In Derrida's reading, that is one of Heidegger's major *philosophical* irresponsibilities in the period of the Rectorate speech: to try to ward off that unilaterality by way of the crossing-through of *Destruktion*. In this chapter we see "the epoch of" – both the era of and the bracketed-in philosophical region of – "subjectity" given the adjective "Cartesian-Hegelian" (OS 55). And, in the passage quoted at length, the deconstruction of ontology in so far as it unseats the Cartesian-Hegelian *spiritus* – by withdrawing it from subjectity – is claimed to be threatened, or rather compromised, by the animal. It is in this context that Derrida brings up the question of a specifically political responsibility again. Let us see how.

Between the stone and *Dasein*, the animal is "the living creature."

> [P]rivative poverty indeed marks the caesura or the heterogeneity between non-living and living on the one hand, between the animal and human *Dasein* on the other…. [This] absolute limit between the living creature and the human *Dasein*, tak[es] a distance not only from all biologism and even all philosophy of life (and thus from all political ideology which might draw its inspiration more or less directly from them) but also … from a Rilkean thematics which links openness and animality. Not to mention Nietzsche … (OS 55, 54)

Derrida does not mention Nietzsche much in this book. But here is one indication why, for him, Nietzsche remains a less dark figure, for Nietzsche reckons with the living animality of the human. As for Heidegger, Derrida asks:

> What is being-for-death? What is death for a *Dasein* that is never defined *essentially* as a living thing? This is not a matter of opposing death to life, but of wondering what semantic content can be given to death in a discourse for which the relation to death, the experience of death, remains unrelated to the life of the living thing. (OS 120)

It is not only that *Destruktion* cannot be used to avoid the unilaterality of subjectity when spirit is bound by a stand taken in its name. That, as it were, is the limit above. It is also that, not being able to fill life and therefore death with meaning, not having made room for the animal-in-the-human, Heideggerian philosophy cannot be a philosophy of life. That, as it were, is the limit from below.

We must keep these earlier elaborations in mind when Derrida discusses Heidegger's refusal of evil to the animal because evil is spiritual (*geistlich*) (OS 103).[28] By Derrida's reading, I can suggest that "we should now have to say of evil what Derrida says of spirit for the animal: the animal is poor in evil [*Bösarm* as it is *Geistarm*, as it were], it has evil but does not have evil and this not-having is a mode of its being-able-to-be/have evil" (see p. 66).

The discussion of the animal emerges in *Of Spirit* in the wake of a
typographical gesture, the crossing-out. We may now be ready to read
the passage about the fully Heideggerian text:

> To dream of what the Heideggerian corpus would look like the day
> when, with all the application and consistency required, the operation
> prescribed by him at one moment or another would indeed have been
> carried out: "avoid" the word "spirit," at the very least put it in quota-
> tion marks, then cross through all the names referring to the world
> whenever one is speaking of something which, like the animal, has no
> *Dasein*, and therefore no or only a little world, then place the word
> "Being" everywhere under a cross, and finally cross through without a
> cross all the question marks when it's a question of language, i.e., indi-
> rectly, of everything, etc. One can imagine the surface of a text given
> over to the gnawing, ruminant, and silent voracity of such an animal-
> machine and its implacable "logic." This would not only be simply
> "without spirit," but a figure of evil. (OS 134)

Deconstruction or *Destruktion* cannot become a matter of obeying
and applying an obsessive typography, and no philosophy can give itself
over to an animality that is "its own." No typographical arsenal can
recall that limit, of qualifying everything one reads, writes, or says:
"everything, etc." One must recall that these typographical gestures are
ways of *recalling* limits that one cannot cross rather than acting out theoretical safeguards against all previous philosophy. The spirit cannot be
bound by politicizing in its name, but Heideggerian philosophy cannot
give itself over to its own open animality either; and it has no typographical arsenal for recalling that limit. And therefore, since the paragraph I quote above is constructed by indicating the "logic" of something
like a dreamwork, it is that unprotected flank that provides the name of
that text where every wish of a *destruktive* philosophy is fulfilled, everything you want to say is eaten up, the Nietzschean philosopher's self-
modeling on the cud-chewing (ruminant) cow goes out of control, not
responsible before the spirit but taken over, not by the animal (for it is
out of reach) but an animal-*machine*, that is crossed-through before
crossing-through.[29] Remember the animal cannot *be* evil by this philosophy. Therefore, in the dream of its fulfillment, the (surface of the) text
controlled by the animal (machine) is (a figure of) evil. To get the force
of "figure" I can, once again, turn to "Shibboleth," my vade mecum of
responsible reading.[30]

This is an indictment of Heidegger's irresponsibility to and in philosophy, the irresponsibility of that philosophy from its powerful start.

It is not the cop-out of: philosophy good, man bad. An ex-Derridian said to me at that time: Heidegger was a Nazi, and Jacques should have said it.[31] This assumes that Derrida should do deconstruction when he philosophizes, and turn it off when there's need for plain talk. It seems more responsible that, instead of falling back on the deceptive simplicity of a proposition (Heidegger was a Nazi) and taking that as sufficient fulfillment of his philosophical responsibility, this philosopher, who has unceasingly deconstructed propositions, would philosophize with all stops pulled out, without denegating his complicity, to present Heideggerian philosophy as *pharmakon*, what could have been medicine turned into poison.[32]

It is not necessary to utter that proposition, after all. Heidegger simplified matters by taking out party membership.

The liberal Euro-US academic, unceasingly complicitous with the text of exploitation, possibly endorsing child slavery every time s/he drinks a cup of tea, paying taxes to destroy survival ecobiomes of the world's poor and bomb innocent Afghan villages by mistake, sometimes mouthing a "marxism" liberal-humanized out of existence, and *talking* no doubt against US military aggression, profoundly irresponsible to the academic's one obligation of not writing on something carelessly read, cannot understand the complexity of this verdict. To them belongs the happy euphoria of being in the right. That their relationship to dominant capital is not unlike deconstruction's to Heidegger and therefore involves "responsibility" is not something they can arrive at through their own thinking, which will not open itself to what it resists. And they are certainly not willing to see if they are able to learn it through deconstruction. For them deconstruction remains caught in the competition of whose sword is sharper.[33]

Of Spirit is concerned with philosophical argument, semantic content, rhetoric, and typography; all of which recall limits (and all of which must remain open to "setting-to-work"). It is therefore noteworthy that the dream of the saturated Heideggerian corpus is given unconnected to an argument, as a momentary and declared pause in square brackets in a long footnote about the "markers and signs" in Heidegger, of "imperceptible – for Martin Heidegger as much as for anyone [–] ... strata appear[ing] prominent after the event," concerning an "example ... more and other, than an example," regarding "the very origin of responsibility," – signs and markers that "assign ... so many new tasks to thought, and to reading ... not only for *reading* Heidegger and serving some hermeneutical or philosophical piety. Beyond an always necessary exegesis, this rereading sketches out another topology for new tasks, for what remains to be situated of the relationships between Heidegger's thought and other places of thought ..." (OS 132–3). In other words, the dream floats up where Derrida appears to be rescuing his thought by way of his "new politics of reading," which may seem to be a case of: thought salvageable, man limited.[34] Trying to learn "the silent dramaturgy of pragmatic signs" in deconstruction in my own way over the years, I have followed the track of markers and signs in *Of Spirit* (the "dream-work," as it were), to offer an unauthorized "wild analysis." I cannot forget that Freud's main criticism of wild psychoanalysis was its irresponsibility, its ignoring of the robust response-accountability structure of transference.[35]

Is it simply this feeling of unease that makes me sense a similar moment of unease in Derrida? He openly censures Heidegger for his disloyalty to Husserl, again in terms of irresponsibility to his own philosophy of crossing-out: "And the fact remains, beyond any possible contestation, that he erased [he didn't cross out this time, he erased] the dedication of *Sein und Zeit* to Husserl so that the book could be republished, in a gesture which reconstitutes the erasure as an unerasable, mediocre, and hideous crossing-out" (OS 121). But in the same note he points out (and to me as a product of imperialism this is a rare courage) that, in a "text delivered in 1935 in Vienna ... [r]ight after asking the question 'How is the spiritual figure of Europe to be characterized?' Husserl adds: 'In a spiritual sense clearly the English dominions and the United States belong to Europe, but not the Eskimos or the Indians of the travelling zoos or the gypsies who permanently wander as vagabonds all over Europe'." He is even aware of the hierarchization and racism internal to an imperialist mind-set:

> It is apparently necessary, therefore, in order to save the English dominions, the power and culture they represent, to make a distinction between, for example, good and bad Indians.... and this reference to spirit, and to Europe, is no more an external or accidental ornament for Husserl's thought than it is for Heidegger's. It plays a major, organizing role in the transcendental teleology of reason as Europocentric humanism... The question of the animal is never very far away: "just as man, *and even the Papuan* [my emphasis – J.D.] represents a new stage in animality in contrast to the animals, so philosophical reason represents a new stage in humanity and in its reason ... (OS 121–2)

Having pointed this out, Derrida engages in balancing the two sides: "Would [Heidegger] have thrown the 'non-Aryan' out of Europe, as did he who knew he was himself 'non-Aryan,' i.e. Husserl? And if the reply is 'no,' to all appearances 'no,' is it certain that this is for reasons other than those which distanced him from transcendental idealism? Is what he did or wrote worse?" It is then that I can hear unease. "Where is the worst [le pire]? That is perhaps the question of spirit."

Why does he cite the title of his book there? In French the monstrative is even stronger: "voilà peut-être la question de l'esprit."[36] Is it that an exercise in judgment, weighing the good against the bad, cannot not be, in a certain sense, a failure of the open-endedness of responsibility or the indeconstructibility of justice? I cannot know, but I mark the moment with my own "judge not, that ye be not judged.")

Let us return to the note on the animal-machine. At the end of the dream-pause, before marking the end, Derrida writes: "The perverse reading of Heidegger." Perverse but possible, not idiosyncratic; the perverse reading.[37] The article is not indefinite. And the French – "la lecture perverse de Heidegger" – even allows "Heidegger's perverse reading."

It may of course be said that Of Spirit attempts to converse with Heidegger, to turn with him into the dark, perhaps perverse, recesses of his philosophy as it juggles with spirit. I could take "perverse" in the colloquial sense and contrast it to Derrida's critique of the eminently sane supporters of the later Heidegger.

Let us turn to the structuring of this long footnote, which deals precisely with the question: has the question been preserved in another form in the later Heidegger? The sentence which this long note divides runs as follows: "Language, always, before any question,* [note reference] and in the very question, comes down to [revient à] the promise" (OS 94). The note is a note to the thought of what is anterior to the question. And it prepares us to weigh the next sentence: "This would also be a promise of spirit."

Let the reader work out the citing of the title of the book again at this juncture where the promise (thought must obey it to be thought) is judged harshly over against the question (thought must recall the responsibility to be answerable).

In the footnote proper, Derrida lets texts of the later Heidegger lengthily point at the now "pre-originary pledge [gage] ... [which] engage[s] ... [the question] in a responsibility it has not chosen and which assigns it even its liberty" (OS 130); but then he offers his own comment, in tones of unmistakable emphasis:

> But it has to be admitted that the thought of an affirmation anterior to any question and more proper to thought than any question must have an unlimited incidence ... on the *quasi*-totality of Heidegger's previous path of thought.... this step transforms or deforms (as you like) the whole landscape to the extent that that landscape has been constituted *before* [devant] *the* – inflexible – *law* of the most radical questioning.... [L]et me recall that the point of departure of the analytic of *Dasein* – and therefore the project of *Sein und Zeit* itself – was assigned by the opening of *Dasein* to the question; [– here Derrida again brings up Cartesian-Hegelian subjectity –] and that the whole *Destruktion* of ontology took as its target, especially in post-Cartesian modernity, an inadequate questioning of the Being of the subject, etc. This retrospective upheaval can seem to dictate a new *order* ... to construct a quite different discourse, open a quite different path of thought ... and remove – a highly ambiguous gesture – the remnant of *Aufklärung* which still slumbered in the privilege of the question. (OS 131)[38]

I have encountered many uncomprehending readings of this text: particularly from readers who imitate the snazz without working on the intimidatingly precise argument. The point is, of course, that it is not an open denunciation, but the double bind of deconstructive responsibility, practiced in the philosophizing, hard to shoulder, hard to recognize. But what is one responsible for? For the understanding and applause of impatient academics? I therefore take the liberty of recommending a slow reading of the next sentence: "In fact, without believing that we can henceforth not take account of this profound upheaval, *we cannot take seriously the imperative of such a recommencement*" (emphasis mine). He gives his reasons, and it is after this that he proposes a "new strategy," "another topology," and, strictly speaking, begins the last movement of *Of Spirit*, deconstructing Heidegger, for his "schoolmates," those who have learned that deconstruction is not exposure of error but "a new politics of reading." In the footnote, he says no more about new strategy (although the text will henceforth and gradually, declare his own (de)construction of Heidegger more and more), because "my purpose bound me to privilege the modalities of avoiding (*vermeiden*) – and notably the silent dramaturgy of pragmatic signs" (OS 133).

Curiously enough, it is after this enigmatic sentence that the footnote pauses upon the dream of the full-dress production of the drama of pragmatic signs: a figure of evil. And this dream of a figure comes before the final paragraphs of the footnote, which seem to admit that even in the later Heidegger, "the proper of man arrives only in this response or this responsibility" (OS 135). Derrida is duty-bound to admit this, for "at the Essex conference ... Françoise Dastur reminded

me of this passage of *Unterwegs zur Sprache,* which indeed passes question. I dedicate this note to her as a pledge of gratitude" (OS 136).
A philosopher's responsibility is to acknowledge a counter-example to
his general argument. In order to show, I think, that it is no more than
a passage that passes question – utters "Shibboleth" with the correct
accent, as it were – Derrida launches this elaborately orchestrated note
to show further that the only way to respond to the thought of responsibility that Heidegger betrayed is to deconstruct *Destruktion*: another
strategy ...[39]

In keeping with the strategy of the deconstructive project this chapter in Derrida's book has already begun to chip away at the identity of
the man named Heidegger. First by constructing Trakl as Heidegger's
ventriloquist, upon Derrida's own contestatory authority, as follows:

> What is spirit? the reply is inscribed in maxims which translate certain
> poetic statements by Trakl.... [F]or lack of time I will have to restrict
> myself to the gross affirmation which I think is hardly contestable:
> statements like those I have just cited and translated by *spirit in-flames*
> are obviously statements *of* Heidegger. Not ... productions of the subject
> Martin Heidegger ... (OS 84–5)

Next, by imposing the word *revenant* upon the Trakl-Heideggerian
stranger whom the spirit follows on a "journey [which] would permit
an interpretation ... more originary ... than ... the origin and deca-
dence current in the dominant, i.e. metaphysico-Christian interpretation" (89). "His step carries him into the night," writes Derrida, "like a
revenant.... '*Revenant*' is not a word of Heidegger's, and no doubt he
would not like having it imposed on him because of the negative con-
notations, metaphysical or parapsychic, that he would be at pains to
denounce in it. I will not, however, efface it, ..."

At this stage in the text there is no serious attempt to justify these
impositions. And in a couple of pages, a crucial sentence will be divided
by the long footnote we have read. (What is it to say "for lack of time I
will ... [make] a gross affirmation" when one is looking forward to a
beautifully shaped seven-page footnote?) "Martin Heidegger's" authority
is being deconstructed here, his text taken over (or cathected?) by "another
strategy," a greater responsibility than allegiance to a proper name.

If Trakl's statements are statements "*of* Heidegger," what does it
mean to say, as Derrida will in the next chapter, after a careful discussion of what "origin-heterogeneous" (in place of the earlier position of
the question at the origin) might mean in Heidegger, that

the gestures made to snatch Trakl away from the Christian thinking of *Geist* seem to me laborious, violent, sometimes simply caricatural, and all in all not very convincing.... It is with reference to an extremely conventional and doxical outline of Christianity that Heidegger can claim to de-Christianize Trakl's *Gedicht*. What is *origin-heterogeneous* would in that case be nothing other – but it's not nothing – than the origin of Christianity: the spirit of Christianity or the essence of Christianity[?].

No, it's not nothing. The final Heidegger (is it the one with the proper name?) is being delivered over to that very metaphysico-Christianity which he mightily contested. And after this the book launches an exchange between Heidegger and his Christian apologists, – "[s]ince I'm doing the questions and answers here, I imagine Heidegger's reply" (OS 111) – each vying to claim the other's space, casually ecumenical, this Heidegger even accommodating the Judaic "spirit" (*ruah*) with an "I am opposing nothing ... no[t] even (I'd forgotten that one) [the discourse] on *ruah*.... I said it is on the basis of flame that one thinks *pneuma* or *spiritus* or, since you insist, *ruah*, etc." (OS 111, 112). "Those I [Derrida] called theologians," had, in their turn, enthusiastically invoked "my friend and coreligionary, the Messianic Jew. I'm not certain that the Moslem and some others" – Heidegger's "etc." matches this – "wouldn't join in the concert or the hymn" (OS 110, 111).

In this easy multicultural chat, a whitewashed Heidegger answers reproaches with "I follow the path of the entirely other" (OS 113). The call of the entirely other, to which one bears responsibility, and which the question recalls, has now been made into this caricature. And "crossing is not a neutral word," Derrida writes, "– [it] runs the risk ... of recalling the cross-shaped crossing-through under which one leaves being [*l'être*] or God to suffer" (OS 112; word-order changed). The crossing-through itself is given over to Christian metaphysics as Christ the man (*Dasein? l'être* is in lower case) is crossed-over on the Cross as God under erasure. Perhaps I am speaking irresponsibly here, but this last movement of the book seems to me to confront European Christianity in its profound anti-Semitism even in its self-consciously ecumenical pose.[40] Indeed, introducing this last moment is a fairly straightforward passage:

One can, then, imagine a scene between Heidegger and certain Christian theologians.... It would in truth be an odd *exchange*.... We are talking about past, present, and future "events," a composition of forces and discourses which seem to have been waging merciless war on each other (for example from 1933 to our time). We have a combinatory

whose power remains abyssal. In all rigor it exculpates none of the discourses which can thus exchange their power. It does not leave a clean
place open [*ne laisse la place nette*] for any arbitrating authority. Nazism
was not born in the desert [as were Judaism, Christianity, and Islam?].
We all know this, but it has to be constantly recalled. And even if, far
from any desert, it had grown like a mushroom in the silence of a
European forest, it would have done so in the shadow of big trees, in
the shelter of their silence or their indifference but in the same soil....
In their bushy taxonomy, they would bear the names of religions, philosophies, political regimes, economic structures, religious or academic
institutions. In short, what is just as confusedly called culture, or the
world of spirit. (OS 109–10)

"Whose power remains abyssal." The word "abyssal" combines
both the nuances of the abyss and the interminable counter-reflection
of the *mise en abyme* – the facing mirrors on the heraldic blazon. The
potentiality for something like Nazism (and I, quite without authority,
would include here the demonization of that other People of the
Book, Islam accompanying varieties of politically legitimized violence) is an always possible potential in Christian Europe's cultural
heritage. When, at the end of the book, we read that the only hope is
in the shuttle of dialogue – "it's enough to keep talking, not to interrupt" – we cannot forget the grim description of such exchanges in
the passage above (OS 113). The imagined exchange between the final
Heidegger and his contemporary interlocutors can achieve nothing.
And *Of Spirit* ends with a deliberate disregard of Heidegger's philosophical cautions, even as a parody of Heidegger's first principle is
offered: the spirit will do the rest. But this spirit is a ghost (there is an
interesting printer's error in the translation, almost as if the translators cannot brook such irreverence), it is in flame as well as ash, and it
is unavoidable. In the version of *Of Spirit*, Martin Heidegger and the
question dead-end in this shuttle, a caricature of the response-struc-
ture of responsibility. The deconstruction of Heidegger has taken off
elsewhere, following the track of a responsibility Heidegger himself
gave up, halfway to its testing in its setting to work. One must learn to
read in order to see it happen, to respond to the argument. This is not
the conflation of literature and philosophy.[41] It is the use of the
resources of writing to philosophize.

And this unauthorized formalization of the silent dramaturgy of *Of
Spirit* is no more than an intermediary stage. I want now to offer another
instantiation of what I have learned from this text of responsibility: the

animal-machine of fully programmed information, and a "European"
combinatory whose power remains abyssal, so that the two sides seem
to engage in an interminable conversation, while a specter does the
rest. I am, of course, miming a progression of images rather than,
strictly speaking, following an argument. Is this responsible to the text?
But concept and metaphor are in each other.[42]

II   Conference on the Flood Action Plan in Bangladesh, European
Parliament, Strasbourg

I do not read here, as does Derrida, reading, the silent dramaturgy of
pragmatic signs which convention considers decadent to "read" because
it is nothing but the transparent scaffolding that supports the text of
reason. I read rather the dramaturgy of the apparently unrehearsed
staging of what convention regards to be (the transparent textuality or
theater of) facts, and "dialogue." I rush in to supplement where Derrida
wisely postpones:

> And as, since the beginning of this lecture, we have been speaking of
> nothing but the "translation" of these thoughts and discourses into
> what are commonly called the "events" of "history" and of "politics"
> (I place quotation marks around all these obscure words), it would also
> be necessary to "translate" what such an exchange of places can imply
> in its most radical possibility. This "translation" appears to be both
> indispensable and for the moment impossible. (OS 109)

The "moment" in that last sentence may be standing in for the
indefinitely differential prow of the present on the move. But I literalize.
I aim to sidle into the parenthesis to see what script puts quotes around
those obscure words in one text, not only translated from Europe but
transferred, yet remaining the same: history, politics, translation. I read
the unfolding of a small conference arranged by the Green Party at the
European Parliament.

So much has been written about the relationship between orators
and rhetors that it seems unnecessary to labor the point. Derrida himself has written on the elaboration of that topic in Rousseau.[43] The
parliamentary setting, with its representatives who must *vertreten* (represent) rather than *darstellen* (represent) has been exposed by Marx by
way of a sustained theatrical metaphor.[44] What is also surely obvious is
the monumentalized role that the delicate and irregular beat of respon-
sibility-as-accountability plays here. The Members are responsible to
their constituency. Derrida has indirectly written about the conventions

of the representation of "the public" to whom the representative is responsible in "Call It a Day for Democracy."[45] And later, as "the public" being the one place where democracy gives "the right to irony."[46]

Let us also remember the other, slightly odder sense given to "responsibility:" the transference of "responses" volleyed from one subject to another, drawn by a *mise en abyme*. There is a *mise en scène* of this in the structuring of a *parlement* – a place where men (typically) reason together.

Let us add to this that the conference was arranged by a group – with a representative in Parliament – that feels responsible to Nature (animal as well as a world worlded as "earth") as the Other of the Human – a group self-consciously responsible for the picking back up of the abdicated responsibility of being human-on-earth, as it were, and representative of those who have recalled this responsibility, those human beings who are fully human, at last. It may, I think, be said that they speak in the name of spirit against technologism and capitalism. Does this "re-inscribing of spirit in an oppositional demarcation" make it a unilaterality of subjectity? And how terrifying is the contamination?

If at an academic conference one's ostensible responsibility is first to "truth," secondly to oneself – since it is oneself that one must represent, and thirdly to the audience – to whom one must communicate, – and all these have, as we know, their attendant practico-philosophical problems – a conference with a registered audience (who are, in such a situation, Rousseauistically called "participants"), where the obligation of the speakers is to represent a specific national perspective through international concern, as they are ranged in a facing space, carries the representation (*Darstellung*) of direct "responsibility" (as if *Vertretung*) into a certain abyssality by borrowing from the resources of the theater; resources that are freely discussed in the planning and recognized in the event even as they are automatically dismissed by protocol.[47] This last awkward sentence must be given the flesh and blood of empirical detail. But there is yet another codicil to be added to the account of how "political" and "human" responsibility was in this case bound to a structure.

(And the very thought of the codicil calls for a caution. There can be no assumption that "pure" responsibility can appear, unstructured and unstaged. The call is a gift, but the response is, unavoidably, an exchange-effect. This is the stimulus of a persistent critique, which must forever try to maintain the precarious balance between construction and destruction: deconstruction.)

The codicil, then: the entire set described in the text was staged as a dialogue, between the forces of "Development" and the voices of a "developing nation," charging the Developers with constructing a theater of responsibility to disguise the mechanics of unrestricted capital investment.

("Dialogue" is in fact the accepted proper name of responsibility as exchange-of-responses, implicitly understood as the flow of propositions or *constatations* rather than responses from both sides. It is a word given status and currency by the participatory movements in the sixties which have displaced themselves in the New Social Movements of the seventies and the eighties, of which the European Green Party is an inheritor.[48] I have already indicated a possible scenario of responsibility that can be constructed out of the Party's presuppositions, broadly understood. This other feature, the implementation of that responsibility through dialogue, is the translation of the presupposition into technique. The thinking of relationship (or non-relationship, or "relationship") between justice and law inaugurated by "The Force of Law" inevitably determines my understanding of the relationship between responsibility and dialogue.[49] For I think it is right to say that in that word, in this particular Anglo-US usage, the "false" etymology of "dia" as the two that converse mingles with the "original" sense of something coming about through the telling, the middle voice of *dialeges-thai* mingling also with telling as in a calculus.[50] But let this remain a parenthesis. For to dwell on this would restrain us from the empirical narrative. Yet let it be said that the often repugnant and smug congratulation that the inclusion of empirical narrative brings to an academic in the Humanities is even less productive when unaccompanied by such musings.)

And indeed the conference was organized for the establishment of a dialogue. The word "dialogue" (and "confrontation," about whose relationship to responsibility much could be written) was repeatedly used in the conference literature precisely as the phenomenon the establishment of which would be the first step toward the restoration of responsibility. Let me quote a sentence which will highlight the justice/law, responsibility/dialogue route that must be taken as given in order to decide, necessarily in the night of non-knowledge: "The legal basis for public consultation and people's participation must be ensured first ... [in order] to have a meaningful dialogue with the World Bank."[51]

I am speaking of a conference that has been described in the following way: "In a victory for Green Party activists from France, Germany and the Netherlands, the European Parliament will host an unprecedented open debate of the merits of the FAP May 26 and 27, 1993, where project opponents will have an opportunity to present their case directly to many of the governments funding the scheme."

Let me give the bare bones of the situation. (If Derrida had been obliged to give gross affirmations for lack of time, I am obliged to summarize because I can expect no familiarity with the background of Development in the readership of deconstruction.) Bangladesh is a small fertile country continually in the making by the play of huge young rivers. These young rivers rise in the neighboring countries and gather force until they reach Bangladesh on their way to the Bay of Bengal. They deposit enormous quantities of silt as their waters divide into innumerable tributaries as they reach the open bay. It is quite like the way the great blood vessels finally break into capillaries to disperse into the skin. The entire country, apart from the mountains to the North and East, is thus soft alluvial deposit and the coast is a collection of many small shifting deltas covered by mangrove swamps.

Because these rivers are young and strong, they move.

When the Brahmaputra River is at maximum flood, for example, bed-forms up to 15m[eters] high migrate downstream as much as 600 m/day. ... Lateral channel movements as high as 800 m/yr are common. ... Many experts consider the confinement of such rivers to be impossible. ... [This is also] one of the world's most earthquake-prone locations. An active fault line lies along the northern edge of the delta, at the foot-hills of the Himalayas. The largest earthquake on land known to seismologists, registering 8.7 on the Richter scale, occurred in this region in 1897. ... Witnesses reported that the quake caused plumes of water to gush from the ground. ... In areas of recent sand and silt deposition with high water tables, such as the Bengal delta, earthquakes lead to liquefaction, the temporary loss of strength of sands and silts, which behave like viscous fluids rather than soils.[52]

It may be said, only half fancifully, that the grounding of the ground is evident here as one thinks from the worlded world. What is crossed out has been already and is being crossed out by the moving weave of water.

At Bangladesh, the land mass of the Indian subcontinent narrows and the Himalaya is squeezed up into its highest peaks. Thus the monsoon winds here travel much longer over ocean and sea, gather force in the incopious width of the Bay of Bengal and dash more quickly at a much higher mountain wall. It is a country of great rains.

In this combination of turbulent flowing and pouring – keep the distinction in mind for later – the Bangladeshi fisher-folk and grass-roots peasants have been used to living with water, even yearly flooding, for ever. Every thirty years or so there are devastating floods. They have learned to bear this, not quite to cope with the extraordinary inundations, but to bend with them and rise again. As for the yearly floods, they have learned to manage them, welcome them, and build a life-style with respect for them. Indeed the moving flood-waters leave algae that alleviate the need to fertilize and Bangladesh notionally produces enough to feed the entire population. (I must keep to the point of the essay and therefore cannot speak of the internal class-exploitation and lack of interest in land reform.) I will touch upon this later in the essay.

And the Bangladeshis' main source of protein is fish. The grass-roots fisher catches fish in rivers and waters that are still common property.

(On my level of miming the logic of the concept-metaphor, is it absurd to ask if the relationship between *Dasein*-animal-world is different here from Heidegger-lizard-stone? It is in the context of the Flood Action Program in Bangladesh that I began to get my kind of handle on Derrida's obstinate insistence in the face of learned participants in his seminar who cited Heideggerian passages apparently to the contrary, that Heidegger never speculated on eating. And his equally insistent refrain: What is it to eat?[53] If in a certain conventional theology to eat God's flesh is to establish exchange with spirit, what is established by eating mere flesh (or fish)? Is the argument on the fetish, contrasting the two, akin to the humanist teleology of (Heidegger's) Christian metaphysics in the differentiation between *Dasein* and the animal? When the anthropologist learnedly transforms the racist language of the fetish into the scientific discourse of the totem, how much by subreption (as in Kant's analytic of the sublime) does the psychoanalytic set subl(im)ate all of this from "real" castration to circumcision as (recalling the fear of) "castration" so that the self-conscious (super-egoic) sense of responsibility, recognizable as such, takes quite another form?[54] How does the ecology of fish-eating in the geology of turbulent youthful rivers transform the eating of sacrificial flesh in Islam, of which these circumcised subalterns are devoutly observant in season, as far as means will allow? Because these people are poor, are they not human enough for philosophizing on the basis of their lives, as did

Heidegger, starting from the generally human? Especially if they occupy Derrida's question to Heidegger – "What is it to eat?" – from a position that is not-quite-not fetish/totem yet marked by sacrifice and circumcision?[55] How does the question of woman complicate each one of these categories? Has Heidegger ever been faulted because today's Bavarian grass roots may not think as he does?

But I am dragged beyond my summary by the problematic of (wo)man-fish-water. Let us resume.)

In 1988 there was a disastrous flood – one of the three expected in a century. It is alleged that Danielle Mitterrand, who was in the country at the time, spoke of the devastation to her husband – of course she knew nothing of what this chapter has summarized so far – and François Mitterrand – ironically, his name means "middle landowner," a traditional small-time class-exploiter of the common-property land-less grass roots – decided to make flood control in Bangladesh the centerpiece of Third World Aid at the Paris Summit.[56]

FAP (Flood Action Plan) 25, the first French plan, is an allegory of right reason (see figure 2.1). To impose upon the changeful riverscape the straight lines of massive "Pharaonic" embankments is the plan.[57] A total of 10.1 billion dollars were circulated to generate further capital according to the changeful laws of the International Monetary Fund. The governments of the Group of the then Seven were involved as "donor" countries.[58]

(If "dialogue" bears a mark, so does "donor." Who deserves that appel-lation? Who gives or can give? The gift is a limit that permits and annuls all recognizable human giving.[59] But here, far from that limit, the name of giving is scientifically appropriated for coercive lending, solicited by comprador capital and a compromised State, used as staging props for a nation seeking alms.[60] Is responsibility to be produced by a debt trap?[61] This monstrosity – a bonded donation – mortgages the future of the country.[62] I foolishly read philosophy as blueprint here: "Know still what giving *means* [*veut dire*, lit. wants to say], *know how to give*, know what you want and mean [*veux dire*, lit. want to say] when you give, know what you intend to give, know how the gift annuls itself, commit yourself [*engage-toi*, stake yourself?] even if commitment is the destruction of the gift by the gift, give economy a chance."[63])

The World Bank coordinates the effort, shored up by innumerable business enterprises and consultancies and government allocations

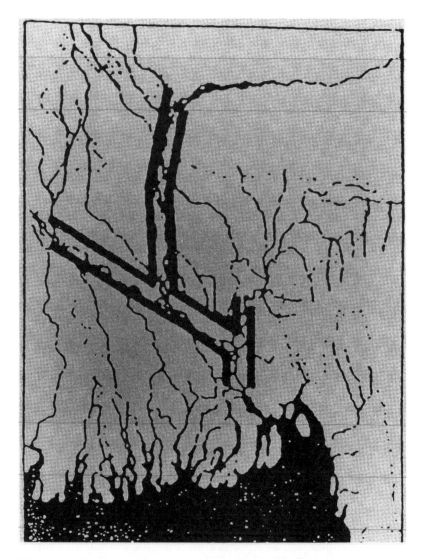

Figure 2.1   Flood Action Plan. James K. Boyce, "Birth of A Megaproject: Political Economy of Flood Control in Bangladesh," *Environmental Management* 14.4 (1990), p. 424. With permission of Springer Science and Business Media.

and international agencies. The country is "consultantized," the possibility of agitation for peoples' rights effectively blocked, since the de facto law is in the hands of the donors via a Flood Protection Coordinating Organization set up by executive decision of the Ministry of Water Development, which describes itself as an ad hoc staff body, directed by the "donors'" own policy requirements. There is, in other words, no accountability here. It is not conceivable that some First

World consulting agency will, first, be tracked down after the Organization has been dismantled; and, second, respond at the subaltern's call.[64] (In other words, the element of legal calculus of one sort in the name of a collectivity of individuals conceived in terms of tirelessly gathered details of life and living has been blocked. The certainty that Justice always eludes these calculations makes it all the more important that their possibility be sustained. "[I]t is just that there be law."[65])

We must recall that Development is the dominant global denomination of Responsibility: the story is that the rich nations collectively hear the call of the ethical and collect to help the poor nations by giving skill and money. There are therefore elaborate and visible structures of public consultation in place. The ways in which these structures are manipulated – well-publicized occasions of exchange which are minimally disseminated or not disseminated at all, promises that are made without intention of performance ("pure" performatives), and in-house decisions not to honor the results of consultation being only a few – can be documented.[66] It was to redress the imbalance between structural rights and the possibility of their exercise that the European Green Party called the most public meeting it could devise.

Knowing that responsibility in its setting-to-work can never reduce out the unilaterality of subjecity, we still compute how the form of complicity of the Green Party on the one hand and the World Bank (shorthand for all the parties involved in the FAP) on the other, are "not equivalent."

Undoubtedly these are two "European" ways of helping the "people" of Bangladesh. For the World Bank the "people" is the name of the final instance of justification for its enterprise. The justification, always crudely formulated, is a parody of Marx's conclusion, based on Victorian Britain, the herald of modern imperialism, that capitalism maximizes social productivity. Marx was involved in working out how the interest of capitalism could be diverted from capital to the "social," how poison could be measured into medicine. I have discussed elsewhere how the concept-metaphor of the "social" betrayed Marx.[67] An irresponsible thought of responsibility can come to supplement that betrayal.

The World Bank is not involved in the diversion of interest from capital to "social." The "people," rather far from Marx's tough rationalist definition of the "social," remain a promised possible beneficiary of the trickledown from capital-intensive "social productivity." The real interest remains the generation of global capital through consultant and contractor.[68] The World Bank does not merit the deconstructive reading and supplementation that Marx's attempt commands. We owe it no such responsibility. It falls far short of the call.

The Green Party as such, on the other hand, whatever the sympathies of individual members, does not act in the name of the "people" as the last instance. Their last instance is "Nature," even though it is always Nature-for-the-human as the human-for-Nature.[69] Here we can take all the precautions against imagining that Nature can ever be anything but that which comes back after and before the human. As an animal-machine.

This said, we can now notice that the elaborate dramaturgy of the parliament/conference structure of responsibility/representation keeps the Party on the other side of the subaltern as well. Yet we certainly will not consider this distance equivalent to the rapacious doubletalk of the World Bank. One can act "politically" to make the distinction clear. Yet one must also acknowledge the repetition of, not simply the rupture between, Party and Bank. That is the harsh lesson of deconstruction, always asymmetrical in interest. An abyssal double bind; to close it off is of course convenient.

(Thus, in inchoate recognition of this lesson, perhaps, somewhat haphazardly selected members of the Bangladeshi opposition to the FAP responded positively to the Party's call. But they felt it inappropriate to sign the resolution drawn up for the support of the Bangladeshi people by interested members of the European Community.)

One might think that pointing out this complicity between the Party and the Bank is enough proof of "a combinatory whose power remains abyssal." These are two faces of "Europe" after all – global and bloated on the one hand, earthy and ascetic on the other. But one must note, once again, the former's formal refusal of responsibility, even as "exchange." The following principals sent belated letters declining the invitation to the conference, pleading an indefinite obligation: J. I. M. Dempster, Panel of Experts; Fritz Fischer, German Executive Director (World Bank); M. H. Siddiqi, Chief Engineer, Flood Plan Coordination Organization, Ministry of Water Development and Flood Control, Government of Bangladesh; John Clark, International Economic Relations (World Bank), Joseph Wood, Vice President, South Asia Region (World Bank), Ross Wallace, Resident FAP Coordinator (World Bank). Others, such as the representatives of the French Government, declined with telephone messages. A Mr Van Ellen, whose designation is not immediately clear from his faxed communication, offered the most interesting response: "I consulted in The Hague with the

Netherlands Government and here in Dhaka with the Government of Bangladesh (FPCO), the World Bank and panel of experts. I have been advised not to participate and as a consequence I have to decline your invitation." The World Bank's Water Resources Advisor (Asia Region) W. T. Smith's refusal was the curtest: "I regret I will not attend since I am not currently involved in the FAP."[70]

The monumental structure of any conference attempts to control the turbulent flow of new and old thought in the name of intellectual and professional responsibility. Let us attempt to draw an analogy between this and the nature of the Flood Action Plan. I have already indicated the broad similarity: the monumental pharaonic concrete hard structures are built in an attempt to control the turbulent young waters of the great rivers. We will see at the end how both – though not in equivalent ways – serve to silence the subaltern. But now let us take the analogy in another direction.

Let us think of these stupendous drains, driving the continually shifting text-ile waters by the violence of reason into the shortest route to the sea as the violence of Reason itself, driving the continually differentiating text-ile of meanings into the shortest route to Truth. But the absolute fulfillment of these drain-dreams and their attendant systems would be the perverse dream of Reason against that principle of reason which is obliged to give an account of itself, fulfilled in every detail, for itself: the absolute fulfillment of the drain-dreams are an animal-machine comparable to Heidegger's dream of the typographically self-protected philosophical text; with all inconsistencies programmed, the land reduced to whatever can be fed into Geographical Information Systems, its surface given over to that ruminant gnawing. This implacable logic began with the systematizing of land into survey in early modern Britain, the condition and effect of conquest and imperialism.[71] The worlding of infinite geometries for control of the country as information is its working-out. It is in the interest of this that culture fishery, projected as a replacement for the capture of fish, moving with flood and moving water as common property, will systematize the bounded rivers into private property and export, establish the systematization of agri-capital.

This is a dream that requires the kind of unconnected monitory pause that a deconstructive censor let slip in that long footnote of *Of Spirit*. Nazism, which showed the risk of *Destruktion* literalized was, ostensibly, defeated, although the demonization of Islam and the progressively militant xenophobia in Euro-US give proof that the "big trees" in the "European" – by Husserl's expanded definition of Europe – forest that sheltered Nazism can still be, however confusedly, called "culture, or the world of spirit."[72] This dream, the animal-machine of exploitation fully transforming land into information for a manipulation that will obey myriad minute rules of programming also belongs to that culture, that spirit, in the name of Reason – the public use of reason – "white" mythology.

It is the subaltern, the fisher and the grass-roots peasant who produce a constant interruption for the full *telos* of Reason and capitalism, for those who have the patience to learn. I will tax my readers' patience with one example among many.

Living in the rhythm of water, the Bangladeshi peasant long sowed two types of rice paddy seed. One of them survived submerged in water, the other came to full growth after the season of rain and flood. In 1971, agricultural reformers introduced a different variety of rice for a single high-yield crop. In the intervening years, the peasant has quietly and gradually shifted the time of sowing of this modern crop to Phalgun-Chaitro (February–March). As was their established custom, accommodating the play of land and water, they now sow pulses and vegetables before this. And now, at the reaping time of the new crop, the old flood-seed is sown, so that in the rain and flood-time, the fields are once again full of that submersible paddy.[73] (By contrast, the land "protected" from water by the embankments loses the fertilizing algae, thus providing an opportunity for the enhancement of the debt trap and the destruction of the ecobiome by the peddling of chemical fertilizers.) I hesitate to call this silent interruption "flood management" by exporting a metaphor of Nature as the "great *laboratorium*, the arsenal which furnishes both means and material of labor...," coming from (what is confusedly called) European culture, producing an evolutionary account.[74] I hesitate to denominate the responsible deconstruction (learning critique from within leading to a new setting to work, as in Derrida's reading of Heidegger) as "technology transfer," as if a "gift" from a superior civilization.

Count this interruption in the nature of a permanent parabasis, the peasant's rather than the philosopher's disarticulated rhetoric, a setting-to-work, not an explication, of the philosopher's dream.[75] Ask the question again: what exactly does the fulfilled dream of Reason bring about on its way? If the subaltern offers us, say, learning, and the ecological deconstructor supplements this with the persistently intermediary stage of its transformation into exchangeable but internalized knowledge (not merely knowledge of knowledge), the "murderous" supplement of the animal-machine bypasses the implication of responsibility with subjectity, even freedom of intention, and substitutes information command. This is the "human" that the unilateral thinking of "animal" produces. This thinking, of the subaltern human-as-animal(like), this figure of evil continues the work of imperialism by destroying, what is, no doubt confusedly, called "culture," in this case a popular culture, traditional learning and knowledge, traditional agronomic patterns, and, what I have left until last, the traditional pattern of subaltern women's freedom on the impermanent floating islands or *chors*.[76] In place of the destroyed culture of learning, a continually expanding amount of money continues to be spent, on the aid–debt model, to collect hydrological data, as if nothing had been known. A large section of the post-colonial subjects of Bangladesh is of course crazy about Geographical Information Systems, and not in the service of accountable reason. They provide the "European" interminable dialogists the opportunity to invoke "the Bangladeshis" as the willing beneficiaries, just as the interminable dialogists at the end of *Of Spirit* had invoked the "Messianic Jew … and the Moslem" (OS 111).

The question or affirmation about the intractable agency of the specter is left open at the end of *Of Spirit*, since its textual function is nothing more (and nothing less) than the transcription of spirit as ghost.[77] Elsewhere Derrida has written on spectrality in connection with Marx.[78]

Is it possible to imagine that, since responsibility must bind the call of the ethical to a response, one must act here as if responsibly to the specter called "commune-ism," whose threat Development must desperately hold at bay? That setting-to-work need not call on a European left monoculture.[79] This space of intimate learning, of human-animal-watery ground, is after all an ongoing response to the weave of land and river by the landless and on common waters. Nothing but an intermediary question can be posed and left suspended in the space of an essay.

Because we have less power than the World Bank, and because some of us are of color, when we confront the World Bank, we sometimes claim that the subaltern speaks. Also, as I have indicated before, if an academic includes empirical details in her essays, joins demonstrations, participates in international conferences with political-sounding titles, and engages in solidarity tourism, we think of her as an activist. Such assumptions might be put in their place by the fact that (1) the World Bank took little notice of the organized protesters at the conference; and that (2) in order to locate the subaltern, the heterogeneous collection of subjects in the space of difference – from the two "Europes," *and* from those who can protest at a conference at a parliament, – we will have to cross other frontiers. This conference was, however, an intermediary stage of strategic and tactical setting-to-work that involved a range from heads of the donor States all the way down to low-level functionaries of the client State, people involved, directly and indirectly, in making decisions and implementing them: decisions making clear that "the night of non-knowledge" did not mean "not knowing one's intentions," decisions that affected the subaltern.

To address (a) concretely, I cite extracts from an internal memo circulated by the Deputy Director of the Environment Department of the World Bank. This is his answer to the question: "What happened at the Conference?":

> There must have been 30–40 Bangladeshis present (all seemingly opposing FAP), with a smaller group of about 6, who were official speakers. These, I understand from Ross Wallace, are the standard characters appearing at all the FAP events in Dhaka. They are, as you know, extremely articulate, and complement each other very well. Professor Shapan Adnan gives the fact in great detail, K[h]ushi Kabir gives a sociological perspective (giving emphasis to the income distributional and women's issues) [Ms Kabir had in fact been surprisingly silent about women this time]. Dr. Hashemi (a very sympathetic person I thought) gives the economic, Mohiuddin Farooq[ue] presents the legal questions (a very nice fellow, but didn't make much sense), and a young woman (Mushrefa Mishu) who is president of the Student Unity Forum, gives the passionate anti-colonial anti-establishment stuff, which the adults wouldn't get away with.[80]

This is a silencing of protest, of course. Anti-imperialist discourse is put in its place with cynical flippancy. In case the World Bank should be obliged to back down (the protest meant something, after all), as they were in the case of the Narmada Valley Project in India in March, 1993, a formula for re-coding defeat as victory is given in advance:

> A clear statement from the Bank on the size and composition of the program emerging from the Regional Studies could perhaps help position us better from an external relations standpoint – although perhaps not with the government. Absent that, the opposition will strengthen in Europe and possibly in the US, and if a year from now a much more modest program does emerge, the NGOs [nongovernmental organizations, presumably Bangladeshi] will claim victory.

This makes it clear that the interminable exchange is indeed between Europe and Europe. The "others" can be dismissed as poor players, a stale act. But we must also note that the issue is how to claim responsibility for a "victory," to stage recapitulation in such a way that it looks like a responsible response to reasoned inquiry. All responsibility is a simulacrum of responsibility, perhaps. But all complicities with this necessity are not equivalent. And what Derrida has, with justified irritation, said about those who respond to responsibility with the cant of the decentered subject is nothing compared to what can be said to those who act out the reasoned responsibility of Europe to the people of the rest of the world in the interest of the self-determination of international capital:

> Whence comes the law that forbids one to forgive whoever *does not know how to give*? "I saw then clearly that his aim had been to do a good deed while at the same time making a good deal; to earn forty cents and the heart of God; to win paradise economically; in short, to pick up gratis the certificate of a charitable man. … to be mean is never excusable, but there is some merit in knowing that one is; the most irreparable of vices is to do evil out of stupidity."[81]

The first of "seven broad points" to which the Deputy Director of Environment reduces "the myriad grumbles about FAP" is that the "talk about participation is just that – talk. There is no genuine effort on the part of anyone to ask the rural poor what they think or want." It is to be noted that no remedy is indicated for this problem anywhere in the memo. No genuine effort can of course be made by the programming dream of the perfect animal-machine to accommodate the singular rhythm of human/animal/water. And, on the mundane register, it is absurd to think that the ethical rhythm of responsive transference with the Bangladeshi subaltern can ever become the necessary but impossible goal for the functionaries and associates of the Bank. The infinite care with which Derrida had compiled a list of the duties of the new Europe, and then reminded the self-same Europe that a list of quite other duties silently supposes it, can never become a part of the Bank's investment in Development.[82]

The point is, however, that even when the Bank is questioned by the representatives of a Europe that is responsible to the human being in Nature, the subaltern is silenced. In conclusion, a few hints.

The feasibility of sane technology transfer by building on traditional flood-management methods was elaborated with care and precision by the President of the International Rivers Network, based in

Berkeley. No one but the Bangladeshis knew that in the overlong Bengali speech of Abdus Sattar Khan, an aging leader of the peasant movement, this flood management technique, and the detailed account of all the major rivers in Bangladesh, was already given in an old-fashioned perorative way.

I am not romanticizing this particular person, beyond remarking that his death in the intervening years was mourned by many. He was not a "great leader," and was apparently not specifically associated with the mobilization against the Flood Action Plan. I certainly do not know enough about him to credit him with authenticity simply because, in that company of card-carrying international activists and Development officials, he seemed a guileless old man. But there can be little doubt that he was staged as a slice of the authentic, a piece of the real Bangladesh.

If the World Bank's internal memo represents the silencing of protest, the misfiring of the staging of this elderly man is also a species of silencing. The way the shape of his words escaped the monumental structuring of the theater of Old Europe, which determined the "dialogue," was pathetically trivial. But even here we are not in the register of the speech of the everyday frustration of the quietly "flood-managing" fisher and farmer at the incomprehensible giant systematically destroying their established rhythm of existence.

It is often forgotten that the persuasive accomplices of the World Bank are, in appearance, well-meaning educated Bangladeshis extending help to these subalterns. The first impulse that comes from below is of trust-in-responsibility. And, indeed, Sattar Khan had come trusting to the conference, trusting that his old-fashioned fact-filled speech against the FAP would be heard. And, although in his case the trust was not in principle misplaced, there was such a great gulf fixed between his own perception of how to play his role in a theater of responsibility and the structure into which he was inserted that there was no hope for a felicitous performance from the very start. In order to hear him, "Europe" would need him to represent responsibility, *by reflex*, in "Europe's" way. In other words, change his mind-set. That is how the old colonial subject was shaped. When we do it, we call it education.

To begin with, the European Parliament had no provision for simultaneous translation from the Bengali. An absolutely unforgivable lapse in responsibility on the part of the benevolent Europeans. This man had been brought to the Conference – not to be heard but seen. Like a child. Or an animal. In the event, an imperfect English translation was read out of synch by a Bangladeshi who was attending ("participating in") the conference, and it was this imperfect well-meaning amateur production that was available through the headphones in simultaneous translation in the other conference languages. For the first time, the hall was full of impatient hubbub: "European" discipline was breaking down. The man's style, practiced on a lifetime of subcontinental popular oratory – another theater that Kipling was already mocking in the nineteenth century – declaimed with now-ridiculous passion to an absent audience. (The Bangladeshis present, from a younger more professional generation, swung between embarrassment and sympathy.) Of course the paper far exceeded the 20 allotted minutes. In the monumental structuring we inhabit in old Asia, the exceeding of allotted time is negotiable and depends on gender, status, and the temperament of the moderator. In this case the benevolent egalitarian young US moderator cut the speaker off. Sattar Khan responded, in generally incomprehensible Bengali, with a "Friend, I am a poor peasant," – which was not strictly speaking the case, but under the circumstances a fair rhetorical representation, and I have no doubt infinitely more effective in those simulacra of parliamentarianism that we encounter in former colonies, where the battle *is* between who is and is not a colonial subject rather than on grounds of cultural difference – "you must hear me out!" Therefore, he was of course allowed to continue by way of a gesture of benevolence toward someone who could not understand the rules. He read now at breakneck speed, and the entire ad hoc effort at translation collapsed.

This incident can only stand in for the subaltern's inability to speak. For Mr Sattar, a middle-class peasant party leader, was far indeed from the landless peasant and the grass-roots fisher, however "indigenous" he was by contrast with the other participants. It stands in successfully, however, by virtue of the fact that the subaltern's inability to speak is predicated upon an attempt to speak to which no appropriate response is proffered.[83] It is in fact a failure of responsibility in the addressee which can be reckoned irrespective of the fact that all communication is infected by *destinerrance*.[84]

In 1991, before I had read *Of Spirit*, I had written as follows about the subaltern inhabitants of the cyclone- and tidal-wave prone Southeast coast of Bangladesh:

If this was an eco-logic where the unlikely material subject was the pulse of the tide and the rhythm of the water-logging of the wind,

I was in no way ready, daily encountering these very people's savvy discussions of the US Task Force ... simply to narrativize them as an earlier pre-scientific stage where the proper help was to "control" Nature so that these people could be redefined as passive. ... What would it be to learn otherwise, here? Better offer the contradiction: they will not move except as unwilling refugees. ... I could respect the relief workers' bemused on-the-spot decision that this other kind of resistance to rehabilitation must not be allowed to develop into an aporia. But the vestiges of intellectual sophistication I possessed saw through with distaste the long-distance theorist's dismissal of the aporia as anachrony or his embracing of it as the saving grace of a-chrony. I was adrift.[85]

This unwillingness to leave the land is rather easily accounted for by the "good Europeans" as a justified fear on the part of the poor that they will "be deprived" of the land by evacuating, or "the increasing lack of waged work in rural areas." I am not satisfied with so easy a reasoning.[86] Was there no lesson there at all to learn, then? Is the subaltern transparent? This may seem inconsequential to the reader, but it is precisely this type of uncaring damming of a drift that marks Heidegger's generalization of the animal. There is, according to the view I am discussing here, no gauge of intention but rational expectations, logical self-interest, reason small r written by something confusedly called European common sense. Moral outrage for Europe, self-interest for the subaltern. Teach them the latter, what you yourself propose not to practice. The subaltern mental theatre is deemed no bigger than this, just as for population control, the subaltern female is deemed nothing but a crotch. There is something like a relationship between this and the perverse dream of fulfilled Reason, although all complicities are not equivalent.

No doubt the easy generalities of the European/Bangladeshi elite activists come out of exchange with local people, sometimes through relayed networking, rightly perceived as a contrast to the World Bank's structured alibi for consultation with the subaltern. Yet the complicity is in that abyssal power of "European" exchange, for responsibility is still traduced here by impatience and inattention. I will close with an example of the silent gnawing of such a betrayal.

In "Birth of a Megaproject," James Boyce, an authoritative witness against irresponsible Development, claims that "[t]he Bengali language distinguishes between the normal beneficial floods of the rainy season, which are termed *barsha*, and harmful floods of abnormal depth and timing, which are termed *bonna*. The English word flood conflates these two very different phenomena."[87] The sources cited are Bangladeshi. Boyce's observation is repeated in a number of subsequent Western articles, I am presuming that Boyce is the source of this. His interpretation of the information is incorrect, in a way common to genuine but anthropologistic Euro-US benevolence, as if someone, hearing people use "see you later" and "see you soon" interchangeably, should claim for the English language a profound philosophy of time where "soon" and "later" were identical.

Professor M. Aminul Islam, who is cited by Dr. Paul, Boyce's direct source, writes as follows:

> In all the three study villages flooding is referred to as barsha and bonna [This idiosyncratic construction carries a trace of the names of two different kinds of times, perhaps]. ... *Barsha* (June–October) is a normal inundation and is taken as a benevolent agent. ... *Bonna* is perceived as disastrous ...[88]

Neither of these native Bengali-speakers is making a claim for Bengali (or indeed, any north Indian language). *Barsha* – Sanskrit *varsā*, a nominal construction from the verbal root *vrs*, meaning, roughly, to drop *down* – means "rain" or "rainy season." What they are claiming is that, in their study area and in "ecologically similar" areas, when the subaltern says "the rains," s/he includes a certain normal inundation. If time and historical circumstance had obliged the English-speakers to take as much trouble with Bengali as a foreign linguist has to with European languages in order to venture a remark about meaning in published prose about the general language, this "authoritative" comment on Bengali would not have been offered. And I am not speaking of high Bengali either, but of the mother-tongue spoken by the illiterate expert of "flood-management." "Monthlies" and "bleeding" are not good and bad words for bleeding in the English language, although the former may indicate menstruation, or, in women of a certain age, "normal" bleeding.

In the context of this water-borne land still in the making in the rough theatre of mountain and wind, the strict differentiation between rain and flood fixed in the (Indo-)"European" mind-set, is persistently deconstructed, the one implying the other. When the balance is disturbed so that the opposition begins to come clear again, the signification is: disaster. However sympathetic the intention, to rob the mother-tongue of the subaltern by way of an ignorant authoritative definition that is already becoming part of the accepted benevolent lexicograph is a most profound silencing.

These words, too many, can only point you toward such silences.

Chapter 3

1994: Will Postcolonialism Travel?

When I was asked by the editor to place what follows in the inaugural issue of the *Armenian Forum*, I politely declined. I did not know enough about Armenia. Yet, without too many revisions, I have included it, for at least two kinds of reason.

First, in our effort to pluralize our Asia-s, we will inevitably be less knowledgeable about areas that are not immediately in our experience, areas that general official histories have marginalized. Transnational *literacy* is not *"knowledge."* If we do not expose our scrupulous effort at working within and beyond these limits, the sanctioned ignorance of geopolitical players will work at will, since specialist knowledge is either self-insulated from geopolitics, or, worse, is selectively on tap. It is my hope, as expressed in the Foreword, that my well-meaning generalism will draw some specialists into a constructive criticism that will bring us collectively into the mainstream that is now increasingly managed only by the policy mavens in the academy, while the cultural theorists, like frogs in a well, debate "universality."

The second reason is the very hyphenated appropriation of which I spoke in the last chapter. Hannah Arendt wrote that when the machinery of the state turns to genocide, we witness radical evil.[1] She was working, thank God, with only one example. In these times, we have come to see that all merely rational structures are structurally susceptible to such a turn – because, in order to function, they must necessarily suppress the part, not of unreason, but of the matricial element of the human and beyond, that does not derive as the opposite of reason, a "part" that exceeds the "whole." Indeed, if there is radical evil, it would belong to that matrix, where it may be indistinguishable from its opposite. We cannot make reason our ally if we do not protect it from such susceptibilities. In the reasonable confines of the state, the word "genocide" provides the possibility of an international alliance and, as I have been suggesting in this book and earlier, it is the metropolitan diasporic from those states who consolidate the alliance. Considerations of Armenia allow us to think this outside Africa or the holocaust.

As our sense of the present has become more informed in space and time, we see more and more examples of mass killings apparently based on ethnicity in the world, not unconnected with so-called democratic structures. If earlier political philosophy defined this as the breakdown of the ethical into radical evil rather than the defining transgression of merely reasonable (state) solutions, it has now become part of the juridico-legal calculus, and evidentiary detail can be accumulated to decide if a situation, past and present, qualifies as "genocide." Such decisions are important. The law demands that "cases" be constructed before action can be taken. But they do not bring closure. Because the effort to establish a name becomes all-consuming, the fact of what remains after naming is ignored. Unless we think of such exclusions, we will not be able to understand why President Kageme of Rwanda wants to get on with healing his country, why some African-American victims of hurricane Katrina (2005) did not wish to qualify as "refugees" in order to receive aid.[2]

The question is not simply: why can Black on Black not have a Truth and Reconciliation Commission; or why will the US not allow the juridico-legal category of "internally displaced." For those too are only legal questions. If we look at why ignoring what remains makes complete redress impossible, in the case of Armenia we will see a fierce nationalism getting in the way of facing globality. It will show us that postcolonialism is too deeply tied to the idea of a national liberation. In other words, some version of postcolonialism may travel, but that is not the point. Earlier, the critique of postcolonial reason was in terms of the usurping of the place of the native informant by the metropolitan diasporic. That critique stands, of course, but now, as postcolonialism spreads to the Balkans and the Caucasus, warnings against mere nationalism must be raised in a new way. The matter of the Armenian "genocide" is more and more appropriated by metropolitan diasporics, aligned with those for whom US unity among metropolitan migrants, from diverse national origins, seems the most urgent task on the agenda. That sort of cultural nationalism remains the staple of the US diaspora. Additionally, the question comes up for the politically inclined diasporic in the context of the international civil society which generally bypasses a state's constitutional obligations. The Republic of Armenia flounders under the weight of Nagorno-Karabakh and the international oil scene.[3] The ideology of that conflict is also produced by a coherent historical narrative where the genocide of 1915 is a contributing factor. Under the circumstances, it seems important to pay heed to the first point above and pay heed to Armenia as part of our task to pluralize Asia rather than to integrate the US, the latter doubtless a good goal within the US as a multicultural nation-state. Indeed, this chapter closes on an open end. Armenia is not in the news, although it has a strong and divided lobby in Washington, and the question which led to the following piece was asked by second-generation diasporics who have moved to other work. Yet other new immigrants, not necessarily academic intellectuals, are asking versions of the same question, not necessarily recognizable as such.

Armenia, pluralized in diasporas for many centuries, guarding its "nationalism" under such circumstances, offers a crucial lesson in contemporary globality.

"Why is there no Armenian postcolonialism?" asked Anahid Kassabian and David Kazanjian.

And I felt compelled to reply.

The question was posed with reference to their essay, " 'You Have to Want to Be Armenian Here': Nationalisms, Sexualities and the Problem of American Diasporic Identity," on the film *Back to Ararat*.[4] Kassabian and Kazanjian have moved on to other though not unrelated concerns. The film itself has taken its place among ethnic identitarian films produced for diasporas. In an extended study, one would have to consider such films as Frunze Dovlatyan's *The Yearning* (1990) and Atom Egoyan's *Ararat* (2002). I have kept the question alive, because, in 1994, the time was ripe for it. After the dissolution of the Soviet Union, "private US interests had been awakened as regards the oil of the Caspian Sea. ... '[A] preoccupation with the four 'nuclear successor states' prevented the Caucasus ... from getting much serious attention until 1994."[5]

Since then, this has been remedied, and Armenia is deemed one of the places most ready for "democracy." The specifically "postcolonial" question is produced from a US ideological position, minoritarian, identitarian, and left-liberal.

In the "Economic and Philosophical Manuscripts," Karl Marx's object of investigation is *Nationalökonomie* or "national economy."[6] The first volume of *Capital* begins with a reference to "the wealth of societies" – an obvious rephrasing of "the wealth of nations" – and the object of investigation has changed to "political economy." Since Marx's project is to establish a rational definition of the "social" (hence socialism), this is not without significance. In the rational plan for socialism, there is no room for nationalism. Armenia, a small land-locked Christian country in the Southern Caucasus, teaches us that, if we want globalization to be more socialist than capitalist, we must negotiate nationalism better than merely suppress it, as did the Soviet Union.

The story of Marxism and nationalism is a complex one.[7] Here it is enough to note that through certain sections of the *Grundrisse*, Marx attempts to understand the question of the nation, posing it in his obstinate bottom-line way: What is it about ground and blood that they constitute such an extraordinary bond? What, in other words, is this irrational affect that brings the rational to ground?[8] He is unable to find an answer. The section ends abruptly. The question is not seriously re-considered. When the pre-history of industrial capitalism is considered later, we are reading the narrative of modes of production, a different issue (C1 877–8, and C3 440–8, 728–48). Yet Marx's dominant example has to remain one nation-state – Victorian Britain, although the implicit teleology is international.[9] The posthumous setting-to-work of Marxian theory decided against the feasibility of immediate internationalism and, only partly in response to opposition from international capitalism, transformed internationalism into expansionism. Dominant nationalisms played a considerable part in this saga. It is agreed on all sides that Marx did not theorize the revolutionary subject.[10] The rhetoric of an extraordinary paragraph in "The Eighteenth Brumaire of Louis Bonaparte" makes clear that the subject is produced by the times. This "subject" is neither the individual nor the collective. Like labor-power, it is not even constitutively human, but rather designated as the "proletarian revolution." The deliberate miscitation of Hegel misquoting Aesopian wisdom at the paragraph's end may carry the suggestion that the revolutionary response may necessarily be in misprision with conceptualizing Reason as the grand Rosicrucian consolation of philosophy to be found in the Hegelian passage from which Marx takes his quotation; as it acts in accordance with what it thinks are the imperatives of the historical moment.[11]

The "subject"-position of revolution therefore remains a textual blank, always dependent upon "the conditions." Marx had described the transformation of industrial capital into commercial capital as an

Aufhebung – a sublation – a destruction and a displaced preservation (C3 742). With the accession of finance capital to the place of the dominant we might once again be in an *Aufhebung*. The subject position of the revolution can no longer be – only – the proletarian on the factory floor. Indeed, the factory floor has been pulverized by informatics. Although the metropolitan working class is made to believe that "outsourcing" is only a "nationalist" issue, it is the nation-state which is today only a moment in the telecommunicative embrace between finance capital and world trade, with a judicious mixture of Caspian Sea oil. One can, of course, call the search for the displaced revolutionary subject in the new conjuncture "postcolonialism." But in order to do so, one would have to move from the nationalism-based version of postcolonial theory. National liberation from the "Turk" is not the postcolonial. Let us resume our reading of Marx.

It is not without interest that the rare passage on proletarian revolutions in Marx is contained in a piece on the function of nationalism in the development of the state. Thus it is possible to imagine that, already in 1852, Marx was not unaware of the power of nationalism, just as, a few years earlier, he is able to presuppose a specifically *German* ideology. But Marxian theory had turned aside from the question of the nation and its ideological weight upon the new state. In the event, the necessarily compromised elaboration of that theory worked itself out on ground that had been and was being worked over by three unevenly pre-capitalist imperial formations: the Habsburg, the Ottoman, and the Russian. Imperial policy exacerbates and mobilizes something that we would recognize today as "nation" thinking, a thinking of collectivity that is at least related to something like a nation, at least in the custodians of ideology, though not necessarily in the "people" in the subaltern sphere.[12]

For us to assume that the nation is no more than the turn away from Latin Europe imposed upon the rest of the world by way of the European Enlightenment metonymically grasped in the Peace of Westphalia (1648) – and thus to assume that its fate in peripheral places was no more than a series of ill-fitting catachreses, is to turn aside again from Marx's road not taken.[13] It seems more responsible to turn that way rather, recalling that every event represented as a rupture – here the imagination of nation where there was no such possibility before – is also a repetition. It is even worth speculating upon the possible ethico-political interest that would determine the initial assumption that a nation was only the peculiar collectivity spawned by the West

European narrative. Could it be in the interest of suggesting, even from a politically contrary position, that history, here the very possibility of the historical, begins with colonialism? On what grounds do "nationalist discourses ... claim that the nation has existed for eternity?" Kassabian and Kazanjian reminded us that the root word in "nation" is "natio," "birth" (KK 20). The Birth of a Nation is to situate or propriate birth. How was it done by a people before Europe sold them the latest model, only a little used, one size fits all? Should we forget that "nation" relates, through an easily recognizable consonant loss and shift, Greek *genesis*, English kind, kin, king, Sanskrit *janma*? I am averse, of course, to mere etymologism. Yet the move to locate in a Latin word the birth / origin or seal of a concept is to obliterate a forgetfulness. Nation cannot be separated from blood-kin, the ground of racism. As the generations pass, this kinship is deconstructed and expanded, "blood" metaphorically at once conserving and questioning the pseudo-biological ground of race, as well as revealing and emphasizing the difference in so-called "literal" blood-kinship. "Diversity" in "citizenship" negotiates this deconstruction.

Let us consider *ethnos*, the word with which such negotiations operate.

In the Greek-English Lexicon, the trick of the alphabet brings *ethnikos* ("foreign, heathen, gentile"; and a much later construction) before *ethnos*. The contradiction inherent in the older word, in the thought of an insider group tied by common birth or common birthplace – blood or land – comes clear by this chance. It is not only birth but keeping in by keeping out that is at issue here. Not only time but space. If one considers the connection with *ethos*, in its various forms relating to habit, habitual living together, this most bloodstained word shows some signs of not necessarily being about birth or blood but about a chance clustering in space: *synoikismos*. Once we get out of the obligatory location of the origin of nationalism in imperialism (trivially true in its current recognizable form), we begin to see the lines of conflict laid down in the way the meaning of the word shifts on the page of the lexicon. The desire to establish "genocide" takes its place within these lines.

This remains an important goal, for political manipulation, economic reparation, and historical vindication. It is, however, not an end-point, except for those uninterested in the detail of the postcolonial state. "Despite the work of intellectuals, some Armenians and Azerbaijanis have articulated an alternative version of history, which suggest that after centuries of cohabitation within the orbit of the Persian Empire, there is more that joins than divides them."[14] Richard Hovannisian, while not denying the genocide, offers a picture that comes close to the moment of antique cosmopolitanism in *Back to Ararat*. Women saved as sexual partners are among the survivors he interviewed in Southern California. Their life stories are often indistinguishable from the force of "normal" marriage. His conclusion: "The Young Turks were extreme nationalists, but they were not racists in the Nazi sense. They wanted to create a Turkic empire and to eliminate all obstacles to the realization of their goal."[15] Even as we acknowledge the power of pieces such as "Shame," underscoring the tragedy of survivorship, we must attend to current geopolitical matters, especially as feminists.[16] I will come to this at the end of the chapter. For now, let us recall that "the expulsion of Armenians from Azerbaijan and Azerbaijanis from Armenia have produced more than a million refugees and internally displaced persons."[17] This is where "Eurasia" will break, and Armenia will be the fulcrum, even more than Turkey, geographically the cape of Asia into Europe. Here the exhortation to think other Asias is to turn the head of the European angel homeward and remind ourselves that more is to be gained by anti-ethnicist, anti-colonialist regionalism than putting ethnic narratives ahead of everything.[18]

Of course the words *ethnos, ethos, natio* do not "really" mean anything. The tiniest bit of common sense shows that no word can "really" mean anything. And yet they do mean.[19] The shape of the word, the transfer of words in the history of the language, can make us think of how this happens. The Lexicon tells us that *ethnos* was used of "a band of comrades," "a host of warriors," and even, by association, of "swarms and flocks of animals." (This reminds us of "Asia" in Homer – see p. 200.) If we want to think of a common birthplace as uniting these warriors and comrades, we have to presuppose what we call "nation," and, of course, women. The 1987 edition tells us that in Homer *ethnos* is used in the sense of a "nation." The 1874 edition, unaccountably, cites *ethnikos*, as used by Polybius, to mean "national"; and transfers *ethne* to the sense of *goyim*. And tucked away in the middle of the columns: "in general, a nation, a people." A sense of a common male-focused destiny is certainly at play somewhere here. Like most classical dictionaries, the Greek-English Lexicon is a cluster of examples. But that hidden general sense in the 1874 edition carries no corresponding example. Is this absence of example an example of the fact that the lexicographers were themselves in the grip of the posterior concept of the "nation," or that *ethnos* did in fact, generally, and also (it is sense number 3) mean something like "nation"? The inevitable coupling of nation and state leads us astray here.

The ethnos–nation displacement tells us rather little about the Armenian case, if we consider language the element of collective presuppositions, presuppositions that go from blood to politics, rubbing out women all the way. (In the Indic case, for example, one is often told not to translate *jāti* as "nation.") On the other hand, the displacement tells us a good deal about Armenia if we figure that a nation is not necessarily a nation-state, that *ethnos* relates to a city-state, whose trajectory is confused, to say the least. And how about the other way around? How about teasing out *jāti* in the history of the language(s) – especially since this is another one of those Indo-European cognates hidden in "nation" – to see why the imperialist displacement did not quite catch? Kassabian and Kazanjian's brilliant piece had not considered such questions, and people still do not. The debate rages around the Latinate word. History as such begins with the European Enlightenment, whatever that might be, communities are imagined on the European national model, and the theorists, at best with an anthropologist's or a migrant's hold on the language, cannot think by way of its labyrinthine history and geography.

The vicissitudes of the thinking of ideas kin to nation have not been generalized in the history of the Armenian language. It is a vicious circle, for this absence of generalization is itself no doubt dependent upon the dismemberment of Armenia before the "nationalist" empires. If this is taken into consideration, then it would be difficult indeed to get a grip on the Armenian case. Then the questioners' just remark: "While significant work in this field has come, for example, from historians and theorists of Palestinian and Indian nationalist movements, we have not yet found similar scholarship on Armenian nationalism" (KK 21) would begin to make a different kind of sense. *Natio* is Indo-European. There's the Indian connection. Why doesn't it travel to Armenian, the language being Indo-European as well? We begin to see that history gives words meaning, not just the other way around. The point may not be that Armenian, being an Indo-European language, should have entered the ranks of the nation-game, since collectivities think something like nation and "nation" is an Indo-European word. The point may rather be that it was William Jones, colonial administrator as well as the founder of the Royal Asiatic society, who announced the common ancestry of Sanskrit and Greek in 1786, at the first anniversary of the society, thus establishing a common Aryan bond between caste-Hindus and Britons.[20] In quite a different way from Afghanistan or Thailand, Armenia was never a "colony." Unsuccessful introjection by multi-ethnic pre-capitalist empires, reversed by extermination, is a different pattern from the one established in the historical dominant. And as for Palestine, the point may not be merely that the Arabic and Hebrew words for "nation" are not so far apart from each other. That may animate the Israel–Palestine conflict. But in the area of postcolonial criticism, the fact that Edward Said was trained in British Literature of the nineteenth century and that his humanist politics were anchored in the best traditions of that time and place, is altogether more relevant.

In the case of India, a broad argument (with all the attendant problems of broad arguments) can be assembled as follows:

The construction of India as a site of British colonialism was rather different from the construction of "Africa." The difference as well as the relationship is argued in Mahmood Mamdani's *Citizen and Subject*.[21] Romila Thapar has persuasively shown how the myth of a shared "Aryanism" was used to justify the British colonial adventure as a historical reenactment of a manifest destiny.[22] At the other extreme, this notion of more similarities than differences allows the powerful Cambridge historians almost to argue away colonialism as a major oppressive force.[23] Unmistakable alliances – as with a *pharmakon* that is both medicine and poison – can be remarked between this narrative and the narrative of Indian nationalism, the force of Indian feminism, the importance of Indian Colonial Discourse Studies, and the role of Indian intellectuals in the study of hybridity and transnationality. Even subalternist historiography, in spite of disclaimers, must work with these narratives.

In the case of Palestine I speak obviously with less "responsible" involvement. The consolidation of the field in the Palestinian case has something to do with the magic date – 1948 – of the establishment of the State of Israel. It is always dangerous to tie worldhistorical or geopolitical events to specific dates. Yet a date invites us to insert ourselves into events ostensibly locked in an unrecoverable past.[24] (It is thus that Bulgaria enters postcolonialism – read post-communism – in terms of the Soviet occupation in 1948 – rather than 500 years of Ottoman rule.) As if in response to that invitation, let me suggest that the mid-forties may be taken to mark the beginning of the shift from territorial imperialism to neo-colonialism, the beginning of the apparent dissolution of imperialism into Development and World Trade, the passing of the torch from Britain (and France …) to the United States. This is a big story and it is still unfolding. It was the establishment of a New World Order in which (the breakup of) Bolshevism was a major contributing force. But world(hi)story unfolds behind the players' back, underground like molework.[25] At the time Britain undertook some consolidating holding actions, writing with the political language woven by the old order: the establishment of Israel in Palestine, the partition of India. The myth of the return to the Holy Land, rather a tenacious topos in the European Imaginary, opened a resurgence of the demonization of Islam.[26] As this Christian story – where Jews were unevenly ranged with Muslims as the other side – shifted historical focus, brutally rearranged by the Holocaust, the British role in the establishment of Israel authorized the displacement of the Jews on the same side as the Christian dominant. Derrida, caught within this narrative as he has frequently reminded us, has narrativized this in his own way by charting the necessarily unwitting complicity of the German Jewish intellectual. The rupture of the Holocaust linked a repetition-in-the-making into a different concatenation in the chain of displacements. The emergence of the Judeo-Christian dominant was legitimized. Anti-semitism persists as a hardy residual, never identical with the variety of "anti-semitism" that hates the Arab, read Muslim. Derrida's insistence that Heidegger was complicitous with the very Christianity that he distanced himself from, adds another twist to this linking.[27] Part of the shifting was a continental drift. The geopolitical protagonist in this *geste* was not, finally, Britain but the US. It is, to repeat, a story that has bold outlines and can be grasped. And the grasp was made magisterially clear by the entry into the not-yet-emergent field of global cultural studies of Edward Said's *Orientalism*.[28] The figure of the US-based "exile" as spokesperson for postcolonialism was born. The intense located struggle of Palestinians on all levels was written into the discourse of postcolonialism.

Postcolonial discourse was now the enablement of "the irreducible face-to-faces" in the force field of the ability-to-know (*pouvoir-savoir*) with two major dominant articulations of "the same," from which all postcolonial engagements seemed to draw energy: Raj in the past: metonym of Britain; Aretz Israel in the present: metonym for the United States. Nagorno-Karabakh and Azerbaijan, Armenia and the Turks cannot find such fit in the permissible narratives. Although Armenia was handled cynically by Great Britain, and the massacre of Armenians by the Turks was prepared for by Czarist policy, what is remembered upon the specifically postcolonial scene is that Armenia represents "a break in the continuity of Islam from the Bosphorus to Central Asia."[29] In the contemporary context, Russia, as well as the United States, find in Armenia a satellite/ally because of their fear of political Islam.

I spend time on language and the rememoration of nation, because, when we talk about European-style nationalism, we are talking about the concept of *nation* that coded and backed up the dynamics of the capitalist *state*. (I use "rememoration" to mean the invocation of a collective past as if each one of us held it in memory.) One must agree with Marx that one is obliged always to speak from capitalism. But one must also attempt the necessary but impossible task of grasping the before and the outside – the "without" – without acknowledging our capital-determination as the better and more realistic model. Armenia has no prehistory specifically of this.

The Armenian intellectual cannot stage the nation-state within "the scholarship of nationalist movements," which requires the script of industrial capitalist colonialism→imperialism as the master model for a reactive and imperfect nationalism. This is the requirement of the current model of postcolonial theory that is being broken in the Balkans. In order not to remain a satellite within a great game not of its own making, "Armenia" must displace this model into a regionalism that I present in conclusion, undo a neatly balanced power-play: Russia-Iran-Armenia, US-Turkey-Azerbaijan. My generation keeps thinking of non-alignment. Multi-ethnic empires with different "nationalisms" under the same state may themselves be thought of as an earlier displacement, of the city-state mindset that made Aristotle a Stygian.

Looking at inscriptions in the streets of a Harlem disappearing under Development, I had begun to understand social textuality as an incessant process of lexicalizing.[30] To lexicalize is to separate a linguistic item from its supposedly appropriate initial grammatical system into the conventions of another grammar. A new lexicalization involves a delexicalization as well. This is a constant and ongoing process and we cannot necessarily fix a positive or a negative value to it. In the emergence of the new postcolonial subject we witnessed a relexicalizing of India and Palestine. About the latter, a reviewer recently commented on "the full pathos of the situation of the Palestinians, a people forgotten by history who found themselves involuntarily caught up in another people's great drama."[31] Paradoxically, it is into this great drama – a commingling of the extermination of the Saracens and return to the Promised Land – that the other signifier, India, hardly a people forgotten by history, is being coded. I was writing with trepidation in "Terror," a piece about September 11, 2001 that took me forever to finish: The conflict that emerges in the visuality of our everyday, in the context of the War on Terrorism, is Kashmir. But if, in the

Palestinian case, it is seldom mentioned that the West Bank is occupied territory, in the Indian case, the state of Gujarat, where genocidal violence against Muslim citizens is condoned by state and police, does not make it into the visualization of our public culture. Indeed, *The Economist* calls the Hindu attacks on Muslims in Gujarat "true but irrelevant."[32] Hey presto, here is Zbigniew Brezczinski now in the mainstream press: "Hindu fanatics in India are also quite eager to conflate Islam in general with terrorism in Kashmir in particular."[33] A straw in the wind, evidence of lexicalization at work.

By contrast, Armenia's narrative reach into the Euro-American Imaginary is dispersed, and millennially dispersed; and its entry into what is recognized as "nationalism" is anchorless and young. Where would we fit Armenia? In the region, and especially by the Russian policy makers, Armenia is integrated into that narrative as the only Christian island in a sea of Muslims. The US can displace it into "most ready for democracy;" and "Armenia is actually the second per capita recipient of US aid in the world after Israel" (SN 370) but this is not a postcolonial telling. A film like *Back to Ararat* seems to take as its emotional fulcrum a thoroughly eclectic longing for community, mobilizing an ancient Armenia which was more "tapestry-like."[34]

PeÅ Holmquist, a Swedish filmmaker, made this film a year before the Berlin Wall fell. The point of the film is to establish the fact of the genocide of 1915 through the representation of various groups: Soviet Armenia as "Christian," generally reclaiming the souls of the victims with elaborate orthodox ritual. (There is a general aura of good (Armenian) and bad (Turkish) violence in the film; the Soviet Armenia sector has rather unnerving shots of smiling children with crosses on their foreheads, sketched in the blood of a freshly slaughtered – shown on film – Paschal lamb.) Old Armenian men in a small French town weep over an older brother murdered in 1915. "Neutral" and thoroughly integrated Armenians in Beirut hand out machine guns on guard duty. Terrible Turkish officials deny genocide and insist it was a civil war. A man who had killed the Turkish Ambassador ("good violence") to Yugoslavia, stoic in his wheelchair, turned "creative," is shown sculpting. Militant diasporics, demonstrating – in Paris, at the European Parliament, in New York – most specifically at the UN. It seems peculiar, at least to this viewer, that the Azeris are accused by the voiceover of "killing Armenians" as did the Turks. It is, after all, agreed on all sides that the conflict over Nagorno-Karabakh, an Armenian majority enclave in Azerbaijan, was initiated by Armenian nationalists and there is fighting on both sides. It is also clear that where the original names the violators as Chechen or Kurd, the voiceover invariably intones "Turk." There are Armenian critics who believe that the ideology for this war was a tradition "invented" by intellectuals.[35] In the Lebanese sector, a lesson in Armenian history and nationalism is being given, by diasporics, in Armenian, in the US, in English. The main man (and woman – they get married in the end) is all for "doing something," and praises the military initiative that started in the seventies – good violence again. At crucial moments we are shown Mount Ararat, serene in the distance, home of the ancient Armenians, by strong symbolic implication the site of the first settlement after the Flood. (The Bible figures prominently once or twice.)

Women who live "womanly" lives often (though not necessarily) relate unsentimentally to nationalism, especially displaced nationalism. There are two noticeable moments of such unsentimentality in the film, from very dissimilar sources: a middle-aged Armenian-American mother, and an old woman, member of an Armenian minority community in a city from which Armenians were purged in 1915. The first one reminds the young man that all this call for "our land," "feeling Armenian," "support for armed struggle" and the like is practical only if exiled Armenians go back to a newly constituted and expanded Armenia, presumably situated within its "ancient" outlines. The young peoples' response is interesting: the Armenian-Americans won't leave the US, but others will. The second one, from the other end of the diasporic spectrum, exiled in her own hometown, says repeatedly to the off-screen questioner, presumably the same Armenian-American young man: "forget all that, it is history, they will kill you!" The answer to this is a dismissive chuckle. Let me call this common sense a low-grade cosmopolitanism – an attitude that assumes a cosmopolis or world republic perhaps because exogamy structurally makes territorial boundaries fluid for "woman."

Let us draw a lesson from it. The film's theme of "return" seems to link it to the Zionist vision of Israel, which would not sit well with the mainsprings of postcolonial theory. Indeed, because of the strong theme of "return," and the powerful diasporic Armenian lobby in Washington (about which more later), Armenia is supposedly called the "Israel of the Caucuses [Caucasus?]."[36] (Metropolitan diasporics, even if they themselves do not return, push for return.) For better or for worse, the message of the film links itself with age-old European conservatism as well.[37] In order for Armenia – territorial and diasporic – to become the subject of postcolonial theory – this chosen subject position would need to be displaced. A subject position is "assigned," others "read" it, well or ill. But one can move toward a collective effort, in the hope that something will have happened, even if not as a direct result. In the field of agency, the results are more direct, the passing of laws, the adoption of resolutions, the drafting of declarations. Indirection is all we have when we aspire to meddle with subjects. The rest of the chapter is no more than such an attempt, to outline the rearrangement of desires, to think "Armenia-in-Asia" rather than "Armenia" as deployed by "Armenian-America." To think, further, "critical regionalism" rather than nationalism. This immense imaginative labor is the only work that will sustain us in confronting the easy internationalism of the non-state networks, backed up by the UN, the newest face of the workings of capital. It must hack away at old tough hostilities, rather than only prove guilt. Here the integrative aspect of the US diaspora can help neutralize the culturalist nationalism and join the located radicals, perhaps.[38] As it stands now the Diaspora is on the other side, the other side therefore also of radical postcolonialism, if there can be any. "[P]ro-active public relations efforts regarding assistance programs appear to have found a natural market within the Diaspora and have found a natural home in [the] US Embassy, Yerevan."[39]

It should perhaps be added here that diasporic Armenia, with a highly powerful lobby where two Armenian political parties push for the same ends in Washington, carrying ideological rather than financial strength, already creates a sort of "postcolonial" identity: "[T]he presence of allies is strengthened by the Armenian lobbies' unified policy objectives: recognition of the genocide, independence and aid for Nagorno Karabakh, maintenance of Section 907, and aid to Armenia."[40]

We keep our eyes on the relatively less remote past, the seedbed of postcolonialism. In the division between the Ottoman and the Russian empires (the two pre-capitalist imperialist formations in that area, neither of them "Western"), the Russian Armenians were the more "enlightened," the more "free." *Back to Ararat*, the film that was the efficient cause of these speculations, seems to reflect this in its choice of Soviet Armenia as the scene of absolution for the victims. Given the current demonization of Islam, it is difficult for mainstream postcolonialism to code the destruction of Armenians, dating from the weakening of the Ottoman Empire in the late nineteenth century. As an Indian, who suffers from the official representation of the country's Islamic imperial past as necessarily and almost uniformly oppressive, I cannot not consider the general problem of "covering Islam." I am not competent to make a judgment here. But this much may be risked: In the coding undergirding the "scholarship on nationalist movements," the historical narrative of Armenia slots in, however unfairly, as a Christian nation seeking to protect itself from Muslims. As I have mentioned above, the alliance with Russia also reflects this conviction on the part of Eurasian Russia.

Section 907 of the Freedom Support Act, mentioned in the passage quoted above, is a case in point. It spells out a withholding of aid to Azerbaijan. After the fall of the World Trade Center towers on September 11, 2001, George W. Bush determined a limited waiver to this section in exchange for Azerbaijan's help in capturing terrorists. It is as if the Christian/Muslim theme expanded, and in the process reversed itself: rhetorically, we would call it a chiasmus.[41]

Turkey itself, in the context of current German xenophobia against Turkish immigrants and migrants, is difficult to dramatize as an oppressor; especially since much (though not all) of the theoretical impetus of the scholarship of nationalist movements privileges migrancy. The only other source would be the evaluation of Turkey's human rights record by the European Union. This too cathects the wrong vector in the received moves of postcolonial theory: faulting Turkey as the EU does, only more so.[42] The human rights lobby and postcolonial discourse are often and perhaps in principle at odds. Thus the staging of Kurds is not postcolonial but rather postimperial, as the object of the benevolence of the international civil society, and overdetermined by contemporary US coding of geopolitics.[43] It should also be added that in the area, Turkey is now sited in terms of the strength of its strong alliances with the West, rather than its Islamic identity.

The long history of Armenia's repeatedly dashed hopes in Britain and France against the Ottomans also proves uneasy. It *can* be read as the machinations of international capital, but that angle is either never sufficiently developed or takes second string in the scholarship of nationalist movements. Again, as an Indian, our sense of the general Armenian tradition, rightly or wrongly, is of the first "Europeans" on our soil, intermarrying with other Europeans, making treaties with the East India Company in order to share trade, advising the Company in its early days and, in 1935, at the time of the Government of India Act, asking the British Government in India for full European status against the indignity of the limited rights of the Eurasians, still a cut above ourselves, the natives.[44] Understandable gestures from a small community looking to protect itself. But bad press for US postcolonial theory.

The fact is that the British played them false repeatedly in the Indian theater as well. And it is also true that Indian nationalism joined hands with Armenian nationalism. About the class alliances of Indian nationalism much work has been done by the subalternist historians.[45] The point I am making here is that, in the matter of successful insertion into the coded infrastructure of scholarship, so to speak, the indeterminate "Europeanness" of the Armenians provides a methodological obstacle. The Irish, with nothing but the British to face on the other side, have no such problem. The only possibility of recoding that one glimpses is through such bold ventures as Aparna Sen's film *36 Chowringhee Lane*, which foregrounds a Eurasian woman sympathetically over against the postcolonial Indian bourgeoisie, or Francis Rolt's book, *The Last Armenian*, which presents Joseph Khatchyan as a *white* man profoundly involved with the oppressed Bangladeshi tribals.[46]

The specific history of the ruthless treatment of Armenians in the Kemalist period in Turkey is also difficult to fit in, for Kemalism is widely coded as liberatory. (Indeed, the new "constitutionality" of the Ottoman empire had kindled hopes for a little among Armenian revolutionaries themselves.[47]) And even here, the nations and sub-nations of choice are the Balkans, where the memory of an Ottoman past has produced Muslim victims, objects of sympathy.

The greatest difficulty is posed by Bolshevism itself. It is hard for the postcolonial scholarship of nationalist movements, generally leftist yet post-Marxist in tendency, not to code Bolshevism as having given way to oppressive and even imperialist policy. You cannot know precisely how the ideological minefield (the subindividual force field substantiated as *pouvoir/savoir*, or ability to know aggregated as the power/knowledge apparatus) of the *socius* is going to judge the decision to "apply" a thought-field from between the covers of a book to a field of action.[48] The reasonable principles of Marxism fell in the ideological field of great imperial formations, at different stages of growth or decay. It is a question-begging naturalization and an over-simplification to think of them in terms of the opposition between nationalisms and an internationalized model of the imagination. The theories of nationalist movements, looking at Bolshevism from the perspective only of Czarist oppression and organized capitalist opposition until it was obliged to change its face, codes it as basically positive-to-negative-under-duress in its earliest days.

The contrast between that image and the one that takes account of the imperial lines, with the Allies queering the pitch in terms of the dynamics of "the self-determination of capital," reflects, among other things, the academic subdivision of labor, and the particularisms of general theories of nationalist movements.[49] Its "real life" counterpart, the contrast between Lenin's genuine concern for the Armenians and the general cruelty of Ottoman and Bolshevik alike, reminds us that Lenin was an intellectual who believed in the vanguardism of theory in its application, rather than its vulnerability to the field when set to work.[50] "Armenians" thought of entry into the USSR as a freeing from Turkish oppression, grateful for the closed Soviet market for Armenian molybdenum and copper, which built up the economy. The Armenian genocide is flanked by Shoah on the one side, and African and Balkan ethnic cleansing on the other; both more readily decipherable as post-colonial. The sober Armenians have always had a lukewarm press in the West, as two pages from Lady Mary Wortley Montagu's Turkish letters would show.[51] In 2002, at the time of first revising, a general post-Soviet postcoloniality was somewhat more on the agenda than it was at the time of first writing, in 1994.[52] Yet, for reasons that I have been rehearsing, Armenia may not figure prominently in the lexicon of the revised agenda. It is neighboring Azerbaijan, Turkmenistan, Kazakhstan, that can be placed within the contemporary politics of Islam.[53] And, if we look at the contemporary narrative of the global, Armenia, Azerbaijan, and Turkey are all members of the Council of Europe, the first two since January 25, 2001, and Turkey almost since its founding. The difference in dates is significant, but would take us too far afield. How does the Council of Europe relate to "other Asias"? The western edge of Asia is Eurasia, and the Asia-Pacific includes the US West Coast. This too adds to the importance of thinking a plural-ized Asia in terms of critical regionalism rather than identity!

When the permissible narrative will not fit the case, we take a step back – short of already-formed narratives, as it were – and look at the broad strokes by which such narratives are put together.

If we try to imagine the texture of the time that one might call the remote pre-history of contemporary theories of global hybridity, all the evidence seems to suggest the kind of conflictual co-existence that one discerns in other areas of the pre-capitalist world, neither politi-cally correct nor willingly hybrid, nor yet syncretic, but at best inter-ested and at worst violently grudging acknowledgement of difference which allows a symbiosis against the grain. (Speed-reading "to learn about one's culture" makes a mockery out of those centuries of [in]tolerant symbiosis.) The potential difference marked by those square brackets can be mobilized today by the confusing imperialist semiotic we are discussing here.

In the journalistic coding of the breakup of the Soviet Union, with little helpful maps that isolated a bit of land with broad cognitive indicators, the conflict between Armenia and Azerbaijan over Nagorno-Karabakh was given some publicity, though the transCaucasus could not generate the same violence as the Balkans. It is interesting that both conflicts were marked by a "consistent reliance on an inappropriate Christian versus Moslem framework.... [T]he term Moslem [is not used in these areas] in the generic religious sense but as a synonym for Turk."[54] These available explanatory resources, confined to the resurgence of "ethnic" and religious conflict with the lifting of totalitarian control, cannot code Armenia as a site of postcolonialism either. The history of the "Armenian subject" cannot be recovered from such gestures. Let us rather displace thoughts of postcoloniality to the broad lineaments of contemporary postimperialism. We must be able to think that "the dynamic course of the new US-Russian relationship ... may ... forge a new Russian role ... in the form of a strategic division of Eurasia ... [and] ... the mediation of the Nagorno-Karabakh conflict" may be an important move in this course.[55] (No one ever mentions, these days, that the Soviet system had a Nagorno-Karabakh Autonomous Oblast, which was abolished in 1991. The troubles had started almost immediately after the collapse of the USSR, without "the dissolution of ... the old ethnically-based Soviet administrative structures," with some violent movement of peoples worked in.[56]) Yet it must be said that the Soviet/Russian provocation could not have succeeded without the strong ethnico-religious identitarianism between Armenia and Azerbaijan. So much so that one critic says that "the zero-sum relationship between Azerbaijan and Armenia is what has enabled foreign actors to get a foothold in the Caucasus by supporting one state against the other" (SN 393). It is, if you like, a direct outcome of a tributary gesture of the Great Game (see p. 111). And, because of this pattern of counter-regionalist divisive moves in a region thick with ethnicities, "[n]o comparable conflict in the world today arguably has the potential to involve as many regional and global powers as does the Armenian-Azerbaijani conflict" (SN 408). Again and again, we are suggesting that the aggregate of this conflict can act as the lever or *mochlos* that will blind the monocular monster – capitalist globalization – if its energy is redirected into an anti-ethnicist regionalism, a genealogical deconstruction, questioning the authority of mere blood as guaranteed by reproductive heteronormativity and sacralized and expanded by religion.[57] Instead of which, a Soviet habit of internal passports or propiskas is retained, subalternizing displaced persons into ethnic statelessness, denying them services.

Just as the functioning of a metaphor is dependent upon conceptual logic and vice versa, so is the logic of transnationality dependent upon the holding force of the (metaphor of the) nation-(in the logic of the so-called) state. The crossing of the nation-marked individual into the unyielding civil structure of the United States, a state perceived to be safer, richer, and more enjoyable if made to yield, is a figure contained within this larger warp-and-woof, this larger text-ile, a weaving repetition in a change of displacements, rather than only creating a rupture into postnationality from nation thinking.

Let us meditate for a moment upon those arbiters of transnationality in the New World Order: the World Bank and the International Monetary Fund. In the post-Soviet moment, the race is on for the World Bank's favors. Armenia has been negotiating with the World Bank and the IMF for over a decade. The question of transnationalization was the question of the IMF's role in a new systemic transformation for the new nation-state. And therefore the monetary structure of the Central Bank was one of the initial threshold questions in the years after the dissolution of the Soviet Union. But the eligibility of Armenia for entry into the *clientèle* of the masters was dependent upon "the conflict in Nagorno-Karabagh." "Armenia is being held hostage until there is stability in that region. Armenia is being assigned the political responsibility for peace in that region. Armenia has supported all of the Russian-mediated peace proposals. But in the face of blocking by Azerbaijan, blockade by Turkey, and the absence of deep-pocket Western assistance, Armenia's point of view cannot be heard." This was the gist of a fantasmatic conversation with a knowledgeable middle-level diplomat in Washington in 1994. A 2003 conversation describes the Nagorno-Karabakh situation as a "freeze," increasing privatization as necessarily corrupt, dependence on the Moscow-Chechen-Georgia circuit being recoded by way of George W. Bush's mandate for a global war on terror, lobbying for Armenian and Azeri politics in Washington, hope for new and forward-looking leadership, and, above all, oil, oil, oil: the Baku-Tblisi-Ceyhan (BTC) project, a new version of the Great Game, between Euramerica and Russia.

The Great Game is a reference to the tug of war between the great European powers for control over the transcaucasus and the frontiers of the Himalayas. It is supposed to have begun in the time of Peter the Great (1672–1725). It will be discussed at greater length in the next chapter. In the strategic moves to win the control of oil today, we encounter the old players, in a version of the old game, even of the old moves. It is not just "theoretical" academic language that would call this a displacement in a chain of repetitions. Even if Armenian and Azeri hang together in New York or Chicago in the name of a fantasmatic globality, or decathect in Paris or Los Angeles in the name of an equally fantasmic nationalism, it is this scene of nation/transnation/state in the financialized globe that the postcolonial theorist manages to exclude. It was Armenia, uncertain nation, that gave me the clue. Other places will work for others, depending on preparation and location and, most of all, "being-responsible-in," a more careful substitutive description of "identity."

The wisdom of the voluble old woman in Soviet Armenia, or the realistic mother in first-generation US migration, as depicted in *Back to Ararat*, is a group-conscious but non-nationalistic realism. It situates the diasporic longing for entry into postcolonial theory. It is a frail and improbable perspective in the context of the fierce nationalism of Nagorno-Karabakh, the region that claims the Biblical Ararat. Paradoxically, this nationalism, by producing violence in the Southern Caucasus, stands in the way of the continuous narrative of the Great Game, as it has been playing out in the region at least since the mid-fifties, the date of the Soviet proposals that led to the establishment of the Conference on Security and Cooperation in Europe (1971), changed into the Organization for Security and Cooperation in Europe. The OSCE is the source of the establishment of the "Minsk Group," which was supposed to provide a forum for the conflict over mountainous Karabakh. The Conference could not take place. Karabakh and Azerbaijan kept fighting too hard, ceased fire in 1994, then froze. This does not stop the Minsk Group from negotiating for a political solution, without Armenia and Azerbaijan. Like its parent organization, the OSCE, it has no legal status, but that is not a problem today with the "good" side of imperialism. It works with the axiomatics of the United Nations-cum-International Civil Society. This is now one of the sites of negotiation for the Great Game, with the players displaced, Russia wishing to use it to contain NATO, the United States preferring to keep it civilian.[58] The Caspian pipeline passes through Tblisi (Georgia) and Baku (Azerbaijan), the long-standing local-tuned Soviet and pre-soviet oil capital on the one hand, and Armenia as beleaguered and longstanding Christian culture, on the other. It is within the horns of this dilemma that the sides are *culturally* coded as "Islam-Warlordism" vs. "Christianity/democracy," even as the military-industrial complex favors Azerbaijan.[59]

If we read the Southern Caucasus with Afghanistan (which will be discussed in the next chapter) and Iraq now, the positions in the Game are not always culturally predictable. It is only an end to nationalist conflict that will make it possible to imagine a regionalism that can in turn imagine players' roles in the Great Game as never before: Najibullah's dream, as we will see in the next chapter. Indeed, Armenia's positive relationship with Iran makes it clear how politicized the question of Islam is. "Armenia's Iran policy is shaped by blockade and isolation, most apparent in the exclusion of Armenia from all regional energy plans."[60]

My answer to Kassabian and Kazanjian's question would then be indirect: "Armenia" cannot lean toward existing theories. It cannot be comfortably located in the generally recognized lineaments of contemporary imperialism and received postcolonialism. It has been too much in the interstices to fit such a location. Indeed, that is its importance. Its history is diversified, with many loyalties crosshatching so small a place, if indeed it is more a place than a state of mind over the centuries. Is it increasingly representative of the contemporary predicament, where mere postcoloniality may be caught in a time-warp and nationalism must enter into an economy of regionalism and globality? A regionalism that displaces ethnic histories is the only way toward neutralizing the Great Game. One may call it the new non-alignment, itself a re-territorializing of genealogical deconstruction, a step beyond the nation-state, vindicating Hannah Arendt's prediction against capitalist globalization.[61]

In "Can the Subaltern Speak?" – now incorporated in a revised version in the chapter on "History" in *A Critique of Postcolonial Reason* – I had suggested that without institutional validation, a "position" cannot be recognized. "Armenia" is in a position of relative subalternity, in so far as it cannot be recognized as postcolonial. The young woman in "Can the Subaltern Speak?," who had attempted to send the (unrecognized) message of resistance through inscribing the body-in-suicide, taught me that the imperative was to learn to build infrastructure, a lesson that led to the work described in the first essay in this book. Since the "subalternity" of "Armenia" as space of postcolonial critique is calculated within elite academic discourse, the imperative is different: to generate a persistent critique of the freezing of postcolonialism/multiculturalism/critique of globalization along the line of least intellectual resistance, the story of the eighteenth- and nineteenth-century nation-state. The profoundly diasporic historical "identity" of the

Armenian, and its attendant cultural nostalgia, can be reexamined as a narrative which may stage the inability of a national narrator to constitute itself as such. Perhaps the received stories of postcoloniality will not seem simply "true" then. Any theory of postcolonial hybridity pales into insignificance when we consider the millennial ipseity of the Armenian, existing in uneasy double bind with the hybridity imposed by the locale. The fact that the road over the mountains connecting Karabakh to Armenia has been modernized and secured by the diaspora carries a symbolic value beyond mere postcoloniality. Perhaps, once again, it is the exceptions, the counter-examples, the strategically excluded narratives that will disrupt the dominant, this time the postcolonial, story. We may perhaps be able to glimpse, then, without nervousness, that postcoloniality is not a euphoric claim tied to multiculturalism for "the Third World" in the First World. It is a warning, a reckoning, a responsibility that reminds us that the future is not here when some of us enter the civil society of an exploitative state and load its cultural self-representation with references to our own. The future is always around the corner, a site of negotiations, a message for the metropolitan diaspora, my initial questioner.

How little we compute in terms of the Austro-Hungarian, Russian, and Ottoman imperial formations is clear from the enduring public inability to imagine the Balkans.[62] And Armenian migration into the US does not therefore have the narrative authority that would constitute an "identity" for others, although, as we have seen because of its old left and newer right loyalties, the two ruling parties among Armenians have a surprisingly powerful divided lobby in Washington, holding up global justice in the Caucasus.[63] Here is nationalism without postcoloniality. The other displaced narrative of imperialism – Trade and Development – is beginning to inscribe Armenia within the dominant text, again as interstitial member (satellite of Russia) in a region dominated by Russia. From within the volatility of the Great Game, however indirectly, the success of that initiative will encourage liberal Armenian Cultural Studies. The need for Business and Development to "learn the other culture" is so pervasively declared in the metropole that I need not labor the obvious. The corollary of this appropriative need is liberal national-origin validation in the metropolis, and a place for Armenian Colonial Discourse Studies as an academic sub-field. Kassabian and Kazanjian are to be praised for raising the question, pretty early on, of Armenia and/in transnational Cultural Studies. That too is different from postcolonialism. Yet here as well, the Armenian question should perhaps be raised as a critique of the enterprise itself. Armenians moving to the US in the twenties described themselves as "immigrants" rather than "refugees," obliterating the massacre. Armenia is now an emergent nation-state. We have looked at the diasporic's aspiration to the country's ancient outlines, condition and effect of modern Armenia's denial of its Western border with Turkey. In the contemporary context, through the narrative of Development, Armenia is poised where Eurasia and Europe contend. The antique cosmopolitanism is ready to give way to a subordinated globalization.

The desire for a critical discourse on Armenian nationalism and Armenian Cultural Studies, coming from Armenian-Americans at the inception of Armenia's negotiations with Development, may be a powerful wedge in dis-locating, say, Indian and Palestinian fulfillments (as perceived by my two questioners) of that desire, if directed in certain ways, against "American intellectual expansionism." It will build itself on the history of American postcolonialism, not on the history of Armenia. It is possible to argue that, otherwise, and in spite of their ostensible position against *Back to Ararat*, the authors (my questioners) will remain complicitous in the larger text, if only because their demands for revision of the film's presuppositions will be tabulated by a peculiarly US grid of corrections. American intellectual expansionism contains postcolonialism. Will they consider the fact that this ancient nationalism is now dealing with an infant state (as did Israel in 1948) and the combination is dangerous?

It is to flesh out the idea of this containment in another way that I cite a passage from the end of Smadar Lavie's *The Poetics of Military Occupation*:[64]

[In] the late winter of 1978, Michael Caine, Peter Ustinov, and the beautiful black American model/actress Beverly Johnson were in the South Sinai with their Swiss producer, American director, and supporting actors from France, India, Israel, and Africa to shoot the Sahara Desert scenes for the movie *Ashanti*. … "Look what they've made us into now," complained the thin bony Mzeini fellow … He wiped his sweaty brow with the rolled sleeve of his costume. "Just so our kids can eat, we have to play slave traders. But it is *we* who are the real slaves! When those Westerners hired us on our camels, they were so surprised and angry that we didn't dress like the Bedouin they had in mind, that they decided to ship these Touareg clothes all the way from somewhere called France. We can hardly move in them and they make our tongues hang out like dogs in summer heat, even though it's still winter. And just because they couldn't let us be Bedouin in our own clothes, they docked our wages." "So why do you do it?" I asked. "If my only other choice is to wash dishes and clean toilets and streets for these people, I'd rather be in their movies. At least I get to be *some* kind of a Bedouin."[65]

These are the last words of the book. The Bedouin in the case is not a migrant but a colonial subject. This is not the moment to expand upon the displacement of the colonial subject into the Eurocentric migrant, and its various political investments; nor to comment on the fact that a "world historically" anachronistic colonial subject in the 1990s is in a different semiotic field from the one in the nineteenth century, although that assumption is in the pores of this chapter.[66] Suffice it to say that the position of the migrant as subject of Cultural Studies shuttles between the Bedouin-American – who s/he? – and the "Bedouin." And that is where the importance of the Second World, which is up for a ticket on that shuttle now, cannot be underestimated.

There is a marvelous bit in the Lavie book that serves as epigraph for its last section. It is spoken by a Bedouin ex-smuggler: "You and your work ... And the university ... Since Israel occupied these lands I've seen so many people from universities – collecting stones, plants, mice, rain, even hyena dung ... God! you make me laugh!"

A graduate student in my class, himself an Asian from that region, here for professional validation, asked if it would not have been more appropriate to have ended that book there. In my estimation, that would have been less responsible. Writing the book for publication in the US, Smadar Lavie, its author, clearly could not believe field research to be simply risible. She takes the epigraph quoted above as a challenge to attempt a "poetic *re*construction of military occupation." By ending the book where she does, she not only acknowledges her complicity with the filmmakers, she also, and honorably, reveals the acknowledged complicity of the Bedouin. Giving this a final reading while Israel destroys the nation-state of Lebanon in 2006, it seems that the idea of a "poetic reconstruction" calls for tragedy.

Kassabian and Kazanjian correctly point out that three-world cultural theorists are unable to imagine the former Second World, as over-reported now as it was under-reported then. Before we pass on to the globalizing appropriation of the former Second World, let us consider the implications of this failure of imagination as it relates to the slightly earlier semiotic of transnational cultural studies.

Deleuze and Guattari said 30 years ago that capital was the abstract as such, and that the agents and patients of capitalisms re-coded and re-territorialized systems of meaning already to hand, to make the abstract palpable and persuasive.[67] (As to whether this abstract is ever disengageable as such is an interesting issue.) By this reckoning, the three-worlds argument belonged in the cultural-political re-codings and re-territorializing of the abstract dynamics of capital. In the event, we did not investigate the abstract mapping sufficiently but mired ourselves in the re-codings and re-territorializings at face value, ruling the abstract calculus out of court.[68] That is generally the critique of the three-worlds system as an explanatory model. Yet the positioning of the "other" subject (how much confessional guff we have had to endure in the name of subject-position claims!), in the First World or the Third, can still be given an initial screening by way of the felicitous coding of that abstract calculus as class; wanting inclusion among the exploiters or refuge in their bosoms in the first case, or relief – in both senses, thereby hung a politics – from them in the second. And now that there are, in the abstract, no more than Two Worlds – North and South – the former Second World – still out of synch, a violent third term that cannot hold together as Asia/Eurasia/"Europe" – must be remembered with, I hope, all these lessons learned. A number of times I have cited the chapter in the third volume of *Capital* that argues that the holy trinity formula of "capital-profit ... , land-ground rent, labour-wages" is "historically specific" (C3 953–70), to understand that race/class/gender does not "mean" the same thing across different historical periods. Extending that method we must now learn this precarious two-world divide. The irony of the female Armenian-American in *Back to Ararat*, thinking *that* nation in *this* civil society, about to facilitate citizenship – in its minimal manifestation, as "papers," in the calculus, for the man – can then perhaps be seen amid the labyrinthine abstractions that put the Bedouin in *Ashanti*.

It is as if the young woman in *Back to Ararat* is getting her "Armenian" from the restricted fragmentation of the news media, scooping from the homogeneous empty time of the nation. News (in this case of the place of the exodus) is not a deliberately fragmented narrative form. The newspaper is simply obliged to a restricted fragmentation. The relationship between the novel and the newspaper may well be read as a crude allegory of the relationship between nation and migration. If we grant for the moment that the timing of the novel is a metonym of nation-formation in that it is homogeneous, empty, and simultaneous (a proposition philosophically difficult to grant), we cannot say the same of the contemporary metropolitan national newspaper. These timings are cases of the general temporizing of narrative that enables individual and collective life. If we expand this into videography and the unmotivated graphematics of the Internet, the scene complicates itself.

It may indeed be true that all newspapers, in their layout policy, assume an ideological subject that may as well be called the national subject. When the diasporic claims a nation different from her state of citizenship, it makes visible the imbrication of metropolitan transnationality with the argument for nationhood – in many different ways. The positioning of the reading subject on that grid of imbrication is crucial for that other imbrication – of the abstract three-(or 2+?)world and the intimate heterogeneous. Indeed, the "national" origin is as fantasmatic in view of the governors of the globe as of the undeclared cultural supremacists, who argue nationalism from imperialism, as it is from the point of view of village or "fief."[69] (I put the quotation marks because the feudal or semi-feudal mindsets of peripheral places are of course never identified with proper European feudalism, which is taken to be on the way to the proper model of the nation.) And the weaving or text(il)ing of the immigrant, old and new, is itself placed differently, by history, geopolitics, and stage of transnationality, on this grid, which is at once a double and an indefinite grid, which resembles no literal grid we may have ever seen, where a shifting from one future falling due in the time of one narrative to (an)other(s) is rather different from what is assumed by the novel.[70] Kassabian and Kazanjian have an important discussion of the constitution of nationalist identity, not necessarily noticing the state–diaspora divide. We add to that the abstract North–South dynamics of Development and Trade, where "nationalism" is transformed into different sorts of geopolitical cathexes. It is the re-coding and re-territorializing of abstract capital as "experience" that geo-politically cathects these variables into various kinds of "identity," thus ensuring support networks. These mechanics draw on the longing for the gift of time (temporalization) annulled and celebrated in marking time for a future; as indeed those re-codings and re-territorializings invest the justification for war. The nation at war, trade, and development draw their sustenance from this originary longing.

Here is a baseline version of the general timing of the narrative that enables individual and collective life: it thrusts us into womanspace, not usually introduced into discussions of the Great Game. When we are born, we are (born into) the possibility of timing: temporalization. This possibility we can grasp only by timing a life – thinking and feeling a before, which through a now, will fall due in an after. Our (mother)languaging seems almost coeval with this, for we are also born into it. Since it has a before before us, we take from its already-there-ness. And since we can give meaning in it, we can think ourselves into the falling-due of the future. It is this thought, of giving and taking, that is the idiomatic story of time into which the imposition and coun-tersigning recognition of "identities" must be accommodated.

Since it is usually our mothers who seem to bring us into temporali-zation, our life-timing often marks that particular intuition of origin by coding and re-coding the mother, by computing possible futures through investing or manipulating womanspace. The daughtership of the nation is bound up with that very re-coding. It is no use merely faulting the filmmaker PeÅ Holmquist (as do Kassabian and Kazanjian) for the shot of the Armenian-American woman contrasting "serious-ness" – the self-conscious need to "feeling" Armenian in America – to putting on makeup. It is also with those semiotics that the American in Armenia will situate herself in a nostalgic seriousness committed to a future that might seem that little bit made-up to those who stayed behind. It is precisely making up, the theatricality of the everyday, an alteration of the national self in iteration, upon which the migrant woman committed to a national origin must turn her back (or, which comes to the same thing, must extend the warmest embrace, as in "ethnic dressing").[71] The generations – and the mother re-coded by dif-ferent intuitions of origin, different projects of timing – will ring the changes on this disavowal, a chain of displacements yet once again, working with the following binary opposition: performativity (the real) and performance (making up). What disappears and yet lingers, as common sense, is that womanly cosmopolitanism in exogamy. It survives as mere common sense: the fairly representative and voluble old woman in the film, who sings history, forgives depredations, and counsels live and let live; and the wise mother in the US. It is this that gives way, again and again, to the simulacrum of a national voice.

Another example of marking time toward a future that will fall due is of women as holding the future of the nation in their wombs. It comes from the obvious narrative of marriage. Consider the limpid Romeo and Juliet story, where love across religions and enemy-"national" boundaries, between the young upper-class Muslim man Ramzi Bey and the self-reliant Armenian Christian woman Efronia Nazarian is made impossible, finally, by World War, as it is packaged to become a text of cultural studies. This poignant autobiography, inter-spersed with commentary by the protagonist's Swedish daughter-in-law, translated with delicate sympathy by her son by another man, her husband, published after Efronia Nazarian's death in northern California, is first in the series on women's memoirs in translation, published by Northeastern University Press.[72] This book is in the advance guard of a new wave of testimonials from former Soviet Asia. I will be forgiven if I think that this too will be read in multiculturalist euphoria.[73] (Inter-racial and inter-religious marriages can be seen as genealogical deconstruction, on the other hand, rather than sentimentalized within an affective version of reproductive heteronormativity.)

These life-timing narratives lexicalize Armenia as a hyphenated "nation-of-origin" in the US diaspora. This may bring in its wake a "post-colonialism" where "colonialism" is a general name for white racism. Armenia is now part of the "teaching tolerance" program of the Southern Poverty Law Center. As a founding member of this program, I certainly endorse it. On the other hand, this is proof that Armenian-Americans are being assimilated into the map of minorities in the United States, working toward a unity *as* minority-American.[74] As I have insisted in every chapter, "Asia" is thus "unified" because the emphasis is on a shared Americanism.[75] A unified Asian-America is only excellent if we want a "rest of the world" to be "at peace," if it does not mistake itself as an "Asianness" that is centered in the subject's national origin, however remote, negotiating a restricted "Asian-American" diversity. It is in fact only excellent as a classed position local to the United States. If we keep imagining a just *world*, we must work for pluralized Asias, even in poverty and obscurity.[76] Armenia will not be, or will not want to be, called into that unity. I draw it into pluralized Asias by going against the Armenian grain. To ask for tolerance abroad is to give tolerance at home. The conclusion to this chapter will show how historically Eurasian Armenia, resolutely European in its Christian ego-ideal, is in fact sharing an "Asian" plan in globalization and to what extent it is a task for feminism to engage itself in that problematic.

International Feminism will consider, for example, the woman-related activities of UNESCAP (United Nations Economic and Social Commission for Asia and the Pacific) in the Southern Caucasus and Central Asia.[77] Here Armenia is indeed in an "other Asia."[78] The feminist point of departure would share the limited reliability of single-issue feminisms everywhere, allowing gender to become an alibi for interventions of every sort, scale, and scope. If one looks at the details of these activities, they reveal themselves to be, among other things, a way for ISAR (Initiative for Social Action and Renewal in Eurasia), a subsidiary of USAID (US Agency for International Development), to enter the field.[79]

UNESCAP's chief role in the area seems to be to promote Information Technology [IT]. I have presented a criticism of unmediated cyber-literacy in "Megacity." More detailed critiques are certainly available.[80] Audrey N. Selian suggests that the "neo-nomenklatura ... in Armenia are very concerned ... [to] portray a cosmetically (i.e. technologically) enhanced version of government and state ... to ensure that donor funding streams continue to flow – in what is without question a donor-driven economy."[81] "Understanding the dynamic of non-western polities," she writes further,

> requires an approach that transcends falsely intuitive analytical frameworks based on western experience alone. It also requires a capacity to account for traits and trends that are embedded deeply within specific cultural and historical contexts. Accordingly, the view of technology as a neutral force in a polity is not unquestioned . ... [For] the world Bank [on the other hand,] ... [f]rom web presence, to the facilitation of interactions, to the eventual transformation of institutions to an "ideal" (exemplified by optimal levels of political participation), ICTs are considered as tools for facilitating "progress" along a continuum of institutional change. ... [I]t is critical to avoid making assumptions of this sort that can allow for a deterministic ICT paradigm to supersede the reality of participating in technology projects in transition countries. ... The development of ICTs in government – in the support of systems both backend and front-end – should come not only from the united front of a coordinated and coherent donor stream, but in conjunction with genuine efforts to promote organic (as opposed to transplanted) growth strategies.

I have written of alternative growth strategies in the first essay in this book. My metaphor is not organicist but rather that of learning the rituals of democracy, but my convictions are with Ms Selian.

Upon the scenario of IT for the women of Caucasus, what we see, in the reports distributed electronically, is a record of the breakdown of the Soviet welfare system and then, without transition, a record, not of how to join local efforts to salvage it, but, of access to IT. The information from the area is electronically received. A Catch-22. A thoroughly detailed analysis of the NGO-phenomenon in negotiated postcoloniality, the unacknowledged move into international capital, its connections with older, more site-specific and committed activity, especially in the name of woman, is imperative here. Feminism requires a follow-through on the addresses of these NGOs, and a consideration of the "missions" (sometimes "not available"). In the overwhelming majority the mission descriptions are produced by the uninspired style of the questions, a style untouched by any research in questionnaire-sociology.[82] A responsible transitional feminism will tease out the relationship between these and the list of 64 august and enormous NGOs given at the end – ending with the World Bank, custodians of reconstruction, the civilizing mission of world governance. On another part of the spectrum, "the Government's Poverty Reduction Strategy Paper (PRSP) [spearheaded by the PRSP of the World Bank] foreshadows a decrease in the number of families on poverty benefits as economic developments and economic growth continue to improve"; without any consideration of the many studies, from left and right, of the lack of connection between the two.[83]

Genocide or no genocide, this low-grade and often welcome infiltration, especially of woman-space, is more alarming to students of the history of imperialisms. In this respect, the memory of genocide can still allow the Armenian, male or female, to claim a separation from the other, Muslim, beneficiaries of UNESCAP – although not from the economic scope of the "other Asia." This is the micromanagement of the Great Game in the name of gender. Now the fault lines in the initial question from Kassabian and Kazanjian connect with the project of *Back to Ararat*. The film represents the production of a cultural memory that the question demands. "Was it a genocide?" "Living" memory sustains us because it privatizes verifiability, effectively canceling the question, making testimony continuous with evidence. The incessant production of cultural memory aspires to the public sphere. The problem, at any rate, is not so much truth and falsity as public verifiability of culture by/as history.[84]

I have argued repeatedly that the specifically postcolonial questions do not fit Armenia. It is of the former colonies that one could ask, if one ignored the seductions of globalization: Why is it that, in this context, the former imperial masters think they can make it all better for us again? What greed, gullibility, innocence, ambition makes us collude? In the case of the Southern Caucasus and Central Asia, we are looking at a displacement of the Soviet Union into the Russian Federation – re-coded through NATO and permanent membership of the Security Council of the United Nations – and the plans for regional governance are dispersed into those nineteenth-century imperialisms that have no history in this area. Regional governance turns into global geopolitics through re-territorializing the Great Game. This cobbled imperial history makes the area an appropriate terrain for a new anti-ethnic regionalism that may undo the Great Game. Capital, the most abstract, codes materiality – oil, land – using the seemingly most concrete – ethnicity and religion (negotiable through the sedimented abstractions of nationalism). The sign-system by means of which these negotiations operate is reproductive heteronormativity. You cannot destroy this semiotic, for it also keeps us alive and makes the ethical possible. It is a *pharmakon*. You regulate it, imperfectly, uncertainly, through pedagogy, through situational (textual, relating to the text-ile web of events) practice. Genealogical deconstruction is what sustains anti-ethnic regionalism and shifts gears from the management of ethnicity to the equitable management of capital and the sources of capital. As long as class-mobile metropolitan migrancy is its only vehicle, by its very dynamic it will work against preparation for it in subalternity.[85] Contemporary European demands for universalism or multitudes float high over this terrain. Anti-ethnic, nationalism-critical regionalism tangles with the closest thing to universalism that the primate world knows – reproductive heteronormativity. Although my own birthplace was ravaged by partition along religious-ethnic lines – and, although divided Ireland was my doctoral area – and, further, Palestine's suffering by this problematic supplemented my fall into postcolonialism through my friendship with Edward Said, it was my amateur investigation of Armenia from 1994 to 2006, in a field prepared by close reading of *Politics of Friendship*, that taught me to think thus. This, too, is a reason for turning to, and with, *other* Asias.

By contrast, the international civil society, the new vanguardists who span the right and the left, proceed here with a geopolitical savvy that thinks "culture" takes no more than a briefing to be learned. Even experienced journalists like Thomas de Waal seem somewhat clueless when they "try to identify ... [the] reasons for the 'reluctance' of the presidents of Karabakh and Azerbaijan to promote peace."[86] I tend to agree with Richard Giragosian, whom I will quote later, who thinks that the new state in globalization needs to secure itself socio-economically against the forces of globalization, which include, with some relative autonomy, the political engineering of the international civil society.[87] Mere nationalism is no answer to this. Once again, we are looking at a critical regionalism where old disputes must be negotiated through genealogical deconstruction. The need for good regionalism in this area is well-known.[88] Yet, just as teacher training in the form of teaching is hardly ever mentioned in the Right to Education debates (see chapter 1), so also confronting the ethnic outlines of reproductive heteronormativity is hardly ever touched upon in the context of regionalism.

The specifically postcolonial questions provoke a thought of re-inventing regionalist "state" structures in the global South rather than pushing IT, at all cost, or ignoring the history of the power politics of non-governmental activity.[89] That is an argument for another book. To re-invent the state structure and make it work for subaltern and dominant alike, the minimum needed is the "reasonableness" that is produced metapsychologically. It is not our master (as humanism would claim), but a fragile and vulnerable "logic," something like formal consistency, that may be more or less shared by a very large number of human beings.[90] This is a better instrument for genealogical deconstruction than high humanist rationality.[91] This is what is used by the "cosmopolitan" women in *Back to Ararat*. It is this project, not a culturalist one, that Armenia can join. It is of course dependent on subaltern education, about which I have written in the first chapter, but also, in the short term, upon a sustained effort to wrench the state away from "rational choice" alone, the most conservative though also most efficient method in economics, political science, and business administration in all its branches.

If we have ears to hear, we hear the cry for the state from activists who are not necessarily nationalists. I heard Sima Samar at the Asia Society in New York on October 21, 2002 make this plea for the new state of Afghanistan. On that occasion at least, no one picked up on her plea. Now the state is being managed behind the back of a puppet president, by a US diasporic who can "speak to the tribals." The US management of the elections of October, 2004, is an open secret.[92] The role of the US diasporics in the constitution of the new Iraqi state after George Bush's war on Saddam and the resultant civil war is too well-known to labor.

The interest of the metropolitan diasporic need not necessarily coincide, and is usually divergent from, the interest of the state in the global South. The use of the returned diasporic for world governance is an important modification. As I have indicated above, since Armenia is millennially diasporic, the role of Armenian diasporics in the invention of nationalism predates this narrative. I have commented on their current role whenever possible. The question I am answering in this chapter is, of course, a diasporics' question. Richard Giragosian and Khatchik Dhergoukassian, themselves metropolitan diasporics, lament the decay of the Armenian state with a strong critique of dependence on non-governmental international intervention.[93] We must of course "read" such gestures, not simply believe them. But we must also be able to understand, when we look at UNESCAP feminism, that telecommunication is pushed for the same reason that the Romans built roads, the British built railways, and the World Bank builds roads again.

Michael Moore makes the point crudely and powerfully in *Fahrenheit 9/11* when he mentions the export of telecommunication to Iraq.[94] Of course, there are trickle down advantages. Even apartheid breeds solidarity; I spoke of "enabling violation" some years ago (see p. 15). What we have to notice is that an epistemic violation is in progress here. There are repeated exhortations to establish the legal infrastructure for purchased virtue (corporate philanthropy) and deregulation by using powerful extra-state organizations. In other contexts, we speak of governmentality and the production of colonial subjects. Academic subdivision of labor does not allow us to see it here. This is not just Western feminism behaving badly toward third-world women. We are speaking of the instrumentalization of gender and the diasporic in the new imperialism, so that a gendered collaboration can be produced. To hold the state accountable can too easily be recoded as a "post-soviet mentality[,] always expecting someone else to resolve problems."[95] The *New York Times* says with critical confidence: "There are ways to bypass corrupt local governments, and funnel aid directly to those on the ground who need it."[96] This is incorrect. The international civil society decides the direct recipient according to the level down to which it can communicate. In fact, giving money to the ones who actually need it often ends in chaos because they have never seen any serious amount of money. The solution is to concentrate on cleaning up the state through citizens' participation, critical regionalism, and the painstaking change in the quality of the education of the subaltern ("those who actually need it"). As a comparativist, I must insist that in this endeavor, the activist must enter the "lingual memory" of the regional language.[97]

Earlier in the chapter I have spoken of the pre-history of hybridity. In these last pages we have considered only agential matters – where we think of the human being as acting through institutional validation. Agency involves at least the assumption of a contingent collectivity.[98]

We recall two things here: one, that the adventures of the international civil society prove the more than millennial axiom that gendering, shorthand for reproductive heteronormativity, is the supplest instrument of institutional validation, and, two, that the production of the subject (rather than the agent, an old note that I keep striking, not to much avail) is altogether more mysterious, much of it not under the agent's control (therefore meta-psychological), and not within the neat outlines of the individual. Gendering in the service of the state allowed the Soviet State (seemingly in the service of Reason itself and attentive and effective in detail to women's health, education and welfare issues) in the Southern Caucasus to encourage and reward women for having many children – "Hero Mothers" – as it allowed the People's Republic to do the opposite. Nagorno-Karabakh (seemingly in the service of enlightened nationalism) follows this policy, declared on its Web:

> In order to stimulate natality and possession of many children, the Nagorno-Karabakh authorities realize a special program, according to which a target deposit account is opened in "Artakhsbank" for every third and subsequent child. Also, habitations are provided, compensations of different types are paid and so on. [527 such accounts had been opened by May, 2004.] Additional accounts of 5000 US dollars have been opened for each of 3 families with 10 children.[99]

I have heard committed Hawaiian nationalist and Middle Eastern national liberationist friends, one female and male, both academics, make similar statements, one repeatedly in public, and one exhorting a student. Now these are not merely agential policies, waiting to be corrected. They affect gendered subject-production. How are we going to gauge this? How place this with the coding of abortion and enforced contraception? The slow work of entering the details of language and idiom, even if it were remotely possible for the quick-fix self-confident gender specialists of US NGOs, is foiled by the happy and willing Americanization of local class-enabled woman activists. ICT is an instrument of upward class-mobility. Check out the pathetic list of "jobseekers" on an Azeri server enthusiastically noted in the ESCAP report, as one example among many. We have forgotten the political lesson that systemic change is unrelated to nice relationships between US visitors and local women. As a teacher of the humanities for more than four decades, I am obliged to say that a program like "Artists Against Trafficking," however well-meaning it may be, has almost no effect on the actual traffickers, many of whom are women. Such interventions routinely stand against women surviving by creating a well-structured sex-work environment, and the role and use of the US State Department's "Trafficking in Persons Report" to keep a certain control over the various nation-states of the world remains troubling.

> Independence from the Soviet era resulted in high cost of poverty rate of 43–51 percent, unemployment rate of 18–76 percent which resulted in migration of over 1 million people. Women were left alone with no financial support to survive and had no choice, but to separate from their family in search of a "better living" in foreign lands. ... 80 percent

of the village women and young girls fall into trafficking by choice, only to run away from a miserable living condition.[100]

Here is womanspace waiting for a postcolonial spin.

Kassabian and Kazanjian, my first interlocutors, have wisely moved off to other fields of interest. I have kept following the question they asked me. I have emerged into this vast space – where ignorant armies clash, and world governance and international civil society come in to redress the obvious evils of cultural difference. I close the text where it should open, rewriting postcolonialism into globality through critical regionalism.

Chapter 4

1996: Foucault and Najibullah[1]

Foucault's *Discipline and Punish* opens with a public hanging. Foucault contrasts this with the Panopticon.[2] The book traces the story of our times as the story of the rationalized individual and of the development of (the) discipline(s). "The carceral network does not cast the unassimilable into a confused hell; there is no outside" (DP 301). It is the story of the emergence of "man as object of knowledge" (DP 24). It is indeed the story of our time. The book was first published in 1975. Today we might say that the narrative was to produce the "wo/man" of Human Rights, in the name of which power legitimizes itself repeatedly. Here is a summary of Foucault's narrative by way of two passages from the book: "In the ceremonies of the public execution, the main character was the people, whose real and immediate presence was required for the performance" (DP 57). This is the initial moment. And then:

> It is as if the eighteenth century had opened up the crisis of this economy and, in order to resolve it, proposed the fundamental law that punishment must have "humanity" as its "measure," without any definitive meaning being given to this principle, which nevertheless is regarded as insuperable. We must, therefore, recount the birth and early days of this enigmatic "leniency." (DP 75)

"I shall choose examples from military, medical, educational and industrial institutions. Other examples might have been taken from colonization, slavery and child rearing," writes Foucault.[3] It appears from the body of the book that he has in mind the establishment of penal colonies overseas or the deportation of "delinquents, undisciplined soldiers, prostitutes and orphans ... [to] Algeria, ... Guiana ... New

Caledonia" (DP 279). But even if we give Foucault the benefit of a doubt here, the application of the analysis to colonialism would trace the production of the colonial subject, whose best examples, in the French case, would be Ho Chi Minh, Frantz Fanon, and Assia Djebar, the critics of colonialism who allow the emergence of the cliché: imperialism produced its critics. In this chapter I have asked: what escapes this naming of wo/man? How shall we plot the excesses of world history?

In an earlier essay, I faulted Foucault and Deleuze for a romantic populism. Here too Foucault puts the reason for his enterprise in the hands of "prisoners," confined to France and the Western world (although he speaks of "the world" in general), assigning, one cannot help feeling, a meaning to their actions that would suit his argument. There is little discussion of the actual prison revolts, certainly nothing like the loving documentation that the "past" receives; the lesson of the book

> is a lesson that I have learnt not so much from history as from the present. In recent years, prison revolts have occurred throughout the world. ... What was at issue was not whether the prison environment was too harsh or too aseptic..., but its very materiality as an instrument and vector of power ... that of the educationalists, psychologists and psychiatrists. ... I would like to write the history of this prison ... if one means writing the history of the present. (DP 31)

Whatever Foucault might have intended, it has led postcolonial critics to embrace his critique of governmentality without regard for its sphere of study. We who are interested in alternative Development propose an ab-use (not abuse) of the Enlightenment (understood in shorthand as "the public use of reason"), a use from below. Marx had tried, but, as I have mentioned earlier he was too much the organic intellectual of industrial capitalism to have broken through to the question of agency; his proletarian remained a straw figure when Communism became a form of (repressive) government(ality). This allowed intellectuals like Foucault to throw Marx out with the Enlightenment, although in this relatively early book he articulated his narrative in terms of "the bourgeois revolution" and made certain connections: "If economic exploitation separates the force and the product of labor, let us say that disciplinary coercion establishes in the body the constricting link between an increased aptitude and an increased domination" (DP 138).

Today's solution in the Development lobby (including, as we saw in the previous chapter, United Nations universalist feminism) is simply to make the world multiculturalist American.[4] It is ignorant of Foucault of course; when necessary, it knows to be against "post-modernism," whatever that might be. Its unacknowledged prophet is Cecil Rhodes: "I contend that we are the first race in the world, and that the more of the world we inhabit the better it is for the human race. ... If there be a God, I think that what he would like me to do is to paint as much of the map of Africa British red as possible."[5] *Mutatis mutandis*: territorial imperialism is no longer convenient; economic restructuring for exploitation will do, with "sustainable development" as the palliative description of how much exploitation and how little good imperialism. When necessary, exterminate the brutes, like Conrad's Kurtz, to produce the docile ones, to produce our simulacra.

I wrote all but the last sentence five years before the events of September 11, 2001. At that time, the complaint above seemed suffi-cient. Although I have changed little of what follows, now I see that the entire pattern of our postcolonial vision was changing. The era of the one-nation colonies that gave us postcolonialism was getting revised. The breakup of the Soviet Union undid the largely artificial rationali-zation of the old multicultural multiethnic empires, without the ben-efit of national liberation movements of the postcolonial variety. My confusion over Armenia taught me this. The United States played a large role in organizing the NATO allies who in turn jockeyed the UN to "keep the peace" militarily among the "nationalities" – hardly nation-states – that emerged as the detritus of the Ottoman, Habsburg, and Russian empires. September 11, focused solidly on the US, brought out a relation that, assisted by the personality of President George W. Bush and the constitution of his advisers, transformed this peacekeeping into full-fledged imperialist intervention. Laws internal to the United States began to be extended internationally, not only the economic, as formerly under the auspices of the World Trade Organization, but also in the political sphere. The Republican party, domestic to the US, has this to ask in a questionnaire distributed to its members: "Do you think that US troops should have to serve under United Nations command-ers?" Now, obviously, they want the stalwart GOP (member of the US Republican party) person to say "no." "Do you support the use of air strikes against any country that offers safe harbor or aid to individuals or organizations committed to further attacks on America?" And the expected good answer is "yes."[6]

Afghanistan, presumably housing al-Qaeda, became the first state to be reorganized. This was, of course, a continuation of the role of the United States in the region for more than two decades – first to get rid of the Soviet presence and now to quash the Taliban to institute a puppet government. The cynical would say all this was in the interest of the oil route and in the body of this chapter I will link US behavior with a political tradition in the area that has been called the Great Game, of which I have written in the previous chapter.

At this point, it may be interesting for the reader to see how "Afghanistan" had attempted to insert itself into the production of the colonial subject – from Abd-ur Rahman Khan (fl. 1880–1901) to Najibullah (1947–1996), the last Communist president of Afghanistan. Guantanamo Bay, where the Bush government kept their captives in cages and tried them in secret military tribunals even while resisting and encouraging small powerless nations from ratifying the international criminal court, occupies a different space and a different trajectory from Foucault's penal colonies. These prisoners could not be produced to testify in court for the possible innocence of Zacharias Moussaoui, the alleged nineteenth hijacker.

In my account, Najibullah, the last Communist President of Afghanistan, would be trying to break the cycle of imperial power-play to achieve national liberation through knowledge. But in the familiar postcolonial scenario, national liberation is organized by colonial subjects. Again, we will look at the attempt to establish such a production in Afghanistan's quest for modernity. Here let us mark Najibullah's unfinished translation of Peter Hopkirk's book, *The Great Game*, of which we will read below, on that road. And today we might say that the push and pull of that power and play were themselves another version of that attempt.

In the Sunday *New York Times* for October 6, 1996, there is an item called "Afghanistan Reels Back Into View" by John F. Burns. There is a picture of "[t]he bodies of Najibullah, left, and his brother hang[ing] from a Kabul traffic post." There is a crowd of peering men from behind, looking as much at the cameramen as at the backs of the bloody bodies, as far as one can tell. What is the lesson of this public spectacle?

In the months before Afghanistan's new rulers marched him from a United Nations compound in Kabul and summarily beat, shot and hanged him, Afghanistan's last Communist President, Najibullah, spent much of his time preparing a translation into Pashto, his native language, of a 1990 book about Afghanistan, "The Great Game," by the English writer Peter Hopkirk.[7] Mr. Najibullah told United Nations officials that he wanted Afghans to read the Hopkirk text because of what they would learn from it of the 19th-century struggle between imperial Britain and imperial Russia for influence in Afghanistan. "They can see how our history has represented itself," he said. "Only if we understand our history can we take steps to break the cycle." (p. 24)

For me, "the Great Game" is a reference to Kipling's *Kim*.[8] A child plays spy for industrial capitalist imperialism, as if it is a feudal game. The particular scene is a Russian and a Frenchman in the Himalayas, where the Russian points at the monstrous colonial subject (my ancestor, M. A. from Calcutta University), and says that they, the Russians, know the Orient and can govern them. Hopkirk tells us that the term "great game" was invented by "Lieutenant Arthur Conolly of the 6th Bengal Native Light Cavalry ... [who], aged 16, ... [had] joined his regiment as a cornet" (GG 123–4). Najibullah, no doubt waiting for a violent death, knew these books and thought that reading them might help. The Soviets had failed him. His revolution had failed. The Taliban thought they had come to power, although they were as reliant upon the CIA as he had been on the Soviet Union. What did his execution signify in the end? Success for the Taliban? In 2002, this question takes on historical poignancy and looks forward to other reversals of fortune. This is why Najibullah wanted "his people" to understand that Afghanistan could not act for itself.

In the context of the student uprising of May 1968 in Paris, calling it "A Symbolic Revolution," Michel de Certeau asks: "Where is the fiction? Where is the real? The line between the 'events' and 'order' engages the relation that we have with ourselves, both individually and collectively."[9] Najibullah's generation went to University in the sixties. It is therefore not inappropriate to ask de Certeau's question not only about French students, but in the context of a worldwide change among left student radicals, what is it for a revolution to be "real"? Are failed revolutions more "symbolic"? What is it for a revolution to succeed? Najibullah's problem was a common one, a class problem, indeed a problem he might have shared with Lenin. As a student radical from a poor (Eur)Asian country, he was in touch with revolutionary thinking, but out of touch with the subaltern in his own country.

The Great Game is a book of riveting popular journalism. What it does demonstrate in as narrative a mode as *Discipline and Punish* (albeit with fewer theoretical pyrotechnics) is that Afghanistan (as part of Central Asia) was a pawn in a game between the Russians and the British – both eager to win a passage to India. The book suggests that the Game began in Russia's reaction to "the 'lost' Mongol centuries" (ca. 1206–1553; GG 16). This is to plot the story not by economic modes of production (as in Marx and the Foucault of *Discipline and Punish*) but by great movements of people (as in Samir Amin).[10] Today this seems altogether persuasive.

The production of the colonial subject in order to administer a settled colonial possession could not appear on the agenda in this region. The examples I have chosen – Mohandas Karamchand Gandhi, barrister, also comes to mind – support the truism that it is in this class that nationalist resistance took root. But Afghanistan was never "colonized," and, it can be surmised that Najibullah, by translating this book, was trying to produce something like that subject in his country; a subject that will know that to take sides in that theater is simply to agree to be a plaything in a game that neither began nor ended with the Cold War. In the event, he became a public spectacle in a discourse – military, political, economic – that he could not signify. In the New World Economic Order of electronic capitalism, the separation "between force and the product of labour" has become aporetic, displaced itself into operative virtuality. That Afghanistan, the only part of Central Asia that was not a member of the USSR, had a role in the consolidation of the end of the Cold War and thus the establishment of the New World Economic Order cannot be doubted. Yet the separation between this failed state and the success of globality is so vast, that in this public spectacle, the people do not countersign the "super-power" of a monarch, as in Foucault's Early Modern France. They face the photographer of the super-power, furtively, once again providing evidence of a "coming anarchy," indistinguishable from a presupposed archaic violence.[11]

Why did Afghanistan not emerge as a modern state? If "[a]n event is not what can be seen or known about its happening, but what it becomes (and, above all, for us)," the situation in the *New York Times* photo still stages a bifurcated subject.[12] What it roughly becomes for the photographer and the broader scenario is not what it becomes for the men in the background, relating in various intensities to a contained and ruptured script. Women will not see the spectacle. They are not subjects for this history of the present as event in becoming.

Why should this be so? This is not necessarily an ideological imponderable, for questions of state-structure relate, precisely, to structural abstractions. I am not a historian, merely an expatriate South Asian reacting to a story in the *New York Times*. Yet it does seem striking that, although Abd-ur Rahman, the last nineteenth-century Amir of Afghanistan, had struggled to establish something resembling a "constitutional government" in Afghanistan, precisely in order to preserve something like "national identity," he had imported English men and women to train up Afghans, rather than encourage the production of the pharmakontic (medicine as well as poison) enabling violation of the full-fledged colonial subject by sending Afghans abroad.[13] The Afghan "national identity" is a provisional moment, of course, in the alternative inter-nationality of Islam. It is fascinating to read the Amir's awareness of the diversity of Islam and yet its provision for thinking a collectivity. "[T]he struggle between imperial Britain and imperial Russia for influence in Afghanistan" was not unknown to him; as it was not unknown to Muhammad Mahfuz Ali, an Indian Muslim who translated his own book *The Truth About Russia and England: From a Native's Point of View* from Urdu into English in 1886, a move that Najibullah was obliged to reverse, as it were, by translating from English into Pashto. It is interesting that even the Indian, on the one hand a loyal subject of the Crown, and, on the other, a Muslim, though inimical to the Amir, spoke of "the national spirit of the Afghan people." The Urdu text is unavailable after considerable research. What interests me is that Mahfuz Ali, very much the colonial subject – at one point he writes of "the oriental mind" – what had that phrase been in Urdu? – had thought that the appropriate translation of the Urdu word was "nation." Yet it is also quite clear that he was aware that Abd-ur Rahman was not an initiate of colonial knowledge. For in the same passage he calls the Afghans "a savage and united race" – that last word too is interesting – and Afghanistan a "wretched country." What had he meant by the word "race," applied to someone who did not share his own epistemic enclave?[14] How does Hamid Karzai, the first "American" President of Afghanistan, whose education is Indian, straddle the gap?

With respect, the problem with the brilliant body of speculation undertaken by Benedict Anderson and Etienne Balibar is that it cannot acknowledge that such questions, finally unanswerable, inhabiting the cusp where the rupture of colonialism is also a repetition, are worth pondering. The word that is translated "nation" names a hardy "residual," not an "emergent" which would allow us to claim that "citizenship" – the model of which is much more directly linked to the development of civil societies in Northwestern Europe – "and nationality have a single, indissociable institutional base."[15] I am suggesting that varieties of nation-think, indistinguishable from other identifications, pre-exist and variously assist the emergence of the state structure sustained by citizenship.

What characterized the para-colonial theater loosely called Afghanistan, was that upon that stage, the masters masqueraded as the native. As in *Kim*, the Great Game was almost invariably played in disguise. Hopkirk's pages are strewn with pictures of British and Russian soldiers in Afghan, Persian, Armenian dress. This planned indeterminacy, like the indeterminacy of the demographic rather than territorial frontiers in this theater, is much closer to the postcolonial hybridized globalized world of today than the nationalist colonialisms, which were as much a historically contained phenomenon as Bolshevism. If in Foucault's story, the transformation of the soldier into a docile body "could become determinant only with a technical transformation: the invention of the rifle" (DP 163), the rifle clinched no great narrative in Najibullah's. Plate 35 in *The Great Game* shows a British officer in native dress surrounded by Afghans. " … [M]any minor players," the caption runs, "were involved in the Great Game. An anonymous political officer (rifleless), hardly distinguishable from his companions, is seen here with friendly Afghan tribesmen," who all carry rifles, but are not called "soldiers."[16] This picture is outside of Foucault's beautifully organized system, so beloved by the disciplines, but also "inside," for this is the wild counter-narrative, rifle-toting tribesmen and rifleless white soldier, that keeps the story of efficiency and leniency going in the metropolis. Abd-ur Rahman, importing Englishmen to teach the Afghans to assemble Henry-Martini rifles, and introducing a European ranking system into his army, marks the spot.[17]

Colonial subject-production within nation-state colonialism goes the other way. The native mimics the Master. That bit of common sense is useful in thinking India, not Afghanistan (*mutatis mutandis* Algeria, not South Africa). Foucault's story is European – largely French – and must ignore these dynamics until the postcolonial arrives in France.[18] Kipling (as, later, Rushdie) constructs the (post)colonial as monstrously comic. Peter Hopkirk, the author of Najibullah's text, cannot understand the colonial Mirza Shuja at all. Like Kipling's Hurree Mookerjee, the Indian Mirza Shuja is part of

an elite group of handpicked and highly trained Indians … [who were sent] into these forbidden regions[.] They were far less likely to be detected than a European, however good the latter's disguise. If they

140   FOUCAULT AND NAJIBULLAH

were unfortunate enough to be discovered, moreover, it would be less politically embarrassing to the authorities than if a British officer was caught red-handed making maps in these highly sensitive and dangerous parts. (GG 329–30)

"Just what drove men like Mirza Shuja to face such hardships and extreme dangers for their imperial masters has never been satisfactorily explained" (GG 332), says Hopkirk. I see in Mirza Shuja the Indian my intellectual ancestor, fooled by "white mythology," serving intellectual ambition rather than his imperial masters. Afghanistan was not a locus of the large-scale production of such trained subjects, male in the Great Game, but male and female in the disciplines.

Between 1919 and 1929, after the dissolution of the Russian empire, Amanullah, the grandson of Abd-ur Rahman, did try to establish the condition of possibility of a latter-day colonial subject in Afghanistan. A good part of the argument of this chapter deals with the city and the country. It is therefore pertinent to note that "[w]hereas Abdul Rahman [sic] had taken the throne himself, his grandson Amanullah was born and raised in Kabul city and had virtually no contact with tribal Afghanistan."[19] Having destroyed the structure of the authority inhering in diversified collective authorities by a counter-intuitive, benevolent, and unilateral "constitutionalism," Amanullah set about to "transform ... [an] absolutist state ... to [a] nation-state." Such modernization by fiat is no substitute for the slow *pharmakontic* violation operated by territorial imperialism, breeding class division and collaboration, as well as an inimical intimacy that opens the ethical and the non-ethical. How derisive then, for the US to try it, with no cultural intimacy, and no appeal to history.

Curiously enough, because of the centuries of propinquity ("'the monstrous hybridism of East and West,' the Russian replied. 'It is we who can deal with Orientals'") as well as the shared hostility to imperial Russia, the Soviet "occupation" of 1979 might have produced such a forced birth, anachronistically.[20] Earlier empires had been more multicultural. Later empires, wanting to make minds ready for the spectral rationality of capitalism or state socialism, produce an "impoverished catalogue of models, and at the same time ... an infinite composition of these few models on almost any situation."[21] In Inner Asia, Russia remained poised between the old mode and the new.

In accessing the new mode of few models and infinite application, "Moslem women came to constitute, in Soviet political imagination, a structural weak point in the traditional order: a potentially deviant and

hence subversive stratum susceptible to militant appeal."[22] Consider
now this passage from *Out of Afghanistan*:

> Cavalier treatment of Muslim divines suspected of opposition to the
> regime, together with reforms affecting the status of women, gave the
> regime a reputation for "godless" disrespect toward Islamic traditions.
> Like its economic reforms, the regime's social reforms were mild by
> Western standards but aroused predictable convulsions in the Afghan
> context. One of the government's most controversial decrees,
> denounced bitterly by the *mullahs*, required the consent of both parties
> to a marriage and placed a limit of 300 Afghanis ($9) on the amount of
> *haq mehr*, or "bride money," [literally, "rightful reward," converted by
> social practice into the other meaning] that could be paid to the father
> of the bride in return for his daughter. The money went to the bride,
> not to the father, if the contract was broken, a revolutionary concept in
> Afghan society. *Feminist leaders in Kabul hailed the reform.* But in the coun-
> tryside, where *haq mehr* was sanctified by centuries of tradition, the
> amount paid for a bride was a measure of her purity and social position.
> When arrests were made for violation of the decree, violence erupted.
> The *mullahs* were also able to discredit rural literacy campaigns by
> charging that the city women conducting these campaigns, often clad
> in skirts, were spreading immoral ideas.[23]

Who are these already-existing "feminists"? Were they the descendants of those who profited from Abd-ur Rahman's introduction of
the registration of marriages? Or of his conviction "that ...
Afghanistan can never make full and complete progress unless its
women are educated?"[24] Was their position a stand for what Islam
"really" meant – that the *mehr* belongs to the bride – or a stand against
Islam as a generally masculist religion – or yet a stand against religions as masculist – or, finally, for gender-sensitive secularism as the
policy appropriate for the state? In a generalist's book, there is no
room to consider such questions, altogether appropriate to the argument of the book, especially since some of the most important
reforms of Amanullah's brief reign, where interest in modernity
seemed perfectly coherent with friendship with the new Soviet
Union, were in the area of literacy, education, and the general emancipation of women. (The other two were coercive constitutionalism
and hothouse capitalism.[25])

Returning to a position against the Soviets and against the King's
enemies produces, through historical amnesia or ignorance, a concern
for women's emancipation, the reason for which is simply called
"Islam," implying that it is essentially "Afghan-cultural," and therefore

justifies Euro-US intervention. As Polly Toynbee wrote just after September 11, 2001:

> (No letters please from British women who have taken the veil and claim it's liberating. It is their right in a tolerant society to wear anything including rubber fetishes. ... The pens sharpen – Islamophobia! No such thing. Primitive Middle Eastern religions (and most others) are much the same – Islam, Christianity and Judaism all define themselves through disgust for women's bodies.[26]

Toynbee sees "Afghan women" as already constructed as a subset within a general set "women in religion," by which she, interestingly, means "women in the Abrahamic religions, monolithized." In fact, reproductive heteronormativity is the broadest, most ancient, most amorphous institution in the world, and its agency is not confined to visible violence against women.

How this potential for gender oppression will be used is situational. (This is why Toynbee's reference to Christianity and Judaism is disingenuous.) Societies (of men) systematize themselves by treating women and non-men as signs.[27] When Hashim Kamali writes that an Islamic takeover in Afghanistan would involve "[a]n Islamic constitutional order, an ulema dominated judiciary, and a return of the classical Shari'a law of personal status," he is obliged to devote more than half his book to the last item which means, of course, "Matrimonial Law." As he himself acknowledges, the first two items have taken his attention "due to the promulgation of two new constitutions and a civil code in Afghanistan during the subsequent [between 1976, the year he completed his dissertation at London University and the Russian presence, beginning 1979] years."[28] Here is the *New York Times*:

> Last week, ... the Taliban ... began constructing their new state along strict Muslim fundamentalist [Islamist nationalist] lines – complete with the closing of girls' schools and beatings for improperly dressed women, as well as at least one public display of a man punished with amputation. ... [The US State Department] voiced American concerns about the protection of Human Rights, "especially women's rights," but added, "We will have to judge them by their actions." ... There is logic in thinking that Washington will not be unhappy with the prospect of a government in Kabul that may limit Iranian influence in central Asia ...

Universalist feminism will take up the cause of these women and congratulate itself on being radical and, once again, with various photo

opportunities, make the world safe for capitalism recoded as democracy. (A US company opened negotiations with the Taliban for opening
a pipeline through Afghanistan for Central Asian oil.) Not much will
change for the woman at the bottom.

It is interesting to read these words in 2003. I was not far off the
mark. The oil circuit has claimed more blood. There I was wrong.

Already in 1975, at the inception of today's electronic capitalism,
and in the year of publication of *Surveiller et punir*, the Report of the
World Conference of the International Women's Year declares: "True
peace cannot be achieved unless women share with men the responsibility for establishing a new international economic order."[29] Since
then, the construction of a general female will for economic restructuring has been the central thematic of international feminism.
Afghanistan will be brought to stability by the gendered subject of globalization. In the previous chapter, we have examined the story breaking in the Southern Caucasus. In 2003, Thomas Friedman represents a
consensus as he justifies the devastation of Iraq by citing conversations
with Iraqi women. If she is grassroots, the US has given her a voice.
(This is Friedman's interpretation, because she "wears a veil." What, in
Mr. Friedman's interpretation, is a veil? What does that have to do with
having a voice?) If she already "has a voice," she is "Harvard-edu-
cated."[30] Plus ça change …

Such historical questions as "How did Islam in the Afghan case, as in
other particular cases, become such a tremendous oppressor of women?"
cannot be answered with correct narratives. I am trying to follow in
Foucault's footsteps. He seemed to think late eighteenth-century
governmentality could be held responsible for policing the body. My
question "How did Islam …" has been asked by many contemporary
Muslims. I know no Arabic, but common sense tells me that a people,
when they begin to be defeated, fall back on gender oppression to
declare their difference. In matters unconnected with gender (is anything?), namely the seeming collapsing of the mysterious relationship-
in-rupture between the open-endedness of ethics and the systematicity
of the Law, I have consulted Fazlur Rahman.[31]

Melanie Klein suggests that when a group of men is oppressed by
another group, against whom it can do nothing, Envy makes it turn
against women, especially the imago of the Mother.[32] This is a complicated argument, and I will not try to lay it out here. But it is a good
working hypothesis against the racist argument that Islam is essentially oppressive. If, as I have stated it, this is seen as too simple a

cause-and-effect model, let me point out that Foucault himself often
uses an equally simple cause-and-effect model, in completely different contexts, of course – with reference to the development of "peasant illegality" (DP 274), of the "delinquent," and of "specialized
criminality" (GG 274–5); as here we point at the emergence of a
sexist Muslim collectivity.[33]

Another sentiment comes from colonially settled areas: that the
conquered civilizations were not put to respectful rest, were not
mourned, when the culture of imperialism brought the nation to a
new frontier. I will offer a poem and a bit of a novel. Can poems and
novels argue? Before we consider how literature advocates, let us
consider a "reasonable" version of the argument, namely, that the
glass is half-empty. In that negative mode and 100 years ago, a full-
fledged Indian colonial subject of the British wrote of the Russians,
who in his view were too contaminated by the Orient, as unable to
internalize the mindset imposed upon them by internal imperialism. I include the comment here because it teaches us a lesson we
would do well to remember today: the line between colonizer and
colonized is indeterminate, especially when the informant is the
colonial subject, today's "diasporic," rather different from the merely
"ethnic":

> As Mr. Wallace forcibly puts it, "No institution can work well unless it
> is the natural product of previous historical development." Hence all
> those institutions, formed under imperial auspices for purposes of
> political discussion, in imitation of the constitutional methods of
> Western Europe, were often more like school-boy Clubs.[34]

In 1995, a postcolonial Indian citizen makes a similar point about his
new nation:

> [w]e must remember that many of the famous universities of Europe
> had existed for centuries before the Taj Mahal was built in India. They
> have evolved and grown with the societies they were part of. By and
> large they have also responded to actual societal needs and grown in
> relative harmony with their surroundings.[35]

These are examples of the haphazard production of colonial subjects when the previous cultural formation is insufficiently "mourned,"
and change is felt as rupture rather than iteration. New and alien values
are internalized through educational institutions, and seemingly from

the ambient air, and the old ways become a place of shame. In the new world, we have learned to call a certain packaging of the old ways "culture," even, embarrassingly, "heritage," but that is a story for "Moving Devi," later in the book.

Indeed, the law of change is impatient and subliminal. There never can be more than "half-mourning" (*demi-deuil*).[36] Our epistemic effort is to produce a judgment of the glass is half-full variety, so that it can continue to quench, rather than be crushed under imperialism as development. This is how one begins to use the Enlightenment from below.

How does one "half-mourn," knowingly? Melanie Klein suggests that the infant's access to the whole person – rather than part-object perception – is the condition and effect of a reality-testing that is a simulacrum of primary mourning.[37] This can be understood as half-mourning, for what is being mourned is the access to the "normal" ego. What is half-mourning is also half-jubilation.

In that affirmative mode, a practical, secondary, and accountable supplement to this primary (gift of half-)mourning is children's education. In the postcolonial context, one variety of "mourning" may be the introduction of subaltern children to a literacy that carries the remote possibility of bearing witness to the intolerable burden of a history whose explanations have not, so far, involved them.

Until the Soviet presence, Afghanistan was ex-orbitant to this narrative, thanks to the Great Game. It was of but not in the colonial orbit. Hence Najibullah's translation project, looking toward a stable state with no sustained colonial precedent.

It is the past as the unburied dead that calls us in postcoloniality.[38] It is in response and responsibility to that call that the postcolonial must strain to gain access to cultural responsibility along a broad political and educational spectrum. In the rock and roll of US versus USSR, and Russia versus France and Britain before that, Afghanistan did not experience a "death" – of culture or colony – that would inaugurate the call. Farhad Mazhar, a Bangladeshi poet, can be our example for the Indian colonial past, altogether unlike the shuttle-diplomatic history of Afghanistan. Mazhar contrasts the contemporary Bengali archaeologists – working in the restricted arena of academic freedom, more "British" than the Royal Asiatic Society, – to the poet-persona forever guarding the unburied corpses of the Sepoy Mutiny (1857), the first battle of independence on the subcontinent, "national" by a logic that Abd-ur Rahman had longed for and that was achieved in Mahfuz Ali:

> Lord, Dhaka's mosque is world-renowned
> Much varied work on pillar and cloister. In British days
> the Whites, right or wrong, put in place
> th'Asiatic Society and researched it all
> Here. In the white eyes
> Of whites the new Bengalis dig now
> And look for things we see.
> I wish them good luck. But doctor's degrees,
> Make them twice
> As wily as their White forebears.[39]

> Lord, I'm an unlettered fool,
> Can't grasp the art of architecture, paint,
> Yet my heart aches empty
> As I stand by the old Ganga.
> The Sepoys seem to hang still on hangman's ropes
> Waiting for last rites, the ropes uncut,
> Their bodies still aloft, none to mourn,
> To perform *zannat*.
> Don't you mock me with minaret and arcade,
> Me, the corpse-keeper of revolt.[40]

Foucault never quite tells us what we should do about Damiens the regicide. For this poet, a task remains undone; as it was for Najibullah.[41]

Assia Djebar is a writer from Algeria, another country with a straight colonial record. She complicates the metaphor of incomplete mourning with the double difficulty of regaining an active perspective for women in the unperformed burial rites for the dead old culture when the colonial culture seemingly gave access to the new. A scene of men fighting and women mourning is all that Djebar stages as a recovery: "The body, not embalmed by ritual lamentations, is found dressed in rags. As an echo the cries of our ancestors, unhorsed in forgotten battles, return; and the dirges of the women who watched them die, accompany them."[42]

These passages should make clear that I am not attempting to bring the dead to life, but rather to be haunted by the ghost of one past so that we can reasonably invoke another. Rather than find in Najib some latter-day Damiens (enemy of Afghan monarchy) – a move Foucault would not have endorsed, I think – we might try to understand what it was that he, and before him Abd-ur Rahman tried to negotiate, with the incoming tide of governmentality, without the presence of territorial imperialism: willing a transformation to modernity as they understood it. Of course, it was without democratic structure, but so was colonialism, in another way. Our question is: did it make a difference for those who did not or could not access this change?

Writers such as Djebar and Mazhar urge us that the unlamented corpses of colonized cultures proper must be lamented anew as we attempt to theorize their history, as lived by their unaffiliated living after-runners (not their "proper inheritors"), by the (gendered) subaltern, not the colonial subjects. The "proper inheritors," the research workers of Mazhar's poem, have expanded their reach. They now claim "subalternity" by way of the international philanthropic interest in minorities. (What is it to live a history? I do not venture up to the perilous necessity of confronting the impossibility of answering that question, given the globalized benevolent opposition.) I have never been at all interested in designating "proper" inheritors of anthropologized older cultures so that they can be distanced from the advantages of colonizing culture and its indigenous collaborators. Hence ethnic identitarianism is rather far from my concerns. In a place like Afghanistan, it only breeds internal feuds, mobilized by the mere mouthing of democracy as vote control.[43] In the absence of sustained unification by colonizing violence, tribal identities and loyalties, in male and female alike, have been alive and well in whatever you call Afghanistan, thinning out to little more than descriptive labels as one ascends into the tiny intelligentsia. There is nothing left for Afghanistan to mourn. And 10 years after Najibullah was hanged, circumstances dictate that an empire-fancying former left-of-center Canadian intellectual like Michael Ignatieff recommend American imperialism in the area.[44]

Again and again in this text, putting together Melanie Klein and the ravages suffered by the subaltern in today's world, I have been proposing that a practical, secondary, and accountable supplement to the primary (gift of half-) mourning may be children's education. "Literacy" is now everybody's favorite project. But, as I have also insisted, because the projects are focused mainly on (what is inevitably mechanical and rote) reading, the imagination is not exercised, worldwide class apartheid is protected, and there is not even the remote possibility that this education will bear witness to a history whose explanations have not involved them. I have written of this in the first chapter. Let me repeat in broader strokes and make further connections. Considerable importance is attached to memorizing – the alphabet, multiplication tables, poems and so on. If I am right, the children will often "read" something different from the page they are following with finger and eye. To "correct" them from above undermines the entire delicate effort. Yet those interested in the eventual subject *for* freedom, and for national liberation as a moment in globalization – student radicals like future Najibullahs – must devote some of their energies to these sorts of details because there are not enough resources at this ground-level for the kind of individual attention for which one might agitate under more favorable circumstances. And, on the other side, when a banalized version of the Enlightenment is used as allegiance to a minimal rationalization by rote, we get the public use of reason travestied as private enterprise on its way to a financialization of the globe. This goes hand in hand with a "privatization" of the transcendental in the name of secularism, or its inefficient suppression in the name of Communism. Arrived here, it is the class-separated (though not necessarily race-separated) universitarian who must learn and change, rather than the impatient and roving international humanitarian. The task is not to cheat the subaltern schoolchild. What one is testing is a teaching system compromised by an "unmourned" tradition, leading to a troubled and alienating "modernity," not the child.

If the girl-child is asked to write her own message to someone, the emphasis on memory and reading does not come to her aid. And yet, when after three years she is confined to home, yard, and perhaps field and stream, soon to be married, she finds no books in her rural household. If in those three years, emphasis had been laid on writing, and not merely copying out what is in the book, it is at least remotely possible that, when deprived of her education and yoked to household labor and childbirth, she would have had a companion, in the secret skill of writing. We have examples of slave narratives and women's secret writing to corroborate this. The patriarchally severed minute effort at the constitution of the gendered subject for the long term of the narrative of history may perhaps (there is no guarantee) find shelter in this small sustained change in the teaching of female children. And yet the change is not easy to make. For once again, we must remember that the limit case teachers who will engage in primary teaching in the peripheries of the periphery are themselves from the rural subaltern order and seldom with more than inferior secondary education, conditioned by the obedience-to-authority to which responsibility is reduced by its delegitimation in war and "fundamentalism." Photo ops lie.

It is in this context, and with all the vicissitudes of university students in developing countries in mind, that one still asks for their periodic intervention in the task of training the teachers. As long as they themselves are taught self-interest alone, they cannot think this of importance. The state is maimed, the intelligentsia Americanized, and the subaltern learns, at best, a crude nationalism that is the other side of tribalism.

In such small ways we make provision for a continuity of the potential for freedom to match the changing polity.[45] A poor provision at best. But if "[a]n event is not what can be seen or known about its happening, but what it becomes (and, above all, for us)," this is the tiny beginning of the animation of an alternative subject for whom the event's becoming can challenge the broader scenario of global *Realpolitik*.[46] Otherwise class apartheid remains in place forever. And those who rise become, as I repeatedly point out, in Paulo Freire's memorable phrase, "sub-oppressors."[47] It is therefore not necessarily less important than the inspirational prose of culturalist academics confined to a colonial/anticolonial historical scheme in euphoric postcolonial space.

By digressing into children's education, I have been speaking of supplementing Najibullah's effort to make already-literate menfolk aware. Now I would like to touch upon what had to be undone in order to produce a Najibullah.

In the archives of the old Royal Ministry of External Affairs in Kabul were lodged 194 "covenants" given to Abd-ur Rahman on August 17, 1896, by various groups that made up "Afghanistan." Hasan Kakar included the one given by the Mohammadzay *Sardars* (lit. headmen), since they were of the Amir's own clan (*qawm*, people related by blood and "otherwise," who can "stand together," to trade, to fight, to recite their genealogies).[48] "For those who read Farsi," he adds, "the Persian text is also printed because English renditions can only approximate the meaning of the original."

The Amir named the day "Festival of Unanimity." The name names a desire rather than its accomplishment. Let us remember the constitutive hybridity of that "unanimity." The document in Kakar is no singular Declaration of Independence where the performance of the signatures was rused as the constative statement of the existence of the signatories as declarers, specifically of a specific gesture, here unanimity, as there independence.[49] There were, after all, nearly 200 such covenants. The example of the Mohammadzay was followed not only by "other groups [*qwams*] throughout the country" but also by "Hindus, artisans, businessmen, *maldars* (nomads [more specifically herdsmen, roving proprietors]), soldiers, civil and military officials."

Any translation of the Great Game from English by Najib, the regicide-by-proxy (the Marxist Government ousted the royal line), into Pashto must take into account the "approximations" of this translation, from Farsi into English, for the sake of the *Padishah*-by-proxy, Najibullah as President. For the relationship between Farsi and Pashto, there is no *De vulgari eloquentia* to guide me.[50]

Let us see in this "covenant" the non-achievement of a shift from a system of responsibilities to a system of rights, although we do so in the same mode of approximation that we are deciphering here. (To call it a shift from feudalism to the possibility of statehood seems too evolutionist. I am trying to see the glass half-full.) The non-achievement is at least partially effaced in the use of the same English word "covenant" for *tahrir* and *taqrir* in the opening sentence and *"ahd-nameh"* in the description of the file-category in the archives. The first couple signal a proclamation – a writing and a reciting – that the true definition of our birth-placing has changed; because Truth has selected our *qawm*-leader as King of Afghanistan; in other words, the *qawm*-leader's true description has become "King of Afghanistan," in the event the *Amir*, or "prince," of Afghanistan. This change from a *previous* state of truth is translated into a *founding* social contract by an archivized collectivity. The timing of the change thus goes unnoticed in the English. That it has not been completely effaced – as it would be in the colonial case – is indicated by the note left by Kakar, a modern Afghan who sought validation at the School of Oriental and African Studies at London University, even as his text was being translated into Russian.[51] In my fancy, this festering of the residual under the scab of the emergent is disclosed in the furtiveness of the gaze of the spectators before the European photographer at the execution of the regicide-by-proxy, the picture in the *New York Times*. (The real "King," no longer a *haqdar* – a word whose significance I discuss below – but a charming ineffectual French-educated Afghan gentleman, had of course been "unking-ed" by history.)

By the presuppositions of the signatories of those firmans, the human being is born into a "para-individual structural responsibility". This structural space defines us. Indeed, in this connection, the word "responsibility" itself is an approximation, even a catachresis – a word used in translation because no psychological referent can be found – because this structural positioning can also be approximately translated as birth-right. Whether it is right or responsibility, it is the truth of my being, in that not quite English sense my *haq*. And the *Amir* holds the subjects' *haq*. He is the *haqdar*. The word that is translated "God" in the second lines of paragraphs 1 and 2, "our right" in the next to the last sentence of paragraph 1, and "real" as in "real King" and "real promise of the day" in paragraph 6 is, equally, *haq*. Thus, what in the English is being staged as the emergence of a (God-given) right is, to put it altogether approximatively, a change in our profane truth because of a move of sacred truth in filling the structural place of the obedience-commander (*moqtada*, tr. "Leader") of sacred and profane management (*din wa dawlat*, tr. "Religion and state") by the person of our *qawm* who is to be followed (*matbu*). Each of these translations is a rich cultural field of "problems" that are testimonies to history.[52] The zeal to announce modernity undoes the patience of mourning. Comparative literary practice must make translation a part of language-learning.

The "true [*haq*] king" and the "true [*haq*] promise of the last day" are, of course as "has been mentioned in Holy Writ." That we are dealing with the culture of Islam here – which does indeed keep *din* and *dunya*, sacred and profane, Church and world, resolutely together by divine decree, associated in the only use of the word "Islam" in the Koran – is effaced by the translation, perhaps in its zeal to record the emergence of the possibility of modernity.[53] Today, when the realization is spreading that the separation of public and private, Church and State, are not tough enough instruments, that they are specific to a restricted time and place, and that, most difficult of all, we must keep working for a secularism with room for intuitions of the transcendental and thus revise modernity, the consequences of such an effacement are written in blood and bombs. The zeal to announce modernity is most evident in the translation's rendering of the fourth vow – where the proclaimers speak and write as *mamārdom* – "we the people." We the people swear to cultivate and not to disregard our King's gathering up and using the reins of our religion according to the truth (*haq*) of God and his prophet. This becomes, we swear "not to dispute the right of the religion and to strengthen our religious arrangements of God and Prophet." The translation takes us toward "render unto Caesar," when what we are witnessing is an important shift in social order: from clan-leadership (*primus inter pares*) to authority. The *matbu* has become a *moqtador*. To translate both as "sovereign" effaces the shift.[54] The shift was practically denied by the Amir's grandson Amanullah (who declared himself "king"), with disastrous consequences.

And indeed the unconsummated shift to a declaration of new rights (in English) is actually the declaration of an expansion in the Farsi, a change in the nature and order of, approximately, obedience. By the structural truth of belonging to the *qawm* we were responsible for the *mtaberat* of this *matbu* (tr. "following" and "sovereign" – the latter clearly in excess, since "follower" and "leader" inter-define through the root *tabe* here). Now, however, with the move made by sacred Truth, the other *qawms* of Afghanistan are also of his following (*tabe'*, tr. "subjects," somewhat incorrectly, because this following precisely does not entail a king). Therefore our *haq* (right-responsibility-truth) has moved into the *eta'at* that is a part of *mtaberat* (an entailment, a metonymic rather than semantic/semiotic relationship), to the extent that, by virtue of our *qarabat* (relationship by blood and standing) of clanship, the other *qawms* owe us *mtaberat*. Again, it is not a shift in the sense of following, as the English translation suggests. It is a shift in social order: from clan-leadership (*primus inter pares*) to authority. The *matbu* has become a *moqtador*. To translate both as "sovereign" occludes the shift, within the same discursive formation, which could, of course, have no future. This is not unimportant, since a real shift in meaning, what the translation suggests, might have involved the episteme. As we have noted above, "Citizenship," according to Balibar, "is indissolubly linked to the nation-state." When Farsi creates a word for citizens (*tabeyat*) from "following as *tabe'*," and Mo'in, the big Farsi-to-Farsi dictionary, gives as the *last* definition of *Millat*, the word translated as "Nation" in the last line, this very word *tabeyat* (the first two being the Law [*Shariyat*] and people who follow the law respectively), the indissoluble link is displaced to another narrative structure. The supplement to Najib's translation is to re-translate "following" and "obedience" into a truth that makes right-and-responsibility indeterminate, in children's education to reinvent tradition as historiography, to a reconceived modernity.[55] That epistemic undertaking is what allows "half-mourning" to put "the past" behind us, again and again.

I resist the temptation of commenting on the play of sacred and profane time in the document. A word on gendering.

I have elsewhere compared the frenzy of the soldier for his country to the gendering that can support *sati* or widow suicide in India (CPR 244–311). The *sardars* prove my point by having to designate their duty not to be unfaithful to the legitimate King in the feminine (*lazemeh*). The King-in-his-Court has the same sort of relationship to his followers as men to women, having the latter's honor (*namus*) in their safekeeping as their right-responsibility. (If indeed Farsi *namus* comes from Greek *nomos*, how much of the polymorphous aura of that word traveled in that derivation? I cannot know.) In this, they are *haqdars* (truth-keepers, clumsily translated "acting in accordance with the heavenly dispensation") of an attribute (approximately) that women can lose, but men have as a ground for shame (*rosva*). Since reinventing the tradition as historiography will keep women's *haq* still fixed as subject-separation from the losable object, always defined as an indeterminate yet defining predication of the tactile and fungible body, women must train for a resistant modernity, elsewhere. Thus the gendered gift of writing, however private the space of women's learning in theocracy, applies in this theater as well.

This chapter has been uneasily shuttling between the two foci of resistance: the aggregative apparatus of the postcolonial state; and the *pouvoir/savoir* (ability to know or episteme) of the rural girl-child in literacy. The two meet in the arena of "Development." But Najibullah and his brother seem to be hanging in some other space. They are casualties of a Game that consolidated, rather than participated in, the narrative of conquest/colonialism/postcoloniality/globalization; which in its turn served to consolidate the emergence of the Foucauldian "man as object of knowledge." This narrative also leads to "Development" as the history of the present – modernity virtualizing into postmodernity. But Afghanistan stalls short-circuited in a buffer zone where the masters, masquerading, did not permit the shadow play of native mimicry fully to run its course.[56] The detritus of the Bolshevik experiment, coded into the Russian part of the Game, reached it too late, and was quickly recoded into the order of the *Cold* War, a horrible misnomer in the periphery. This chapter only signals toward the conjuncture of the present, the nation-state vanishing into the "good imperialism" of US world governance, Afghanistan a colony at last, globalization-style.

Earlier I have considered the question of a reactive Islamism in classic postcoloniality. In the Afghan case, as has been endlessly discussed, "Islamism" was as much constructed by US opposition to the post-'79 Soviet-backed Afghan state and sustained US supply of arms, as was the construction of "custom" by colonial powers in Africa.[57] There is no radical anticolonial hybrid space in the Afghan metropolis for the public proclamation of the intellectual as, in Réda Bensmaïa's felicitous phrase, "phantom mediator."[58] As the subtitle of Barnett Rubin's

1995 book would have it, Afghanistan goes from "buffer state to failed state." (Bringing this sentence up to date in 2006 would involve rewriting the chapter.)

Abdur Rahman's "Festival of Unanimity" had used the dynamic of the kind of pre-capitalist "secularism" that classical Islam characteristically practiced in positions of power. I am not idealizing the "Absolute Amir."[59] But he was no Taliban.

On the other hand, the Afghan left was constructed at the unanchored university that followed in the wake of Amanullah's constitutionalism. Kabul University was founded in 1932, three years after Amanullah's deposition. It is still "unanchored," since the slow work of the uncoercive rearrangement of the desires of the subaltern (which affects gendering), their insertion into the intuition of a public sphere (which affects democracy), and the production of a "general will" for a culture-specific modernity, could not, of course, be undertaken. This is not the story of "Afghan essence," but of the ways of class-formation and now, with US influence, the story, once again, of the complicity of colony and class. It is in this context that the muted plea to university students to be aware of class apartheid by engagement with subaltern education is muted indeed. One begins to understand the destructive impatience of Mao's cultural revolution, to be distinguished from the impatient efficiency of the animal-machine of the international civil society, negotiating technical solutions for every aporia.[60]

I have been a graduate student in the United States, and a full-time university teacher for 40 years. I teach now at Columbia University. I also happen to be rather well acquainted with the highly politicized scene of tertiary education in Bangladesh, split precisely between the "Left" and "Islam," when it is not split between the two chief political parties, with not many issues to choose between them that an outsider can glean. (The case of India needs a different analysis.) Therefore, the fact that the first Communist President of Afghanistan (later assassinated by the Soviets), had been the head of the Afghan Student's Association at Columbia, that Gulbuddin Hekmatiyar, the fundamentalist "resistance" leader whose views were the opposite of the Communist Najibullah, as well as Najibullah himself, were university students whose studies had been interrupted by jail terms, gives me a sense of how distant this world would be from so unglamorous an issue as the methodological detail of rural literacy. Thus Najibullah's exemplary nationalism was itself a reactive construct, no doubt owing rather more to the tremendous underground internationalism of the Eurocentric radical student movement of the sixties than to a connection with the Afghan subaltern. The hijackers of 9–11 were graduate students as well.

That is the burden of our supplement: Unless the slow process of using "the Enlightenment" from below is emphasized and engaged, there is no hope that anyone will question the identity of the monster painted by John F. Burns, the *New York Times* correspondent: "Mr. Najibullah, who in life served the KGB's efforts to eliminate opposition to Marxism, died a death as miserable as any his secret police meted out." Under pressure from both the USSR and the US, possibly because he was a capable and convinced man, he had resigned on the promise of a government of unanimity. When that was not forthcoming, he had sensed his vulnerability and made arrangements to leave his country. He was stopped at the airport. He turned himself in to the UN. Commenting on his demeanor on the eve of his resignation, Diego Cordovez, the former Undersecretary General of the United Nations who negotiated the Soviet withdrawal from Afghanistan, remarked in 1995: "He was not a scared or a nervous man; quite the contrary, he seemed serene, fully in control, and ready to face all the ominous eventualities that could follow the Soviet withdrawal."[61] In less than a year, the *Times* had written his epitaph: a flunky of Stalinism. A Swiss anthropologist had apparently noticed "primary school students changing out of their traditional clothes into their Western-style school uniforms while on the way to school."[62] In my fancy, that quick-change is grotesquely reversed in the difference between the smiling and plump Najibullah, dressed in suit and tie, shaking Gorbachev's hand – Gorbachev sold him out in the end – and the emaciated man, dressed in Afghani costume, hanging from the traffic post in Kabul. If we are to credit the second volume of the *Life*, Abd-ur Rahman had attempted to substitute trim European clothing for the voluminous attire of the male Afghan.[63] No translation from English to Pashto must ignore the translations from Pashto to English in an earlier dispensation. And the woman is elsewhere, even on this terrain.

In the New World Order, where there is only North and South rather than East and West, it is impossible for a new state to escape the constraints of a "neo-liberal" world economic system which, in the name of Development, removes all barriers between itself and fragile national economies. And then the disappearance of the state is deplored as a sign of racial inferiority, and indeed, accountability is shifted from the state to a self-selected international civil society that looks for "freedom" for the implicitly racially inferior folks – inaugurating a new era of good imperialism, otherwise known as world governance.[64] As we have seen, the advance guard of world governance is often information and communication technology, and the alibi often women. On the other hand, as I have stated above, the actual, although remotely potential front against these forces is located in a subalternity condemned (or celebrated, depending upon your politics) as a mere enclave of tradition, or ignorance. In fact it is upon this terrain that the resistance to "Development" has been organizing. Since resistance to "Development"-as-an-alibi-for-exploitation is by no means a refusal of development as such, its connection with the (ab-)use of the Enlightenment – reconstellation from below and in the interest of gender equity – should by now be clear. The only bulwark against the rear-and-plunge of unregulated competition and monopoly fostered by the three controlling global agencies – the World Bank, the International Monetary Fund, and the World Trade Organization – is a reinvention of the accountability into which a responsibility-based ethical system must repeatedly appear as determining, with all the risks attendant upon translation. Without this the well-meaning arrogance of enforcing Human *Rights* is a pathetic reliance upon the Enlightenment notion that an ennobled sense of self will not be able to brook the suffering of the other. This effort at reinvention animates the persistent short-term initiatives of local self-management that run interference against the financialization of the globe, which become possible through a politics that brings subalternity to crisis.[65] This is where we locate the long-term double-sided effort of rural literacy, building not only for struggle against political oppression, but for a sustainable future as well, where what is being sustained is not the expanding limits of global capital alone. It is thus that we place together the concept that in the New World Economic Order the new state is obliged to veer away from any redistributive functions, and the metaphor that postcolonial culture must actively mourn the pre-colonial, which has remained so long without funeral rites. In my fancy, Najibullah was trying to provide a means to educate the people of Afghanistan to want a public sphere, and to mourn a violent past. We supplement it by reminding his ghost of subalterns, of women, *if* we deserve that haunting. It is hard: for the languages are Farsi (Abd-ur Rahman), Urdu (Mahfuz Ali), Pashto (Najib)! This is where British colonialism is an enabling violation; it provides a connection, as did something called "Communism," with Najib. I go scrounging in the field of "enabling violations" and pick up the structure of the state as site of accountability – a thing to be effortfully reinvented, against the depredations of cultural conservatism and mere nationalism.[66]

In 1996 I felt that if one went below the big NGO networks, the very texture of everyday tugs of war would convince one that, because these local initiatives in fact ran interference with transnational capitalism and are therefore of global impact, it is not possible for the postcolonial state, mortgaged to the global agencies in the New World Order, to take the main initiative. Therefore, I then thought, the so-called New Social Movements must build up an alternative inter-nationality that will stand behind the state. Today, with the global movements appropriated by the international civil society, "standing behind" the decimated and repressive state has little purchase. What follows must therefore be read as fears realized: Here again, we see a difference between claiming rights as an end and valuing the right to the insertion into responsibility to the ecobiome – to Nature seen as containing human species-life, rather than opposing human species-being.[67] For the subaltern of the South, the issue is not conservation and recycling, it is ecological survival through claiming responsibility to Nature. The sacredness of animist space can prove a liberation theology, but not if it is museumized from above, only if we learn space as a name of absolute alterity, an alterity that is effaced as it is disclosed in the difference between Gross National Product and Gross Natural Product.[68] These words may also be too late. Environmental issues are being defined by way of the security paradigm. Soon they will be another way of legitimizing Northern interventionism.[69]

(Incidentally, developing subsistence and small- and large-market farming, which is a practical outcome of such efforts, is important for the constitution of the subject for academic and democratic freedom in another way as well.[70] Without such a support system, a large part of the population is obliged to engage in migratory– rather than merely migrant – labor. I do not have to recount the soul-devastating effects of this cosmopolitanism. Let me say the obvious practical thing: if there is no class to teach for six months in the year, a literacy drive is hopeless. But today even this is jeopardized. In 2004, the consumer market in India is second only to that in Russia and foreign direct investment is actively solicited.[71] The bottom will remain good for vote-fodder alone. The relationship between this and the revolt of Cancún in 2003, where a new alliance – roughly Brazil, China, and India, agitated against Northern internal protectionism, must be taken into account in any extended consideration of these problems. All we can say here is that such interventions are impossible to imagine in Afghanistan today, which seems to be engaged in a simulacral and restricted constitutional patriotism, about which more below.)

Am I suggesting that academic and democratic freedoms, rather than inalienable formal rights of an already constituted "human being" who must be tacitly assumed to be undifferentiated and "naturally social," might, assaulted by the dynamics of globalization, be rethought within the paradigm of global Social Movements working to rescue the structure of the state? I am close to that. But does not such a suggestion transgress the very concept of a "freedom"? This is indeed the point I have been driving at in this section. It is this political insight that the "properly" postcolonial sector can hope to be ready to offer to Najibullah's ghostly and incomplete legacy.

Academic "freedom," like all rational formal freedoms, can only be exercised by its own transgression, by being "bound" to content. Pure "freedom" is "guaranteed" by the exercise of the constitution of a possible subject, already the commitment to a content. We in the United States have experience of a society of largely unexercised guarantees, a society just by default.[72] In the wake of 9–11, even this model no longer applies. Civil liberties are now actively threatened. We must continue, however, to think that a robustly just society is where the members, when acting self-consciously within rational and privative norms – never adequately possible – see freedoms not as ends but absolute means to protect their transgression, which is also their exercise. No justification of the *exercise* of (academic) freedom can be drawn from within (academic) freedom understood as "free" and without content.[73] It comes into being in its own binding. We cannot read Foucault – as offering a free rational argument guaranteed for application – without accounting for Najibullah. And the question of (academic) freedom in Afghanistan is more than ever compromised by the de facto Occupation.

A word here on the draft constitution of Afghanistan drawn up in 2003 in the wake of the Bonn Agreement of 2001. Its apparent matrix of "secular Islam" never confronts the contradictions between serving two masters within a "modern" constitutional framework. Women are mentioned only once. Considering that gender justice was one of the chief alibis for the US intervention, and that Amanullah's constitution perished on the question of female honor, this seems a lot of blood shed for a little security in the future. Female honor, as we have seen, was the weakest link in his grandfather's Farman. The Soviet constitution of Afghanistan bypassed the internal culture and placed women's agential equality within the cradle-to-grave welfare system. We have seen how this system is compromised on various fronts.

We have touched upon the consequences of Amanullah's constitution of 1923, modeled on the Napoleonic Code via the "Young

Turks," who internalized the admonitions of the legacy of imperialism in order to legitimize it by its reversal: nationalism. As has been abundantly pointed out, Marxist fundamentalism in Asia and Africa, finding in simplified doctrine the touchstone of political explanation, has also had unhappy consequences. In the Afghan case, Soviet intervention spawned, with the mediation of destructive violence, this latest constitution – now the US code rather than the earlier European attempts, first as internal class-generated support and, second, as offer of leadership. I should like to think that Najib's prison translation tried to undo this, even undo varieties of the Nasser-Qutb polarization.

After our reading of Abd-ur Rahman's firman, it should be clear why I insist on languages. Indeed, the authorities know it is an issue. On every page of the draft constitution is the caution: "Unofficial Translation. Please refer to official Pashtu and Dari texts for accuracy."[74] No one who reads Dari (an Afghan form of Farsi) or Pashtu because s/he does not know English will be able to understand the level of Dari used there, unless they are learned clerics, for whom the conceptual fabric will be alien. Often, the peculiarities of the Dari idiom suggest that an English "original" is being literally translated.[75] In the Preamble of the Constitution, the list of adjectival and adverbial clauses for "We the people of Afghanistan" contains, half way down the line, that very word "qawm," now given the US multiculturalist politically correct "translation" "ethnicity." Work it out – the located care of the Iron Amir to break the circle, take a step out, as contrasted with this careless imposition of a discursive history of politically correct metropolitan multiculturalism in the guise of a mere translation.[76]

Many years ago, as I was taking the first halting steps toward thinking gender and colonial productivity together, I was struck by the flattening out of the four part Hindu legal "system."[77] Articles 120, 130, 131 of the draft constitution offer examples of such flattening out of various schools of Islamic jurisprudence. I cannot offer a reading of the immense steamrolling, but experts can.

Finally, the peculiar place of "Islam" in the constitution. Secular Islam is a problem – primarily because the two parts of that phrase come from different universes of discourse. The space between them has been made inaccessible by violent politics. Abd-ur Rahman was trying, within his discursive framework, which combined the system of ethical convictions (*al din*) with the system of juridico-political action (*al dawla*), to fashion co-existence. To alter Bessie Head's mad

Elizabeth's words only with a different geographical proper name and a pluralization, he was trying to make his brothers (sisters are a different story), *as* Afghans, be just anyone.[78] And now, US puppets. For him, Afghanistan was more a state of mind to be created and fostered, since territorial boundaries were up for grabs with international powers. In my fancy, this difference is marked in the difference between *Afghanistan wahd wa yakporcha* (united and single Afghanistan) in the interim constitution, and its English "translation" – Afghanistan *is* a single and united *country*.

We do not celebrate the public spectacle in the *New York Times* which, removed from the uncontested authority of the European narrative, cannot produce "a history of the present," as Foucault promised. Unlike Damiens, who illustrates the story, Najibullah can be read as desperately trying to negotiate its elements. He cannot stand as an illustration of the abstract movements of electronic capitalism. How had he understood Marx as he was caught in the crossfire between Moscow and Washington, so that the last resort seemed to be to translate a "political" text that takes from "fiction" its model? Western Marxism either ignores this or gives a contemptuous answer; you will do neither. The paracolonial subject of academic freedom cannot afford merely to excoriate a governmentality whose benefits it quietly enjoys. Let us hope that the rural schools of Afghanistan will one day yield such subject-formation. In this essay, written five years before 9–11, I had closed in the name of a freedom in the future anterior, where translation of uncontested narratives is, as usual, necessary, impossible, and perhaps foredoomed. To end thus seems altogether more urgent now.

Chapter 5

Megacity – 1997: Testing Theory in Cities

In order to subsidize constant travel to devise a philosophy of education that would be practically accessible to rural teachers, an effort
described at length in "Righting Wrongs," I accept improbable invitations. I like interdisciplinarity. I am an autodidact. These gigs make
me learn things. It is thus that in January 1997 I found myself in
Hong Kong, speaking on megacities. Take this chapter as a trave-
logue, then, caught in a moment in the siliconization of Bangalore,
one among India's five megacities.

In Bangalore I encountered the social class described by Robert Reich
in an interview that year: "Electronic capitalism ... enables the most
successful to secede from the rest of society. It is now possible for top
level managers, professionals and technicians to communicate directly
with their counterparts around the world ..."[1] This secessionist culture
has many faces and they do not necessarily resemble each other. Many
of the children of the "model minorities" among New Immigrants to
the United States (who came after Lyndon Johnson relaxed quotas in
1965) now belong to this group. Members of the new "International
Civil Society" of collaborative non-governmental organizations, give
backing to this secessionist network, busily producing its human face:
universalist feminism is active here; we have seen its network connection in chapter 3. In Bangalore I met another kind. He was the Deputy
Managing Director and Director of Business Development of one of
the largest Indian software companies, a man who had perhaps just
touched 40, at the moment heavily jet lagged from a recent trip to the
US. This man gave me the usual potted account of why Bangalore
became the Silicon City of India. This is the view from the North of

the South, rather far from Armenia and Afghanistan. Much metropolitan radical literature collapses such differences.

In the late forties and early fifties, as India's map was being reshuffled immediately after Independence, a number of science institutes, such as the Indian Institute of Science and the Asian Institute of Development, were established. The Indian Institute of Advanced Studies was set in Bangalore, for reasons having as much to do with Bangalore's pre-colonial and colonial history (a small town with a developed civil structure) as with its climate and demography. This created a certain technical base which drew large national electronic firms under India's First Five Year Plan. In the late seventies and early eighties the industry shifted into software. The relationship between this and Lyndon Johnson's relaxing of the quota system remains to be investigated. Between 1971 and 1981, the growth rate of Bangalore was 76 percent, the fastest in Asia. Software companies – among them Digital, Hewlett-Packard, IBM, Verifone – reevaluated India as the place for software investment. Foreign companies who wanted to get their software developed in the Third World because of the "cheapness of labor"– a phrase that must be persistently unpacked by all global cultural studies persons – began to buy it in India instead of doing it themselves. (This scene is changing just now, but is beyond the scope of this book. We will continue with this slightly earlier history.) The relationship between this and the European Recession of 1973 as well as the electronification of the great international stock exchanges is now the prehistory of virtual money. In 1987 Texas Instruments moved in. It was the first company in India to use satellite communications. The cost of uplinking – $300,000 a year – to operate a circuit was prohibitive for indigenous capital. To lower this was the competitive lure. Here the plot of "secession from society" thickens. It was helpful that movements "internal to the industry" – another phrase for cultural unpacking – brought the cost down dramatically to about $30,000 per half-circuit.

(Although this actual player, my informant, brought up "cheap labor," a Cultural Studies activist from Bangalore said in March 2000 that there was "no working class" in the cyberindustry in India because it was "all software." This is of course "correct" if you are thinking nation-state. "No working class" can be compatible with "cheap labor" if "cheap labor" means software engineers working for one-tenth the salary of American counterparts who are upper-class by Indian standards. The problem is that cyberconsciousness is supposed to globalize nation-think into postnationalism. The fact that Southeast Asia *does* have a hardware-related mostly female working class means nothing to Cultural Studies in Bangalore, located in *South* Asia.)

In 1991 the Karnataka State Department of Electronics – in other words the public sector – established an Earth Station. And, already in the late eighties, Development Financial Institutions – "private" companies coordinated by the World Bank but with some government shares – began to set up venture capital by financing 15-year loans as seed capital for startup software companies.

Thus spoke a representative of the secessionist culture of Bangalore Silicon City. There are several thousand software managers in the City, mobile among the companies, who do not resemble the "average Indian," that impossible figure. (By silencing the anguished question of a woman broadly from this community, put to me during a discussion session – "Why do our children want an American identity rather than an Indian one?" – I am myself cutting off an immensely important question about gender division of labor in the culture of the megacity: for the husband business and globalization, for the wife childrearing and Americanization. The connection remains unmade.)

My informant, this relaxed good-looking man, going slightly thick in the middle with stress and easy living, described himself, in effect, as a member of the culture – very good telecom links abroad, traveling abroad incessantly, making a dollar salary but living in India, free to be globally mobile in skills, with aspirations clued in. If they live only virtually in the real space called Bangalore, the words "real" and "virtual" belong to an earlier semiotic. Every rupture is also a repetition.

No doubt software development is virtual, people in different places can work together without physical dislocation. Yet, this in itself is not virtuality in a completely new sense. The fact of working without physical dislocation is after all the selling point of homeworking, post-fordism, the breaking of the working class. And, looking at it another way, communication has always been tele-communication. Today its instrumentality has become indistinguishable from the circuits of finance capital. I have written of this elsewhere.[2]

In *Capital* I Marx described the entailed subject structure of capital – Foucault would call this an "assigned subject position" – via Goethe's *Faust* as "an animated monster which begins to 'work,' 'as if its body were by love possessed'" (C1 302). Marx's solution to this was a reconstellation of the position in the interest of redistribution, not a Luddite ego-idealism, as a postmarxist view might too easily suggest.

Marx wrote about industrial capitalism. Lenin shifted the base to point at the importance of commercial capital. Saskia Sassen suggested in her early work that authority and legitimacy have passed to the finance capital market, which she calls the "economic citizenship."[3] And, if Marx had described the subject-structure of industrial capital, we are here describing the subject of electronic secessionist culture, the Economic Citizen as "person," as a displacement of the Marxian system. S/he carries the entailed subject structure of the finance capital market. S/he trumps common or garden variety postfordism because her or his product is virtual. This is a displaced version of Marx's discussion of the special place of transport as industry in *Capital* 2, where the product is not the goods transported, but displacement itself (C2 135). My informant had not read this, of course. Like the radical left and the modern state, he also speaks of nation, or better, location. We have been project-based so far, he cried, our specifications laid out by others, and we produced to their requirements. Now we must make products according to our projects, call the shots. We have been global in customers, now we must be global in capital.

The southern citizen of the virtual megacity is deceived here. In the economically restructured postcolonial state, the barriers between the fragile economy of the state and international capital are being removed in the hot peace. As telecommunication grows into postmodernity, the dreams of decolonized modernity are being shut off by the crisis-management activities of the World Trade Organization. The protected economy written into the 1947–9 Nehru–Mountbatten Constitution of India would *de jure* allow the manufacture of semiconductor chips. Under economic restructuring, this hugely expensive undertaking, will be taken up by US-based entrepreneurs. We are talking about the place of the nation-state in the real space of the globe as it relates to the machinery of virtualization. Bangalore is not "really" only Silicon City. It is indeed the home of the third richest man in the world, who, despite his wealth, is still at the receiving end of global capital. And the ranking is ephemeral, exceptionalist.

Thus the "culture" or "subject" of the virtual megacity is not only diversified in the usual race-class-gendered way alone, but also capital-fractured in agency. The culture-subject-agent trinity remains as necessary as it is impossible. If the subject does not dream of the controlling agency of capital, capital does not move. In the intervening years, this subject's dream of capital control moved far enough to be perceived as threat. Outsourcing is a common concern at all levels. The weakening of the state-structure has been consolidated as Indian capital becomes

successfully global. Manmohan Singh, the finance minister who opened
the country to restructuring in 1991, has been Prime Minister since
2004. George W. Bush has given India limited entry into the nuclear
club in order to retain control over the nuclear balance of power in
West Asia. The subaltern is still not speaking.[4]

This particular concatenation of subject/agent was not then representative of "India." A year later I was at a Subaltern Studies conference
in Lucknow and used the words "electronic capitalism." Because of the
general sexism of a handful of Left conservatives at the conference, who
felt this phrase came from my US elitism, I was not given time to reply, but
did at least utter these words: if you had had a few people from Bangalore
at this conference, you would have known what electronic capitalism
means. Bangalore is not in India, it is the open end which goes way out of
a national left argument. You *cannot* know what is meant by what makes
you archaic. The city of Hyderabad has now entered the lists.

By November, 1999, the mainstream Left intellectual knew about
Bangalore, though the term "electronic capitalism" might still have
seemed alien. (Today they are well-acquainted with "globalization,"
without necessarily connecting it to that earlier description.) The
Bombay (subsequently Mumbai)-based *Economic and Political Weekly*
(*EPW*) produced a critique of the civil polity of Bangalore without
much concern for the cityscape or its special relationship to federal
funding as a megacity.[5] It is a good critique, and it establishes this
rupture as also a repetition, susceptible to classical Marxist analyses of
exploitation, as revised for postfordism and specific feminist analyses:
"[T]here is ... concern about whether developing countries will continue to occupy the same lower levels of the international division of
labour in IT [information technology] as they did in the more conventional sectors."[6] (There is now concern on the other side of the threat
of the opposite.)

I am not devoted to the cause of making every Marxist a poststruc-
turalist. I mention here some Derridian reminders of repetition-in-
rupture, strewn throughout his work, at least from the publication of
The Post Card, for a specific reason.[7] Artificial intelligence requires these
reminders in order that an inter-diction may be launched. An inter-diction in Roman Law was to come between two contenders to break up
a dispute. It is a convenient name for a practice that does not take sides,
but uses what is strategically important.

Here, then, are the Derridian reminders, digested in my own fashion: that the structures of tele-communication are already present as

residual elements in the cultural process, for all communication is structurally tele-communication, however slow. If one allows that the work of the psyche produces the "I," one may be able to grasp that that work can be described by more and more complex manifestations of the machinic potential of the silicon chip, that this meta-psychological work blurs the distinction between "natural" and "artificial." If the inter-diction is set to work, it can help grasp the inadvisability of accepting seductive promises of unmediated cyberliteracy as a shortcut to general education in developing countries. To elaborate this here would take us too far from the megacity, into Armenia, the Southern Caucasus, and Central Asia! For those with already existing post-structuralist sympathies, let me add that the Derridian work can revise and enhance the brilliant work of Saskia Sassen, when she claims a new instantaneous temporality for politics based on the Internet, or the category of "presence" for the visibility of formerly "invisible" resistance.)[8]

As I indicate above, the activities of UNESCAP must complicate this grid.

The editorial in *EPW*, fairly representative of the liberal left in India, ignores the fact that urban development in Bangalore, one of the five Indian megacities, is supposed to be funded largely by the central government. When, therefore, *EPW* comments: "State governments and urban development bodies are investing vast amounts in providing infrastructural support – infotech parks with hi-tech communication networks and wired up residential colonies," it may be ignoring a much broader fact than that "broader social and welfare issues ... are not being addressed with adequate seriousness." That fact is globalization: global electronic capitalism steps in to manage the affairs of the *nation*-state as it helps build an infrastructure for its own optimal functioning and no more. Here the field includes the so-called rural theater. As I have already said in the opening of this chapter, I am not an expert here. I therefore offer my "experience," in the absolute confidence that the writings of experts such as Sassen and Vandana Shiva will bear me out.[9] The argument, as I have repeatedly made it elsewhere, runs something like this.

The non-Eurocentric New Social Movements, working for ecological agriculture against biopiracy, for women's general health and infrastructurally supported family planning against pharmaceutical dumping and population control – to name only two fronts – are rural and local by some residual binary opposition that cannot go beyond the new buzzword "glocal." These movements directly confront the global and produce the inter-diction between global and local. World-systems theories locating the emancipatory potential of these movements still chart a systemic telos for them. In fact, the movements operate an inter-diction between the repressive and/or decimated state and the often exploitative agenda of the self-styled International Civil Society. To think a systemic telos is to forget that these movements arise because of the weakening of the state in globalization. To place uncritical faith in an international civil society is to forget that the claim to internationality endorses the weakening of the state and therefore of constitutional redress on the part of resistant groups when the transnational agencies discriminate among nation-states in terms of their shifting location on the grid of geopolitics and the financialization of the globe. Once again the Group of Seven – globalized – can work in the interest of globalization by dealing with the Group of 77 on an uneven nation-state basis. (In the middle of the first decade of the twenty-first century, the power-blocs have shifted, but uneven nation-state development as a base of action has not. I am keeping these parenthetical updatings at a minimum. Even so, it should give the reader an idea of the importance of transnational literacy as a continuing task. This kind of work is a persistent economy of repetition and rupture.) The place of "nationalism" for the ground-level resistant groups, as a precarious resistant catachresis, has not yet been theorized. The postcolonial "rural," often separated from nation-think in coloniality and postcoloniality, is its theater. This is because, as the early work of the Subaltern Studies group has shown, in much of Asia and Africa, the peasant was not integrated into thinking of himself as part of a "nation" at the time of the national liberation struggles. The struggle was on the terrain, to quote Lenin's famous phrase, of "the progressive bourgeoisie." Therefore the nationalism on behalf of the weakened state in globalization for the redress of the virtualization of the rural can be distinguished from earlier anti-colonial manifestations that often lead today to a justification for religious nationalism. This is abundantly visible, as in a theater – to borrow a metaphor from global war. It is also the task of theory to make rationally visible what the so-called authority of experience may hide. Speaking an urbanist post-state globality is to forget that task: the task of persistently keeping a functioning state free of mere nationalism, the task of fostering a desire for critical regionalism.

Here's the scene: the actual *networks* of the loosely strung social movements spanning many nation-states in the South entertain nationalism on the way to internationalism. The great bourgeois movements for *national* liberation largely left the rural poor alone. The *trans-national* agencies still count the state as a separable guarantor as the databasing, patenting, and genetic devastation of the rural mediates the virtual and the real. Thus "nation"-talk must now emerge again as an always risky moment in the consolidation of these inter-dictions. The "nation" is under erasure (crossed out but visible) if the rural and urban are put in inter-diction. Indeed, unlike religion, nation-talk on this register cannot mobilize into the kind of conflict that may serve as reason for military intervention in the name of Human Rights; for the goal of these movements is global, and nation may contradict more archaic identity-claims. These movements are in a space of cultural difference but separated from metropolitan culturalism by their class alliances. The triumphalist manifest destiny position of the United States as last resort of "cultural rights" cannot help the project of making-visible this concatenation of resistance, and indeed helps define its terrain as nothing but "cases" of state-based or cultural human rights violations. They deserve a more responsible reading: that in the appropriate sectors of the South – and South Asia is one such – the imperatives should be broadened to take in the rural-global rather than only the national-urban as the determinant. For the fashioning of the general will for the real space of the megacity is in the interest of the virtual, consolidated not only by the destruction of biodiversity but by the incursion of foreign capital into the agricultural sector, making it even easier for foreign companies to buy land. What does resistance look like here? Among the items included on the Bangalore megacity project that year was an international airport. There was a hearing scheduled on January 13 and Babu Mathew, a law professor who is also a labor activist, assured me that exploitative land acquisition for this project would probably be halted through a favorable judgment. (In the event, the airport was not built. The existing one was "modernized.") Yet Professor Matthew was solemn. "Why?" I asked.

His answer should warn us against vanguardist romanticization of collective memory. The workers and organizers were of course euphoric about the legal victory. But in fact the small landowners had been completely won over by the mega-prices offered by the Development Financial Institution. So the mere halting of the construction of the airport was no more than a skirmish. The bigger battle had been lost. A voluntary basis of support for the World Bank as it coordinated private capital had been gained. Any of us who have confronted the World Bank and other transnational agencies in public know that we are silenced in this way: The poor Bangaloreans want it, who are you? This is the construction of the general subaltern will for the virtual megacity.

In the strictest sense, the "rural" is the inter-diction of the local and the global-in-urban-space. The play of electronic capital blurs their binary division. As all global "people's alliances" know, and as I have already argued, biopiracy, seed-patenting, genetic engineering, pharmaceutical dumping by way of chemical fertilizers (the list could go on) make the rural so fertile a database today, that it is a direct front of the global on virtual terms. The megacity initiative, in all its forms, tries to lift the inter-diction, gives the urban a "proper" access to globality via the electronic, and transforms the "rural" into a metaconstitutive outside for the "urban." Hence Babu Mathew's gloom.

The local urban vision – both official and resistant – seemed remote from the global. The municipal vision of the megacity project is sectorialized. The City Development planners use land use plans – the metropolitan authorities use structural plans. The land marked for the international airport had no water. Let us build dykes as in Holland, said the high-level government official, even as he admitted that this was unreal. But, he continued, it would be easier to build because half the land is owned by the government. This land is Reserve Forest, and the problem is water! And so on. Such sectorialized judgments have little to do with the "professionally popular idea [of] ... the megaform, in which the city is one single, vast, three dimensional structure, instead of being separate elements, supported directly on the earth."[10] Sectorial judgments depend on questions of budget allocations. The only general point in the uniform guidelines handed down by the Central Government to these five altogether heterogeneous cities – Bangalore, Chennai, Kolkata, Hyderabad, Mumbai – is that 50 percent of the investment be coordinated through global tenders, by those development financial institutions that work on behalf of the secessionist culture of the virtual megacity.

The Indian vision of the megacity was then the city-state of Singapore. Following this model, the floor space to height ratio of public buildings was changed in Bangalore and encroached further upon the so-called slums. "Slum clearance" or "new townships" are megacity projects in both Bangalore and Kolkata. Hong Kong was discussed, even by fairly low-level government functionaries as a colonial city-state confronting the problem of reinsertion into a nation-state. But the reverse problem of the Singaporeanization of Indian "megacities" was never discussed. I visited a public forum of resistant architects. The alternative to Singapore-talk seemed peculiarly "cultural."

What sort of cultural forms should Indian architects use as models? I have suggested elsewhere that the use of the word "culture" in radical multiculturalist struggle is comparable to Foucault's use of the word "Power": "to name a complex strategic situation in a particular society" (CPR 353). Radical resistance to globalization uses "culture" similarly, except with a 180 degree turn. "Culture" is a word that suggests motives beyond reason. In migrancy it is used to cover a desire to enter a civil society whose felicitous subjectship is claimed by Anglo or Anglo-Clone supremacists. In postcoloniality it is used to discuss access to an unmarked modernity, for the Western is "modern," and culture is "traditional."

The government is, of course, resolutely "modern." Charles Correa's culturalist Urban Commission Report was quietly dropped by the Indian Planning Commission in 1987, the year Texas Instruments moved into Bangalore.

Prem Chandavarkar, my friend the resistant architect, knows better; but as associate in a successful, Bangalorean architectural firm, he is hounded by the question of cultural models for an unmarked modernity. When left to theorize in peace, he produces a theory of architecture as absorbing rather than intending meaning, a critical version of the split between intention and consequence. And, when he leaves his office to resist, he engages in making accountable the 74th Amendment to the Indian constitution, the Nagar-Palika Act, and locates in the ward, the smallest urban unit, the desired unit of local self-management. The Nagar-Palika Act, pugnaciously local, is resolutely sidetracked by municipal authorities and ignored or sabotaged by the trans-national agencies.

Yet, just as the question of cultural models leads away from unmarked modernity, the urban ward-based resistance fails to create a city-base. Babu Mathew, the activist Law Professor, notices that, at the moment, the looming problems of housing, transport, health, education, although understood by vanguardist radicals, were not a need felt by the workers. They have had too little too long. Land, only land, was seen as a problem and the trans-nationals were solving it. Construction of a general will. One agenda is in a residual binary with that "rural" South, the persistent undoing of the "urban" South mediating the virtual megacity into real space: to a futurism that only appears to be Luddite. Professor Mathew's phrase, for activating this resistant binary, is strategy-driven rather than crisis-driven globalization. At this stage, and to repeat, the strategy called for seems to be a persistent critical regionalism.

For the non-Eurocentric New Social Movements alone can no longer be an invisible corrective for the International Civil Society. The point is not to locate the ward as the smallest unit of urban self-development, but to broaden the perspective into the local as interrupting the global. The good NGOs – people's alliances – are the ones that have enough momentum to continue on, in however limited a way, if aid stops. They can become regionalist in scope. Resistance would be organized clear out of party politics. As a result of what I have summarized all too briefly, radical architects as well as the municipality might do well to rethink the rural as they try to hold on to the city as city. The rural is not trees and fields any more. It is always on the way to data.

It is our hope that if imperatives are thus shifted, the task (in so far as the architect has a task) – of constructing culture (in so far as it is possible, or necessary and impossible) – will of course run texturally by "the old rules" judged in its setting to work, as does all accountability. We will at least not confuse US nationalism with the (benevolent) global as such. A classless vision of ecological justice made in the USA is hopelessly inadequate to come to grips with the spectralization of the rural.

(In 1997, in a world not yet ravaged visibly by the undoing of the difference between the malevolent "bad" imperialism of war and the benevolent "good" imperialism of reconstruction, I had more hope. Now it seems that without the persistent reinvention of the state as structure, shared regionally, those moral undertakings have little chance of real survival.)

In the first chapter, we have read about the impossible project of educating against such dangers as the fabrication of a general will to mediate between the virtual and real megacity, against the obliteration of the globalizing inter-diction.[11] I have hinted at its necessity by way of Derrida, above. Here I remind you that the trip to Bangalore was undertaken to collect material for the conference in Hong Kong that was subsidizing one among many voyages in the interest of labor-intensive work for this project. The trip to Bangalore was thus doubly instrumental, and to that extent a remote and idiosyncratic constitutive outside for that unrepresentative corner of aboriginal India, where Kolkata seems an altogether luxurious metropolis. But the entryway is caught in idiom, and there are no guarantees. That corner cannot enter the space of this essay. Thus whatever critique I offer of the megacity as custodian of globalization is restricted in scope.

I live in New York, which thinks of itself as a megacity because of the growing diversity of its inhabitants, and its command of the world financial as well as cultural scene. Yet the size of the subdivision at the ground plane is so much richer than the height of buildings on an urban block in New York that technically, the old description of New York as a bunch of neighborhoods is still in the running. There is indeed an ongoing virtualization of the City, an effort to reconstruct it as the nexus of electronic capital, as the recent redoing of Times Square, and general rezoning, bears witness. But New Yorkers are fighting to sustain the older definition, even as they change its class-composition. That struggle, in all its ramifications, is theorized in Rosalyn Deutsche's *Evictions*.[12] Even as the odd newspaper article reports artists as caught between the homeless and the gentry, the artist himself offers Brooklyn as the new Left Bank – P.S.1 trumping the Whitney Museum.[13] Eurocentric economic migrants mingling with old minorities is the culture of old New York, rewritten. Let it be a site of conflict for the forces of the megacity. In this respect, I still remain a bit retro, I guess.

Cut to another scenario and another player, from my second home-town to my first. The government of India, the so-called modern post-colonial state, has five megacity projects. These include the two new silicon cities – Hyderabad and Bangalore – but also the three old colonial Presidency capitals – Chennai, Kolkata, Mumbai. Upon this palimpsest, with its own historical ironies, there is also the peculiar clash of the old sectorialized bureaucratic vision of the named "megacity project" and the forces of globalization.

I am from Kolkata, which is a designated megacity. And there are certainly members of the aspiring secessionist class inhabiting (if that's the word) real Kolkata space as well. Yet Kolkata is still perhaps an example of how nation-state particularities remain pertinent to the universalizing thrust of the discourse of the megacity. Often it is because the native informants are unwilling or incapable to take such particularities into consideration that we dismiss them as archaic. And of course *Kolkata 300* lacks the superficial glamor and patter of silicon alley journalism.[14]

Here then is my concluding experience-talk, back in my first home-town. The person at the Kolkata Metropolitan Development Authority who was most knowledgeable about the Ford Foundation's finally abortive attempt to civilize Kolkata since the sixties was also the only person in my entire amateur fieldwork who asked me: "What is an academic definition of a megacity?" I phoned him from Hong Kong and said the jury was still out.

Kolkata is in the state of West Bengal, run by a left coalition government for over 30 years. It has not been a most favored state for the central government. The megacity deal, with its special relationship to central funding, is not run with particular enthusiasm here, though under the pressure of globalization, the city is giving way. By all accounts, the state government has done well with the rural five-member self-government units. (If I retreated to that unrepresentative corner of aboriginal India, where Kolkata seems an altogether luxurious metropolis, this success would become crosshatched with prejudice, but that is too micrological.) This is old real-space town and country relationship. Rural West Bengal is not as strikingly prey to global spectralization as rural Bangladesh. Monocultures and fertilizers came here with an earlier wave of "Green Revolution," not as engulfingly because of the state's leftist economic structure. Resistance is not strongly organized and the effects of globalization are felt less keenly in the rural sector. There is no West Bengali working class in New York City.[15] (The rural is now the theater of a violent industrialization that this book cannot encompass.)

I continue to feel a clandestine comfort that the megacity-effect is resisted in New York and Kolkata is somewhat resistant to it. It is the terminal comfort of a person out of joint with the times.

Postscript

The jury is still out. In the meantime, experts seem to define the megacity in two ways: first, simply as cities with megapopulations; and secondly as cities connected by the virtual network of telecommunication. What was noticeable in India was that the central government was making an attempt to share in the international or global pull of the second definition above. In the chapter I have made the point that government bureaucracy seemed not to be fully aware of the forces with which it had to contend. Reading about megacities in the international context, it is clear that the state is not in the running at all. The country-to-city scenario of progress has long been taken for granted. The new twist seems to be the absence of the nation-state. This is where the Indian example is interesting, although the competition between "city-states" and the nation-state figures there as well. These city-states are different from the classical examples in that they form a global network.

The theorists claim that virtuality has achieved an epistemic revolution. These new sociologists of knowledge suggest that, as a result of
the explosive advances in information technology, our very way of
knowing, our very way of intuiting space and time, have changed.
The most noticeable thing is the absence of the rural from this
advance. And yet, the constant transformation of "the rural" into data
in the field of genetic engineering, the line between virtuality and the
terrain is constantly deconstructed. I have called this "inter-diction" in
the body of the chapter. If we look at rural as "place" rather than
"space" (Castells's distinction), the Indian example offers the Panchayat
solution, the five-person body for local self-government selected by
direct popular election. The Nagar-Palika Act, mentioned above,
brings this structure into city governance. Here the state tries to raise
as many obstructions as possible, since direct elections are a threat to
political ambition.

On the other side, in New York City, there are attempts to bring about
quality of life changes through non-governmental initiatives. The best-
known among them, Janice Perlman's Mega-Cities Project,

> concentrates its efforts to make cities more socially just, ecologically
> sustainable, politically participatory and economically vital in four high-
> priority areas: 1. Environmental Regeneration (toward circular systems
> for water, sanitation, garbage, food, and energy). 2. Poverty and Income
> Generation (toward alleviating poverty and strengthening the informal
> sector). 3. Decentralization and Democratization (toward greater local
> participation in planning, service delivery, resource allocation, and
> urban management). 4. Women's Empowerment and Well-Being (toward
> greater choice, access, and voice).[16]

Would such old-fashioned attempts qualify as within the postmodern
episteme of the real (virtual) megacity dwellers, celebrated by Castells
and others?

I had thought "Megacity" was an occasional piece, written to facilitate the attempts to build another Asia. Now it seems that this may
well be the wedge that breaks Asia apart – into the network of global
cities and the rest receding. This too is an "othering." In spite of Castells's
argument that culturalism is a reaction to this, metropolitan diasporic
culturalism is actually comfortable with this development, especially when
it is connected to the new global museal practice. In the next chapter,
I unpack this comfort as, myself: a metropolitan diasporic subject.

Chapter 6

Moving Devi – 1997:
The Non-Resident and
the Expatriate

This chapter describes the difference between the broad-stroke culturalism of the upwardly mobile immigrant Indian and/or the South Asian art historian on the one hand, and my own jumbled cultural productions on the other, nostalgic for the rural woman, struck by the strength of destitute widows. If the reader finds ingredients for religious violence here, I can only say this: you can find such ingredients anywhere. Censoring the religious produces more violence than these scattered ruminations of mine, which start from the fact that there was a lavish show at the Smithsonian. Perhaps in what follows there was even an attempt to show how unrestrained cultural studies might be, if left to the diasporic, in this case myself. Perhaps it was a feeling that all speculations on religion should not be confined to the Abrahamic. The piece was written at a relatively less menaced time, before the outbreak of violence in Gujarat, before the events of September 11, 2001, but after the demolition of Babri Masjid, about which I wrote in "Love, Cruelty, and Cultural Talks in the Hot Peace."[1] I'll try harder next time to be politically absolutely correct. For now, I invite the Hindu Right to read my piece on secularism.[2]

Moving Devi: Meera Nanda, This Is To Save "Hindu" Culturalism From Hindutva![3]

"Moving Devi" is linked to "Can the Subaltern Speak?" The link between the two essays is a life-link.

In "Can the Subaltern Speak?" I had tried to engage pre-colonial Indic material for the first time. It meant pushing away my allegiance to "French theory." To keep working with Derrida, I had to endorse him, to make sure he survived my new engagement with that new material, which I saw, not as identity, but as making use of the extra-curricular "knowledge" I had because of the accident of birth. I knew nothing of the Indic material in a disciplinary mode. I proceeded with my serviceable Sanskrit and little else. I located the "subaltern" in the middle class, in which I was myself "responsible." The essay itself was a resolute suppression of the autobiographical, in ways that I have subsequently revealed.[4]

By contrast, in "Moving Devi," some 17 years later, the Western stuff is digested, for better or for worse. It does not oppress, it is not a thing to quarrel with. I am also at ease with the Indic material, not a little because of the calm guidance and encouragement of my late friend, Bimal Krishna Matilal, whose name I will take again in the essay proper. I am no longer beset by the need to occlude the traces of the irreducibly autobiographical in cultural speculation of this sort. It will be harder to take sides now. There are many subalterns in the pages of this essay, their speech is still unheard, but not one of them resembles me.

In 1998, I was asked to write an essay for the catalogue accompanying an exhibition on the great goddess (Devi) at the Arthur M. Sackler gallery in Washington. "Moving Devi" emerged in response. A shorter version was published in the catalogue.[5] This unwieldy hybrid essay is as much about the authority of autobiography in the problem of reading as was "Can the Subaltern Speak?" although the earlier essay was not yet ready to betray this. My understanding of the autobiographical subject is a position without identity. How that computes in the writing is for you to judge.

I have just been reading a lot of writing samples for a postcolonial position. It seems that many younger scholars now refer to metropolitan migrant writers as "subaltern." Yet Gandhi and Nehru were not "subalterns" for the Subaltern Studies Collective.[6] (It goes without saying that the historians themselves did not claim subalternity.) The term "subaltern" has lost its power to indicate people from the very bottom layer of society excluded even from the logic of the class-structure. This may indeed be one of the reasons why I take the museum visitor from the model minority – sometimes myself – as a constituted subject that forgets the other in its haste to claim otherness, only with reference to the metropolitan majority.[7]

Every critical conviction persuades me that if I were representative of anything, I would not know that I was. Yet, surely, I must at least represent the passage, in migration, from *ethnos* to *ethnikos* – from being home to being a resident alien – as I write on the great goddess as she steps into a great US museum? I will allow "myself" to occupy this stereotype as I think about her. Surely it is because of this stereotype that I was asked to be part of the catalogue?

I have moved from a Hindu majority in the center of Hinduism to a Hindu minority in a new imperialist metropolis where Hinduism was, until the day before yesterday, in the museum. Yesterday, when the active polytheist imagination accessed the mind set of the visitor in the museum, a colloidal solution, shaken up between here and there, was surely secreted? I want to ruminate upon this transference from care-less participant to uneasy observer. I speak of Devi, from somewhere upon this transference-circuit, not as an expert among experts.

I have no disciplinary access to knowledge about knowledge upon this topic. I must write of/from that frailer base – "making sense." I am an educated "native informant," the peculiar subject of metropolitan multiculturalism. I must destabilize the constitution of the Devi as yes-terday's object of investigation. I must not say what standard textbooks say: "The Great Goddess, or Maha-Devi as she is known in India, burst onto the Hindu religious stage in the middle of the first millennium of the Christian era."[8] That is yesterday's talk. I am in the history of the (globalizing) present. I must let foolish common sense interrupt the power of knowledge and declare: "There is no great goddess."[9] When activated, each goddess is the great goddess. That is the secret of poly-theism. Intellectual Hinduism – to speak of it thus in the singular is to assume too much – seeks to emphasize its monotheist, monist, jurid-ico-legal singular version. A certain line of Hindu thought has striven to see the polytheist moment as a more or less divine and playful alle-gory of the philosophico-theological. With Buddhism, that moment seems to become altogether extra-orbitant, until Mahayana Buddhism brings it back in.[10]

For some of us, the more interesting aspect of this impulse is its replication in varieties of the dominant – orthodox Brahminism, Puranic syncretism or, finally, semitized reform Hinduisms reactive to the British. If today's metropolitan immigration is linked to this chain of displacements, the effort of the "Hindu-majority-model-minority" is to reconstellate this something called Hinduism as "a living heritage as ancient as it is modern."[11]

These displacements signify great waves of cultural politics. Does "being in a culture" bring with it a special way of feeling in thinking? Twenty five years ago, Raymond Williams thought that the way to observe culture where it is in the making is through "structures of feeling."[12] And more recently Derrida has reread Marx's thought within his own (and Marx's) Abrahamic cultural fix of messianicity – the possibility of welcome structuring the human as human.[13] Can we make some such claim for a "Hindu" way of viewing, thinking of it "culturally" rather than from within a system of belief? Common sense tells us that any such claim is necessarily behind the time of its possibility. Surrendering ourselves to that inescapable necessity – that we cannot break through into the vanishing present – let us venture a guess as to what an everyday polytheist structure of feeling might be.[14]

I am drawing now upon my conversations with the late Professor Matilal, who was one of the greatest international authorities on Hindu religious and philosophical culture. Discussing the *Mahābhārata* with him, I had suggested that the active polytheist imagination negotiates with the unanticipatable yet perennial possibility of the metamorphosis of the transcendental as supernatural in the natural. To my way of thinking, this seemed to be the secret of the *dvaita* structure of feeling: the unanticipatable emergence of the supernatural in the natural – the tenacious dog on the mountain path is suddenly King Dharma for Yudhisthira in the last Book of the *Mahābhārata* – rather unlike any sustained notion of incarnation. Perhaps this is why the Sanskrit word for "incarnation" (*avatār*) – has nothing to do with "putting on flesh." It means rather – "a come-down [being]." Everything around us is, after all, "come-down," if we assume an "up-there."

It is not too fanciful to say that a possible *dvaita* "structure of feeling," if there are such structures, would be the future anteriority of every being as potentially, unanticipatably, *avatār* in the general sense. It is within this general uneven unanticipatable possibility of *avatarana* or descent – this cathexis by the ulterior, as it were, that the "lesser" god or goddess, when fixed in devotion, is as "great" as the greatest: *ein jeder Engel ist schrecklich.* How did Rilke know? Perhaps "culture" is semi-permeable by the imagination?[15]

In Mahasweta Devi's lovely story "Statue," a passage about Manosha, a late Puranic almost-human snake-goddess, catches my drift. Manosha, although a minor goddess, is everything for her particular protégés: "The brass Manosha, with her wide-open indifferent brass pop-eyes, has been hearing the prayers of devotees for two hundred years. She hears them still."[16] For the families Manosha had devastated previous to this passage, she was the presiding goddess of the household and, when in action, she was the great goddess, the goddess of everything. The dark consequences of a *dvaita avatarana* – where the moment is sustained into stabilized worship of an unfortunate young female person – are represented in Satyajit Roy's 1960 film *Devi*.

When I first read about the Greek pantheon and its division of labor in college, I therefore had a problem. Was not each god or goddess the god or goddess of everything when s/he was cathected in devotion or worship?[17] I felt convinced that the commentators had got it wrong, for they did not know polytheism in cultural practice. The difference between "Greece" and "India" seemed only knowledge, unsustained by the responsibility of experience. The authority of autobiography (as well as knowledge) must remain forever problematic because that binary opposition does not hold at the limit, either way.

Our word is *dvaita* (two-ness, with the secondary meaning of doubt – in this case about the stability or constancy of the apparent), not *poly-theist*. Since *each* other being is the only other being, there are always only two, not many. For the *dvaitin* or twoness-minded, radical alterity is in an impossible invagination in every instance of the other.

Invagination. When you think anything can be contaminated by the super-natural, by alterity, "[i]t is precisely [by] a principle of contamination, a law of impurity, a parasitical economy." Para-sitically to the merely "real," alongside its ecology, runs this unanticipatable possibility of alteration. "A participation without belonging – a taking part in without being a part of ... the boundary of the set comes to form, by invagination, an internal pocket larger than the whole."[18] The super-natural in the pocket of the natural, *dvaita/advaita* in action, a structure of feeling folded in, again and again, to alterity.

In usual cultural explanations, classical and modern, the austere transcendentalization of radical alterity in Indic monism is made to coexist with these invaginated representations of the quick-change into alterity by way of an argument from allegory. I am suggesting that the relationship is ironic rather than allegorical, if by irony is understood "the permanent parabasis of an allegory (of the *advaita*) ... the systematic undoing, in other words, of the abstract."[19] The politics of polytheism as the politics of relative subalternity, as it were. The *dvaita* episteme or mindset, the "structure of feeling" that shelters the invaginated radical other as perhaps already descended in what surrounds us, interrupts *advaita*. And an *advaita* or non-dual impulse establishes itself imperfectly when a cathected god or goddess occupies the entire godspace.

"*Dvaita*" and "*advaita*," especially the latter, are here being used as common nouns. With or without the "allegorical" explanation, they (especially *advaita*) have been perceived as proper names of doctrinal *ensembles* that are, at best, in a binary relationship, offering historical possibilities of openness and/or closure in response to their negotiations with the profane, at all social levels. Indeed, a more dialectical vocabulary of forms of appearance (*Erscheinungsformen*) of essential structural relationships (*Verhältnisse*), would probably fit the case better. However that complex binary is perceived, the idea being advanced here is that perhaps the *dvaita* and the *advaita* are also lowercase names of a sleight of mind, a cultural mind-trick where the outlines bleed into each other in the mode of a permanent possibility of a parabasis in the future anterior. The *dvaita* will have pierced the *advaita* already, perhaps; and vice versa, asymmetrically. It is in this structure of feeling that devi(s), and deva(s) too, of course, have their spectral being.

Thus in the structure of feeling-thinking, the attempt is not only at the transcendentalization of the figure of radical alterity, which is all that is evident if we examine comparable movements among peoples of the Book. The polytheist moment (not invariably identical with the *dvaita/advaita* [non]relationship) is not often invoked there, except as an originary violent female pre-history, before binaries can be launched. Freud is of course the most monumental example, but other instances can be found.[20] Our suggestion has been that, in an effort to stabilize the future anterior, "Hindu" polytheist cultural practice attempts to *presentize* the uneven but permanent parabasis of the natural by the supernatural, thus making phenomenality resonate with its transcendent double, where the double (*dvi*) stands for an indefiniteness that is not merely the opposite of one as many. That originary indefiniteness is celebrated in the fact that the one itself is *a-dvaita* – non-dual – rather than singular.

Let us now examine an extreme and eloquent case, where the *advaita* is the abstract God of Islam:

> Let the lips utter non-stop
> *La ilaha illella* [the Islamic credo: There is no greater God than God]
> The Lord's prophet sent this law.
>
> But keep form and name as one
> In spirit, and say it over thus.
> If you call without form-sign
> How will you know your Lord?
> [translation mine]

This is Lalan Shah Fakir (1774–1890), chief among Bengali counter-theological lyricists. The hazy margins of South Asian Islam will yield other examples. What is important on the track of the Devi is the possibility that, when the *dvaita* interrupts the abstract, the feminine enters.[21] If Lalan can interrupt his abstract and imageless Lord with the *dvaita* urge to *rupa* (manifestation, "form" in my translation), he is a step away from suggesting, in another song, that Khadija – Muhammad's eldest wife – is Allah: *je khodeja shei to khoda*, that one cannot determine the coordinates of Prophet and Lady separately: *ke ba nobi ke ba bibi*, that it is a marriage of transaction between the same and the same, othered. Not formless (*nirakar*) but one-formed: *ekkarete moharana*.

As Muhammad's chief wife, Khadija is here the chief goddess, as it were. She is chief player in the play of *advaita/dvaita* in Lalan's hymn. But this is tightly structured poetic counter-theology. The *dvaita* impulse is at work to mark out (or in) the borders of Islam. The 14 wives of the Prophet are suddenly the 14 worlds of Indic mythology, without any attempt at establishing allegoric continuity. Lalan is no blasphemer. Three of the wives were before the *kalema*; before, that is, the Islamic revelation. And therefore it is of the 11 within Islam that Lalan the Islamic *dvaitin* sings: *egaro jon dasya bhabe Lalan koi kore upashona*: Lalan says that the 11 worship in the servant's way.

Lalan writes this scene of woman within the script of *bhakti* or devotion, widely recognized as a historical challenge from within to the caste-fixed inflexibility of high Hinduism.[22] *Bhakti*, creating affective links between the subject and the invaginated radical alterity of the *dvaitin* mindset, inscribes and assigns the subject's position within a taxonomy of phenomenal affect: the word literally invokes this taxonomic division. When Lalan iconizes the 11 wives of Muhammad as worshiping him in the servant's way, he is not guilty of *naturalistic* sexism. He is speaking rather of the various assigned subject-positions within the text of *bhakti*, themselves undoubtedly related to the highly detailed taxonomy of the *rasas* (names of implied affective responses to texts) available within the general Indic aesthetic.[23] *Dasya* or servant-ness is one of the affective roles cultivable within the script of *bhakti*. It is not a natural attitude to be developed as a virtue, and it is not gendered.

Bhakti is thus a parabasis or interruptive irony of rule-bound high Hinduism as well as of the *advaita* mindset.[24]

Permanent parabasis. As I have indicated, it seems to me more and more that this may be a name for the most effective and plural way of dealing, from below, with the repeated mortal experience of nonpassage to the other side.[25] The plurality in this plural way is fragile and irreducibly uneven – dependent upon an "institution" that can be as amorphous as "culture" (gendering plus religion? I risk a definition of culture's bottom line) of which we can speak only by begging the question. The various and much-negotiated *dvaita/advaita* sleight of mind may be the experience of one such nonpassage. (When *bhakti* lived in the crannies of culture where it could give the lie to caste and scripture, it did so – and does; and it opened doors for women's agency. There were woman practitioners and teachers. It must, however, be admitted that these women were exceptional. Mirabai, the fifteenth–sixteenth-century aristocrat, leaves home to be *Krishnabhakta* [it seems interesting that *bhakta* – the adjectival noun from *bhakti* – (division in) devotion – admits no feminine], in the *dāsya* (servant) or *madhura/gā rhasthya* (wife) mode. The maternal mode is also possible.[26] But within the Orissa-Bengal *bhakti* tradition of Sri Chaitanya (1486–1533), out of 191 devotees listed in one reference book, only 17 are women, 5 of them members of Chaitanya's direct family. Of 100 poets, only 1 is female.[27] The most striking characteristic of this group is the near-institutionalization of sexual indeterminacy. But the chief appearance of this phenomenon was in men affecting the feminine. The most superior *bhāva* was the *sakhi bhāva* toward Krishna – to be Krishna's girlfriend. Many of the male *bhakta*s were also called by female names. This identity-crossing and troping of the sexual self did not touch gendering. The object – Krishna – remained male. When Madhavi Dasi, the only named female poet, mourns Chaitanya's death, she laments from within untroped female gendering: "Whoever sees that golden face floats in waves of love/Madhavi is now deprived by the fault of her own karma"[28] Affecting Radha, Krishna's chief girlfriend (that is what *sakhi* is, I mean no disrespect) in Rādhā *bhāva*, remains similarly drag-troped.)

Speaking of epistemo-affective specificity ("structure of feeling" in thinking as a presupposition), I have been denying the great goddess exclusive "greatness" in the experience of the culture. But if "culture" may be the name of an amorphous/polymorphous "institution" which holds us (*dhr* = to hold, gives *dharma*), it – again that question-begging – is also disclosed in institutions of a more systematic and formal structuring: festivals are among them. And no person from Bengal – as is the present writer – can deny that, in terms of goddess festivals – Durga and Kali mark the year much more flamboyantly than any other divine figure.

But that feeling, of half-belief or "suspended" belief – that the metropolitan middle class in India (mostly the origin of the immigrant museum-goer who was my "implied reader" for the catalogue essay) may attach to the festivals of Durga or Kali – is not what travels to the metropolitan museum in the United States. This is not due only to the willed epistemic emphasis of Eurocentric economic migration.[29] It is also because, the colonial museumization of Indian "culture," with its roots in German comparative religion, is an altogether more specialized affair. Its starting point may be loosely assigned to a positive evaluation of what Friedrich Hegel had called, negatively, a *verstandlose Gestaltungsgabe* (a mindless gift for morphogenesis) in his *Lectures on the Aesthetic*.[30]

If one steps upon that established scholarly terrain, the blithe assertion of "Durga and Kali, of course," begins to get muddled, for we step into the enclosed garden of Art History, not to mention the history of religion. On the other hand, for the educated native informant from Eastern India, Durga and Kali, Durgapuja and Kalipuja, remain distinguishable. Too much learning would here make present certainties indeterminate.

There are hyphenated and/or expatriate South Asian art historians of South Asian art, of course. How does their learning complicate the certainties of cultural competence? I cannot know. No doubt such experts negotiate the culture/discipline divide by way of some variation of the unevenly pluralist parabasis of which I have already spoken, complicated by the fact that their authority sometimes takes on extra weight by that very negotiation, a move from story to fabula, as it were.[31] "Religious" denomination and gender complicate the issue further. The comparison is with long-resident Americans and American Studies of various kinds.

Let me quote a learned passage, written for British academic validation, by a located female South Asian Asianist, born a Seventh Day Adventist in Kolkata, by political conviction a Communist. A labyrinth opens there ...

> *TA* [the Taittiriya Aranyaka] x:18 tells us of an unnamed wife of Rudra; *TA* x:I of Durgā Devi Vairācani (Virācana's daughter); *TA* x:I: 7 of Durgi, Katyāyani and Kanyākumāri; *KU* [Kena Upanisad] III: 12 of Umā Haimavati. *TA* x:18 has a parallel Dravidian text which makes Rudra Umāpati (Uma's husband). *MU* [Mundaka Upanisad] 1:2:4 mentions Kā li and Karāli among the seven tongues of fire. The *SGS* [Sānkhāyana Grhya Sutra] II:15:14 and also *Manu* III:89 mention Bhadrakāli. These texts, as is shown from their vagueness, are inconclusive even if taken in their totality; the epic-Puranic Durga did not develop from any one of them, but from all of them and also from many other elements.[32]

Why have I gone into all this and not started comfortably with feminist reminiscences moving inexorably toward a foregone "postcolonial" conclusion? I think because I have a strong sense of straddling a transitional historical moment, and political correctness would arrest it. All historical moments, whatever they may be, seem and are transitional. Historians judge between transitions. I will account for the specific transition I surmise. It is that soon the generations of US-born Indian-Americans, descendants of the first big wave of Indian immigrants after Lyndon Johnson relaxed the quota system in 1965, will have changed the conventions that allowed culture to function as such (performative conventions, in a colloquial rather than Austinian sense) into a performance. The possibility of performance (citation) inhabits the performative. Yet the two are not "the same." In this case, it involves a willing exchange of civil society. The performative restricts the event. Performance may (only may) open it into singularity.

Hedged in by this framing, then, I give witness to the great goddesses, Durga and Kali. You will work out my negotiations.

> "I" is only a convenient term for somebody who has no real being. Lies will flow from my lips, but there may perhaps be some truth mixed up with them; it is for you to seek out this truth and to decide whether any part of it is worth keeping. If not, you will of course throw the whole of it into the wastepaper basket and forget all about it.[33]

In this mode of lying truth (fiction in the underived robust sense as the authority of autobiography), Durga and Kali will remain different. For Durga I will choose the story of the dismemberment of Sati. For Kali, an illustrated translation of a hymn by Ramproshad. I will give an account of the "little mothers" of Bengal, of *vāmāchāra* and the *Chandimangal*, and close with a hesitant dedication. To begin my fiction, I caution again.

It is difficult to deny that something like a history leaves its mark on "us"; but this mark, in a time of migration, seems a dynamic. Thus even if there is a "structure of feeling" that can, vaguely, be called "Hindu," it would not be identical with the "Indian" structure of feeling, of course, whatever that might be. If we insisted, we would be inhabiting *Hindutva*, the slogan of Hindu nationalism upon the subcontinent. In the United States would this be something like a dominant residual? I think more and more that a critical vocabulary for describing culture is only good for the person who puts it together.

If ever I had a *dvaita* sense of my city, it came from the story of Durga.
A bit of her body had fallen upon Kolkata, and made it a place of pilgrimage. I knew that the Durga who had been dismembered should be
called "Sati." I knew that the ten-armed, familial, annual autumn image
celebrated in the high holy days could not be called "Sati." This plural
naming of alterity – some minimal identity presupposed somewhere,
just to hang the names on, is taken for granted by the *dvaita* mind set.
Being "in a culture" is to pre-comprehend, pre-suppose, even suppose.
The question of belief comes up in crisis, but even then perhaps in
performance rather than in a strictly cognitive assent. This is why
accusations of fundamentalism should be careful.

Here is the story, told by Sukumari Bhattacharji, the source of the
learned passage above, now for children:

> One day, while Sati was sitting outside her house, she saw a number of
> gods and goddesses passing by... "Where are all of you going?" They
> answered, "Don't you know of Daksha's magnificent sacrifice?" ... [Sati]
> could not believe that they had been deliberately overlooked. ... Sati
> asked her husband if he could explain her father's abnormal conduct.
> Shiva was sure he could. ... Daksha intensely disliked Shiva and his
> unconventional way of life... So, Sati ran to her father, ignoring the
> banter and sneers directed at Shiva, and said to Daksha, "What kind of
> sacrifice is this, father, where the supreme god Shiva has not been
> invited?" The status-conscious Daksha ... replied sarcastically, "... You
> have married beneath your social status, my child. I cannot insult these
> assembled dignitaries by asking that lunatic loafer to be here!" ... Unable
> to bear the insults uttered against her dearly beloved husband she fell
> down in a swoon and died. ... [Shiva] was mad with fury and ... rushed
> to Daksha's sacrifice. ... Shiva tore Daksha's head from his neck and
> threw it away. The sacrifice itself assumed the shape of a deer [lovely
> *dvaita* touch!] and fled. Shiva with his Pinaka bow in hand, chased and
> shot it. ... Shiva now came to where his beloved Sati lay dead and an
> uncontrollable fit of madness seized him... [P]icking up Sati's body, he
> walked, jumped, danced and traversed long distances for many days on
> end, oblivious that the mortal remains of Sati were dropping off, bit by
> bit, over many places. All these places, including those where parts of
> her jewellery fell, later became places of pilgrimage.[34]

In most Puranic accounts Sati's death is more theologized than in the
intuitive popular story. In the *Kālikāpurāna* she meditates a moment
upon the undivided pre-semic possibility of utterances, – *sphōta* not
mantra – splits the top-center of her skull, and gives up her life.[35] In the
Devibhāgavata she burns herself through the fire of her concentration

(*yogāgni*) in order to satisfy the ethics of good-womanhood (*satidharma*) because her father had engaged in unseemly sexual behavior under the influence of a magic garland indirectly conferred upon him by another one of her fictive manifestations![36] In one the dismemberment is motivated by the other gods' caution rather than the husband's frenzy. In the other the gods enter the corpse, cut it up from the inside and make the pieces fall in specific places.[37]

Classical iconic representation makes no effort to grasp the drift of a story. And indeed, the stories are not starting-places. They are pluralized presentifications of the *dvaita* episteme at odds with the theological impulse. The mode of existence of the icon as meaningful, from the point of view not of the scholar but the culturally competent observer (a vast and many-tiered sprawling space of agency always "after" culture but also its condition of possibility) is something like a submerged genre-"painting." The culturally competent (in this sense) may provide some generic narrative dynamic to move the Devi and her companions along the stream of "history." It is in that assumption that a few generalizations will here be advanced.

I have cited Freud as dismisser of polytheism, defining it as pre-history and the intolerable rule of powerful women. If we take Freud as everybody's father (or anti-father), we are working with the axiomatics of imperialism: Europe gives the model of every knowledge. On the other hand, if we relax Freud's chronologic to a logic, we will see Freud's brothers, or at least male cousins, in these Puranas. There can be no doubt that the general cast of the "authorship" of the Puranas is male.[38] Women speak in them but the frame-narrator is generally masculine. There can also be no doubt, I think, that there is a degree of "relative autonomy" to the great social text of sexual difference which overflows cultural frontiers, without losing specificity. It is therefore not surprising that, in the pores of these authorized versions of Sati's dismemberment, there are efforts at controlling the feminine as female. Relative autonomy is relative; it is not a postulation of universal deep structures of human sexual dynamics. It is in the sector of the relativity of the relatively autonomous that we look for cultural specificity.

These considerations made, we see in the Puranic texts that the female empowers, but males act. At the end of the chapter previous to the dismemberment story in the *Devibhāgavata*, there is a vertiginous spiraling of such empowering and acting which comes to a halt when the two male gods of the Puranic trinity think they act on their own and thus are cut off from empowerment through their hubris. The third calls his sons, they pray to the female fictive power, and the entire spiral starts again, with this supernatural division of gendered labor intact.

Within this division, in the high Puranic texts, male gods are allowed elaborate courtship privileges. Brahma is represented as publicly (although transgressively) spilling his semen on earth, lusting after Sati. But the Devi celebrated in the Puranic account is the pleasureless mother. Sati punishes herself for pleasuring others.

At the beginning of this essay I suggested that the unanticipatable and irregular presentification of the slippage into *avatarana* (or descent from a transcendental semiotic) is the work of the *dvaita* episteme. The denaturalization of the goddess that has been tracked in the last few paragraphs can be seen as a counterpull: to stabilize the *dvaita* episteme by reversing the *avatarana* into reminders of *arohana* or ascent. Thus the *Devibhagavata* loosens the connection between death, mourning, dismemberment, descent of body parts, inscription of geography: "The pilgrimages created by Sati's body parts have indeed been spoken of, but also those that are famous on earth for other reasons."[39]

This loosening of connection between Sati's body parts and natural space comes at the end of a torrential list of pilgrimages which began with the following declaration: "Wherever the cut limbs of Sati fell, in those very spots Shiva established himself, assuming various forms." The loosening of connection is accomplished through a double-barreled list of 108 items, place-name in the locative case with the accompanying body part mentioned only in the initial one: "Vishala kshi [the large-eyed one] at Varanasi lives on Gauri's face" (55). (Gauri is another name of the Devi.) The subsequent references are not necessarily to a body part. And soon the "poetic function" takes over, making the repeated couplings seem dictated by sheer euphony.[40] The pairs start looking like ordinary epithet-subject couples rather than located body part couples as the formality of the verse gathers momentum, and various rhetorical moves are made. Now the subject is enclitic upon and contained in the epithet. Now the so-called "subjects" are themselves epithets, dependent upon the location of the so-called "epithets" as condition, respectively qualifying and modifying an absent subject, by now fragmented, by force of rhetoric, at least 108 times. Intact manifestations, belonging to other narratives, are sometimes introduced, perhaps to dilute the force of the dismemberment story. Consider these two pairs, among many: "sex-loving at the door of the Ganga [*gangadvare ratipriya*]" (68) is clearly a riff on the woman's body as geography, but not of the Sati's body part story. The subject is an

epithet entailed by the overtly metaphorical locative: the river mouth as
vagina. And "Rādhā in Vrindāban forest [*Radha vrindābane bane*]" (69),
refers to a completely different story, thus negating the narrative and
generative force of the dismemberment. The final names are not connected with the dismemberment story at all: "Among good women
she is Arundhati, among charming women she is Tilottamā. In the
mind she is named Brahmakālī and among all embodied [beings] she is
Shakti" (83). From names to attributes. There is no Devi here. As we
saw in the opening verse, it is Shiva who is sited in the *pithas*.

This would be the bits of narrative and anti-narrative within which
the images are set. Such Puranic references are archaic rather than
functionally residual in metropolitan hybridization. For the specialists
they find their place in the academic subdivision of labor, unevenly
divided among continents.[41]

Among the four broad "kinds" of Indian scriptures – Purana ("ancient")
is a temporizing claim to antiquity – whereas Veda is "known," even
"known by heart," Smriti is "remembered" and Sruti "heard as revealed."
The double-structured pull of the *dvaita* is felt within the Puranas.
Some are more a tabulation of the thingliness of the signifier, others
more inclined toward the mindiness of the signified. The tension is
generally coded as less and more brahminical respectively – what
Raymond Williams would code as the dominant incessantly appropriating the emergent.

This is the kind of difference that is usually noted between the
Devibhāgavatapurāna and the *Mārkandeyapurāna*. The former more airy,
the latter more earthy. We have just noticed how the body-part-real-
space referential narrateme was unevenly sublated into a locative con-
dition-dependent logical structure of potentially reference-undermining
naming in the *Devibhāgavata*'s account of Sati's dismemberment. (This
is the kind of sentence that irritates conservative Indianist scholars
muscle-bound by their discipline as well as racist Left conservatives of
whatever color. In the mean time, the dominant passes everything off
as transcendent high culture.[42])

The list in the fifth chapter of the *Devimāhātmya* section of the
Mārkandeyapurāna – read by Birendrakrishna Bhadra on All-India Radio
in the fifties – is well-known to most culturalist Hindus. It comes closest to the always deferred possibility of a sublation of the Devi into her
attributes. But the list is here directed toward a Devi who is located in
all that is, and the reciter/reader performs his respects by enunciating
that directedness. To the goddess who, in all that is, is well-established
as consciousness, respectful greetings, goes the first line. A marvelous

series of parallel lines follows: respectful greetings are given to her as she is well-established as intelligence, sleep, hunger, shadow, power, thirst, patience, birth, modesty, tranquility, faith, beauty, grace, activity, memory, compassion, contentment, mother, and the best of all, error.[43]

Yet this powerful song of praise is narratively framed as Visnu's *Māyā*. I propose to translate *Māyā* as "fiction," an English word philosophically unconnected with prose. Like all translations, this translation too "is a movement ... that transports [the] language beyond its own limits."[44] But *Māyā* in the limited sense or translation of "illusion" has given trouble to readers and believers through the centuries. *Māyā* as "fiction" would carry the paradox of the range of power of this antonym to "truth."

However the great goddess is made to occupy the place of power, it is always as fiction, not as "truth." It is not a question of the multiplicity of manifestation; gods and goddesses share it; it is a *dvaita* world. It is not even a question of doing – both do. But she does through fiction and they – the singularity of the Puranic male *isvara* is nowhere near as grand as the singularity of the morphogenetic multinominated Devi – through method. If *Māyā* is understood as fiction, this is how the empowerment–activity dyad, mentioned above, would be re-grasped. There is never an exception to this in all the male–female binaries strewn through the Puranic corpus: *prakrti/purusa* (comparable to *physis/nomos*, matter/consciousness, *hylè/morphè*) and *prajnā/upāya* (wisdom/method) are only two of the best-known.

The name of that fiction or *Māyā* is the apparent magic of fertility – animate and inanimate. This is seen as unitary, even before the human-image propriation of the supernatural. Therefore, for the Hindu, whatever that may be, it is different to be identified with the worship of different male gods – a Shaiva is different from a Vaishnava, a Brahmavādi is loosely an *advaitin* until the nineteenth-century reformist Brahmos took the slot. But if you are a *Shākta*, Durga and Kali must be acknowledged as the same. The acknowledgment of this always unitary female power (at the time of first writing, the Indian film star Hema Malini was pushing her dance drama on Durga by cluing on to a culturally conservative feminism as "the strength and power of the woman" on the New York TV channel "Eye on Asia") is yet another way of attempting to control what Freud would call "the uncanny."[45] Such acknowledgment cannot be translated into normative social attitudes toward female human beings. And indeed, women cannot feel fertility as the uncanny in quite the same way. For reverence for fiction

(*Māyā*) as female to be unleashed, the *dvaita* trick must happen, and the female subject exit sociality. More of this later. For the moment let us note that the name of the version of the great goddess who animates the section of the *Mārkandeyapurāna* that is called *Devimāhātmya* is Chandi – the "irate." Indeed, by displacement, this section of the text is also called *Chandi*. In the mode of glorification, each of the "little mother" goddesses of Bengal is also a chandi. *Ein jeder Engel ist schrecklich.*

To encounter specifically female focalization in the *dvaita* presentification of the goddess in her biotic sphere, we will have to leave the great goddess, and turn to these "little mothers" of Eastern India, surrounded by their specific flora and fauna.[46] The high pantheon is dominantly male-focalized.

When cathected in ritual, each small goddess is the great goddess. The cycle of her praise and worship is much shorter than the annual festival cycle of the great ones: daily, weekly, or by the phases of the moon. She relates not only to the house (there are male deities who bless and curse a particular foundation) but to the household as it is run by women, often by women in subordinate positions, such as a daughter-in-law or a virgin daughter. Even widows worship these "little mothers," although for them the male greater gods come into social focus again.

There is no doubt that the addition of "chandi" to their names respects what I have already remarked: each goddess, when cathected in worship, is the great goddess. But, with specific reference to the minor goddess Sitala (this remark would, *mutatis mutandis*, apply unevenly to all the minor goddesses of Bengal), a commentator adds: "This Chandi is not Durga, rather she is the hunting deity of the hill-tribes of Chhotanagpur of Bihar. Purulia, as it was formerly under Bihar, hence, the Chandi of Bihar of the aboriginal groups spreads her impact in Purulia district."[47] Yet "*candi*," even as a common noun, as presumably here, is a Sanskrit word. It is not possible to separate the Aboriginal and the Indo-European on the occasion of the goddess. They share a heartbeat: "that which, from moment to moment, *from one moment to the other*, having come again from an other of the other to whom it is also delivered up (and this can be me), this heart receives, it will *perhaps* receive in a rhythmic pulsation what is called blood, and the latter receive the force to arrive."[48] Except in stratified social practice, where "Indo-European" and "Aboriginal" have been forcibly kept separate for millennia. And perhaps in the museum.

Most of the regional accounts of the historical emergence of these minor goddesses are also accounts of resistance and flexibility: resistance to the increasingly caste-bound ritualism of high Hinduism. Scholarship tells us, of course, that even these great gods and goddesses owed a good deal to the aboriginal cultures already in place on the subcontinent when the Indo-European speakers began to settle; and that "Hindu" history is a history of the imperfect obliteration of traces. But the emergence of the gendered secondary pantheon as resistance is part of a cultural self-representation that is not necessarily scholarly. I am not "responsible" in Hindi as I am in Bengali, my mother tongue, and English, the object of my reasoned love and a general instrument of power. I am therefore better acquainted with a portion of the considerable writings in Bengali and on Bengal about the coming into being of these gods and goddesses of field, stream, forest, hill, and household. Not as a specialist but as a "Bengali," whatever that might be.

These goddesses, who came to be worshiped in the house without a priest and in Bengali rather than Sanskrit, are seen, in a certain kind of Bengali writing, as aligned to the aboriginal descent of the Bengali, to a resistance to the great tradition, as a sign of ecumenicism. The vision of Bengali identity captured in this temporizing points to a gender-liberated, egalitarian, and humane people, domesticating Buddhism as high Buddhism moves to East Asia, coming to terms with Islam as Bengali Islam opens its doors to the oppressed outcastes, acknowledging the body as the iconic representation of the universe. The account consolidates the *dvaita* "structure of feeling" (if there be such a thing) by bringing it within a calculus of representation and practice, by removing from it the element of chanciness, by constituting it as the evidence of an "identity," not of Indian culture so much as of Bengali humanism. It is a tempting exercise, especially when garnished by such open-ended statements as this from the first extant text in "Bengali," composed between the eighth and twelfth centuries: *jetoi boli tetavi tal/guru bo se sisa kal* (the more said the more error/guru says the student deaf).[49]

Let us now leave the labyrinthine "truths" of this temporization of identity, and look at a text in the history of the present, aligning it with the ones we have already assembled in these pages.

If one believes that "the synchronic" is at least a methodological possibility, a pamphlet entitled *Meyeder Brotokatha* is also part of "our" present.[50] The book was bought at a fair for the aboriginal Sabars in Rajnowagarh in West Bengal, organized by the local Sabar welfare committee. Rajnowagarh is a relatively remote place. Most of the Sabars, except for a handful of adults and schoolchildren, are illiterate. The few "regular" Indians present at that feudally "activist" organized fair were from the urban middle class. Rural Hindus and Muslims do not mingle with the Aboriginals by choice, for pleasure. In other words, the itinerant bookseller on a rusty bicycle, from whose horde a celebrated "activist" bought me a bunch of books, had no real buyer at that particular fair. But it is conceivable that at the more usual rural fairs, organized around festival days or around the weekly or bi-weekly market day, men buy these books for their wives and daughters, so that they may learn the religious authority behind their ritual practices. In the last decade, I have touched the normality of this grass-roots readership, and try always (with no guarantees, of course) to compute their distance from the New Immigrant spectator of the Devi icons in the museum, of Hema Malini at Lincoln Center, in order not to speak nonsense in the name of global feminism or hybridity.

Forty six household rituals are listed in the book – broto-s (from Sanskrit *vrata* = restraining practice), not *puja*-s. Women's rituals without a priest. I quote the opening lines of the poem accompanying one to give the reader a sense of the performance in it. I had read them before, in a novel by Bibhutibhusan Bandyopadhyaya, that Satyajit Ray translated into film in his *Apu* trilogy.

> Pond of good works, Garland of flowers
> Who worships in the morning?
> I am Sati Lilabati
> Lucky girl with seven brothers

and so on.

The text as it was used in Bandyopadhyaya's novel (as opposed to the pamphlet bought at the fair) was not "real" but cited in a fictional frame to signify "village girl." But if and when a "village girl" utters this within an appropriate performance, she is also citing fiction, in our English colloquial sense of course, but also because the performance is in the frame of the *Māyā* of the world. She acts two parts in the script – the questioner and the answerer-performer, specifically named: I am Sati Lilabati. "Sati" is a word in the language – meaning, presumably, a paragon of the specifically womanly virtues; and the expert will give me a list of Lilabatis; it's a common enough moniker.

What matters to us is that there is something moving in the self-bestowal of that grand theatrical appellation – Sati Lilabati – upon a young girl, even as her good fortune is carefully designated as the possession of seven brothers. O my mute inglorious Antigones! Behind these broto-s are quite often stories of women saving their men. There is indeed a degree of (the representation at least of) agency on this register, validated by traditional gendering, securing domestic loyalty.

The ostensible goal is a good husband. There is something like a relationship between this and the personal columns of newspapers, seeking partners. Chance and choice are at play here. The personal column relies on a theory of the subject of decision, only apparently ungendered. The broto relies on propitiating the animal world as much as anything else. The ritual begins with offerings made to snakes and frogs. The connection between such gestures and fertility remains enigmatic.

There is a broto listed here, for example, involving the goddess Earth. The chant commemorates the dvaita moment, within that "structure of feeling," not just the dead metaphor in "mother earth." The Earth is a devi: "Come Mother Earth, sit on a lotus leaf." The chant goes on to praise her husband, the king of the universe, in the hope of marrying a king.

These performative pieces, without need of an officiating priest, organize woman's time theatrically. The connection with the ostensible purpose – good husband or good fortune – is thin, less focused than the personal column or lottery tickets. And, these temporizing stagings of the woman's being in and of the oikos do not produce an affective relationship with the great goddess as such. As the great goddess of the male imaginary recedes further and further into distanced and fixed visibility (as in Lacan's reading of Antigone), the invaginated dvaita episteme uses its part-containing-the-whole resources to create a space of theater for the women who sustain rural society.[51]

This sort of little mother ritual is the staging of the woman's day. The great goddess festival is a grand exceptional event. And indeed, at those festivals, the womenfolk are the preparers of food and the ingredients for ritual detail, not the human protagonist.

In Meyeder Brotokatha, the pamphlet of little mother rituals, there are narratives that invoke the high pantheon. They are perfunctory tales, using the dvaita principle of quick shifts from human to other-than-human at random, to end inevitably in an injunction to perform the specific broto, with no noticeable logical buildup. The ritual seems the remains of some other text, whose meaning is errant here. Was that textuality an indeterminate weave of aboriginality and the para-Vedic Puranas? I like best the eccentric scholar who writes: "Bengalis, like

Indians in general, had their origin in Negrito or Negro-Bantoo race,"
and points out repeatedly that it is only in southwestern Bengal that
the "little mother" Sitala – goddess of smallpox – is worshiped fully
in the aboriginal way, and points at the sliding scale of ritual and
imaging that she is offered.[52]

No "Indian culture" here. No great goddess as such. No serious ethnography either – just a traffic in regional identity in the name of
women, in the household.

When the story of the dismemberment of Sati turns up in this
pamphlet, it does not continue on to the establishment of *pitha*-s or
places of pilgrimage. There is no account here of the limning of a
sacred geography upon a place we now call South Asia. The region
does not exist here, only the courtyard and the field. This women's
mulch is far indeed from projects of "critical regionalism." We cannot
ignore that liberatory political work will bring these women into
"citizenship" (they already vote if of age), promote intuition of the
public sphere, and bring the little-mother rituals into performance
rather than the performative, at best. History is what hurts. For now,
we note that there is a hiatus between the end of the Sati's-death
story and the injunction for the particular *broto* to which it is unaccountably attached.

As the new immigrant woman crosses the threshold of the museum,
she reads the images in the museum as cultural evidence or investment, even as proof of a feminist culture. "Interest in the feminine
dimension of transcendence as revealed in mythologies, theologies,
and cults of goddess figures throughout the world has been keen in
recent years both among those concerned with 'Women Studies' and
among religion scholars generally."[53] I want now to leave the rural
theater, and to flesh out this viewer's look, by referring to my own
childhood. Autobiography is at best an example, no authority.

"Indian" cultural evidence is in the children's story. Professor
Bhattacharji has distilled Bengali popular tradition there. The Sahitya
Samsad Dictionary of the Bengali language lists the 77 places conse-
crated by Sati's body simply as part of the definition of the word *pith*
(Sanskrit *pitha*) or "seat."

As it provides the modern place names beside the ancient, there is
no hesitation in the dictionary. There can be no doubt from this lexi-
cography that the naming was yet another way of consolidating settlement in a new land. If one follows through, one sometimes comes up
with a geographical information system that uses a woman's body to
bring under one map self-contained aboriginal settlements. I feel my

lack of expertise rather strongly here. But consider the place where Sati's upper lip came to rest: "Bhairavaparvata (Avantidesa near Ujjain). The country of Avanti, much of which was rich land, had been colonized or conquered by the Aryan tribes who came down the Indus valley and turned East from the Gulf of Cutch."[54]

Behind the fictive authority of autobiography, and the ecstatic celebration of the yearly Durga puja in Kolkata, there is the shadow of the first colonial conquest of India, by "my own kind":

[A]ll over the world there was the cult of a holy family – composed of "mother and son" at first, but later (when the man's contribution in the procreative process was recognized) of father, mother and son. In India this family consisted of Siva, Parvati and Kartikeya. Later the family grew to include Ganesa, Laksmi and Sarasvati, who constitute the group now worshiped in India in the autumn.[55]

What did this mean in my childhood and adolescence? New clothes for every day of the five-day festival, drinking mescalin-paste milk in the bosom of the family on the fifth night, visiting and comparing innumerable images all over town, complaining about and loving film-soundtrack and amateur theater blaring over loudspeakers, and going the rounds of visiting extended family and friends, abruptly cut off when I left India in 1961. It is possible to connect to simulacra – citations within a general metropolitan civil performative – here in the United States, but I am not given to the expatriate staging of national origin for a culturalism that removes the nation-state of origin from independent transnational consideration. Lest I seem to suggest that the "originary" place is without simulation, I will relate Durga puja ("Devi Puja" in Bihar and Uttar Pradesh) – the sanctioned worship of the great goddess – through a photograph by Kalo Baran Laha that engages a rather different theater.

Mr Laha is a hotel owner in the country town of Purulia in West Bengal. He photographs, with a group of friends, for his own pleasure, establishing a record of the life mostly of Aboriginals living in the region. This photograph, of a boy looking up obliquely at the clay and wattle frame of the image of Durga and her family, worshiped annually, is a little off Mr Laha's usual beat.

A small-town boy or a rural boy, one cannot know. The photographer seems to have caught his subject unawares. The boy gazes at the image. The eyes in the absent, spectral head return his gaze. The knowledge of the return of the image every year directs the boy's gaze;

Figure 6.1 Boy looks at goddess. Photograph © Kalobaran Laha.

a cultural habit that also knows that the image will be destroyed, plunged in the river with great pomp and circumstance at the end of the five days. It is the *dvaita* habit institutionalized – to see in the obviously transient and ephemeral the possibility of alterity – that conjures up the goddess's absent yet gazing, living, head for the boy. It bears repetition: it is not just that the image is not yet ready; it is that even when fully assembled and gorgeous, it will carry its imminent death. The day of triumph – *bijoya* – is also the day of the renouncing of the simulacrum – *protima bisharjon* – of floating – *bhashan* – all words in grass-roots vocabulary. And yet the gazes lock. In fact, if the image had been fully formed, the picture would have signified differently, for the goddess's fixed and stylized gaze (which I, like the boy, can imagine) would be angled at the other corner of the photographic space. The boy's expression does not lend itself to quick characterological analysis; in my reading, there can be none. The *dvaitin* gaze is not phenomenal.

If we read the photo through Sigmund Freud's essay on "Fetishism," we would expect a fascinated gaze, and we would expect a doubled anxiety of castration and decapitation.[56] But that is another "culture," and I hope I have demonstrated that I do not mean that word in some silly multiculturalist way. If our boy had looked between this humble unfinished great goddess's legs, as Freud's boy in "Fetishism" would, he would "see" the absent gaze from the not-yet-assembled human head of the defeated buffalo, in a representation of the *dvaita*-moment caught in the icon. Is this why polytheism (not a good word, but we will let it pass) is scary, because of such powerful females, improbably limbed? What does it "mean" that this representation, of this boy, at least (we must beware of making a singular representation exemplary, although Freud sometimes forgets this lesson), will not prove the case for subject-constitution on an error about genitals? To pose the question is to make Freud "real," an occupational hazard of psychoanalytic cultural criticism.[57]

I will not open my usual Kleinian argument here, since that will divert this line of thought too far.[58] I will simply repeat that the *dvaitin* gaze is not phenomenal, that in every act of Hindu worship or presentification alterity must be instituted in the material – *prāṇapratisthā* – and then let go at the end, and that the relative permanence of built space – which organizes so much Hindu nationalist violence in India today – is irrelevant. The nonpassage between (above? below? beyond? beside? Can there be a relational word here? The *dvaita* gaze forever trembles on that brink) the boy's actively *dvaita* gaze and the metropolitan museum will have remained negotiated without his "cultural" (not necessarily deliberate) participation; that gaze, locked perhaps in the spectral gaze of the great goddess, will have fallen short of the exhibition.

My take on Kali is different.

The Bengali *bhakta* visionary Ramakrishna (1836–86) often experimented with cross-gendered *bhāvas* or affective essences. As a *bhakta*, however, he was turned chiefly toward Kali.

Because of family involvement with Ramakrishna, his wife, his disciples, and the movement in his name, over four generations; as well as because of the sect-orientation of my father's ancestors, I was born and raised in the verbality of the praise of Kali.

The genealogy of the great goddess renders the distinction between "Aboriginal" and "Aryan" indeterminate. But Kali seems to have preserved some especial aura of aboriginality. It is difficult to clothe that joyous, leaping, naked black body altogether. If the buffalo-killing (*mahisasuramardini*) golden Durga is not the object of worship of the aboriginal Indian, Kali has remained so. At least in the aboriginal group – the Kharia Sabars of Manbhum – known to me, non-figurative design is a major part of decorative art. It is perhaps no surprise that Kali has lent herself to the greatest abstraction, in the non-figurative mystical diagrams or *yantras* of *tantric* practice. I lack the scholarship to say this with confidence. In this section, I will consider one such *yantra* as represented by the twentieth-century cosmopolitan artist Nirode

Mazumdar and his coupling of it with a verbal text from the celebrated eighteenth-century religious poet Ramproshad. The text is, among other things, a humanization of the goddess that has something like a relationship with the *dvaita* episteme in the *bhakti* mode. (I hasten to add that Durga too is domesticated in Bengal. Her autumn festival is often coded as the married daughter visiting her parents' home and there is a wealth of songs welcoming her as such a daughter.)

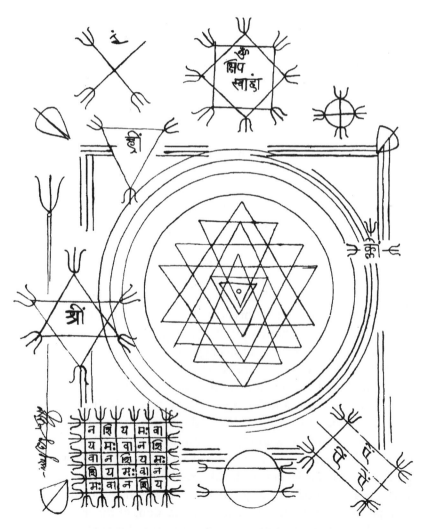

Figure 6.2 Nirode Mazumdar: Yantra. Representation of Kali from *Song for Kali: A Cycle* (translation with introduction of Ramproshad Sen, 18th-century poet), Calcutta: Seagull, 2000. Image courtesy of Seagull Books.

In this hybridized representation of Kali by an Indian artist living in France well before the era of the emergence of today's hybridist epis- teme – the exotic artist in Paris was an earlier stereotype – truth-in- painting discloses itself even as it misfires on its intention: to couple text and image.[59] The "truth" disclosed is that such a coupling would work only for the glance that would see "India" as a stable symbol of the promise of mystical liberation – the Herman Hesse mode – with tantalizing residues of an earlier, more Madame Blavatsky mode, which would hint at the esoteric-as-such. For the middle-class Bengali of *Shākta* (the sect loyal to *Shakti* – power in the feminine – generally understood as Kali) provenance, as perhaps Nirode Mazumdar was, the eighteenth-century verbal text looks forward to the dynamic of Bengali colonial modernity, constituting a female object of the *dvaita* gaze who could straddle the culture of the rural landowners (itself on the cusp of the "feudal"-residual – thus reaching out toward the culture of the tenants – and the "colonial"-dominant); as well as that of the devotional culture of the emerging urban colonial middle class, strati- fied along location-specific lines. The visual text, by contrast, looks back toward the "archaic."

Mazumdar's line drawing is a *yantra* – an instrument. *Yantras* are used to start inspiration in *tantra* practices. The line between the erotic *bhāvas* in *bhakti* and *tantra* is shifting and unclear. When, however, a *yantra* is used to focus ritual, there is a clear distinction from the affect- centered practice of *bhakti*. A *yantra* is a calculus, a diagrammatic rep- resentation of the goddess and the god, male and female together, to help access the human body as itself a diagrammatic representation of the universe, not as a container of affects.

Tantra is the "reverse" method of appropriating the *dvaita* structure of feeling. Instead of emphasizing ascent or *ārōhana* by bracketing the *dvaita* event into "allegory" in a restricted sense, *tantra* attempts to arrest or capture by going *through* the descended flesh. Perhaps *tantra* longs to turn invagination inside out, by literalizing it?

To engage the affects would be, strictly speaking, contrary to the *tantra* endeavor. Theoretically, the body that *tantra* wants to engage is a representation of the universe, not the text and instrument of affects. "The universe" is most often understood as a sexually differentiated force field.[60] The body engages in sex and comes to *jouissance* (*mahā sukham*) and has the skill to experience it as *advaita* transcendence. This skill is *tantra*.[61]

Nirode Mazumdar seems to have drawn a partial version of the most celebrated *yantra* – the *Shrichakra*: "There are nine *yonis* or female organs, five of which have their apex pointing downwards, and these represent Shakti. The remaining four with apex pointing upwards represent Shiva. The *vindu* (dot) is situated in the smallest triangle pointing downwards."[62] In one corner is a hexagram expressing respect for Shiva.

With this *yantra* the artist has coupled the following two lines, by Ramproshad Sen (1718/20–1775/81): "See how the bitch plays, in her own way of acting the secret play/Setting the phenomenal at odds with the noumenal/Hitting stone on stone."[63]

If you knew the significance of the *yantra*, it is conceivable that these lines could be an admiring monstrative description of it. But Mazumdar, like the museum, is reconstellating. The "felicitous" text accompanying a *yantra* would tell the aspirant how to use it. This is why Naren Bhattacharya writes, somewhat querulously: "The term tantric art is evidently a misnomer."[64] You do not celebrate a baseball game for its choreography. Why not? We ask. That would be reconstellation.

Ramproshad Sen, the eighteenth-century poet, is also reconstellating. Working first as a clerk for a new colonial-style urban merchant, and patronized subsequently by a semi-feudal landowner-"king," he can be read as living a nostalgic regression into a social discursivity that was soon to become residual.[65] He writes when the active modes of *bhakti* and *tantra* have already receded from the mainstream. His poems are informed with the *desire* to taste the divine madness of the true *bhakta*. All his songs outline this desire within an enactment of the *bhaktibhāvas*.[66] He is no mendicant minstrel and certainly not a practicing tantric, although he uses the metaphorology of both. His lines are playful, tuned into the affect of sweetness (*mādhurya*) or filiality (*vātsalya*). The "bad language" signifies the familiarity of affection. For this poet-persona a *yantra* would be somewhere between a curiosity and an artifact to be revered. Certainly in his own famous line: "I *yantra* you *yantri*," the use of the word is Bengali colloquial: "I am the instrument you the player." All his *tantric* imagery is filled with the accuracy of descriptive, not potentially performative, passion.

If Ramproshad had written practicing *tantric* texts, they would have been *vāmāchāri* (focused on sinister- or woman-practice), since he invariably used the coupling of Shiva and Shakti as his vehicle. Let us therefore look, not at a learned discussion of the *tantric* heritage, but at a text of grass-roots *vāmāchāri tantra*, written in Bengali, on sale at that rural fair in West Bengal.

Here is the beginning of the text, accompanying a *yantra* altogether less complex than the one we are looking at:

> Penance must be continued for seven days. No food or drink. Only milk. Drinking that milk you must think that I am sucking immortal nectar from the Devi's large firm breasts. You must prepare a *yantra* according to the figure above, with white sandalwood paste. Then worship the *yantra* with karabiflower and vermillion. Get to a hilltop on the ninth night of the waxing moon and constantly recite the *mahabija mantra*. Devi will appear toward the end of the night. Devi strips and undresses the aspirant. To make the aspirant engage in erotic play she kisses, licks and embraces the aspirant constantly. She gives him great wealth. The pure body of the Devi is the aspirant's heaven. The aspirant enjoys this unearthly body for a long time.[67]

The book is full of such injunctions, often very graphic, about how to deal with the different erogenous zones of the female body. The passionless didactic tone is about as far from Ramproshad's funky affective use of *tantric* imagery as can be. It is interesting that, in the opening chapter ("Devi Bagala's Manifestation"), the oneness of the great goddess is asserted: "In addition, it is this Devi who is also worshipped as Kali, Tara, Shodashi, Tripura, Bhairavi, Rama, Bagala, Matangi, Tripurasundari, Kamakshi, Jambhini, Mohini, Chhinnamasta, and Guhyakali" (p. 10).

Who uses these pamphlets? Are there practicing *tantrics* in the rural areas, or among the floating urban sub-proletariat? Here again, we are looking at a long-delegitimized sector of what culturally defines "India." What word would Raymond Williams use for this?

I cannot think that *tantra* ever allowed for women's sexual agency. Although in the supernatural the Devi is dominant, in the *yantra*-inspired activities the actual women representing her are the affectless receivers of foreplay. In the act itself, the goal is to arrest male ejaculation, so that orgasmic pleasure can lead to a transcendental rather than merely organic fulfillment. An actual event of this type, described by an ecstatic participant from the orthodox Bengali middle class, is rather horrible in the implications of what actually happened to the passive young woman involved.[68] If the evidence of this book is to be believed, the female advisers within the system feel no hesitation in acting as procuresses.[69]

Better I think to be the agent of the theater of the domestic in "little mother" rituals than to be the victim or organizer of this curious reverse figuration of the transcendent, upon the woman's body. And better to join the chain-link of re-constellated desire for a cultural "lost object": Ramproshad Sen, Nirode Mazumdar, and the negotiable figure of the New Immigrant Model Minority lady viewer. A politics is involved in how we will represent that desire, how we try to make the images mis-speak, and who gets to represent; by the structures of social empowerment, guaranteed by sexual difference, the lowest level of institutionalization that we can reach: the multicultural relative autonomy of gendering. Perhaps the chain-link should include the *tantra*-impulse itself, appropriating, for a specific practice, the general word for technè as weaving the base thread (*tantu*); resisting the strict theological dominant with the flesh.[70] We are all like the little boy in Laha's photo, looking up at an angle at the absent head of a not-yet-there Devi, making eye-contact with what is not yet there. When *vāmāchāra* in *tantra* needed to set a practical course, suspending affect to go through the flesh to transcendence became learning to withhold male ejaculation on the bodies of doped or brainwashed girls or sex workers.[71] We must keep on attempting to reconstellate, but we must not forget this fact and its corollary: the relative autonomy of gendering, everywhere.

Mazumdar makes a lovely experiment. Yet, whatever the continuities or discontinuities of his visual-verbal couplings, a simulacrum ("citation without literal referent"), at best, of the condition-effect effect, there is no necessarily "female" component in the focalization of their two parts.

I did not engage in "little mother" practices in childhood and adolescence; although here and there, women in my extended family performed them with the required regularity and did not seem odd. If "I" am representative of the shift from *ethnos* to *ethnikos*, am I then deprived of the possibility of occupying designated womanspace in the praise of goddesses? Am I confined, at best, to the cultural re-constellations of the radical sector of the expatriate middle class, such as the experiments of Nirode Mazumdar? Before I ask this question again, let us look at the class-mobile rhythms (disclosed and effaced by the imperialisms that have nurtured our viewer) in *Chandimangal*, by Mukunda Chakrabarti, a Bengali poet of the middle of the sixteenth century.[72] I am observing what Williams would call the "pre-emergent."[73]

This is the best of a series of *mangalkavyas* or rhymed romances of earthly good fortune, celebrating these minor goddesses. *Chandimangal* celebrates our major goddess – *Chandi* – as if she were a minor one.

Only 2 of the 14 sections of the long poem are located in the world of the gods. There is an account of the ill-fated festival of Daksha, but no continuation into dismemberment. The fixing of the sacred geography of the subcontinent is not important here either. This poet steers by a real map. This poem, like others of this genre, is also an account of sea trade.

Barter – what Marx would call the relative value-form – is the medium of trade. An extraordinary passage of exchange valuation or *badol* occurs, for example, in Day Six, section 338 of the poem.[74] And the reader can almost feel the value-form straining toward some version of the general equivalent – the money-form – in sea-trade. In 50-odd years the East India Company will come upon these shores. One of the gradual and necessary achievements of the East India Company was to standardize the many silver currencies in 1835. A uniform paper currency was established by the Negotiable Instruments Act of 1881. Thus with the straining of the value-form in *Kabikankonchandi* we are on the way, however remotely, to globalization – which is the establishment of a uniform electronic exchange system globally.[75]

K. N. Chaudhuri proposes a non-continental "Asia" constituted by unifying trade activities upon the Indian Ocean rim.[76] In my schooldays, the Sri Lanka trade on the Bay of Bengal rim was incanted to establish in our volatile hearts a pan-Bengali culture stretching from Lanka to Indonesia: "Our son Bijoysingha, conquering Lanka, left a signal of his valor in the name 'Singhal'."[77] Kabikankon Mukunda Chakrabarti's Chandi is also the patron goddess of trade.

She is conceived as a competitive woman: "Where will I get the best-quality worship?" is the question that motivates the entire romance.

If relative value trembles on the brink of the general equivalent in the details of the representation of trade, the *dvaita* form of appearance of the actant trembles here on the brink of what Roland Barthes would call "the 'character-person'."[78]

The recognizably European form of the picaro is not available here. A new style of Comparative Studies would, however, catch this traveling Devi by the representation of her dynamic use of the shape-changing already available in the narrative impulse of the Puranas – as opposed to the rhapsodic or legiferant impulses of Sruti and Smriti.[79]

In order to compete for the best-quality human allegiance, this Devi literally manufactures curses so that the inhabitants of the supernatural world can descend (*avatarana* in the general sense) and play in the real world. The *dvaita* has become fully instrumental. We can perceive the realization of that remote structure – the Devi as competitive loyalty-buyer in the context of trade – as the corporate PIO of gender

sidles into the museum, looking around her to make the right moves.[80]
Every rupture is also a repetition.

If this suits her fancy, our PIO might save the residual as it emerges
into the emergent from the depredations of the dominant. For
Kabikankon's Devi is split between two conjunctures. In the first phase
of her descent, she is the forest.[81] In this age of biopiracy and the export
of hunger, the viewer can perhaps cross identity a bit – go from US PIO
to a gendered citizen of the world – and realize in herself the Devi of
the hunters and gatherers, who wished to establish peace in the animal
kingdom.[82]

This gives a partial answer to the question of our access to womanspace. The secure *oikos* of the *broto*-bound woman has been delegitimized by the Green Revolution and its consequences. Our way in is
unavoidably with the dominant – our ally is the elite of the forest as
picara – looking for the better bid. (I do not think of it as necessarily a
way forward. But that is another argument.)

Perhaps there is also an "aesthetic" answer to the question of our
access to this particular womanspace.

I have described above the peculiar positioning of the disciplinary
historian of South Asian art who happens also to be South Asian. To be
an expatriate feminist literary Europeanist who happens to understand
the easier Sanskrit of the ritual practices is also a peculiar designation.
In the last 45 years I have been present at two or three great goddess
rituals among expatriates; sanitized yet not without a certain poignancy
in the framed observance of a deliberately distanced unacknowledged
dvaita mindset. On these upwardly mobile model-minority subcultural
occasions, the general nostalgic gender structure is preserved. Women
who might otherwise hold corporate posts (not invariably of course,
and it was different until the mid-seventies) dress in costume and make
elaborate preparations of food and flowers; some men join, under their
guidance, in the more masculine chores of fetching and carrying, the
male priest(-for-a-day in this simulation) intones, the congregation
repeats, the words are lost, the feast is the best, saved for last.

My stereotype of "myself," knowing the minimum Sanskrit required
for comprehension of the service, combined with an altogether fierce
training in "the willing suspension of disbelief" in 49 years in departments of English literature as a non-native speaker, as student and
teacher, moving through culturally fractured changing classrooms, is
separated from the festive gender division described above.[83] I "read"
the text of the service and address myself as reader to the image as
figure, and animate the ritual as an act of "poetic faith" (Coleridge) in

the broadest possible way. If anyone notices, which is unlikely, the most generous explanation would be: bluestocking, and I choose the colonial word advisedly.

I should like to think that "suspension" in that description of poetic faith means both *"hanging on* and *hanging between, dependent* and *independent,* an 'assumption' both assumed and suspended."[84] And this quivering subject-fix, without its protective gender-skin, can perhaps be donated to the formation of one hyphenated (as in -American) agent among many, as subcultural practices become an increasingly inflexible class-differentiated special semiotic, to be performed (or not) like a dance routine, under special circumstances.

I think it is best, in view of such a hope, to put the historical distance of a great museum between the icons and the multicultural beholder. If multicultural mulch begins to affect museal practice, it will have happened in the middle voice, neither active nor passive, – an expressive instrument we have lost in modern grammars. It will have happened – varieties of the future anterior are the closest we can get to that voice in modern Indian languages – only when the new museal discursive formation – internalized, becomes part of the migrant episteme; as it no doubt will, with much *Sturm und Drang,* as Hinduism becomes one of the minor religions of the United States.

On my wall hangs M. F. Hussein's "Laxmi," which I acquired at the Sotheby's auction in January, 1996, where the NRI (the non-resident Indian, an important category within the problematic I am discussing) entered the auction room to invest in contemporary Indian art. That lovely image of the dismembered Maha-Laxmi reminds me daily that I have not made the epistemic shift to the great goddess in hyphenated America. It is the museums, great and small, that will have led us in.

Paradoxically, it is in this "aesthetic" challenge that I turn once again to the *broto*-bound rural women. The repetitive theatricality of the priestless *broto*-rituals were not necessarily connected, for these women, with a directed goal other than their performance. This can be put two ways: on the Indic register we can say that a *naimittic karma* (purposeful act) became formalized in daily practice as a *nitya karma* (routine act); on the European register, although both sides will object to this transgressive and scandalous reconstellation, we can call these repeated rituals a *Zweckmäßigkeit ohne Zweck* – an aimless purposiveness or, in the new translation "a purposiveness without an end."[85]

Coleridge was wrong, of course. The habit of art appreciation is a cultural *reflex* translated differently in different subjects, not a *willing* (or unwilling) suspension of disbelief.[86] It seems to me more and more, as I go further and further into the rural past and present of my corner of South Asia, that the everyday *dvaita* habit of mind is just such an unacknowledged cultural reflex. The *broto*-bound women can be imagined as bound to this reflex as well. They are not asked to *face* the great goddess in festival. Their theater is the restricted sylvan enclosures in and around their home. We cannot, therefore, substantively share their space, even as it shrinks into the archaic. But I can at least acknowledge the possibility that I am concatenated with them upon a chain of displacements when I animate "ritual" as "poetry"; if not, like them, as the theater that makes the everyday.

Unless one grants the possibility of such aesthetic judgment, one cannot account for the critical edge of the widows' talk, precisely at Vrindaban, the fabled loving-ground of Krishna and Radha, where they are paid in food and a pittance to pass their days in singing *bhakti*-ful adoration of Krishna, in the *dāsya-bhāva* (assigned by Lalan to the 11 post-Islamic wives of Muhammad) as also in *sakhi-bhāva*, girl talk with Radha, the chief girlfriend.

    Pankaj Butalia's documentary *Moksha* is here my text. It is too easy to have a politically correct interpretation of these widows, although the denunciation of the predatory male establishment of moneylenders and petty religion-mongers is altogether apt. Except for the one case of absolute depression where the subjecting script of *bhakti* has failed, the women are in the theater. These women, who would seem decrepit to the merely sophisticated eye, speak with grace, confidence, and authority, not as victims.[87] Their views on marriage, as expressed to these alien questioners, are poignant and innocent. They have come to Vrindaban for freedom, such as it is. The quality of their performance of improvisatory *palakirtan* (an antiphonal and choral narrative song of praise in the Eastern *bhakti*-tradition) is often excellent, the songs in *dāsya-* and *sakhi-bhāva* full of longing and humor. As old-age homes for a female parent, or orphanage for widowed female relatives, these dormitories are harsh indeed. But they are transformed into a space of choice and performance by the gift for theater of these near-destitute widows, ready to inhabit the *bhakti*-scripts that are thrust upon them. There is everything to denounce in a socio-economic sex–gender system that will permit this. But the women cannot be seen only as victims, and the theater of *bhakti* cannot be seen as orthodoxy pure and simple. The contrast between the inevitable sentimental voiceover of the documentary and the dry power of the women is itself an interpretable text. Butalia has done well to begin and end with a song where the cracked tuneful strong voice of the female *kirtaniya* sings as god: "These cowgirls have tied me down, brother ..."

Again, subaltern women in theater. Again, no great goddess to offer an improbable role for women. The invaginated *dvaita* habit is nowhere near a "naturally" feminist narrative of identification with great goddesses. No room for She-god essentialization here. Adoration legitimizes hostility by reversal. The many representations of the great goddess look stunning on the wall. Real women are distanced from her. She is no role model unless, by the cruelty of the *dvaita*, one of us is thrust into that space. I shiver with the icy detachment of words meant and spoken by one who had been so thrust.

I am thinking of Saradamani Devi (1853–1920),[88] the wife of Ramakrishna, whom I have mentioned earlier – an ecumenical visionary (he reminds me of William Blake), playing with gaiety as position without identity, who addressed himself chiefly, though not exclusively, to Kali, in the *bhakti* mode.

Sarada Devi was a village girl who could read some but not write. She was married at 5, joined her husband at 18, and then was drawn into celibacy and the circuit of a tremendous assembly of male colonial subjects who gave her reverence and worshiped her often *avataric* husband. In her own life's detail, in the everyday detail of her marriage, she needed self-consciously to call upon the resources of the *dvaita* episteme in the most concentrated way. We have bits and pieces of her exquisite utterances as testimony.

This remarkable woman outlived her husband by 34 years. In the course of time, his 12 young male disciples established her as the advisory head of an organization that became a monastic order devoted to social work. She performed her role with tact and wisdom, always remaining in the background. Here was a *broto*-bound girl transmogrified into an *avatarin*. Her husband had worshiped her ritually, officiating as his own priest.[89]

It is one of her ice-cold sayings that haunts me, a questioning of the right to possessing the other and of self-determined identity at once: "[action] befitting the situation, [consequences] befitting the person, [gifts] befitting the recipient. No one is anyone's, dear, no one is anyone's."[90] Paradoxically, this admonition without an imperative describes without moralism the passing of the *dvaita* habit of seeing – into the museum. Perhaps it is the female as honorary male who can say this best.

Vivekananda, Ramakrishna's chief disciple, wrote a Sanskrit hymn to her. The addressers, in the plural, are grammatically in the masculine gender. My female cousin and I, when we sang the hymn together in Kolkata in the fifties, quietly changed the gender of the collective singers to feminine, perhaps simply because we were two women incanting. A few years ago in New Delhi, the female religious order founded in her name sang the hymn on her birthday. They had not disturbed Vivekananda's grammar. The collectivity of nuns spoke in male gendering. Sarada Devi had become a Devi – a goddess, the *dvaita* gaze frozen in the artifice of a forever present, standing in for eternity.

For me, whatever she was, remains afflicted by mortality. She could not have known what an art gallery was. Is it appropriate to dedicate these pages to her? You will judge.

Chapter 7

Our Asias[1] – 2001: How to Be a Continentalist

Argument: There is no original unity to the name "Asia." When we claim the name today we are divisive. To repair this, Social Sciences and Humanities must come together. The production of knowledge must be supplemented by the training of the imagination. We respect efforts at unity in Asian-America, but they cannot be our model. In conclusion to the book, I bring the broader political argument into the classroom.

Asia

The general argument of my book has been to regionalize Asia politically. But what is Asia? Should we train our imagination to allow "Asia" to emerge as a continent? The word "Asia" reflects Europe's eastward trajectory. It is as impossible to fix the precise moment when "Europe" became a proper name for a real and affective space as it is impossible to fix the moment when a "European" first used the name "Asia." Did the Hittite Assiuvans call themselves "Assiuvans" in the second millennium BC, down to the last woman and child? Given that that would be nation-think long before its time, such speculation seems useless. *The Oxford Classical Dictionary* tells us that the current rural population of Turkey is palpably descended from the Hittites. What does one make of such visual markers in terms of cultural transfer? The fact remains that Turkey is in a punitive progression toward the European Union. When the word "Asian" is used colloquially, we do not immediately think of Turkey unless the context dictates it. And because of this inexorable move to Europeanity, the break between rural and urban Turkey is a cultural rift.

It is well-known that in that very millennium the Mycenean Greeks fought with the Hittites. Homer, writing about the Mycenean attack upon Troy, a city in Northwest Asia Minor, finds in Asia a natural metaphor for human movement – the movement of Greeks into Troy. It is the first famous picture of a place called Asia, only an adjective and a vehicle: "And as the many tribes of winged birds, wild geese or cranes or long-necked swans on the Asian meadow by the streams of Caÿstrius, fly here and there, ..." Homer uses the same words *"ethnea polla"* – many tribes – for both birds and men.[2] There is certainly no trace in this text of the folks the Myceneans perhaps knew as Assiuvans. The Trojans are built in the image of the Greeks. In the 700 or more years that passed between the Hittites and Homer, the name shunted from Northwest Asia Minor to the hinterland of Ionia. "Asian" in this passage is the name of a sub-cartographic space, nowhere near a continent! I am an Asian Europeanist literary critic. If I go back impersonally, using the disciplinary training that has sharpened my look, in search of the adjective that identifies me, this peculiar landscape, the marshy meadows of Anatolia, is my earliest contact with that name: my "Asia," a place I have never been.

I need not recapitulate the well-known history of the trajectory of the name "Asia" in Herodotus (484–420 BC), Strabo (64 BC–AD 23), Pliny (AD 23–79), Ptolemy (AD 127–45). Medieval Christianity almost swallows up the cartographic imagination: Orosius (fl. 414–17) to Hugo of St Victor (1096–1141). For the medieval Christian the name "Asia" conjures up the place where the border between the real and the imagined, between the profane and the sacred, trembles. Isidore of Seville (560–636), drawing on Pagan sources, gives us a gorgeous fantasmatic Asia.[3] The extraordinary ancient maps produced in South, East and Southeast Asia do not of course have any sense of the name "Asia," although the name "Jambudvipa" for India seemed to have been current in Japan early on.[4]

The Arabs, West Asians themselves, have a more scientific record. But they never used the name "Asia." The prophet Muhammad is supposed to have said: "Seek knowledge even in China" – the name is *Sin* (alternatively *China*) – China being the limit of the Muslim imagination of space in the Christian seventh century. For Al Biruni (973–1048), Ibn Batuta (1304–77), and all those Arab travelers and geographers, India was "Hind." The Polos (Marco 1254–1323; his father Niccolo and his uncle Maffeo) never used the name "Asia" either. For them "Cathay" remained an object of investigation and astonishment, the other as such, domesticated into trading partner, object of conversion, preparing the ideological field for Mercator (1512–94) – object of colonialism, not "our Asia" at all. Why then should we train our imagination to allow "Asia" to emerge as a continent?

Alexander (356–323 BC) came to India in 324 BC, having defeated the Persians. He thought of Persia as Persia, a tough competitor, having rather little to do with Asia, a less real place. From Arrian's (Flavius Arrianus AD 96–180) account, it seems that "India" was abundantly available to Alexander as a name. It did not share the vague spaciness of the name "Asia," a container and signifier of the not-yet-known. The Indian emperor Asoka (268–232 BC) could think "India," knew five Greek kings and composed some of his edicts in Greek and Aramaic. The more learned you are in ancient history, the more connections you discover. Andre Gunder Frank redid his world-systems theory with an Asian focus in a book wittily entitled *ReOrient*, which gives a whole world of such connections and cites many other scholars who provide further elaboration.[5] But as is so often the case, even in the qualitative social sciences, this is a book of corrective knowledge from above. It is a revision of European worldhistory, not an accounting for the history of "Asia"-s present, which passes through genealogy, marking the possible moments when the contacts disappear from public memory and from the geographical imaginary. There is no continuous line from then to now.

In my schooldays, every Indian school child knew that through Asoka an intra-Asian connection was also established. We read in school about Fa-hsien (fl. 399–414) and Hsāen-tsang (602–64), fourth- and seventh-century travelers. In May 2001, when I traveled to a rural area in China, where I was repeatedly assured that no one had seen a non-Chinese foreigner, the bus driver related to "India" as the place where "the Chinese went to fetch Buddhism." Yet, this historically strong connection in popular memory lingers as a lack of contemporary political information rather than as a sign thereof. I have never received a comparable response, personally or impersonally, in speech or in writing, from any Cultural Studies scholar, author, or colleague and/or friend. (Alternatively, a map in Gunder Frank's book shows me that there was a direct trade connection between my hometown and this area of rural China between 1400 and 1800!)

Even at the time of Asoka and the Chinese travelers, these exchanges were not perceived as continental amities, but as establishing connections between far places. The effect was confined to a small section of the elite. Neither the elite nor the subaltern peoples of "Asia" participated in the *synoikismos* (living in a common home) of this named space. Should we train our imagination to allow "Asia" to emerge as a continent?

In *Asia Before Europe*, Kirti Chaudhuri argues that "the identity and the totality of the 'excluded set,' Asia will hold over time only as long as the identity of the 'set of sets,' Europe, is intact... It is impossible to distinguish a continent from an island, a peninsula, or a large land mass."[6]

We react to such remarks generally as a critique of the colonial production of knowledge. Yet, from Asia Minor to Indonesia, the patterns of European colonization are so different that I believe any productive and generalized *cultural* reaction to this is uninteresting now. It is the many bilateral Eurocentrisms of academic knowledge-production, as Chaudhuri's own book demonstrates, that concern us.

There are no ingredients for unification for the regions that are opened up for a generalized cultural production of a revised continent-think. Chaudhuri's example is the Indian Ocean rim. Gunder Frank provides many others. But these are trade routes, breeding an exchange culture that disappears easily. What inclusive cultural matrix exists in the history of the present for producing a region-think here? As I will repeat at the end of this chapter, regional economic initiatives, that may seem unifying, do not provide a specifically cultural cement, but rather produce a global managerial culture that Robert Reich has called "secessionist."

Further, one of the most interesting things about the Asia-*Pacific* phenomenon – a real mega-regional identity with its own archaic-residual-dominant-emergent flows – is that it harbors a China and a Japan, that had no sustained European colonial experience and a historically and geographically differentiated diaspora. Anti-colonial culturalism does not provide a ground-level cultural cement in that initiative. And Sinocentric world-systems theories legitimize Eurocentrism by reversal.

The only cultural cement provided for such unified "anti-colonialist" continent-think is among recent metropolitan migrant communities. In so far as this supports resistance against dominant racial discrimination and against dissension among different immigrant communities, this is a good thing. But (a) at best, it would go beyond the geographic outlines of Asia (for immigrants come from all over the world); and (b) if this metropolitan global-think appropriated the cultural imperatives of the global South entirely, such resistance would lead to another version of the "colonial" problem in the production of knowledge.

The first people to have called themselves "Asian" were Roman colonists of the province of "Asia," fully established 100 years before Christ's
birth. In its heyday it included the provinces of Bursa, Bahikesar, Izmir,
Usak, Denizh, Manisa, all in what would now be Western Turkey.
"Roman republican governors and capitalists exploited the new
province with predatory rapacity. ... The glittering and extravagant
society of the coastal cities, with their wealthy rhetors and sophists,
contrasts with the traditional, rural-based society of the Anatolian
interior" (*Oxford Classical Dictionary*). What else is new? Orhan Pamuk
would ask.[7]

The Gothic invasions of the third century after Christ finished "Asia"
off. Continental reference to Asia, tied to European continental self-
reference, arose with capitalist territorial imperialisms after the fifteenth century. It does not seem that the metropolitan postcolonial
"new empires" are up for violent overthrow soon. (Seems odd to be
revising this sentence the day after the collapse of the World Trade
Center towers in New York on September 11, 2001.) And since I am
part of the biggest of them, I should like to turn to Asian-America in a
moment.

Before I do so, however, let us remind ourselves that, whether in the
global North or the global South, the search for an originary "Asia" for
the ground of our identity leads to nothing. We are not looking for an
Asia before Europe. We are looking at the claim to the *word* "Asia,"
however historically unjustified. To search thus for an originary name
is not a pathology. Yet it must at the same time be resisted. The desire
is its own resistance. Today more than ever, "Asia" is uncritically regionalist, thinks "Asia" metonymically in terms of its own region, and sees
as its other the "West," meaning, increasingly, the United States. After
the death of his wife Harinder Veriah, an ethnic Indian Malaysian,
allegedly caused by too long a delay in life-saving medical procedure in
a Hong Kong hospital, early in 2001, Martin Jacques called Hong Kong
"a bi-racial society in which [only] Chinese and Caucasians are respected
and accepted."[8] Newly arrived in Hong Kong, I could not join the Press
Conference to protest Veriah's death and say *j'accuse*, because I knew
only too well that when we caste-Hindu Indians are in the majority, we
do not necessarily behave differently. And yet to say that in the face of
violence seemed inappropriate. I felt a coward in every way.

We cannot expect root-searching or anti-colonialism to activate a
new continentalism, not pan – but pluralist – imaginary, cultural, not
directly productive of the political, although at the end of politics. We
must educate ourselves as educators to think this mode.

A preliminary conversation with the students from my class in Hong Kong, before the Spring semester of 2001 began, disclosed a desire for mediation and/or counter-discourse between *Chinese* literary and cultural theories and European poststructuralism, which was my announced topic. They cannot be faulted, they reflect a general trend in training. In March, the session called "Critical Acculturation" at the Comparative Literature Association at the University of Kuwait, at the other end of Asia, read as follows: "Papers on critical efforts/models seeking mediation and/or a counter-discourse between classical *Arabic* literary theories and structuralist/post-structuralist Western theories are particularly welcome. The overarching aim of this section is to open a multi-dimensional perspective on critical theorization in the non-Western world."

With respect, I am obliged to say that the bilateralism of these aims gives me pause. It falls into that pattern: my country or region over against "the West." By implication, the entire "non-Western" world is one's own region. I am reminded of the failure of the Uruguay round of the General Agreement on Tariffs and Trades because each member of the Group of 77 entered into bilateral agreements with the old Group of 7, a banal political analogue to Harinder's death.[9]

Our continent is plural. Europe named it progressively.[10] Today we are divided into at least West Asia (the Arab world), East Asia, South Asia, Central Asia, – and Southeast Asia unevenly divided, not only between its two directional components, but also, chiefly through the inter-nationality of Islam, with West Asia.[11] The claim to the name is unevenly divided, yet there is a regionalist claim. We must therefore attempt to think it as one continent in its plurality, rather than reduce it only to our own regional identity. A necessary impossibility, if you like. Or a perspective available only to the imagination, though not to the understanding, which *must* go by way of regional identity.

United States

By contrast, in the United States, there is a superficial and precarious multiculturalist solidarity. This is dependent upon regularized civil rights within the abstract structure of the United States polity. The battle for such regularization is certainly a worthy cause, but it relates to the US as a nation-state rather than the adjective Asian or African in a hyphenated cultural descriptive. The differences come clear in voting blocks at election time and erupt into violence when the New

Immigrants fight the old and vice versa. But even on festive multicultural occasions such as the recent presentation of balagtasan, "a traditional form of poetic debate made famous by Francisco Balagtas, a Filipino poet of the 1920's...[that] was performed...[in March 2001] at Cooper Union in the Filipino language Tagalog and translated into English before a general public," English was the national language by way of which "a multiracial audience of all ages laughed and applauded as two poets debated whether Filipino-Americans should retire here or in the Philippines."[12] This is one random example among millions, of course. Asian-America is not Asia. English is the cultural cement of Asian-America.

In my first chapter, I have commented on Said's and Rorty's faith in the American University. Within that utopian enclosure, "Asian-American" is being expanded from East- and Southeast Asia to include, specifically, South Asia. It is my belief that this is so because the general South Asian diaspora, securing itself after 1965, when Lyndon Johnson lifted the Asian quota, came in as upwardly class-mobile professionals. Writers from this influx have a more direct continuity with radical Brit. Lit, coming from the legacy of the production of the colonial subject, "English in everything but blood," as declared in Macaulay's famous "Minute on Indian Education" of 1842.[13] We are anglo-clone yet Asian – we make a great alibi for affirmative action. Joining the Asian part of Asian-America allows caste-Hindus to enjoy victimage. Amitav Ghosh, a (South) Asian-American writer, has recently fictionalized this group as marked by "a huge indelible stain which has tainted all of us. We cannot destroy it without destroying ourselves."[14] That "all of us" is a synecdochic definition that Ghosh offers with historical irony: part standing for the whole: the colonial middle class projecting itself as the whole region.

At the oral presentation of this piece in Hong Kong, my friend and colleague Fred Chiu made an impassioned statement of identity with India, especially invoking the poet Rabindranath Tagore. Such statements of solidarity go a long way toward undoing the kind of regionalism that probably led to the death of Harinder Veriah. They can connect with the sort of exoticized solidarity that is available in the everyday, the bus driver remembering India as the source of Buddhism or, in a working-class restaurant in Hong Kong, the voluble and inebriated guest lifting his joined palms in a *namaste* greeting when I answered his query in "Cantonese": "Yan-doy-yan": Indian.

But just as such everyday gestures of solidarity melt in the face of economic competition or military or political mobilization, so do gestures such as Chiu's remain discontinuous with or disconnected from his actual politics if not amended by his counterparts (such as myself) from the other place. Tagore was indeed altogether unusual in wanting to claim "Asia" – perhaps the world – rather than India as his home. We must honor that initiative, especially today, even as we notice its legitimation, by reversal, of a more competitive Pan-Asianism. But, because the vicissitudes of such initiatives did not allow the practical struggle, to destroy the mechanisms of class apartheid at home, to flourish, Tagore's admirable efforts eventually worked for its consolidation.[15] Today the divide between the Bolpur (the railway station serving Tagore's university)-Suri-Rajnagar-Ranigram-Shahabad trajectory (to name only one of the many possible ones) and the Kolkata-leaning trajectory of the University itself is relatively inflexible below the (upper-middle) class line. It reminds me of Atlanta's status as a sun-belt metropolis, its lines to immediately adjacent rural North Georgia relatively feeble. What lies on the other side of the line is the largest sector of the potential electorate.

Yes, what lies above the line is the middle class and above, the synecdoche for the nation-state. What lies below is the largest sector of the electorate.

I am making the kind of point about my fellow South Asians that the great West Indian interventionist intellectual C. L. R. James made about his fellow West Indians – such as George Padmore and Frantz Fanon. Commenting on Fanon, James suggested that West Indians did so well in "politics abroad" because they suffered from an oppression not so savage as what "the Negro" suffered in the United States.[16] From the point of view of Jean-Paul Sartre, the benevolent anti-imperialist imperialist, Fanon became identical with his desire for Africa, a French-African; for Said, Fanon is North African – almost West Asia (the Middle East, of course); for Bhabha, he represents national liberationist anti-nationalism – and the deep background is South Asia (read India). These are powerful intellectual interventions, for contextual reconstellations are certainly necessary. It is only when the historicity of the source is altogether neglected, when the metropolitan appropriates the local, that locationist cautions become important, as powerful as they are dangerous.

Such distinctions can be made among the underclass as well. In her sympathetic book *Voices From the Indenture*, Marina Carter reminds us of this with reference to the experiences of Indian migrants in the British

Empire: "The natural alienation which is a core feature of slave diasporas has not the same force in assessments of the indenture migrations."[17]

Martí and DuBois[18]

In order to study such differences, and in order to examine the claim to diaspora as a distinctive property that lies at the base of US Ethnic Studies as a disciplinary tendency, and in order persistently to wrench it away from becoming a study of comparative victimage, we must investigate its vision of a paradoxical postnationalist continuity, now operating in the new name of continentalism. We must insist that this is not to suggest that the so-called nation of origin, or indeed continent of origin, especially when claimed as such, is in itself a repository of any monolithic identity.

A few years ago, it seemed that metropolitan hyphenation – subordinating the nation of origin to citizenship in a metropolitan country – might foster a postnationalist, even post-continentalist, global intuition. Paradoxically, the lines of contact established by the Internet have created a fictive continuity which allows the nation of origin to become a cultural justification for the otherness of the relatively mobile ethnic.

I do not believe that US Ethnic Studies need go quite so far as to turn its metropolitan home into an other space. But it can construct an intellectual critique of unexamined academic/diasporic culturalism that works to support US manifest destiny as the last best hope of cultural rights for the world. It is certainly good to say – for citizens of diverse national origins – in the US we are united in Ethnic Studies, although at home we are at war. But that passive peace has no intellectual purchase.

To combat the desire for an origin in a name, I propose to deal with "Asia" as the instrument of an altered citation: an iteration. Indeed, the possibility of the desire for a singular origin is in its iterability.

José Martí (1853–95), the Cuban patriot, lived in New York from 1881 to 1895, and wrote an influential essay called "Our America." In his writings, he refers to "Spanish America, *his* America, ... [as] 'Our America' and ... Anglo-Saxon America, 'the Other America'."[19] The title of my chapter is an altered citation – an iteration – of Martí's. Martí's essay has recently been reconfigured for Latino/a Cultural Studies, with strong connections to US West Coast Ethnic Studies, in an interesting book called *José Martí's "Our America"*.[20] This is how the

editors of the text reclaim or reterritorialize Martí: "Martí's US writing," the editors write, "belongs to that tradition of exilic representation which counterpoises the lived experience of being 'left alone' in
the Anglo United States with the reconstructed collective memories of
homelands which lie elsewhere." I myself do not believe Martí is quite
so distant from Cuba when he writes from New York; "reconstructed
collective memories" gives a sense of nostalgia, which, for me, is absent
from Martí's feisty text, except as part of the decorum of a nineteenth-
century style. I think part of this sentimentalization is precisely because
the text is now being reconfigured for the "twentieth-century migration
[that] has seen the reassertion of Our America's *cultural* claims to" the
Other America.

Martí could still generalize a binary opposition. We Asian-Americans
are citizens of Martí's "Other America."

(Strictly speaking, I am not an Asian-American, but rather a resident alien Indian citizen. It is worth mentioning that here because I
belong to a peculiar regional formation that is now becoming extinct,
as we saw in the last chapter.) I was born during the Second World
War. In the estimation of my generation in India, the War was, to use
an obsolete German adjective that Marx often uses: *zwieschlächtig*,
the site of a conflict. The horror of the Holocaust was what made it
European. It was a *world* war because for us – with our quarter of a
million dead fighting for the Allies and the highest number of military honors won by any national group – and subsequently for a
number of colonies – the War was a remote instrument for the end
of specifically territorial imperialism. The end of the Second World
War seemed to make it possible for the entire world to become "nothing but neighbors."[21] I come from a generation for whom it seemed
that the control of this could also be grasped by the new nation. This
was the false promise of a (post)nationalist internationalism that
accompanied the euphoria of Independence. That dream has long
turned into a nightmare, the disingenuous metropolitan promise of a
"level playing field."

Any narrativization of the restless limning of a world after the
World War goes through many phases, large and small. Negotiated
Independences redefined themselves as neo-colonialism from the
West. Failure of decolonization at home and large-scale Eurocentric
economic migration began to fix the new world's demographic outlines. Increased Asian migration to the United States after 1965 bifurcated the US community of East Asian origin in the most significant
way.[22] One may mark that as the beginning of the call for re-citing or

iterating Martí's title. Before that East, and to some extent Southeast, Asians were the only groups granted the sobriquet "Asian" by US fiat. Now the "Asian" is broken into old and new. With the Fall of the Berlin Wall and the subsequent events in Eastern and Central Europe, these outlines have become altogether unstable. It is in the attendant demographic chaos that South Asians have breached the frontiers of Asian-America. Indeed, the Hong Kong academic is also US multiculturalism's felicitous "Asian," precisely because of the Anglocentric legacy of British imperialism, and because resistance to decolonization/recolonization in Hong Kong presents itself as unique postcolonial predicament. A cultural studies labyrinth there....

I speak as a person from the very first waves of postcolonial migration. I came to the United States 46 years ago, when the virtualized demographic frontiers of the modern world were not yet set. A bit of anachronistic nationalism clings to me still. However common it may be among European nationals to retain a passport and remain no more than a permanent resident in the US, Asians and Africans emigrate to gain metropolitan citizenship. My small group, however, is in both worlds, deeply, without being quite of them. I believe that slight anomaly gives us a certain distance, which may be valuable.

I had written a version of these words first as an Indian living in the US, speaking to Swiss philanthropists.[23] In the present context, plotting the patterns of global change after the era of territorial colonialisms in general, I must take into account the possibility of an Asia-Pacific as a major phenomenon. This possibility seems still confined to economic connections, easily established in an era of information technology. As I have suggested, the recent phenomenon of Sinocentric world-systems theories, generally equating dominant economic systems with cultural formations, only apparently provides a broader base. The iteration of Martí would especially emphasize a social and cultural change in that theater. I will come back to it.

There is now a nascent academic subdiscipline called "Migration Studies." At its most theoretical edges we don't often stop to think of the difference between the cultural requirements of migration and allocthonic demographic patterns in the United States, and in the European Union, respectively. Those differences should also occupy us, especially in an old Crown colony, with that strong cultural resistance to "decolonization" I mention in the US context above, recoded in Hong Kong itself in many different ways, from academic cultural studies through middle-class stereotypes to patterns of street behavior. But I must get back to Martí, and Asia as the first half of a hyphenated word, the second half of which is "American," a nuanced difference from simply "the US context," European in the dominant.

Martí could still generalize a binary opposition, from the Hispanic cultural matrix of the Euro-Latin American, although he was sympathetic to the presence of the First Nations. We Asian-Americans are citizens of Martí's "Other America." If we binarize some monolithic "Asia" as our Other, or indeed our Self – same difference – we rehearse the problems that I have been outlining so far.

In his essay "The Uncanny," Freud had suggested that the familiar (home-ly – *heimlich*) becomes frightening (uncanny – *unheimlich* – literally un-home-ly) through the operation of repression.[24] I have little faith in using the foregone conclusions of amateur group psychoanalytic diagnoses as evidence for Cultural Studies. But "The Uncanny" is somewhat different because Freud is there stepping into our territory, trying to open up the space between a word and its (formal) antonym. (I say "formal" because Freud starts off from the point that the two words *heimlich* and *unheimlich* do not *mean* opposite things. They are formal, not semantic antonyms – and the motor of this discrepancy is repression.) Freud is presupposing an unmotivated process working in language to which he can only give a psychological name.[25] When native speakers (Freud's patients among them) use these words, the psychological potential in the archiving of the language allows them to signal "repression," unknowingly – via the history of the language.

Freud wrote this piece in 1919. Saussure's lectures for *A Course in General Linguistics* were presumably given between 1907 and 1913. There is an affinity here – one assuming, the other theorizing – the play of impersonal "motivation" and the "arbitrary."[26] The chief question begged or left unanswered is: "What are the rules of the arbitrary way in which meaning enters and inhabits words?"

By deciding to move from actual spatial or locationist reference for the word "Asia" to its use as a place-holder in the iteration of a citation, I have entered the terrain of that unanswered and unanswerable question that must be begged – assumed answered – before we can launch any serious investigation in Cultural Studies. With that proviso, I move to another sentence in the Freud text: "Something has to be added [muss erst etwas hinzukommen] to what is novel and unfamiliar in order to make it uncanny."[27] It is the productive contradiction that splits our continent, bearing the mark of different histories, languages, and idioms "that come forth" each time that we try to add an "s" to the wish for a unified originary name.

Thus, I am not talking about "real" minds (inside) and I am not talk-ing about "real" space (outside). Yet, I am not playing games either. I am writing about the risky ways in which the "real" is produced. This is the slippery terrain of responsible Cultural Studies.

My sustained argument for the last few years has been the heteroge-neity and plurality of so-called homelands. Here I have signaled at the confusion at the origin of the name of a continent. I would like further to suggest that the final "s" that might differentiate "Our America" from "Our Asia-s" may be a sign that if our home-nations were acknowledged in their plurality by ourselves as Americans, however hyphenated, they would become a source of anxiety. (My model is Freud's suggestion that the prefix "un" in the word "uncanny" is a sign of repression.) Unless we suppress the plurality of the many Asia-s as they relate trans-nationally, we Asian-Americans cannot qualify ourselves as "diaspora." Yet the singular is singular by virtue of its plurality – each named region is its own different and singular Asia.[28]

Here as in so much else, W. E. B. DuBois (1868–1963) can instruct us. If he began as an "African-American" wanting to be both African and American, in mid-career he moved to Pan-Africanism and differenti-ated among the various kinds of Black Europeans upon the African continent – Our Africas.

Today, speaking as an "Asian" rather than a New Yorker, I want to turn to W. E. B. DuBois to show how African-American continent-think was pluralized by him. It is interesting that the lesson has not stuck.

The importance of Africa for the African-American is no secret.[29] What I find in DuBois is a starting point from hyphenation in the United States, and a movement toward a pluralization of the African continent in terms of the diversified imperialist history of the nation-states and regions. Through his Pan-African experience, he was able to think "Africa" without necessarily confining it to the outlines of the named continent.[30] I have often remarked that the lineaments of the African-American predicament can teach other hyphenated groups the vicissitudes of a "postcoloniality" specific to the United States.[31] It is possible that what I am seeing in DuBois is shared by others. Like many scholars outside of African-American Studies, I may be assigning the name "DuBois" to tendencies present in less prominent workers in the field of cultural politics.

With that proviso, I should like to comment on these two moments in DuBois: *The Souls of Black Folk* (1899–1901), DuBois's famous early work, is the prototype of the best vision of metropolitan Cultural Studies. It is an American book, an exceptionalist and individualist book. In his questioning of Booker T. Washington, his refusal of a "triumphant commercialism, and the ideals of material prosperity" as the African-American's only future, and patience and forbearance as his or her only present, DuBois was also against the grain. (I have declared solidarity with this position in chapter 1.) Yet the only ancestor that DuBois could claim at this point is "this common Fatherland" – the United States of America –, because he recognizes a "responsibility to the darker races of men whose future depends so largely on this American experiment, but especially a responsibility to this nation...."[32] (In order to find a comparable statement from an African-American woman, we must go to the end of Tony Cade Bambara's short story "My Man Bovanne."[33])

DuBois acknowledges this responsibility because "the [matrilineal] shadow of a mighty Negro past" is unavailable to the children of slavery. Here, early in the century, Africa is no more than "Our Africa."

In a prescient essay called "The Negro Mind Reaches Out," written 25 years later, DuBois pluralizes Africa.[34]

This text is particularly interesting because it is included in a watershed anthology, edited by Alain Locke, called *The New Negro*. The emergence of "the New Negro," the felicitous subject of the Harlem Renaissance of the twenties, has conjunctural similarities with the Asian-American intellectual backlash against the "model minority" image of the Chinese-American – recoded by the mainstream news media to combat the African-American conscientized by the Civil Rights movement and, to a lesser extent, the "Hispanic"-American conscientized by the events so carefully described in José Saldívar's *The Dialectics of Our America*.[35] The rejection of the model minority image produced the New Immigrant movement toward selective and hyphenated Pan-Asianism. I have made it clear that I predate this movement. DuBois was invited to contribute to Alain Locke's anthology as a member of a generation older than the New Negro.[36] I feel an affinity with his message from an earlier generation at a particular historical moment.

DuBois's shift from exceptionalism to egalitarianism is well-known. If, however, we look at the two texts without explicit reference to his intellectual life, what seems most striking is that, writing as a member of the metropolitan minority, DuBois is exceptionalist and individualist; whereas, writing as a member of a global colonial world looking forward to postcoloniality, DuBois is altogether aware that the production of the exceptionalist and individualist colonial subject creates a class-division among the colonized; and that the colonizer often and paradoxically preferred the "primitive" rather than the "mimic man" he himself produced, preferring a synecdoche that reverses the one Amitav Ghosh laments. DuBois speaks of the differences in policy among the various European powers, or, as he puts it more picturesquely, the "shadows" of Portugal, Belgium, France, and England. Africa is seen as historically pluralized.

We cannot know if DuBois was aware that anti-colonialism would not necessarily lead to a pluralized continentalism. If so, he never put it down in published writing.

Asian-American Pedagogy

Over against these monumental considerations, I want to look at something fragile, of the moment, dependent on the classroom. From Martí and DuBois I want to turn to an unusual and fine example of US pedagogy, critical of a specific regionalism, an unexamined claim to "Asia" by East Asian-Americans. I take Leti Volpp, who teaches at the Washington College of Law, as my example, as she describes a course that is "an internal critique aimed at those teaching Asian American jurisprudence." She is describing her own teaching, intending

> to challenge the often unrecognized dominant paradigms that serve to shape what is understood as "Asian American" or "Asian Pacific American." ... Legal scholarship in many ways is lagging behind interventions made by others writing under the rubric of Asian American studies... [There] is [a] sad lack of legal scholarship on Asian American communities beyond Chinese and Japanese Americans. ... Some have referred to this [general phenomenon, the East Asian-American domination of the API rubric] as a form of racism.
>   What are [sic] missing are Filipino, SE Asian, Korean American, South Asian, Pacific Islander communities. What does it mean to teach a course about Asian Americans or Asian Pacific Americans but not include these experiences? ...
>   This is not just a question of responsible politics, it is also an intellectual matter, when we look at how the term discursively produces a category whose existence masks particular assumptions.

Volpp goes on to hit some of the stereotypes surrounding what is generally known as " 'Asian-American' " or " 'Asian Pacific American' ":

for example, "the model minority myth, the immigrant experience, the idea of perpetual foreignness, [the] eroticization of the submissiveness of Asian women."

> [T]o what extent [are these stereotypes] true for Native Hawaiians and Pacific Islanders? ... Their racialization has been primarily accomplished through the processes of colonization, dispossession, deracination, and through claims about the purported primitiveness of their cultures, [not through immigration].... What does it mean to use the rubric of "yellow" to presumptively represent Asian Americans? It signals that the speaker seeks to only represent East Asian American experiences, since those are the communities that have historically been labeled "yellow" in the system of ethnographic taxonomy, such as that invoked by the lower court in *Loving* v. *Virginia*, upholding that state's miscegenation laws – "God made the races white, black, yellow, malay, and red and put them on separate continents for a reason."[37]
>
> Centering Native Hawaiian, Pacific Islander or Filipino/a experiences also opens up the question of the role of US colonialism in shaping racial formation....
>
> Thus, I include course materials about the US colonization about Hawaii, the Philippines, US neocolonialism in Korea and Vietnam, and British colonialism in South Asia....
>
> In the usual courses on Asian-American jurisprudence, it is straight men [who are centered]. The course is often constructed as about race, with gender and sexuality as distant add-ons. I try to set up the course so race, gender and sexuality are understood as mutually constitutive of one another.... In terms of centering gender, the course foregrounds the question of culture, incredibly important in Asian-American racialization, which is a site that is often about women. In terms of naturalization, I am researching now how gender and race intersected in denials of naturalization....
>
> Are these courses spaces for Asian-American students to engage in identity politics/consciousness raising or for students to examine a site of academic inquiry? The ideal is mostly the latter....[I]t is important to differentiate identity politics from intellectual reasons to have a course like this.[38]

I cannot overemphasize the importance of Volpp's distinction between identity politics and intellectual commitment, of her inclusion of questions of gender, cultural difference, and sexuality, especially in the context of an academic professional school (although I must point out the asymmetry of the inclusion of South Asia and the Raj – a history that has been laid to rest by the move to America – on her list). Such unusual interventions, however, must still remain focused, by intention, on the US scene: the repercussions of the denial of naturalization. Within that focus, the continent of Asia can still only be seen, by implication, as the ground for (new) immigrant identity politics. The questioning of identitarianism is in the interest of claiming "Asia" for all who can claim to be *Asian-American*. West Asia is best left to Middle Eastern politics – inner Asia to post-Sovietology. There is not enough critical mass of Myanmar to Indonesian immigrants. Volpp's excellent pedagogic plans depend on the historical demography of the United States. Within those outlines, this is the best example I have found. And this is a unifying, not a pluralizing initiative. "Our (American) Asia" is an effortful achievement. What it has to contend with is the fact that "incidents of sexual violence in the West are frequently thought to reflect the behavior of a few deviants – rather than as part of our culture. In contrast, incidents of violence in the Third World or immigrant communities are thought to characterize the cultures of entire nations."[39]

Efforts such as Volpp's can still be contained within disciplinary sociology: as a move from identity to social relations. The importance of the effort is that it redefines education as a metropolitan social movement. But the matrix of this relocation and the "identity" of the players are provided and determined by the civil society of the United States.

We cannot ask Leti Volpp and other interventionist Asian-American critics to do more.

"Asian" Pedagogy: The Impossible Perspective

The production of a pluralized continentalism is dependent upon a responsible pedagogy in the humanities supplementing disciplinary sociology. Sociological connections, based upon conscientious research data, cannot by themselves address the problem of the desire for Asianism in Asians as something to unlearn and relearn imaginatively. Yet this task is daunting for the Humanities as well. Speaking, as I was in Hong Kong, as an Asian from one nation-state to Asians in another, in front of an Asian-majority multicultural audience typical of a modern university in Hong Kong, I must admit that the effort at supplementation seemed forbidding because there was no matrix, not even that of a common continent, if we considered space and history rather than name. (Next set of revisions waiting for my widow schoolteacher to arrive for training, early morning in a "village" remote from any sort of "road." The anchorlessness of "Asia" is perhaps felt best in subalternity. Last week, the same anchorlessness was evident in the tiny Chinese school at the end of a narrow hill track, run by a woman alone. Shall we dismiss these folks as pre-political when there is so much fantasy at the top?)

There is, of course, an awareness of the many areas of the world – including the many "Asia"-s – in Comparative Area Studies, in International Affairs, in Development Economics, and perhaps even in Comparative Asian History – although my imagination falters there. Because of these seemingly obvious disciplinary connections, the Social Sciences lay claim to a conciliatory role. As I have commented earlier, already in 1959, C. Wright Mills laid claim to the imagination – within strict US outlines – in his famous book. In 1996, in the full flush of globalization, the Gulbenkian Commission published its report on "the opening up of the Social Sciences."[40]

But if we want to talk about a change that is more than institution-structural, a change that might affect the way the next generation thinks, we have to consider pedagogy in the Humanities. Here as else-where, I have a working hypothesis which brings us full circle to the beginning of the book; there below, here above: humanities pedagogy as such attempts an uncoercive rearrangement of desire through the method of its study. When we leave the general field of the Social Sciences and enter into the Humanities as such, we are speaking of a more textured kind of work, entering through friendship with the language(s), able to meditate upon gender and sexuality without the self-conscious arrogance of the gender-trained do-gooder. The real ground for examining and implementing this is of course in classroom and teacher training – language-based close-reading laced with social-scientific rigor.

In *Death of a Discipline*, I have attempted to give examples of such reading. But I have not been able to go as much in the direction of the social sciences as I would like – no doubt because of my own inade-quate training.

I despair at the possibility of breaking through the insular special-ism favored by many humanities departments in the best Asian insti-tutions. At the same time, I cherish a hope that the best fruit of the new generation of (counter)globalizing intellectuals will foster some-thing like what I am suggesting here on the pedagogic front: an enlightened generalism. This remains a goal in view of which a sort of transnational literacy, an intuition of the dynamic geopolitical con-figurations of the globalizing present, may be achieved, again and again, providing a changeful and moving base for the recoding of the ceaseless movement of data as such.[41]

In the Humanities – by which I understand philosophy and literature – basic research *is* the exercise of the imagination. And it is through that exercise that a rearrangement of desires can, perhaps, begin to take place. There are no guarantees here. All other forms of research in the humanities borrow from other disciplines – law, history, anthropology, sociology, and the general craft of databasing. But the textured work specific to the Humanities must be distinguished from both comparativist expertise and the more localized dispelling of ignorance of internal conflict in each region, although that too is necessary. That is a different kind of savvy, not unimportant in its own place.

An article in nytimes.com described the detention of US-related academics in China in April–May, 2001 with a uniform US-focused reasoning, oblivious of the micrologies of internal power. The article spoke of Hong Kong as follows: "The detentions are casting a pall over Hong Kong's universities, which have become a popular base in the last decade for scholars to study China. The former British colony offers a hard-to-beat combination of high salaries, proximity to the mainland and relative academic freedom."[42]

This description, based on ignorance of (or ignoring) internal power lines, offers us a text rich for interpretation. "Relative" to what, one wonders, as that adjective is applied to "academic freedom"? To the United States, one presumes. Additionally, it is possible to assume that Hong Kong, being a *former* British colony, now enjoys only *relative* academic freedom, full *academic* freedom being possible when the *state* is colonized or unfree. I am obliged to insist that a proliferation of specialisms continue to uphold the idea of an academy protected by a repressive state. As I have already remarked once or twice, Hong Kong is marked by a pervasive resistance to decolonization. I did not notice a "general" pall over the universities. There certainly was a contained effort at redress. The article also needed an adjective before the "scholar" who studies China thus, conveniently: "foreign," read US. But we must also be able to imagine that the absence of this adjective, the unemphatic management of "relative" and "general" in the texture of the report, parallels our own metonymic appropriation of the proper name "Asia" only for our region. The denial of Hong Kong passports to those who are not ethnic Chinese, the denial of Pakistaniness to Yemenis, the denial of Indianness to Muslims, the exclusion of Kurds from the rights to the Turkish state, the withholding of inclusion into statehood from Palestine, where shall we stop? The conflict in the Balkans is certainly comparable to this. But the latter is distinguished from our predicament by a desire for entry into European continent-think. If we lack the supportive matrix of the metropolitan nation-state, in other words if we are not Asian-*Americans*, we are also without the potential ideal of a united continent.

In *Anil's Ghost*, the Asian-Canadian novelist Michael Ondaatje attempts to imagine the difference between location and diaspora.[43] Sarath, an archaeologist, lives in the contradiction that the patient aesthetics of his profession must continue even as, as an activist intellectual, he must engage with the violence all around him, and his archaeological skills must operate in that arena as well. Anil, a diasporic Sri Lankan woman holding a British passport, travels to Sri Lanka as a forensic anthropologist for a human rights investigation, and is anxious only for the uncontradictory truth. Anil is the central character of the novel and is portrayed with exquisite sympathy. It is Sarath who is somewhat uncouth, with hints of dubious political connections. Yet at book's end it is Sarath who is tortured and killed, helping Anil presumably to escape, outside of the book's frame.

A training in literary reading teaches us to learn from the singular and the unverifiable. This little vignette from Ondaatje is thus not the general social truth about all located workers and all diasporic human rights activists. To think so is to refuse the invitation to work together with the social sciences, that can produce useful generalizations – however limited – that is one of the main concerns of this closing chapter.

Having said this, let us note that it is in the context of this division, in an indirect free style that signifies Sarath thinking, that Ondaatje gives a description of the foreign press and Asia: "Sarath had seen truth broken into suitable pieces and used by the foreign press alongside irrelevant photographs. A flippant gesture toward Asia that might lead, as a result of this information, to new vengeance and slaughter."

And, even if it can teach us something about the press and the mediatic production of "truth," the novel is still caught between Asian-America and Asia, the diasporic and the located. It does not escape the exclusionary Asian politics that I have commented on above. Qadri Ismail suggests that:

> Since its cardinal actants are all Sinhala and Buddhist, since it minoritizes the Tamils by denying them effective voice in a story explicitly set in Sri Lanka, since it cannot even name its Tamil actants, since it denies therefore the multi-ethnicity of Sri Lanka, since it presents the

JVP [*janatha vimukti peramuna*] sympathetically but not the LTTE
[Liberation Tigers of Tamil Eelam], since it depicts the state's brutali-
ties in the south and not the north, since the only Lankan history it
presents is Sinhala history, *Anil's Ghost* is clearly on the side of ...
Sinhala nationalism.[44]

Thus, although literary reading can teach us political lessons, we
cannot assume this without a more widespread habit of politically lit-
erate textured reading, which is dependent upon training.[45] It is because
I feel that we must *learn* to read texturally even as we produce generalizable knowledge that I call yet again for at least a relaxing of the academic subdivision of labor, not only between Sociology and the
Humanities, between History and Cultural Studies, but also between
the area specialties; at least a truce in the quarrel of the ancient and the
modern, in the interest of an integrative pedagogy that still respects
disciplinary difference. At courses I have team-taught with the social
sciences, the greatest problem has always been to teach how to use
literature as "evidence."

In one part of the academy – a part that is bigger than the whole – an
area-integrative approach is the only game in town. I speak, of course,
of the Business School. Here also specific regions and nation-states of
Asia are connected selectively and the game theory exercises given to
the students connect pretty directly to the "real world" outside the university. The extramural lines remain sectoral – governed by the ambits
of groups such as ASEAN (the Association of Southeast Asian Nations),
flanked by sub-regional groups such as SAARC (South Asian Association
for Regional Cooperation), IORARC (Indian Ocean Rim Association for
Regional Cooperation), BIMSTEC (Bangladesh, India, Myanmar, Sri
Lanka, and Thailand Economic Cooperation), BBNI (Bhutan,
Bangladesh, Nepal and India quadrangle), and the like.[46] This area is so
volatile that a layperson like myself can only report the day before
yesterday's news, and ask questions. What kind of class- and gender-
divided epistemic transformations will take place if the ASEAN dream –
"the world's biggest free trade zone of nearly two billion people?" – comes
true?[47] What new patterns of subalternization will emerge and how
will metropolitan academic radicalism, including Asian-American radicalism, contribute to this? What does it matter that Megawati
Sukarnoputri, an organic intellectual of this field ("Asean must remain
open to the global economy," rather than allow some protection
because China is notionally "nonmarket," she says), is a "third world

woman?" (I cannot forget that her father claimed that she was named "with/of clouds" – meghavati – because she was conceived on a cloudy day. Remember Norman Mailer's conviction that the man knew the day when a child was conceived?)

It is increasingly my sense that we must find some way of critically acknowledging the role of business schools in producing an integrating interface with the "real world," and not keep ourselves confined to magisterial Schools of International and Public Affairs. Corporate philanthropy leads to apparent material solutions to the problems of the disenfranchised, no doubt based on a general knowledge of problems on a pan-Asian basis. But it is a collection of gestures that does not lead to broad-based epistemic change in either the giver or the receiver. The connection may seem stronger than in Comparative Area Studies and the other Social Sciences that I mentioned before, where knowledge circulates in the academy and the contact is fieldwork. But in fact the connections are just as unmoored. It is the "aesthetic" that allows for an attempt at the bridging of the gap, always in a mode of uncertainty and anteriority. In the humanities, we can learn to try to "other ourselves," without guarantees. This can supplement the sympathetic identification and didactic leadership mode of the networking in global social movements which sometimes produces a Luddite legitimation by reversal of exploitative "Development" efforts.

There is a growing body of literature that focuses on the role of the CEO in today's world. I came across former Undersecretary of Commerce Jeffrey K. Garten's *The Mind of the CEO* the day after I gave a shorter version of this chapter as a speech in Hong Kong.[48] It strikes some notes that are common to these kinds of books. In brief, the points to mention are that, although the inevitable nod to "education" is made once or twice, the general tone is defensive, the general plan is "profits and communities," there are no details as we hear paeans to the loyalty of workers in this age of layoffs. The general theme is how to save old-fashioned capitalism in the post-Cold War world of Information Technology. Garten does not collapse economy and culture, as does Gunder Frank. He certainly insists on the unifying world system of the economy – "the Internet ... will create ... a 'new mental geography,' in which distance is eliminated and there is only one economy and one market – global in both cases" – but is quite aware of the cultural differential. This is what he writes as he discusses "communication ... under pressure ... when I was in charge of Lehman Brothers' investment banking activities in Asia ... [overseeing] the restructuring of a gigantic near-bankrupt shipping company headquartered in Hong Kong: I was sure that some of my Asian colleagues were hearing the words but not really understanding them. This wasn't anyone's fault; the American, Japanese and Chinese experiences were just very different. I confess that I wished many times that the team was composed only of Americans like me." "Americans like me," not Asian-Americans. Ultimately, his recommendations in the book are profits plus community, a greater engagement of academic political philosophers (a disciplinary combination of social sciences and humanities), presumably to help make this happen, and, in one ominous sentence, a program that is the opposite of the imaginative othering of the self in which a robust Humanities education can train the imagination: "The mind of the CEO needs to get into the mind of his customers."

My call for integrative pedagogy must not be confused with these lines of trade and finance, haphazardly opposed by global social movements, although they signify a major arena of cultural transformation. These lines of transformation do not necessarily undo Martin Jacques's lament regarding "bi-racial [Asian] societ[ies] in which [only the ethnic majority] and Caucasians are respected and accepted." In fact, such lines of trade- and finance-related transformation, unanchored in the older disciplinary formations, can exacerbate what can perhaps be called "cultural feudalism," where a benevolent despot like Lee Kuan Yew can claim collectivity rather than individualism when expedient, and texts such as *Going With the (Cash) Flow: Taoism and the New Managerial Wisdom* proliferate, to rub shoulders with *If Aristotle Ran General Motors: The New Soul of Business*, to obliterate cultural difference superficially.[49] In the present state of the world, such lines may leave undisturbed classed cultural patterns of gender oppression, opposed by nothing stronger than the unexamined cultural golden-ageism of the middle- or upper-class activist – located, "international," or diasporic. Outside the circle of activism, it can produce a superficial "liberation" from Asian oppression in public behavior, temporary re-definition of protected space for diversified sexed behavior, with no epistemic or ethical change – no change, in other words, in deep mind set, and often no inclination for involvement in the struggle for the juridico-political redefinition of public and private space which remains little more than a facile imitation of Euro-US gendered political behavior unless opened up by the sort of disciplinary change I am imagining here. In the field of *sexual* practice, there is no trace of the sequentially stacked multiple modernities of which Shmuel Eisenstadt speaks so eloquently, although his examples are culled from women's collective behavior in the field of *gender* struggle in the service of national politics.

Islam

Islam is a peculiarly Asian internationality that also embraces Africa, Europe, and, latterly, the United States. Thus, if we have mentioned disciplinary and geopolitical lines of thinking the plurality of "Asia"-s in the previous sections, in closing I mention a revised approach to Islam, not as a self-contained and monolithic exception, but as another historical entry into the plurality of "Asia"-s. This becomes altogether urgent in light of recent events – the demolition of the World Trade Center in New York and injury to a wing of the Pentagon in Washington on September 11, 2001; and George W. Bush's subsequent declaration of "war."

I am revising this by the light of a flickering oil lamp in a dark room in an Asian village where only the teacher knows Saddam Hussein and Iraq, vaguely. This is also true of the one-teacher school villages in China. Yet there are Muslims here, and there. Internationality is not necessarily geopolitical. Let us remember this as we read the rest.

I would like to start this section with a quotation from Charles Tilly:

> Over the time that the world has known substantial states, ... empires have been the dominant and largest state form. ... Only now ... do we seem to be leaving the age of massive Eurasian empires that began in earnest across a band from the Mediterranean to East Asia almost four thousand years ago. To the extent that we regard such international compacts as the European Union, GATT, and NAFTA as embodying imperial designs, furthermore, even today's requiem may prove premature.[50]

Today we are obliged to add US military-political imperialism, and plans of world governance, "good" imperialisms on the sustainability calculus. When I first wrote, the focus was on the postcoloniality announced by the breakup of the old Russian imperial formation, competing with the Habsburgs and the Ottomans, that managed to appropriate the dream of international socialism. The most interesting area of research in this new postcoloniality is neither that fantasmatic space "South Asia," nor that oneiric disciplinary enclave "*Asian*-America," but rather Central Asia.[51] (In a larger perspective, the Balkans and the

Balkan diaspora would be of interest.) I have merely skirted this in the chapter on Armenia, and tried to suggest how the new postcoloniality is on the way to globalization.

The kind of integrative vision that I am suggesting would see Islam as a relief map with a diversified history, read Aquinas as a conservative respondent to the great twelfth-century secularist Abu'l Wahid Muhammad Ibn Rushd, known as Averroes by European mispronunciation. Indeed, this is the advice I gave when Ho Wai-Yip shared his brilliant study of the ethnic Muslim minority in Hong Kong: "Go integrative on Islam. Think not only of West and South Asian and North African Islam, but also of varieties of Chinese Islam, distinct in their diachrony and synchrony."[52]

Attached to the area is the nearly millennial geopolitical narrative – Russia, France, and Britain playing for power there – of the Great Game. To comment on this play by historical play remains a rich field for an integrative Asianism backing up the tremendous impetus of US Ethnic Studies. How does the cultural politics of identity play in the Taliban's destruction of the Gandhari Buddhas? Can we attempt to understand them in terms of the unpublicized destruction of Native American and Pacific sacred places in the interest of "development"? Is the issue different because what is at stake is money – notoriously without identity – rather than "identity" as such, a culture of death against the iterability of being-human?[53] There have been some recent attempts at writing the area comfortably in the past in terms of the Silk Route from Samarkhand even as an anti-Soviet position re-coded religious fanatics as allies in the fifties, and the oil route re-coded the Taliban in a different frame day-to-day.[54] Such recodings have taken on a minute-by-minute dynamic since the events in New York and Washington. What are the intellectual lines that inform the politics of RAWA (Revolutionary Association of the Women of Afghanistan)? A study of a metonymic individual of this group would be a task indeed for the new initiative in the Humanities I am invoking here, something in between socio-politically informed literary reading of idiom and a culturally caught discourse of ethics. Here Volpp's rethinking of the relationship between multiculturalism and feminism can be useful. My model for such a metonymic approach remains Ranajit Guha's study of Philip Francis in *A Rule of Property for Bengal*.[55]

I wish I were as young as my best students, with the time to learn a few languages. For this new approach will not necessarily find the best directions from the proliferating collections of post-Soviet feminist anthologies in translation. First because, like much earlier postcolonial studies, they still follow the lines of empire and therefore Central Asia is likely to find a less than interesting place in the anthology, with little careful historical textualizing or tracing. And secondly, as I have already mentioned the Soviets had made women the vehicle of modernization in the area. Thus the division among women down the tradition–modernity line is one agenda for feminist integrative work as it gives Asia a place in the history of the present for a US-based Ethnic Studies.

Another fascinating area, not unconnected to the lines of a new articulation of feminist culture, is the "Islam"-ization of the area's Islam. As Hamid Dabashi writes: "From the scattered memories of a sacred imagination that once congealed in the Arabia of the sixth (Christian) century, competing 'Islams' were invented by contending political forces dominant from Transoxiana to Spain."[56] The tribalities of Central Asia had paradoxically written a "freer," more eclectic Islam than the more publicized conflicts in the residues of medieval Islamic cosmo-politanism or the recent puritanism and orthodoxy of the Wahabis. Close as I am to Bangladesh, I am very aware of the paradoxical freedoms within peripheral Islams. In Central Asia we can tap the con-sequences of an earlier modernization of women, and a current tradi-tionalization of Islam. As the bankers say: a huge untapped market. ... Farideh Heyat has written of this in the context of Azerbaijan.[57] In my discussion of Armenia in chapter 3, I remark on this change as it comes through the United Nations Economic and Social Commission for Asia and the Pacific reports. Somini Sengupta drives the point home, reporting from Baghdad: "In an air-conditioned bedroom with pink everything on the walls, Yosor Ali al-Qatan, 15, stares longingly at a hip-hugging pair of pink pinstriped pants. The new Iraq, her mother warns her, is far too dangerous for a 15-year-old girl to be seen in such pants."[58]

I have not touched upon the phenomenon of the Caribbean – a space of productive *synoikismos* between Asia, Africa, Europe. I quote my wise colleague Maryse Condé: "As long as the African, European, Indian and Asian elements are not merged, Caribbean identity will not flourish."[59] That peace must also be made if "Asia" is claimed across the disciplinary boundaries.

Conclusion

To sum up my proposal, then: I am imagining something like a plural-ized Asian Comparative Literature – something in between socio-politically informed literary reading of idiom and a culturally caught discourse of ethics – altogether broadly based and working against the obvious identitarian regional divides, ready to work with already existing resources in the Social Sciences. Resources of language teaching would have to go beyond the major European and local language, which are already in place. Such a literary approach to languages places the reader in the place of the reader perhaps implied by the writer in the language. This practice of othering ourselves into many Asia-s can also use the resources of what is by now pretty standard Euro-US literature teaching – close reading. My slender experience with tertiary students and colleagues indicates that the great universities in the PRC teach literature much the same way. At less prestigious institutions there may be a "modern is better" approach comparable to "traditional is better" or "pomo/poco is better" in the Euro-US.[60] We are looking here at problematizing an established approach just as strongly as the identitarianism that has been a largely unintended consequence of *Orientalism* and postcolonial criticism.

In philosophy, on the other hand, the effort will have to be more thorough. The gains of analytic philosophy and pragmatism should obviously be retained (and indeed will be, since it is still the Euro-US dominant). Pragmatism's effort to sanitize and claim a humanist post-structuralism is, however, too close to the declaration of "white mythology" as the human norm to be fostered as an unquestioned good to be seriously reconstructive.[61] The insights of post-Hegelian (European) "continental" philosophy – for requirements of time and space I can comment neither on the connections between the concerns of this chapter and this widely accepted nomenclature, nor on the hierarchy implicit in European "philosophy" versus Asian "values" – need to be unmoored not from their intellectual complexity but from their attendant disciplinary hermeticism. Identitarian culturally marked "Asian" philosophies should be freed from similar separatist hermeticism and/or conservative regionalist isolationism as well as elite diasporic golden-ageism. All of this without dilution into what Jean Franco might call the "light" Cultural Studies approach.[62] And the entire effort – literature and philosophy combined – should be held in the principles signaled by Leti Volpp in her consideration of multiculturalism and feminism.

I am speaking of an effort that must be renewed again and again, with no guarantees, in the name of Asia-s pluralized, where the naming names no real space, but rather names the critical position that re-cites Martí, puts both diasporic hegemony and regionalist unilateralism with the Euro-US under erasure.

Let the Asian universities also become utopias – but not on the US model. Rather than supply the dominant demand for restricted multiculturalism by only focusing on our own region, let us think of a more than merely economically diversified Pan-Asianism, a more than merely "comparative Asianism." Gunder Frank cites Joseph Fletcher describing "integrative history" as follows: "First one searches for historical parallelisms ... then one determines if they are causally interrelated."[63] If the Humanities and Social Sciences supplement each other, interrupt each other productively, then the production of knowledge will not be such a "been there, done that" game. A merely social scientific "frame resonance" – structure – will give way again and again to the attempt to strike a "musical resonance" – texture – and "failure" will be recoded as persistent critique in view of a success always "to come."[64] Of course there are vested interests that will oppose this mightily, kill us with kindness and no funds in a corporatizing trend in universities, but we either do it or we don't. I'm sorry for this lame conclusion on behalf of an impossible project that remains necessary, but I cannot find a rousing one. At any rate, an ongoing project at least assures us that the schools do not close.

Afghanistan, Armenia, Azerbaijan, Bahrain, Bangladesh, Bhutan, Brunei, Cambodia, China, Cyprus, Georgia, Hong Kong, India, Indonesia, Iran, Iraq, Israel, Japan, Jordan, Kazakhstan, the Koreas, Kuwait, Kyrgyzstan, Laos, Lebanon, Macau, Malaysia, Maldives, Mongolia, Myanmar, Nepal, Oman, Pakistan, Paracel Islands, Philippines, Qatar, Russia, Saudi Arabia, Singapore, Spratly Islands, Sri Lanka, Taiwan, Tajikistan, Thailand, Turkey, Turkmenistan, United Arab Emirates, Uzbekistan, Vietnam. Asia. Diversified subject-positions produced by shifting geopolitical lineaments. So far just a list off the Internet, with quotation marks around at least Cyprus, Russia, Turkey – and such absent named contested spaces as East Timor. "Asia" drags the aura of its name – Melanesia, Micronesia – into Australia's sphere of influence. Is Australia in the Asia-Pacific? A labyrinth of investigation there....

After my oral presentation of a shorter version of this essay, Jeremy Tamblin remarked that the incantation of the names of the various nation-states of Asia was reminiscent of Yeats's "Easter, 1916":

> I write it out in a verse –
> Macdonagh and MacBride
> And Connolly and Pearse

Now and in time to be,
Wherever green is worn,
And changed, changed utterly:
A terrible beauty is born.[65]

Yeats is writing in the mode of tragedy – "a terrible beauty." My mode is of the workaday world, people "[c]oming with vivid faces/ From counter or desk ...." Yeats writes in the name of nationalism opening out to exilic regionalism – "wherever green is worn." I write to cite and pluralize the name of a continent. Yeats leaves out Constance Markievicz in his naming, having dismissed her as a "shrill argument[ative person] of ignorant goodwill" earlier in the poem. The woman's part holds everything in my proposal. Some may say I am myself shrill with ignorant goodwill.

Yet it is an honor to have unwittingly borrowed a gesture from so deft a practitioner of the English language. May that power radiate in our efforts to inscribe our multiple Asia-s, again and again, in all our work.

And now for the rest of the world, the spirit of Bandung recoded from postcoloniality to globalization. Kwame Anthony Appiah's important book *Cosmopolitanism: Ethics in a World of Strangers* is just out. I will submit my manuscript before I get a chance to read it. I read a selection and, based on that chapter, I would heartily agree with him that contamination rather than authenticity is what we must prize.[66] I must however suggest that there is a difference between the chosen Europeanist cosmopolitanism of the global elite and the passive exposure to multinationality in the everyday of the global underclass. However much they seem to "choose" and celebrate this by-product of capitalist globalization, they cannot be said to be the agents of it. My critique of cosmopolitanism cannot begin here. Let me point at another item of agreement between Appiah and myself and propose a solution.

"Take another look at that Unesco Convention," Appiah writes. "It affirms the 'principle of equal dignity of and respect for all cultures' (What, all cultures – including those of the K.K.K. and the Taliban?)" I too have no faith in bureaucratic egalitarianism. Speaking in Cape Town right after the lifting of apartheid I had suggested, as I do in this book:

all rational formal freedoms ... can only be exercised by [their] own trans-gression, by being bound to content. We have experience of a society of largely unexercised guarantees, a society "just" by default. A robustly just society is where the members, when acting self-consciously within

rational and privative norms – never adequately possible – see freedoms
not as ends but absolute means to protect their transgression, which is
also their exercise. No justification of the *exercise* of [a] freedom can be
drawn from within [itself]. It comes into being in its own binding.[67]

Elsewhere I have situated the question of cultural rights.[68] My solution is to make it institutionally possible to learn as many of the world's
languages as possible, which is rather different from both preserving
cultural authenticity – "culture is its own irreducible counterexample,"
"culture alive is always on the run" I have written, repeatedly – and
imagining that the presence of people from different places all gradually acceding to the uniformity of globalization is actually affirming
cosmopolitanism as a mindset.[69] I end my book on the promise of a
conversation, on other Africas, on the way to the globe othered, again
and again, from capital to social, through a pedagogy of genealogical
deconstruction reterritorializing the abstractions of an anti-ethnicist
regionalism.

Appendix

Position Without Identity – 2004: An Interview with Gayatri Chakravorty Spivak by Yan Hairong

Gayatri Chakravorty Spivak is University Professor and Director of the Institute for Comparative Literature and Society at Columbia University. She specializes in nineteenth- and twentieth-century literature, Marxism, feminism, deconstruction, post-structuralism, and globalization and has been a member of the Subaltern Studies Collective. Professor Spivak is active in rural literacy teacher training at the grassroots level in aboriginal West Bengal. Among her publications are *Of Grammatology* (a translation with critical introduction of Jacques Derrida's *De la grammatologie*), *Imaginary Maps, Breast Stories* and *Old Women* (translations with critical material of the fiction of Mahasweta Devi), *In Other Worlds, The Post-Colonial Critic, Outside in the Teaching Machine, A Critique of Postcolonial Reason: Toward a History of the Vanishing Present*, and *Death of a Discipline*.

This conversation took place on the campus of the University of California, Irvine. It was the fourth Sunday of May, 2004, but the weather was not as warm or sunny as one might expect. To get away from noise and find a quiet and sheltered space for our conversation, which would be taped, we tried the Humanities Instructional Building. Professor Spivak had the key to an office that she borrowed, but did not have the key to the front door that locks the main office area. The only public and sheltered space available then was the restroom. We brought in two light plastic chairs from outside and made use of this space. It was fortunate for us that nobody else came in to use the restroom during our hour-long conversation.

Gayatri Chakravorty Spivak: Hairong has given me the proposal of the special issue and a number of questions related to it and I am fascinated by the proposal and I suggested that I start talking about the very first question in the proposal and then we'll go from there, and that question is: Why do we need to think about "Asia" as a problematic today?

I have been asking myself this question now for some time, because I know that something has to be counterposed to the main outposts of power. On the other hand, I am deeply troubled by identity politics, so for me it cannot be India, it cannot be Bengal, as a political basis for a problematic, it cannot even be that fantasmatic phrase *South Asia*. On the other hand, in many ways, it cannot be, for me, Africa. I have to think Africa from a guest's position and I have to think Latin America from a guest's position. Asia can be for me a position without identity, not only because the continent itself is so regionalized, but also because by the accident of birth I am one of the claimants to its name. I thought I should articulate it as a position *from* which to view, yes? I'm being personal here. I will go further, but I think I have to begin here. I am a literary person, so the personal, not the personal as it relates to me, but the personal as it relates to any person, the person as a "shifter," is important for me. Therefore let me offer a narrative. After all, it is with narratives that a literary critic negotiates.

This narrative is of young schoolchildren in the forties and the fifties who wrote as they were taught that their country was independent, who wrote in their schoolbooks their names and their school, and then Calcutta, and then India, and then Asia, and then the World. What did they know about Asia? But they looked at the map. It was a cartographic position, without identity. They certainly could not imagine "Asia." I find this interesting in thinking about places in the world. If you move from the personal, you will see that it is a place for negotiation.

I want now to talk about Iraq and then about UNESCAP.

Iraq is a project for Asia. The war began in Afghanistan, which is West Asia. Iraq is also in West Asia. Pakistan is in the plan, which is Southwest Asia. Immediately after that, the axis of evil included not just Iran, but also North Korea. In terms of regionality, the only thing that bound these two places together was that they were part of this fantasmatic Asian theater. Almost immediately after that, it was the Philippines; Southeast Asia. So, *we* don't know what Asia is but we can see that this is an Asian operation [smile].

This is why Asia is interesting and, exactly what you say, problematic. It does exist, geopolitically, and yet, as we know, it doesn't exist. In your own excellent proposal, you, in the second sentence, I'm moving through, you mention "ASEAN plus three, Korea, China, and

Japan, flows of capital and labor in the region." Asia is not a region
and these three named nation states are not Asia, and that's one of
the problems, we tend to think of our part of Asia as Asia. That's
what I was questioning. The idea that this is Asia is US-centric. It
comes from the decision, in the United States, that East Asia, because
of immigration and the pattern of military and political relation patterns, is Asia. People who are not particularly in favor of the US have
accepted this view that a strip of Asia is Asia as such.

Now I want to move to UNESCAP, the United Nations Economic
and Social Commission for the Asia-Pacific.

UNESCAP is very interested in other parts of Asia also. Tani
Barlow was talking about this, but I think because she didn't have
enough time, she was not able to integrate it into older patterns of
control. Let me try to do that. UNESCAP is very interested in the
post-Soviet areas of Asia, in other words, Central Asia and the
Southern Caucasus: Armenia, Georgia, Azerbaijan. It is a peculiar
part of Asia. You move a little further and you come to Asia Minor.
You are moving toward what used to be called Asia by Homer,
Western Anatolia. Troy was on the western coast of Western
Anatolia and across the Aegean Sea was Greece. *You* don't have to
think about it because you're a social scientist, but I think about it
because I'm a literary Europeanist and I see how that word "Asia" is
negotiated – it is a Western word. In Japanese, it is written as
'katakana' – a script reserved for foreign words.

Now let's get back to UNESCAP. When they do interest themselves in Central Asia and the Southern Caucasus, they are coming
into an area where, since the Russian Revolution, nationalities have
been negotiated. The settlement of the area, was, of course, a Soviet
undertaking. Now that the Soviet Union has disappeared, what we
are looking at is a reopening of what is called the Great Game. It's
the fight between the big powers in terms of access to oil. That's
why these Central Asian and Southern Caucasian countries are so
interesting to UNESCAP. And there have been others before them.
That's what you saw me looking at, other organizations there before,
when you came in. And OSCE is one of them, Organization for
Security and Cooperation in Europe. That is Europe now, not Asia,
remember, we're talking about Asia as a problematic and suddenly
we're into the word Europe, this organization which comes from an
earlier organization is now perceived by the Russian Federation as
an organization which can work over against NATO. Just as Australia
is in the Asia-Pacific, maybe – the West Coast of the US is maybe the

East Coast of the Asia-Pacific, so this border area is where Europe can sometimes step in. On the other hand, the US will mind its security in Europe, and NATO is not an Asian organization [smile]. This area is part of the Great Game since Peter the Great, and now the players are Europe, OSCE, and NATO. NATO does military exercises in Georgia, Azerbaijan, and Armenia. Now *that* Asian theater is something we can't just forget. You see how it fractures our sense of identity. On the other hand, nearly all of these Central Asian countries on the northern front of the Caucasus, they share a border with China. Yet the people who are negotiating the identitarian cultural conflicts in that part of the world are playing a different kind of game, as "located" as all of us regionalist "Asians." And for that we have to come to an area of Asia which you probably never think about. Nagorno-Karabakh ... do you know what that area is?

Yan Hairong: No.

GCS: Nagorno-Karabakh is a mountainous area that is within Azerbaijan. Nagorno means mountainous in Russian, but Karabakh I can understand through my Urdu and Hindi. In Urdu and Hindi, it would be Kalabagh, that is to say Black Garden. I've never been there. It's full of Armenians but it's inside Azerbaijan. It has a corridor which goes into Armenia. These folks want to be independent. This fight has been going on since the Soviet Union broke up, but it's a much older fight; it's a fight between Christians and Muslims. We've heard about this fight elsewhere, yes? Not in Nagorno-Karabakh, but think about Iraq, think about Afghanistan, think about the Crusades, think about, you know, what's happening on TV today, in terms of the Abu Ghraib prisoners, etc., it's the same topos except no one's paying attention to it. Most of the Armenians are Christians and the Azeris living there are Shia Muslims and the funniest thing is that of course like elsewhere they lived in amity for hundreds of years, but now it has become clued into this particular fight.

YHR: How did you come to pay attention to this?

GCS: About 10 years ago, two Armenian-American students of mine asked me – one of them an undergraduate and the other a graduate student – why doesn't Armenia have a postcolonial theory? I have remained focused on the question for 10 years and then it flowed into my other interest: finding Asia outside of just the areas that I'm interested in. In the meantime the fight for postcolonialism carries on between Africa, China, Latin America, and South Asia – big players. I have begun to see what you're calling the problematic. Now what I was going to say in terms of Asia and Europe was that since 1992 they have been wanting to establish peace there because without peace the oil stuff is ruined. In 1994 there was a ceasefire which they actually kept pretty well. But what was going to happen there was going to be decided by a conference which would take place in Minsk, headquarters of the Commonwealth of Independent States and the national capital of Belarus. Now the funny thing is that the Minsk conference could never take place because all the people involved in it would not agree to sit down together. Mind you, for hundreds of years they have lived together, but not now. But a Minsk group which is just Europeans and some other powerful groups began to operate without the conference. And now I believe last year that even out of the Minsk group emerged another group which has been initialed HL something High Level which means pretty much United States, Russia, and France. So you see how Asia is not just a problematic, but it's a problem, and so for us to really understand how it is a whole collection of positions without identity and going back and forth, we have to step out of regionalisms. Those of us who, in some way, which I don't quite know how, I mean you and I are talking to each other – Chinese and Indian – in some way we are connected to that name. But on the other hand our obligation, if we want to think about the problematic, is to resist the name as simply describing our identity. So, that's my response to one and two, the first sentence and the second sentence.

Where do you want me to go now?

YHR: I actually have a question derived from your interview with Tani. I suppose one can look at regional economic solidarity as both a kind of resistance to this US form of globality but also interpellation by it. Now in the talk you – both in the interview and the talk you gave in Hong Kong on "Other Asias" – you talked about how we need to undo this economic reality in some way. I was wondering how you would speak to people who are actually invested in this form of resistance. How would you talk to them about this need, or rather "imperative," to undo that economic reality?

GCS: Who are the people who are invested?

YHR: These people who I'm talking about are certain kinds of government officials who are very much involved in forming organizations, for example Shanghai Six involving China and Central Asia ... and also intellectuals who somehow could not see other alternatives ...

GCS: Rather than economic organizations/collectivities, is that what you're saying?

YHR: Yes. Or rather there's a belief in certain kinds of economic realities that are a determining factor in the global game and therefore
this investment in this primary sector. So how would you speak to
this audience?

GCS: Well I would not, I don't believe I have the wherewithal to simply
discourage them. The global game is a game that is not going to stop
because I am saying something. So I think whatever I say will be said
as a comment on it rather than a suggestion to them because they
are not going to listen to the two of us talking in this gendered and
private place. In Shakespeare's *Henry IV*, Glendower comes forward
and says – maybe I said this to Tani also – "I can call the spirits from
the vasty deep" and Hotspur asks him "will they come when you do
call for them?" You know, anybody can make suggestions, but it's
foolish if it has no effect [chuckle]. So I comment on this.

As an old socialist, I'm interested in an international economic
system. I am. Now I have said many, many times and I am not alone
in saying this, that that particular dream ended in 1914 when the
German social democrats, the Marxist party, wanted war credits; in
other words, workers of Germany and Britain wanted to fight, two
small places in Europe could not unite. So we knew that we needed
something other than just the idea of a just world emerging out of
a global economy which would be a level playing field – that idea
was not going to work. International socialism was based on that
idea. Capitalist globalization pretends that that idea will work
[chuckle]. But look now at all this stuff in the US, the unions, agitating against outsourcing. People who don't think it through think
that to support the unions against outsourcing is to be doing counter-globalizing left work. In fact, it is a reassertion of the failure of
that old failed dream. Workers of the world cannot unite. And will
not unite. So in the place of that dream which was a dream of justice, international justice, remember Teodor Shanin saying socialism
is not about development, it is about justice, we put a plan for sustainable development, sustaining what? It is the false promise of globalization as a way which can succeed. Globalization is a false
promise of socialism. It is capitalism pretending to be socialism.
How can we be taken in by that?

So, if we are interested in working for a just world with an international system, it's no use saying give up the global game. What
one needs to think of is in what ways one can constantly train people
to interrupt the global game, to remind it that all of these games are
supposed to be for human beings. They are supposed to be. They're

not of course. But on the other hand, it's like Mary Prince calling on the abolitionists saying this is what you promised: be good to your promise. Now, in fact, these are false promises, so the thing to do is to train people to see that these are false promises. That's the only way to do it, in my view.

It is notionally good if Euro-US hegemony is balanced by other economic blocs. Balance of power is good. But we are talking geopolitics here, competing capitalisms, not about human beings, however you want to plot it.

Secondly, it can't be done today. It's a long-term project. Training human beings is not so easy. You can train them to use information technology but training them to form these kinds of collectivities of political philosophy, and activism which is based on political philosophy, is a very slow labor indeed. We're talking long-term. The more geopolitical stuff can work *only if* in the global south, we reinvent the state as an abstract structure, as a porous abstract structure, so that states can combine against the deprivations of internationalization through economic restructuring. We see in country after country that so-called economic growth does not lead to redistribution. The most quantitative economic analysts and the most qualitative, politically correct discussions are united in noticing these results. You don't have to be a hard leftist to say this. Nobody looks at the possible efficacy of state structures because people have their faith today in everything outside of governments. Remember, I'm not talking about national sovereignty, I'm talking about abstract state structures that are porous. I'm talking about critical regionalism, shared laws, shared health, education, and welfare structures, open frontiers rather than only economic organizations. We can't really even think about what they would truly look like. In August there was a South Asian women's court, a symbolic court, we heard testimonies from survivors, in this case of trafficking and HIV/AIDS. We listened to 40 to 45 women. We made a suggestion to the South Asian Association for Regional Cooperation [SAARC] that they should establish trans-state jurisdictions for the apprehension of perpetrators and also to make victim-friendly legislations. Now those kinds of suggestions are not economic suggestions. They are suggestions that look forward to the state as an abstract and porous structure. Otherwise, to give accountability over to nongovernmental organizations [NGOs] – I don't think nongovernmental organizations should be abolished – can become a way of letting organizations like the USAID [United States Agency for International Development] into a country. Even this afternoon as I was reading about this area that I talked about at length, finally ISAR [Initiative for Social Action and Renewal in Eurasia], USAID, they're entering through the NGO training workshops. The World Bank is an NGO after all. Giving over all of the accountability to this group, which then conspires against the individual states and sees them only as areas of repression is also to take power away from the citizens who can after all supposedly *make* the state accountable. But who listens to suggestions by humanities teachers?

YHR: I think it'll be a useful comment for people who are trying to make certain kinds of critical decisions in our current situation and this is the audience that I think will find your commentary useful. Then ... a question that I'm really interested in is how is the Asia question related to the question of the Third World? I was wondering whether you're interested in this question.

GCS: People like me, from the postwar generation, think of the Third World as a very specific collection of self-styled nonaligned peoples who had some solidarity and therefore could make statements in a divided world. What do *you* understand as the Third World?

YHR: I think my interest is precisely in this question of bringing us back to the 1960s. The formation of the Third World then presumed two things: the first condition was that we had two opposing camps, the socialist camp and the capitalist camp, and the space this opposition created for the Third World; and second was the strong sense of sovereignty, right after national struggles. And today, these two conditions are not there anymore. Yet there are intellectuals today still interested in reviving and invoking it and keep using the word Third World. So I was wondering how do we think about it, and what would be our relationship with that kind of invocation?

GCS: What I'm going to say is going to be again somewhat impractical, but what one thinks about is not necessarily practical. I think it's not just that the division into the socialist camp and the capitalist camp is gone, it's also that we cannot think of sovereignty in terms of last century's nationalist struggles. This is why when I was talking about *reinventing* the state, I was NOT talking about sovereignty. This is why I speak about the global South. All the Asian countries are not part of the global South. Each of the countries has a North in the South in themselves. And the North in the South is in fact more committed to the global game than it is to the welfare of the state space. And the so-called Asian Tigers have recovered. China is in a very special place now, bailing out the US economy. These intranational and international, economic and geopolitical divisions within our continent require the kind of critical regionalism we are talking about. If we do anything on the model of national sovereignty in the name of by now archaic nationalist struggles we are going to get replicas of the global game except now, truly in a scary way, confined to our region. What I'm talking about is sustained resistance, as I was saying, the production of collectivities based in political philosophy, sustained resistance to those kinds of units *recoding* themselves in terms of the last century. I think Marx's *Eighteenth Brumaire* gives a fine analysis of how the 1850s in France tried to recode themselves as the 1790s. I wish people would read that again carefully. I don't think we can talk about attempts to form alternative players in the global game as the reemergence of the Third World.

YHR: I think it relates to what you previously wrote about secessionism.

GCS: Yes, secessionism within the state; yes, of course, remember that secessionism is not my word. It's Robert Reich's word.

YHR: I think you were talking about it in the context of Bangalore.

GCS: I was talking about it in terms of Bangalore, but it is of course true all over the place … To whom one speaks is a very important category. Convenience in communication – method and language – is going to lead us to the North in the South. There is much talk these days of the emergence of subaltern counter-collectivity. I think that is bogus. If you nominate collectivities that are questioning the power of the United States or the power of the West or whatever as immediately a subaltern counter-collectivity, I don't think you really know what it is like where this conflict *can mean nothing*. There are many millions of people in the world to whom this conflict means nothing, except in the lives they are obliged to lead. The search for subalternity has become like the search for the primitive.

YHR: I think sometimes these things are the unintentional, unthoughtful actions …

GCS: And ignorance.

YHR: Yes, and sometimes these are purposeful, intentional mobilizations of these terms. So I'm thinking of the recent AFL-CIO report on China's labor situation in an attempt to represent itself as savior of US workers.

GCS: Absolutely! In English there is the useful simple phrase: a fool or a knave. Either you're ignorant and you don't know what you're saying but you intend to do well, or you know pretty well what you're saying and you intend to do harm in the name of good. You're either a fool or a knave. That's more or less the situation.

YHR: This is something that I really feel should be brought out in the daylight for all of us to discuss.

GCS: I would like to say something about anticolonial and national struggles. I'm reading through your proposal and hitting one sentence after another [smile]. Anticolonial struggles are a thing of the past. You have it in Israel and Palestine: that's an anticolonial struggle and the tragedy is that it does not belong to our times. We cannot take national liberation as a model of anything anymore. We don't support Palestine's struggle because it's anticolonial. We support it because Israel is a geopolitically violent state. In the name of anticolonialism you get the kind of national identity politics that can lead to fascism. Edward Said once said, in response to Donald Davie, quite a few years ago, that "once the state of Palestine is established, I will become its first critic." Now that contained an insight of what I'm speaking of now. You support the struggle against the brutality of Israel, but to support it in the name of national liberation is anachronistic today. Hawaii, for example, is in a colonial situation. There isn't that much talk about it because over against it is the United States. But when I was teaching there last year I tried to say that the separatist idea of the national liberation of Hawaii for native Hawaiians is anachronistic. I myself found the coding of Hawaii as a Pacific state, part of Oceania, with the advantage of being inside the US system, an insider–outsider, much more useful. Because the Pacific is what you folks, the so-called Asia-Pacific, jump over. It's the West coast of the US and the eastern coast of the continent of Asia. That's Asia-Pacific. And what's in-between is in a completely different state from Fiji to New Zealand to the Easter Islands. I felt that Hawaii should re-regionalize itself and not think in terms of national liberation. I mean its history is as scary as the history of Palestine, although its present is confined to legalized racism, blood quantum claims to land, and economic oppression – not overt military violence. In the late nineteenth century, it was *made* to become part of the US by this Bayonet Constitution, which actually made it possible for foreigners to have voting rights [laugh]. What kind of a constitution is that? In the twenty-first century, I cannot connect to anticolonialism as a slogan. We have to think of the deep involvement of all these countries of the world one way or the other in either globalization or the desire to be so. Anticolonialism can quite often work in the interest of terrible cultural conservatism, which is generally bad for women. We haven't talked about gender at all, but anticolonialism is not a good slogan anymore. I just said that national identity isn't either. People talk about a postnational world; the world is not postnational. If it were postnational, then it would be a different kind of world. I want a critical regionalist world, but I don't want these slogans – colonialism and national identity – to be around for us to use.

YHR: Yes, I think we are learning in some ways, the lesson from 1970s onwards in terms of the consequences and aftermath of the triumph of nationalist struggle.

GCS: Yes.

YHR: I'm interested in your book *Other Asias*. What is it in the book? A few years ago you talked about the paper. How did it become expanded into a book?

GCS: It's a difficult … it's a short book, but it's a difficult book for me to finish. The manuscript is finished. I'm doing final revisions because I bit off more than I could chew. I'm not trained to write about these places. On the other hand, I don't think I should not write about them because I have the conviction that specialists in these areas are muscle-bound by their specialism. I've already told you about finding a position without identity in the name *Asia*. This came out, for me, in response to questions asked in Thailand. In Thailand there was among the students deep resentment about the fact that India was a British colony and therefore had fluency in the language. I've heard this also in China and indeed in Latin America.

So I was thinking, how am I going to answer these young men and women? I mean the faculty people knew to be polite, but the young men and women were speaking out. How can I answer these young men and women – I love students – but these young people are full of resentment against a kind of history. What am I going to tell them? That's when I thought on my feet, very carefully, and I realized why I was looking toward Asia as a word. And I shared that with you today in the beginning. So, what I had done was I had gone into Armenia and the Southern Caucasus in ways that I told you, and then I had gone into Bangladesh because I share a language with them, and so it was possible for me to get some experience of global social movements in Bangladesh in a way that wasn't possible in India because India is a multilingual country and the main language in India is Hindi, and Hindi I can speak, I can read and write in Hindi, but badly, less well than French. I was honored by the fact that Bangladeshi resistance against the World Bank chose me as their spokesperson in the European parliament, and so I had a certain experience, something came out of that. And then in 1996 when Najibullah, the last Communist president of Afghanistan, was hanging from a lamppost with his brother, I started writing on Afghanistan.

So I was looking into these other areas of Asia, taking chance as my guide. Armenia that way, through student questions, Bangladesh that way, through the accident of birth and my mother tongue. Afghanistan because I was teaching Foucault, and Foucault's *Discipline and Punish* opened with a reference to a public execution and then construed a European history from it. I asked myself what does this tell us, this public execution in Afghanistan of the last Communist, and all these people watching, what does it mean? And so I entered Afghanistan by that chance, just looking at that picture in the *New York Times*. And in Hong Kong I was invited to be the first Cultural Studies visiting professor, I felt that I had to think of myself as an Asian in some way because I was not interpellated as a US academic there, and I was not going to hang out with the expatriate Indian community there either, I had little in common with them, I had to think somehow of this fantasmatic Asia which mediated the stereotype of myself for those students. The piece about Bangalore, about global megacities, is in there. There is another crazy piece, which also came by chance. The last piece thinks of me as a hyphenated person, Indian-American, although, strictly speaking, I am not one. I was asked to write a catalog essay for an exhibition on the Hindu great goddess at the Smithsonian for which I had *no* qualification – I'm not an art historian – I'm a British literature modernist and French and German comparativist, and completely irreligious, I realized that I was being called because I'm hyphenated, and so I totally let myself go. It is a very crazy piece as to what a hyphenated American can do if she relies on nothing but the fact that she's hyphenated [laugh ...]

Mind you it's me [chuckle]. It's not just any hyphenated American. It's *this* hyphenated American. So the hyphenated American is very nostalgic about her own so-called culture. That's the last word.

So that's what *Other Asias* is all about, but I'm finding it very difficult to do the final revisions because Afghanistan and Armenia, they are so much in the turmoil of today that for me to put the full stop at the end and give the manuscript over – it frightens me. I believe I've done the Afghanistan but the Armenia I want to do as quickly as possible and it's not going as quickly as it should. That's the book. I hope people like it. I've put a piece I delivered at the Oxford chapter of Amnesty International in the beginning. It brings us forward.

YHR: I really look forward to it coming out. It's supposed to come out at the end of this year.

GCS: I was supposed to have handed in the manuscript two years ago and then I promised Blackwell that I would hand it in at the end of April. I'm hoping that by the end of May it will be handed in, and then I suppose it will take four to six months to come out.

YHR: In the book *Death of a Discipline* you talked about postcoloniality, sort of in the Indian style as something of … I'm not sure whether I can put it correctly … a past tense, that we need to go beyond that. Can you talk more about that?

GCS: *Death of a Discipline* is written in another voice altogether. If I'm not able to finish my book on *Other Asias* because I'm not a specialist, *Death of a Discipline* is exactly the opposite case. I write it as a comparative literature teacher. That's the one area that I know. My PhD is in comparative literature. I've been involved with comparative literature now for many, many years. I started directing a comparative literature program in 1975. In that book I'm really writing to a comparative literature community and, within that context, I'm saying that a postcolonial criticism that is based upon the South Asian model is out of date. It began there, people say. People say it was Edward Said and myself and Homi Bhabha … we are generally put together as the founders of postcolonialism. I certainly know that two or three things that I wrote at the beginning of the eighties have been vastly reprinted as postcolonial texts, but I didn't really know that I was doing anything postcolonial and I don't believe that when Said was writing *Orientalism* he thought that he was doing something postcolonial, but this is quite often the case, that people who write at the beginning don't … but in any case what happened was – since the Algerian independence in 1962 and Indian independence in '47, 15 years before that – these were the models of national liberation, big models of national liberation, right, because of that and because neither Homi nor I were thinking much about the postcolonial in a broad way, the South Asian model, which is a rich field, began to take hold. I have nothing against that, but you cannot think about Latin America according to South Asia and you cannot think of what has happened in the post-Soviet world according to the South Asia model and certainly the role of Japan, Korea, Taiwan, in what you call Asia, cannot be thought of by the South Asian model. Critics in the Balkans are very charitable toward me. The Belgrade circle talks about taking the postcolonial position. By that, they mean Said and Bhabha and myself. They are wonderful translators but I tell them again and again that you may teach us as much as we might offer you a model. We can offer a model only in the broadest sense of what Said used to call "speaking truth to power." On the other hand there you have a history of multicultural and multiethnic empires, precapitalist empires, that are quite different from the South Asian model and the funny thing is that India itself can be rethought and should be rethought like that. Because when we only do poco in terms of what Edward, Homi and I would do, what happens is that the caste-Hindus or the big minorities – Muslim, Sikh, Parsi, Dalit – come up as Indians. Whereas, if one thinks of India itself as a multiethnic, multicultural, precapitalist imperial situation and even a millennial settler colony with the Indo-Europeans coming because they were more agriculture-based and so pushing the nomadic or the forest dwellers, the hunter-gatherers aside, then it's a different history.

If I may add to this one proviso. In *A Critique of Postcolonial Reason* which is a much bigger book, I was making another suggestion as well, which I think should be considered as part of an answer to this question. There, I was saying that what used to be the native inform- ant for the anthropologist, that position now has been illegitimately usurped by the upwardly mobile metropolitan migrant as the post- colonial. That is an accusation behind which I still stand. It seems to me that the fact that I found in Kant a repudiation of the aboriginal, and that the aboriginal gave information which had to be closed off in order for his philosophy to flourish, allowed me to go into the trajectory of what I called the impossible perspective of the native informant, which now has been taken up this way. I would say that now you find this kind of South Asia model – although of course competitive with China … – it's tedious. It's tedious. We should escape from that.

YHR: Very much so. I think that in your talk in Hong Kong you alluded to that problem.

GCS: Yes, but now I know it's coming up in ways that are more alarming.

YHR: Yes. Do we have time for one or two short questions?

GCS: Well yes. We haven't gone beyond. I'm still reading this. No, you ask your questions.

YHR: My last two questions are not so well formulated. One is related to my own interest in your writing on value. You work through sev- eral versions on your speculation on the question of value and that notion of value, which I found to be most useful for my own work, links the question of predication in the question of labor and the question of subjectivity, so I was wondering, would it make sense to connect the question of value to the question of Asia?

GCS: The question of value is everywhere. I mean, there is a value theory of everything, not just a value theory of labor. Because value, simple and contentless, is just a form in use when things are made commensurable. I still feel, as I felt some decades ago when I wrote that piece, that the question of affective value is extremely important. At the time I closed it off by saying two things: one, that there is the possibility of investigating affective value if one goes back from the general equivalent to the total or expanded form and that people like Foucault are doing that; and, two, if one wanted to go forward toward the last form of value in Marx's *Capital* because he is dealing with the economic, one can go to the general equivalent, and think of psychoanalysis, because it gives that kind of general equivalent value-description of what one can loosely call affects. I now think that the use of the value-form is mysterious, because of the thing in terms of which other things are made commensurable. People do not look into this. When Euro-US queer theory is imposed worldwide, this becomes important. In terms of what do you measure sexual preference? Marx thought that the value-thing lost substantiality. How does that figure?

Next about the international entry into gender. I was at this conference on gender a couple of days ago, and it was very alarming that nobody ever asked the slightest question regarding what the word might mean, though it was in constant use. I don't think that everybody had to talk only about that, but on the other hand not a single person and not a single sentence! It was completely taken for granted that we knew what the word meant. Gender is the closing off of the site of something, it is sexual difference in the value form. Because [Gilles] Deleuze and [Felix] Guattari felt that the idea of value in Marx was an extremely potent idea, which [Louis] Althusser tended to ignore or dismiss, they redid or rethought the idea of value as that which gives a common measure by way of the word desire. Desire was not tied to an individual subject, not to a subject at all, but as a kind of misnomer for something that ran everything. I feel that the risks of choosing such a word are too great. Today we can think of data as such a ubiquitous empty word. That's the substance of value now. I mean if you put everything into that form it becomes commensurable in terms of the system, the financialization of the globe. What is it for data to be desubstantialized? So, I've given you many different kinds of answers. Some of them go totally toward the … mysterious thickets of gender which is the most global institution with the longest history, it is as old as humankind and perhaps even older. That's one end. The other end I've spoken on is data as the general equivalent. A lot is there in between, and gender is also data.

YHR: The last question I have goes back to the issue you had talked about. It is a question of internationalism. This also goes back to the politics of Marx in some sense that you alluded to before. How do we now think of the possibility for internationalism, now, if before World War I we always thought of international solidarity, what is the possibility today for us even to think along that terrain. What are your thoughts on this problem?

GCS: There is a class that already think internationally. You and I belong to that class. The relationship between international thinking and the thickness of languages is what Derrida describes as aporia. I have been discovering over the last two or three days, because I have to teach the relationship between Derrida and Levinas, I think of that as supplementation. I hadn't realized before, but perhaps it's better to think of it as an aporia because that way you know that the two cancel each other out, on the other hand you always cross in one direction or other, and from there you state the aporia again. Depending on what kind of thinking you do, you can find a way of crossing it, and the crossing always takes place. That's the aporia. I, on the other hand, have been thinking about this as a supplementation. You have to think international. I have been emphasizing the necessity for abstraction. If we are going to fight the data form we fight it through abstractions, we use it to reevaluate, recode, reverse, and displace value. We think the state as abstract. Remember I said keep purging the state from nationalism, fascism, national sovereignty, all that stuff. I think of secularism in that way, too – all of these things that must be kept rarefied and abstract, it's a persistent effort. That for me is the essence of activism. If we don't make reason some kind of god, then we can see that the area of what might be called the minimal formal logic of reasonableness, consistent calculation – is one area of being human and it should be protected. That's where things like secularism, the state, internationalism are lodged. In the area of the abstract. That is supplemented by the extraordinary complexity and heterogeneity of the resistance that is lodged in the many languages – not only the many languages of the world but the many idiomaticities of those languages. I'm not interested in destroying those. I don't see that as an aporia. Perhaps it's better to see it as such. But I find that even thinking of it as supplementation, these incredibly mysterious areas that the humanities keep trying to teach differently, form collectivities of political philosophies that can in fact nourish and cherish the abstract as well. Otherwise, internationalism is class-divided and we can't do anything about it. We impose what belongs to our class, your class and mine, upon the whole world.

YHR: And it's also nationally divided?

GCS: It's not all that nationally divided. That's the secessionist thing I was saying. It's an international class, with nationalist knowledge bases. Generally an intellectual class ... and some business people who do not have enough education in other areas think that they're thinking internationally. They're thinking nationally but operating on an international level. If we impose that upon the whole world then you don't need me to tell you what kind of a terrible mistake that would be. I think we should end there, eh? Good. Thanks for your questions.

YHR: Thank you!

Notes

Foreword

1   My thanks to Rosalind Morris and Henry Staten for reading the manuscript and suggesting changes. My thanks to Gyan Prakash for reading "Foucault and Najibullah" and suggesting changes. Gyan, here is a public apology for not returning the favor with your manuscript because times were bad. Send me the next one.

2   "Scattered Speculations on the Question of Value," *Diacritics* 15.4 (Winter 1985), pp. 73–93.

3   For the construction of a disciplinary Southeast Asia, see Benedict Anderson, *The Spectre of Comparison: Nationalism, Southeast Asia and the World* (London: Verso, 1998).

4   Ninan Koshy, *The War on Terror: Reordering the World* (New Delhi: LeftWord, 2003), p. x.

5   When (and if) future generations look back upon the administration of the forty-third president of the United States, they might notice the play of chance in giving the US a role as "problem-solver," i.e. undoing the mistaken moves (West Asian policy) in a Great Game this book will discuss in detail, by using those chance events: the demolition of the World Trade Center towers on September 11, 2001, and the great Asian tsunami of 2004. One of the main arguments of this book is that the work of education is a responsible intervention into normality rather than solving problems from above. My earlier work examined that intervention into normality that entails training into consumerism. Yet even there, the concept of "enabling violation" in the production of the colonial subject that I invoke on page 9 recognized the role of education as intervention into normality. Now the work points

at the counter-intervention so that the class apartheid generated by the production of the colonial subject can be faced. I bring this up here because the Indian state's refusal of aid does not reflect an undoing of the class apartheid. This book will speak of reinventing a state that resembles the old dream of the welfare state accountable to the citizenry rather than the geopolitical state confronting global challenges.

6   "US at Critical Crossroads with India," communication from Ram Narayanan, May 6, 2006.

7   S. 3709, passed by the Senate Committee on Foreign Relations, awaiting floor vote as of August, 2006. For further developments as of April, 2007, see Somini Dasgupta, "India Debates Its Right to Nuclear Testing," *New York Times*, Apr. 21, 2007.

8   Sun Yat-sen, "Pan-Asianism," in *China and Japan: Natural Friends, Unnatural Enemies*, (Shanghai: China United Press 1941); Prasenjit Duara, "The Discourse of Civilization and Pan-Asianism," *Journal of World History* 12.1 (2001), pp. 99–130.

9   For Shinpei Goto, see Emmanuel Todd, *After the Empire: the Breakdown of the American Order*, tr. C. Jon Delogu (New York: Columbia Univ. Press, 2003).

10   See Michael W. Doyle and Nicholas Sambanis, *Making War and Building Peace* (Princeton: Princeton Univ. Press, 2006) and Edward Mansfield and Jack Snyder, *Electing to Fight: Why Emerging Democracies Go to War* (Cambridge: MIT Press, 2005). For a popularized account of the debate, see Gary J. Bass, "Are Democracies Really More Peaceful?" *New York Times*, Jan. 1, 2006, p. 18.

11   Raymond Williams, "Structures of Feeling," in *Marxism and Literature* (Oxford: Oxford Univ. Press, 1977), pp. 128–35.

12   Jacques Derrida, *Of Grammatology*, tr. Spivak (Baltimore: Johns Hopkins Univ. Press, 1976), p. 93; translation modified.

13   I was struck by this in Peter Hallward, *Absolutely Postcolonial* (New York and Manchester, UK: Manchester Univ. Press, 2001).

14   This is not "privatization." English is not the only public language upon the earth, however convenient it may be to think so. Upon the relationship between the convenience of hegemonic languages and the "public" in languages without power, the text to consult is still Ngugi wa Thiong'o, *Decolonizing the Mind* (London: J. Currey; Portsmouth, NH: Heinemann, 1986).

15   Peter Hopkirk, *The Great Game: The Struggle for Empire in Central Asia* (New York: Kodansha, 1994); hereafter cited in text as GG, with page references following.

16   "Empire, Union, Center, Satellite: The Place of Post-Colonial Theory in Slavic/Central and Eastern European/(Post-)Soviet Studies, a questionnaire." *Ulbandus: The Slavic Review of Columbia University* 7 (2003).

17   Spivak, *A Critique of Postcolonial Reason: Toward a History of the Vanishing Present* (Cambridge: Harvard Univ. Press, 1999), p. 388; hereafter cited in text as CPR, with page references following.

18   Angel Rama, *The Lettered City*, tr. John Charles Chasteen (Durham, NC: Duke Univ. Press, 1996); Jean Franco, *The Decline and Fall of the Lettered City: Latin America in the Cold War* (Cambridge: Harvard Univ. Press, 2002).

19   Wu Hung, *Reinterpretation: A Decade of Experimental Chinese Art: 1990–2000* (Guangzhou: Guangdong Museum of Art, 2002).

20   "Postcolonial Literature and Theory," in *New Dictionary of the History of Ideas* (New York: Scribner's, 2004).

21   This is now a received idea. Manuel Castells, *Rise of the Network Society* (Cambridge: Blackwell, 2000) argues the point passionately and with fascinating documentation.

22   Immanuel Kant, *Die Metaphysik der Sitten* (Frankfurt: Suhrkamp, 1977), pp. 672–3 and passim. In the translated pages, this word or its variants is variously translated "imputed," "responsible," and "accountability"! (Kant, *Religion and Rational Theology*, tr. Allen W. Wood and George di Giovanni, New York: Cambridge Univ. Press, 1996, pp. 74–5). I believe the integrity of Kant's argument is destroyed by such translation practice.

23   In recent years, my analogies for scholarly practice seem to come more and more from old-style social movement activism. I believe this has something to do with the relationship between deconstruction and "setting-to-work," as I have outlined it in the appendix in CPR, pp. 423–31. Arindam Chakrabarti assures me that this is similar to a probative use of *vyavahāra* or "practice" in Indic rationalism.

24   Charles Lamb, *The Essays of Elia* (New York: E. P. Dutton, 1939 [1800]).

25   Vilsoni Hereniko and Rob Wilson, eds., *Inside Out: Literature, Cultural Politics, and Identity in the New Pacific* (New York: Rowman, 1999), p. 8. This book both gives us the problem and points at solutions.

26   Manuel Castells, *The Power of Identity* (Cambridge: Blackwell, 2004).

27   And it is in that spirit that I will open a dialogue with Meera Nanda, who has called me, in good faith, a prophet facing backward

NOTES TO P. 11

(Meera Nanda, *Prophets Facing Backward: Postmodern Critiques of Science and Hindu Nationalism in India*, New Brunswick: Rutgers Univ. Press, 2003; hereafter cited in text as PFB, with page references following). I am that, I think, though not only in the sense that she seems to suggest. ("Seems to" because I remain confused as to who her largely undocumented postmodernists might be.) I want to see a secularism that does not privatize the transcendental. (Neither mourning nor execution is possible without an intuition of the transcendental.) I do not just want to follow the European Enlightenment because, in its generalized form, it gives succor to the upwardly class-mobile colonial subject: "Science gave me good reasons to say a principled 'No!' to many of my inherited beliefs about God, nature, women, duties and rights, purity and pollution, social status, and my relationship with my fellow citizens" (PFB, xii), writes Nanda. I want rather to take my cue from the criticism of the Enlightenment from within the Enlightenment, and see how it can be used if turned around on its own terms. In answer to Nanda's judicious question "why intellectuals should work so hard just to say 'an impossible no' to the intellectual heritage of the West which, by their own admission, is indispensable to their own intellectual and political lives" (PFB 25), this is the answer I must give: I cannot think that what was good for me is good for the rest of the world. I inhabit the structures of the Enlightenment for reasons similar to the autobiographical ones Nanda provides. In order to make its good structures habitable by all, I must open the Enlightenment to what it was obliged to exclude, but not in an uncritical way. One cannot claim solidarity by acting out formulas. Otherwise, that excluded part is open to the kind of mobilization that both Nanda and I abhor. This will explain the dedication to my book. (Incidentally, it is reprehensible to suggest that I thought the Hindus gave sati-s [self-immolating widows] courage (PFB 151). I call the British abolition of sati "in itself admirable!" (CPR 290). My point was that neither side cared about the patient engagement with women's subjectivity and no one could recognize a woman's lonely resistance as resistance. There was no epistemic engagement with the women by Hindus or the British. Did Nanda really miss the fact that I excoriated the Hindus? The epistemic violation performed by the British was an enabling violation for people like Nanda and me. The inheritors of such enabling violation are described on the first page of the first essay.) Nanda thinks of it only as enablement.

Perhaps I should add a further word here about "epistemic violence." On page 151 of her book, Nanda seems to think that I wanted the British to acknowledge the women's courage by asking them to code sati with war and religious martyrdom. I should have spelled it out more. I think war is stupid and criminal and religious martyrdom at best misguided. The British reformed sati because it was an atrocity performed by an alien religion. Reforming sati was in fact as important as pacifism or secularism. That was my point. And, further, that the way to it should have been through engaging with women's subjectivity, uncoercive rearranging of desire.

This morning a reader sent me another piece by Nanda where she faults me: "Indeed, scholar-activists sympathetic to the Hindu worldview, including Rajiv Malhotra and Koenard [sic] Elst routinely cite the writings of Ashis Nandy, Ronald Inden and even Gayatri Spivak as allies in a shared project of understanding India through Hindu categories."

I checked Rajiv Malhotra on the Web. Out of 18 articles stretching from November 19, 2001 to November 18, 2004, I found only one reference to me, citing me as a fashionable deconstructivist corrupted by the West and ignorant of the Indian classics, certainly not an ally in Hindutva! As for Koenraad Elst, checking the index and bibliography of the eleven published books listed in the Columbia University library did not produce a single reference to Spivak.

Nanda is also critical of my support of "strategic essentialism" (PFB 156). I do not believe I should be on anyone's compulsory reading list. If, however, I am going to be held responsible for something in a book published in 2003, then I feel it is imperative for the author of that book to have read the interview, first published in 1989, and subsequently collected in a book published in 1993, where I thoroughly repudiate the idea of "strategic essentialism"!

Nanda's main objection to the postmodernists (and therefore subalternists?) is that they claim there is no "objective science" and therefore they lend support to the rightwing Hindu nationalists who espouse "Vedic" science – referring to the ancient Hindu scripture collectively called the "Vedas." Her main source for this conviction seems to be the rather unscrupulous sting operation on *Social Text* undertaken by Alan Sokal some years ago. All that the Sokal experiment proved was that humanities folks could be taken in by unscrupulous scientists, and that the referee pool of *Social Text* was not interdisciplinary enough. If we want "postmodern" scientists speaking undecidability, my uninformed suggestion would be to go to probability theory or particle physics, or to a text like Ilya Prigogine and Isabelle Stengers, *Order Out of Chaos*, already somewhat dated. I certainly do not remember ever suggesting "there is no objective science." As for Derrida it is always possible he has said something of this sort in material I have not yet read, but I am well-acquainted with his general argument, and I would doubt it strongly.

28   Sayyid Qutb, *In the Shade of the Qur'an*, tr. M. Adil Salahi and Ahaur A. Shamis (New Delhi: Islamic Book Service, 2001).

29   Sumit Sarkar is altogether more astute in "Postmodernism and the Writing of History," in *Beyond Nationalist Frames: Relocating Modernism, Hindutva, History* (Delhi: Permanent Black, 2002). I would add a few suggestions. The tired judgment that Derrida "level[s] the generic distinction between literary and other uses of language" (p. 165) has been discarded even by the one who started it, Jürgen Habermas, whose earlier indictment on those grounds was notoriously based on secondary sources alone (Habermas, "Beyond a Temporalized Philosophy of Origins: Jacques Derrida's Critique of Phonocentrism; Excursus on Leveling the Genre Distinction between Philosophy and Literature," in *The Philosophical Discourse of Modernity: Twelve Lectures*, tr. Frederick Lawrence, Cambridge: MIT Press, 1987, pp. 185–210). Habermas's obituary statement for Derrida – "deconstruction is essentially praxis" (Habermas, "Ein letzter Gruß: Derridas klärende Wirkung," *Frankfurter Rundschau*, October 10, 2004 is not just a bit of pious fluff. Derrida is all about effort, all about setting to work, grafting the performative and constative together. Sarkar does not mention my work and indeed, it is not important enough to be included in a general critique confined to a single chapter. I must therefore speak up for myself, especially since both Meera Nanda (in a negative spirit) and Shrinivas Tilak (in a positive spirit) align me with Hindu nationalism. When Sarkar quotes with approbation Sarah Melzer's and Leslie Rabine's suggestion that "[f]eminists ... need to relate to the Enlightenment ... as 'rebel daughters'" (p. 184), he might cast his glance at my old formula, instantiated in detail, of the "ab-use" of the Enlightenment, using it from below, wrenching it from its felicitous context. The anthropologist Joan Vincent found it interesting enough to have included the piece in

her collection *The Anthropology of Politics: A Reader in Ethnography, Theory, and Critique* (Oxford: Blackwell, 2002), pp. 452–9, specifically because of its consideration of the European Enlightenment.

30   At the "Conference on Autonomy and the Other: Conceptualization of the Israeli-Palestinian Question" (with Edward Said, Jean-François Lyotard, Israeli members of the Peace Now movement, and Palestinian intellectuals in exile), Rutgers University, November 28–9, 1984. Mattiyahu (Matti) Peled (1923–95) was a general, a professor, and a member of the Israeli knesset (parliament). Born in Haifa, his brief service as the military commander of Gaza, during and after the Sinai 1956 military operation, was a crucial turning point in his life. Direct contact with Palestinians led him to conclude, that for Jews and Arabs, who share the country, to reach mutual understanding, it is paramount to know each other's language. Matti Peled decided to study Arabic. Peled was the first Israeli professor of Arabic literature who introduced studies of Palestinian literature into the academic curriculum. Toward the end of his life, he expressed disappointment with the Oslo Accords (adapted from http://www.peledfoundation.com/Mattipeledeng.htm).

31   I look at the recent work of my friend William A. Callahan, for example, and think how much my book would have gained if I had known that in discussions of civil society China is compared to the post-Communist societies of Eastern Europe (William A. Callahan, *Cultural Governance and Resistance in Pacific Asia*, New York: Routledge, 2006, pp. 103–5); or if I could connect Nagorno-Karabakh with the Nanjing massacre, and draw out the lines of gendering in both (Callahan, "Theorizing the Nanjing Massacre: The Visual Politics of Chinese Nationalism and Sino-Japanese Relations," work in progress).

32   Nigel Harris, *The End of the Third World: Newly Industrializing Countries and the Decline of an Ideology* (London: Penguin, 1987), p. 7.

33   Paul Robeson, "Here's My Story," *Freedom*, New York, Apr. 1955.

34   Here a word to my dear friend Tim Brennan might not be out of place. Derrida wrote a great deal about tele-technology throughout the decades. Bernard Stiegler's book *Echographies of Television: Filmed Interviews with Jacques Derrida* tr. Jennifer Bajorek, Cambridge: Polity, 2002) is among the many books that touch upon this. But a greater problem might be to call videography "orality" because it "represents sound" (Timothy Brennan, Wars of Position: The Cultural Politics of Left and Right, New York:

Columbia Univ. Press, p. 129, 290n. 13). The entire early critique of phonocentrism was indeed focused on this sort of generalization. It was in this context that Derrida criticized Claude Lévi-Strauss's inevitably patronizing benevolence toward the oral culture of the Nambikwara by pointing out that the great genealogical memories of robust orality "writes" upon mnemonic material, which is why conventional writing seems as much a repetition as a rupture, a cyber-change as it were (Derrida, *Of Grammatology*, pp. 107–18). I mention this because the subalterns in the entire Fourth World still have a hold on orality and class-mobile artists and archivists use videography and digital inscription to shift mnemonic writing to digital. Pedagogy marks the move in-between, a pedagogy I attempt to describe in "Righting Wrongs." I sympathize with Brennan. The desire for the oral is major. Indeed, in Derrida's staged failed mourning for his mother interrupting Bennington's Derrida, the very first words are "le vocable cru" – the believed in / raw vocable, voiceable, vowel (Geoffrey Bennington, *Jacques Derrida,* Chicago: Univ. of Chicago Press, p. 3).

Chapter 1   Righting Wrongs

1   George Shelton incidentally provides a gloss on the native English-speaker's take on the word "wrong" in *Morality and Sovereignty in the Philosophy of Hobbes* (New York: St. Martin's, 1992), pp. 128–9. See also D. D. Raphael, "Hobbes on Justice," in G. A. J. Rodgers and Alan Ryan, eds., *Perspectives on Thomas Hobbes* (Oxford: Clarendon, 1988), pp. 164–5. Alex Callinicos gives other examples of social Darwinism in *Social Theory: A Historical Introduction* (Oxford: Blackwell, 1999).

2   CPR 217 n. 33. This is a much-revised version of earlier work. The initial thinking and writing of the piece took place in 1982–3. In other words, I have been thinking of the access to the European Enlightenment through colonization as an enablement for twenty-odd years. I am so often stereotyped as a rejecter of the Enlightenment, most recently by Meera Nanda, that I feel obliged to make this clear at the outset. But I thought of this particular method of access to the Enlightenment as a violation as well. In 1992, I presented "Thinking Academic Freedom in Gendered Post-coloniality" in Cape Town, where I laid out the idea of

ab-using the Enlightenment, in ways similar to, but not identical with, the present argument. (Excerpts from that essay are reprinted in Joan Vincent, ed., *The Anthropology of Politics: A Reader in Ethnography, Theory, and Critique*, Oxford: Blackwell, 2002, pp. 452–9. The editor describes it as "prescient" about South Africa, because it was presented as early as 1992. She describes the piece as the "sting in the tail of her collection," because Spivak, contrary to her stereotype, recommends using the Enlightenment from below.) This, then, was a decade ago. Indeed, this is one of the reasons why I hang in with Derrida, because here is one critic of ethnocentrism (*Of Grammatology*, p. 3) who continues, as I remark in the next essay, to indicate the danger and bad faith in a wholesale rejection of the Enlightenment. My double-edged attitude to the European Enlightenment is thus not a sudden change of heart.

3 Mel James, "Country Mechanisms of the United Nations Commission on Human," in Yael Danieli, Elsa Stamatopoulou, and Clarence J. Dias, eds., *The Universal Declaration of Human Rights: Fifty Years and Beyond* (Amityville, NY: Baywood Publishing, Inc., 1999), pp. 76–7.

4 Cited in Thomas Paine, *Rights of Man* (Indianapolis: Hackett, 1992 [1791]), p. 9.

5 The identity of the nation and the state is generally associated with the Peace of Westphalia (1648), often thought of as one of the inaugurations of the Enlightenment. See, for example, R. Paul Churchill, "Hobbes and the Assumption of Power," in Peter Caws, ed., *The Causes of Quarrel: Essays on Peace, War, and Thomas Hobbes* (Boston: Beacon Press, 1988), p. 17.

6 Thomas Risse, Stephen C. Ropp, and Kathryn Sikkink, eds., *The Power of Human Rights: International Norms and Domestic Change* (New York: Cambridge Univ. Press, 1999).

7 I have written about this class in CPR 392. They are not only involved in righting wrongs, of course. At the time of writing, the head of the Space Vehicle Directorate's innovative concepts group, behind George W. Bush's new space war initiative, was a model minority diasporic; hardly righting wrongs!

8 I am not tendentious in being critical of this. Ian Martin, Secretary-General of Amnesty International from 1986 to 1992, is similarly critical. See Ian Martin, "Closer to the Victim: United Nations Human Rights Field Operations," in Danieli et al., *Universal*

Declaration, p. 92. W. E. B. DuBois made the connection between the United Nations and a new imperialism at its founding (David Levering Lewis, *W. E. B. DuBois: The Fight for Equality and the American Century 1919–1963*, New York: Henry Holt, 2000, pp. 502–10 and passim).

9   Risse, Ropp, and Sikkink, eds., *Power*, p. 170. The next quoted passage is from p. 167.

10 Edward W. Said, *Reflections on Exile and Other Essays* (Cambridge: Harvard Univ. Press, 2000), p. xi. It is interesting that Mary Shelley calls imperial Rome "capital of the world, the crown of man's achievements" (*The Last Man*, London: Pickering, 1996, p. 356). I am grateful to Lecia Rosenthal for this reference.

11 Kuan Yew Lee, *From Third World to First: The Singapore Story, 1965–2000* (New York: Harper, 2000); the sentiment about detention is to be found on p. 488. Rorty, "Human Rights, Rationality, and Sentimentality," in Stephen Shute and Susan Hurley, eds., *On Human Rights* (New York: Basic Books, 1993), p. 127. Meanwhile, general pieces like Asbjørn Eide, "Historical Significance of the Universal Declaration," *International Social Science Journal* 50.4 (Dec. 1998), pp. 475–96, share neither Rorty's wit nor the realism of the rest.

12 I think there is something like a relationship between these and the "tutored preferences" discussed in Philip Kitcher, *Science, Truth, and Democracy* (New York: Oxford Univ. Press, 2001), pp. 118–19 and passim. Professor Kitcher is speaking of an ideal community of taxpaying citizens and he is concerned about "well-ordered science," whereas I will be speaking of students in general, including the rural poor in the global South. Even with these differences, I would argue that "transmitting information" (p. 118) would not necessarily lead to a tutoring of preferences. This is part of a more general interrogation of "consciousness raising" as a basis for social change.

13 I had not read Dewey when I began my work with the children of the rural poor. In order to write this piece I took a quick look, too quick, I fear. I am certainly with Dewey in his emphasis on intelligent habit formation and his contempt for rote learning. It must however be said that Dewey's work operates on the assumption that the educator is of the same "culture" and society/class as the person to be educated; my idea of cultural suturing, to be developed later in the chapter, does not reside within those

assumptions. Dewey has a holistic and unitary view of the inside
of the child which I find difficult to accept. I am grateful to
Benjamin Conisbee Baer for research assistance in my quick
preliminary foray into Dewey.

14 I am so often asked to distinguish my position from Martha
Nussbaum's that I feel compelled to write this note, somewhat
unwillingly. In spite of her valiant efforts, Martha Nussbaum's
work seems to me to remain on the metropolitan side of the
undergirding discontinuity of which I speak in my text. Her
informants, even when seemingly subaltern, are mediated for her
by the domestic "below," the descendants of the colonial subject,
the morally outraged top-drawer activist. Although she certainly
wants to understand the situation of poor women, her real project
is to advance the best possible theory for that undertaking, on the
way to public interest intervention, by the international "above,"
who is represented by the "us" in the following typical sentence:
"understood at its best, the paternalism argument is not an argument against cross-cultural universals. For it is all about respect
for the dignity of persons as choosers. This respect requires us to
defend universally a wide range of liberties …" (*Women and Human
Development: The Capabilities Approach* [WHD hereafter],
Cambridge: Cambridge Univ. Press, 2000, pp. 59–60).

It is not a coincidence that Nussbaum became aware of poor
women by way of a stint at the educational wing of the UN (*Poetic
Justice: The Literary Imagination and Public Life* [PJ hereafter],
Boston: Beacon Press, 1995, pp. xv–xvi, 123 n. 4). She went to
India "to learn as much as [she] could about women's development projects," and worked through interpreters in order to find
both a philosophical justification for universalism and to draw
conclusions about the pros and cons of public interest litigation
(her book ends with three legal case studies). These "cases" are
exceptional subalterns prepared by SEWA (Self Employed Women's
Association) – one of the most spectacular social experiments in
the Third World. I have mentioned elsewhere that this organization is the invariable example cited when micro-credit lenders are
questioned about their lack of social involvement (Spivak,
"Claiming Transformations: Travel Notes with Pictures," in Sara
Ahmed et al., eds., *Transformations: Thinking Through Feminism*,
London: Routledge, 2000, pp. 119–30).

If Nussbaum's informants are urban radical leaders of the
rural, her sources of inspiration – Gandhi, Nehru, Tagore – belong

to national liberationist leadership from the progressive bourgeoisie. (She has an epigraph about women from Iswarchandra
Vidyasagar (WHD 242), whose activist intervention in rural education I cite later in this essay. His intervention on behalf of
women engaged caste-Hindus, since widow remarriage was not
unknown among the so-called tribals and lower castes. My great-
great-grandfather Biharilal Bhaduri was an associate of
Vidyasagar's and arranged a second marriage for his daughter
Barahini, widowed in childhood. The repercussions of this bold
step have been felt in my family. The point I'm trying to make is
that, whereas Vidyasagar's literacy activism, aware of the detail of
rural education, applies to the subaltern classes even today, his
feminist activism applied to the metropolitan middle class, to
which I belong.)

Nussbaum certainly believes in the "value" of "education" and
"literacy," but these are contentless words for her. She also believes
in the virtues of the literary imagination, but her idea of it is a
sympathetic identification, a bringing of the other into the self
(PJ 31, 34, 38), a guarantee that literature "makes us acknowledge
the equal humanity of members of social classes other than our
own." This is rather far from the dangerous self-renouncing "delu-
sion," a risky othering of the self, that has to be toned down for
the reader's benefit, which remains my Wordsworthian model
(William Wordsworth, *Lyrical Ballads and Other Poems*, Ithaca:
Cornell Univ. Press, 1992, pp. 751, 755). It is not without significance that her models are social-realist novels and Walt Whitman
read as expository prose.

Wordsworth's project was pedagogic – to change public taste
(ibid., pp. 742–5). There is not a word about pedagogy in
Nussbaum's text. Like many academic liberals she imagines that
everyone feels the same complicated pleasures from a Dickens
text. As a teacher of reading, my entire effort is to train students
away from the sort of characterological plot summary approach
that she uses. In the brief compass of a note I am obliged to refer
the reader to my reading of Virginia Woolf in "Deconstruction
and Cultural Studies: Arguments for a Deconstructive Cultural
Studies," in Nicholas Royle, ed., *Deconstructions* (Oxford: Blackwell,
2000), pp. 14–43; Jamaica Kincaid in "Thinking Cultural Questions
in 'Pure' Literary Terms," in Paul Gilroy et al., eds., *Without
Guarantees: In Honor of Stuart Hall* (London: Verso, 2000),
pp. 335–57; and Maryse Condé in "The Staging of Time in Maryse

Condé's Heremakhonon," *Cultural Studies* 17.1 (Jan. 2003),
pp. 85–97 for accounts of such teaching. The only rhetorical reading Nussbaum performs is of Judge Posner's opinion on *Mary Carr
v. GM* (PJ 104–11). (The piece in Royle will also give a sense of my
activist reading of the poiesis/istoria argument in Aristotle.)

I have remarked that, in the context of "Indian women," "education" is a contentless good for Nussbaum. In the context of her
own world, the "moral education" offered by literature is simply
there (PJ 84). For me the task of teaching in the two worlds
is related but different; in each case interruptive, supplementary.
In the disenfranchised world there is a call to suspend all the fine
analytic machinery that gives Nussbaum the confidence to "claim
that the standard of judgment constructed in [her] conception of
'poetic justice' passes … [the] tests" of Whitman's "general call
for the poet-judge" (PJ 120) and so on. To attend to the unleashing
of the ethical gives no guarantee that it will produce a "good"
result – just that it will bring in a relation, perhaps. As the literary
Melville and the literary Faulkner knew, the relationship between
the hunter and the prey steps into the relational domain we will
call "ethical." The dominant appropriation of the necessary and
impossible aporia between the political and ethical into the convenience of a bridge named race-class-gender-sensitivity is what
we must constantly keep at bay, even as we cross and re-cross.

Although Nussbaum knows the limitations of behaviorism
(WHD 119–35), it is clear from her discussion of central capabilities and, especially, the value of religion – "something having to
do with ideals and aspirations" (WHD 198) – that she knows
about cultural difference but cannot imagine it. Her model of the
human mind is wedded to the autonomous subject, a gift of the
European Enlightenment broadly understood. The emotions are
named. They are yoked to belief and thus led to reason. This trajectory produces Adam Smith's idea of the "literary judge."

For better or for worse, my view of the mind is forever marked
by the common sense plausibility of Freud's "stricture" of repression – the mind feeling an unpleasure as pleasure to protect itself.
Therefore my notion of political agency rests on a restricted and
accountable model of the person that bears a discontinuous and
fractured relationship with the subject. The most difficult part of
the pedagogic effort outlined later in my essay may be precisely
this: that in opening myself to be "othered" by the subaltern, it
is this broader more mysterious arena of the subject that the self

hopes to enter; and then, through the task of teaching, rehearse the aporia between subjectship and the more tractable field of agency.

For us "politics" can never claim to "speak with a full and fully human voice" (PJ 72). Nussbaum's work is thus premised on the asymmetry in the title of the series. My modest efforts are a hands-on undertaking, with the subaltern, to undo this asymmetry, some day. Without this effortful task of "doing" in the mode of "to come," rather than only "thinking" in the mode of "my way is the best," there is indeed a scary superficial similarity (PJ 76, 86, 89–90) between the two of us, enough to mislead people. I admire her scholarship and her intelligence but I can learn little from her. My teacher is the subaltern.

15 Anthony de Reuck comments on the discontinuity between subaltern and elite (using a "periphery/center" vocabulary) as "styles of perceptual incoherence … on the threshold of a cultural anthropology of philosophical controversy" and veers away from it: "that, as they say, is another story!" ("Culture in Conflict," in Caws, *Causes*, pp. 59–63). My essay lays out the practical politics of that other story, if you like. The superiority of Northern epistemes, however, remains an implicit presupposition. Jonathan Glover analyzes the possibility of the Nazi mindset in numbing detail and discusses Rwanda with no reference to a mental theater at all (*Humanity: A Moral History of the Twentieth Century*, London: Jonathan Cape, 1999). Risse, Ropp, and Sikkink vary their definition of the domestic as "below" by considering freedom of expression only in the case of Eastern Europe and not in the cases of Kenya, Uganda, South Africa, Tunisia, Morocco, Indonesia, Philippines, Chile, and Guatemala. The luxury of an expressive or contaminable mind is implicitly not granted to the subaltern of the global South.

16 This forgetfulness is the condition and effect of the simple value-judgment that rights-thinking is superior – "fitter." Social psychology is now producing abundant retroactive "proof" that each separate "developing" culture is "collective" whereas "America" (synecdochically the US) and "Europe" (synecdochically Northwestern Europe and Scandinavia) are "individualistic." This "collectivism" is a trivialization of the thinking of responsibility I shall discuss below. "Multiculturalism" (synecdochically "global" if we remember the important role of upward mobility among diasporics and the economically restructured New World) is now factored into

this authoritative and scientific division, although all comparison relating to actually "developing" countries is resolutely bilateral between one nation/state/culture and the (Euro) US. The sampling techniques of such work is pathetic in their suggestive nudging of the informant groups to produce the required "evidence" (Susan M. Ervin-Tripp et al., *A Field Manual for Cross-Cultural Study of the Acquisition of Communicative Competence*, Second Draft – July 1967, Berkeley: Univ. of California Press, 1967; Geert H. Hofstede, *Cultures and Organizations: Software of the Mind*, New York: McGraw-Hill, 1991; Saburo Iwawaki, Yoshihisa Kashima, and Kwok Leung, eds., *Innovations in Cross-Cultural Psychology*, Amsterdam: Swets & Zeitlinger, 1992; Gail McKoon and Roger Ratcliff, "The Minimalist Hypothesis: Directions for Research," in Charles A. Weaver et al., eds., *Discourse Comprehension: Essays in Honor of Walter Kintsch*, Hillsdale, NJ: L. Erlbaum, 1995, pp. 97–116; Paul DiMaggio, "Culture and Cognition," in *Annual Review of Sociology* 23, 1997, pp. 263–87; Huong Nguyen, Lawrence Messé, and Gary Stollak, "Toward a More Complex Understanding of Acculturation and Adjustment: Cultural Involvements and Psychosocial Functioning in Vietnamese Youth," *Journal of Cross-Cultural Psychology* 30.1, Jan. 1999, pp. 5–31; Arie W. Kruglanski and Donna M. Webster, "Motivated Closing of the Mind: 'Seizing' and 'Freezing'," in E. Tory Higgins and Arie W. Kruglanski, eds., *Motivational Science: Social and Personality Perspectives*, Philadelphia: Psychology Press, 2000, pp. 354–75; Hong Ying-yi, Michael W. Morris, Chiu Chi-yue, and Veronica Benet-Martinez, "Multicultural Minds: A Dynamic Constructivist Approach to Culture and Cognition," *American Psychologist* 55, July 2000, pp. 709–20.) The sophistication of the vocabulary and the poverty of the conclusions rest on an uncritical idea of the human mind. We cannot ask social psychology to become qualitative cognitive psychology or philosophical ontology. Yet these sorts of academic subdisciplinary endeavor, especially when confidently offered up by female diasporics (my last terrifying encounter with this type of scholarship came from a young intelligent innocent confident power-dressed Hong Kong Chinese woman trained in California), directly or indirectly sustain the asymmetrical division between Human Rights and Human Wrongs that informs the series title. The division that we are speaking of is a class division dissimulated as a cultural division in order to re-code the unequal distribution of agency. It is in that context that I am suggesting that the begging of the question of human nature / freedom, much discussed when the question of Human Rights was confined to Europe, has been withheld from a seemingly culturally divided terrain not only by dominant political theorizing and policymaking, but also by disciplinary tendencies. Alex Callinicos, whom no one would associate with deconstruction, places the nature / polity hesitation as the conflict at the very heart of the European Enlightenment, arguing its saliency for today on those grounds (*Social Theory*, pp. 25, 26, 29, 31, 37, 67, 83, 178, 179 and passim).

17 Paine, *Rights*, p. 39.

18 Derrida, "Force of Law," in David Gray Carlson, Drucilla Cornell, and Michel Rosenfeld, eds., *Deconstruction and the Possibility of Justice* (New York: Routledge, 1992), pp. 3–67. Benjamin's essay is included in *Reflections: Essays, Aphorisms, Autobiographical Writings*, tr. Edmund Jephcott (New York: Harcourt Brace, 1978), pp. 277–300. Derrida shows how Benjamin attempts to solve the problem both on the "universal" register (the new state) and the "singular" register (his own signature). In terms of the text's relationship to the subsequent development of a full-fledged Nazism, Derrida offers an alternative reading. Most readings (including Derrida's) miss Benjamin's conviction that "the educative power" is a "form of appearance" [*Erscheinungsform*] of what Benjamin calls "divine power," because it breaks the crime / expiation chain that the law deals with. And yet the educative does not depend upon miracles for its definition (Benjamin, "Critique," p. 297; I am reading *entsünden* as breaking with the unavoidable link between guilt and expiation – *Schuld* and *Sühne* – rather than as "expiate," as in the English text, a translation that renders Benjamin's argument absurd. I thank Andreas Huyssen for corroborating my reading. The reader will see the connection between the guilt-and-shame of human rights enforcement, and our hope in the displacing power of education).

19 Ernst Bloch, *Natural Law and Human Dignity*, tr. Dennis J. Schmidt (Cambridge: MIT Press, 1986). The passage quoted in the next paragraph is from p. 263.

20 Michel Foucault, "The Masked Philosopher," in *Politics, Philosophy, Culture: Interviews and Other Writings 1977–1984*, tr. Alan Sheridan (New York: Routledge, 1988), pp. 323–30; Derrida, "My Chances / *Mes Chances*: A Rendezvous with Some Epicurean Stereophonies," in Joseph H. Smith and William Kerrigan, eds., *Taking Chances: Derrida, Psychoanalysis, and Literature* (Baltimore: Johns Hopkins

Univ. Press, 1984), pp. 1–32. For the Nietzschean moment, see
Derrida, *Politics of Friendship*, tr. George Collins (New York: Verso,
1997), pp. 79–80. It is of course silly to call Zeno and Epicurus
"colonial subjects," or Aristotle – who never became an Athenian
citizen – a "resident alien." The point I am trying to make is that
the removal of the Austro-Asiatic Aboriginals from the Indo-
European colonizing loop – the narrative behind Indian constitutional policy – was active when Epicurus the Athenian from
Samos, hugging the coast of Turkey, whose parents emigrated
from Athens as colonists, and Zeno the Phoenician from Syrian
Cyprus – both places the object of constant imperial grab-shifts –
came to Athens to be educated and subsequently to found their
philosophies. As I will go on to elaborate, these Indian Aboriginals
are among the disenfranchised groups whose contemporary educational situation seems crucial to the general argument of this
essay. I discuss the resultant process of atrophy and stagnation at
greater length below.

21 Gregory Elliott puts together two distanced assertions by Louis
Althusser to sharpen the latter's sense of Machiavelli's uncanny
engagement with this problematic: "Machiavelli's 'endeavour to
think the conditions of possibility of an impossible task, to think
the unthinkable' induces 'a strange *vacillation* in the traditional
philosophical status of [his] theoretical propositions: as if they
were undermined by another instance than the one that produces
them – the instance of political practice'" (Elliott, "Introduction,"
in Louis Althusser, *Machiavelli and Us*, tr. Elliott, London: Verso,
1999, p. xviii). On pages 123–6 of this text Althusser attempts to
fix Machiavelli's place upon this chain of displacements. See also
Adam D. Danel, *A Case for Freedom: Machiavellian Humanism* (New
York: Univ. Press of America, 1997). For the Hobbes–Bramhill
debate, see Vere Chappell, ed., *Hobbes and Bramhill on Liberty and
Necessity* (Cambridge: Cambridge Univ. Press, 1999). David
Gauthier provides an interesting way of linking Hobbes and Paine
(Gauthier, "Hobbes's Social Contract," in Rodgers and Ryan,
Perspectives, pp. 126–7, 148).

22 George Shelton, *Morality and Sovereignty*, pp. 20, 86–7, 175. "Fiction"
and "reality" are Shelton's words. By indicating the slippage
Shelton makes room for my more radical position – that the fiction marks the begging of the question that produces the "real."

23 Patricia Springborg, "Hobbes on Religion," in Tom Sorell, ed.,
The Cambridge Companion to Hobbes (Cambridge: Cambridge Univ.

Press, 1996), pp. 354–60; see also Arrigo Pacchi, "Hobbes and the Problem of God," in Rodgers and Ryan, *Perspectives*, pp. 182–7. Balibar suggests a double Hobbes: one in whose writings the violence of original sin was always ready to burst forth; and another who saw law immanent in natural self-interest and competition (private communication); a version, perhaps, of the discontinuity I am speaking of.

24 In his reading of Rousseau in *Of Grammatology* (pp. 95–316), Derrida has indicated Rousseau's place on this chain. Locke's view of natural rights is another well-known concatenation on this chain (see John Locke, *Questions Concerning the Law of Nature*, tr. Diskin Clay, Ithaca: Cornell Univ. Press, 1990, for how Locke taught the issue; for a scholarly account, see A. John Simmons, *The Lockean Theory of Rights*, Princeton: Princeton Univ. Press, 1992). Balibar suggests that, by "privatizing nature on the one hand [as] he is also socializing it," Locke is able to reconcile natural society and artificial community ("'Possessive Individualism' Reversed: From Locke to Derrida," *Constellations* 9.3, Sep. 2002, pp. 299–317). For a contemporary discussion of the chain from at least Roman law, Richard Tuck, *Natural Rights Theories: Their Origin and Development* (Cambridge: Cambridge Univ. Press, 1978) remains indispensable. This is of course a layperson's checklist, not a specialist bibliography.

25 I have no expertise in this area and write this note to provoke those who do. I am thinking of Bimal Krishna Matilal's attempts to connect with Oxford ordinary language philosophy when he was Spalding Professor there, specifically his unpublished work on rational critique in the Indic tradition. Arindam Chakrabarti continues that work. I am also thinking of Ayesha Jalal's work in progress on Iqbal. When one invokes Kautilya or the *A'in-I-Akbari*, or yet engages in Sinocentric world-systems theory – as in the current different-yet-related work of André Gunder Frank, Immanuel Wallerstein, and Giovanni Arrighi – one is either in the area of comparative specialisms or identitarian cultural conservatisms. These are the risks run by Walter Mignolo and Agustin Lao-Montes as well as by Gordon Brotherston in Americas studies, Paul Gilroy and Martin Bernal in Africana. I compose this inexpert footnote so that my practical-political concerns are not silenced by mere erudition.

26 Alan Gewirth, *Human Rights: Essays on Justification and Applications* (Chicago: Chicago Univ. Press, 1982), p. 128.

27   I have argued this in *Imperatives to Reimagine the Planet* (Vienna: Passagen, 1999).

28   Gewirth, *Human Rights*, p. 45.

29   Ibid., pp. 132–3, 141.

30   Ibid., p. 140. What does the golden rule have to do with what I was saying in the preceding paragraph? For Gewirth, "Human rights are ... moral rights which all persons equally have simply because they are human" (p. 1). For him the Golden Rule is a "common moral denominator" (p. 128). Hence it is a grounding question. In the preceding paragraph I was suggesting that European political theory has stopped considering the relationship between grounding "natural" questions and the establishment of civil polities. I am now suggesting that Gewirth is a philosopher who does worry about it, making the usual disciplinary arrangements. In my estimation, Rawls's separation of political and philosophical liberalism is a way of getting around the necessity for confronting the problem.

31   Derrida has discussed this with reference to Leibniz in his "The Principle of Reason: The University in the Eyes of its Pupils," *Diacritics* 13.3 (Fall 1983), pp. 7–10.

32   Gewirth, *Human Rights*, p. 8; emphasis mine. Reason as "white mythology" is the informing argument of Derrida, "White Mythology: Metaphor in the Text of Philosophy," *Margins of Philosophy*, tr. Alan Bass (Chicago: Univ. of Chicago Press, 1982), pp. 207–71. Ronald Dworkin describes the undecidable moment: "The right to concern and respect is fundamental among rights in a different way, because it shows how the idea of a collective goal may itself be derived from that fundamental right. If so, then concern and respect is a right so fundamental that it is not captured by the general characterization of rights as trumps over collective goals, except as a limiting case, because it is the source both of the general authority of collective goals and of the special limitations on their authority that justify more particular rights. That promise of unity in political theory is indistinct in these essays, however. It must be defended, if at all, elsewhere" (Ronald Dworkin, *Taking Rights Seriously*, Cambridge: Harvard Univ. Press, 1978, p. xv). I believe this indistinctness is generic and the "elsewhere, if at all," is an irreducible alibi. Later in the collection, Dworkin is able to dismiss the discontinuity between "natural rights" and the "best political program" because he is building an argument, not worrying about the justification for the foundation of states

(pp. 176–7). To take his statement here as a final solution to the entire problem is to "confuse the force of his [argument] for its range," a confusion he attributes to Gertrude Himmelfarb's reading of John Stuart Mill's *Of Liberty* (p. 261). Where I find Ronald Dworkin altogether inspiring is in his insistence on principle rather than policy in hard cases. The range of this insistence has an elasticity that can accommodate the force of my plea to the dominant.

33　I use aporia to name a situation where there are two right ways that cancel each other out and that we, by being agents, have already marked in one way, with a decision that makes us rather than we it. There are other, more philosophically complex, ways of formalizing aporia.

34　For a more extensive definition, see CPR 269–74.

35　In the fifties, C. Wright Mills wrote his famous *Sociological Imagination* to suggest that Sociology was the discipline of disciplines for the times. He claimed imagination totally for reason. The sociological imagination was a "quality of mind that will help [us] to use information and to develop reason in order to achieve lucid summations of what is going on in the world and what may be happening within [our]selves" (C. Wright Mills, *The Sociological Imagination*, New York: Oxford Univ. Press, 1959, p. 5; the next quotation is from p. 17). Within a hitherto humanistic culture, reason and imagination, analysis and synthesis, are ranked. That is how Shelley's *Defence of Poetry* starts, giving to imagination the primary place. Mills is writing a defence of sociology, which he thinks will reconcile the inner life and external career of contemporary man. Nussbaum feminizes this model. For the humanities, the relationship between the two had been a site of conflict, a source of grounding paradoxes. Mills cannot find any comfort in such pursuits, because, in the fifties, the quality of education in the humanities had become too ingrown, too formalist, too scientistic. It no longer nurtured the imagination, that inbuilt instrument of othering. Therefore Mills wrote, revealingly: "It does not matter whether [the most important] qualities [of mind] *are* to be found [in literature]; what matters is that men do not often find them there," because, of course, they are no longer taught to read the world closely as they read closely.

36　"The ability to make fine-grained predictions indicates that the task is unlikely to be error-tolerant" (Kitcher, *Science*, pp. 23–4.) The effort I am speaking of must be error-tolerant, in teacher, trainer, trained, and taught, since we are speaking of cultural shift, and thus a shift in the definition of error.

37   Think, for example, of the constructive undermining of triumphalist "we must help because we are better" sentiments to the awareness at least that, to help undo the difference between "us helping" and "them being helped," if the excellent teaching tool "The Rohde to Srebrenica: A Case Study of Human Rights Reporting," which "documents U.S. reporter David Rohde's journey through Bosnia" (http://www.columbia.edu/itc/journalism/nelson/rohde) were supplemented in the following way: in the long run, a literary-level entry into the nuance differences between Muslim and Serb Bosnian, and their relationship to the subaltern language Romani (which can also be accessed with deep focus), in order to tease out the compromised and disenfranchised elements of the local cultures before the most recent disasters, in their "normality," atrophied by waves of imperialisms. This note properly belongs to p. 43, where I speak of learning subaltern languages, and to p. 21, where I assure the reader that every human rights activist is not required to learn all languages at this depth. Here suffice it to notice that the difference between the existing teaching tool and its imagined supplementation is the difference between urgent decisions and long-term commitment. I refer the reader to the difference between "doctors without frontiers" and primary health care workers with which I began. The analogy: short-term commitment to righting wrongs versus long-term involvement to learn from below the persistent undoing of the reproduction of class apartheid and its attendant evils. The reason for avoiding it is its inconvenience, not a good reason when the goal is to establish the inalienable rights of all beings born human. For one case of the subalternization of the Romany, see CPR 406–9.

38   Spivak, *Imperatives*, p. 68. Marshall Sahlins lays out the general characteristics of these defects in his *Stone Age Economics* (New York: de Gruyter, 1972). Sahlins also points at the obvious absence of a "public sphere" in such social formations. I am grateful to Henry Staten for bringing this book to my attention. Given that I am known to have sympathies with postcolonialism and poststructuralism, some might find my invocation of Sahlins unexpected. In fact, I share some of Sahlins's impatience with postcolonialism ("I mean the rhetorical shift to morality and

politics that has overtaken all the human sciences ...," "Two or Three Things I Know about Culture," *Journal of the Royal Anthropological Institute* 5.3, Sep. 1999, p. 403). Consideration of his curious and often ill-documented diatribes against poststructuralism would take us too far afield.

39 Unpublished communication. The survival of some of these convictions in capitalist societies is a point of study.

40 For a discussion of justice, law, and the unconditional, see Derrida, *Rogues: Two Essays on Reason*, tr. Pascale-Anne Brault and Michael Naas, (Stanford: Stanford Univ. Press, 2005), pp. 148–53.

41 As I will mention later in connection with Anthony Giddens's *Beyond Left and Right* (see p. 27), I am not extolling the virtues of poverty, not even the Christian virtues of poverty, as does Sahlins by association (*Stone Age*, pp. 32–3). I am only interested in bringing those virtues above, and concurrently instilling the principles of a public sphere below; teaching at both ends of the spectrum. For, from the point of view of the asymmetry of what I am calling class apartheid in the global South, a responsibility-based disenfranchised stagnating culture left to itself can only be described, in its current status within the modern nation-state, as "a reversal of 'possessive individualism'," the tragedy "of 'negative' individuality or individualism" (Etienne Balibar, "'Possessive Individualism' Revisited: (An Issue in Philosophical Individualism)," unpublished manuscript). It is interesting that the industrial revolution is the one thing Marx does not mention in his discussion of the origins of capitalism in *Capital: A Critique of Political Economy*, tr. Ben Fowkes (New York: Vintage, 1977), pp. 873–940. Hereafter cited in text as C1.

42 Marx, "Concerning Feuerbach," in *Early Writings*, tr. Rodney Livingstone (New York: Vintage, 1975), p. 422; translation modified.

43 Marx, "The Trinity Formula," in *Capital: A Critique of Political Economy*, tr. David Fernbach (New York: Vintage, 1981), vol. 3, pp. 953–70. Hereafter cited in text as C3.

44 I will be developing this concept-metaphor of suturing as a description of practice. To situate this within Marxist thought, see Callinicos's gloss on Marx's discussion of religion: "Religious illusions ... will survive any purely intellectual refutation so long as the social conditions which produced them continue to exist" (Callinicos, *Social Theory*, pp. 83–4). I would not, of course, accept the illusion/truth binary and would therefore activate and undo-reweave from within the imaginative resources of the

earlier cultural formation – often called "religious" – in order for any from-above change in social condition to last. This undo-reweave is "suture," the model of pedagogy "below." What must be kept in mind is that the same applies to consciousness-raising-style radical teaching "above." The problem with "religious fundamentalism," the politicizing of elite religions, is not that they are religions, but that they are elite in leadership.

45 "But how might it be put into place?" a reviewer asks of Joseph Stiglitz's newest book, *Making Globalization Work* (New York: Norton, 2006) (Stephen Kotkin, "Aiming to Level a Global Playing Field," *New York Times*, Sept. 3, 2006, p. 7). "He offers less sense of the powerful stakeholders who will level the field for all," he also writes. Reviewer and author share one presupposition: that nation-states are their political and economic leaders. If we want democracy, we must believe that states are made by the electorate. If globalization is to work, the ultimate and micrological way to secure all ethical macroeconomic plans (an oxymoron, but we will not go there), large-scale education of the sort I am describing here has to be undertaken and continued, on both sides, however inconvenient it may be. If I started cataloging what people actually do in the name of education, this would be an interminable footnote.

46 Interestingly enough, this very passage was used in a speech entitled "Responsibility: The Price of Greatness" by Anthony F. Earley, Jr, Detroit Edison Chairman and Chief Executive Officer, at a conference on "Business Ethics, Integrity and Values: A Global Perspective," on March 23, 1999. Churchill's own speech, made at Harvard on Monday, September 6, 1943, was precisely about the United States as the savior of the world: "one cannot rise to be in many ways the leading community in the civilised world without being involved in its problems, without being convulsed by its agonies and inspired by its causes." I am grateful to Lecia Rosenthal for bringing these connections to my attention. The point of my humble experiment is that the textural imperatives of such responsibility, acknowledged in the national political and corporate sphere, the internalized reflex "to save the environment," for example, do not follow automatically.

47 "Muddying the Waters" (IOR 40/002/1998, Apr. 1, 1998) at http://amnesty.org/, emphasis mine.

48 For a discussion of the contradiction between individualism (rights) and communality (obligations) when they are seen in a linear way, see Tuck, *Natural Rights*, p. 82.

49   Emmanuel Levinas, *Totality and Infinity: An Essay on Exteriority*, tr. Alphonso Lingis (Pittsburgh: Duquesne University Press, 1969; first French edn 1961), pp. 255–66.

50   Derrida, *Monolingualism of the Other; or, The Prosthesis of Origin*, tr. Patrick Mensah (Stanford: Stanford Univ. Press, 1998), pp. 70–2.

51   Indeed, that sentiment is implicit in the very last line of CPR: "… the scholarship on Derrida's ethical turn …, when in the rare case it risks setting itself to work by breaking its frame, is still not identical with the setting to work of deconstruction outside the formalizing calculus specific to the academic institution" (p. 431). It must, however, be said, that in European from-above discussions, it is the so-called poststructuralists who are insistent not only on questioning a blind faith in the rational abstractions of democracy, but also in recognizing that top-down human rights enforcement is not "democratic" even by these terms. See, for example, the strong objections raised by Foucault, Lyotard, and Derrida after Claude Lefort's claim that "[a] politics of human rights and a democratic politics are thus two ways of responding to the same need" (Claude Lefort, "Politics of Human Rights," in *The Political Forms of Modern Society: Bureaucracy, Democracy, Totalitarianism*, tr. Alan Sheridan, Cambridge: MIT Press, 1986, p. 272. The discussion is to be found in "La question de la democratie," in Denis Kambouchner, ed., *Le Retrait du politique*, Paris: Galilée, 1983, pp. 71–88). I have recently read Derrida, "Interpretations at War: Kant, the Jew, the German," where Derrida traces the genealogy of the Euro-US subject who dispenses Human Rights, with uncanny clarity (in Gil Anidjar, ed. and tr., *Acts of Religion*, New York: Routledge, 2002, pp. 135–88). Since this chapter was originally given to Amnesty International at Oxford, I chose Anthony Giddens. The texts for the times are now Niall Ferguson's *Colossus: The Price of America's Empire* (New York: Penguin, 2004) and Michael Ignatieff's *Lesser Evil: Political Ethics in an Age of Terror* (Princeton: Princeton Univ. Press, 2004). The argument against them would be at once easier to make and more difficult to sustain.

52   Anthony Giddens, *Beyond Left and Right: The Future of Radical Politics* (Stanford: Stanford Univ. Press, 1994). The passages quoted are from pp. 165, 247, 184, 185, 190, and 194. "Third Way" was, I believe, coined in a Fabian Society pamphlet (Tony Blair, *New Politics for the New Century*, London: College Hill Press, 1998) confined to policies of a European Britain. (I am grateful to Susan M. Brook for getting me this pamphlet.) It was used by Bill Clinton

in a round-table discussion sponsored by the Democratic Leadership Council in Washington, DC on April 25, 1999. Although this discussion does not apply to the administrations of Britain and the United States in 2004, it is still pertinent to the human rights lobby.

53   Giddens, *Beyond*, p. 197.

54   I have discussed the role of teaching in the formation of collectivities in "Schmitt and Post Structuralism: A Response," *Cardozo Law Review* 21.5–6 (May 2000), pp. 1723–37. Necessary but impossible tasks – like taking care of health although it is impossible to be immortal; or continuing to listen, read, write, talk, and teach although it is impossible that everything be communicated – lead to renewed and persistent effort. I use this formula because this is the only justification for humanities pedagogy. This is distinct from the "utopian mode," which allows us to figure the impossible.

55   John Rawls, "The Law of Peoples," in Shute and Hurley, *On Human Rights*, p. 56. I have a pervasive objection to Rawls's discipline-bound philosophical style of treating political problems but felt nervous about stating it. I feel some relief in George Shelton, *Morality and Sovereignty*, p. 171, where the author expresses similar objections. Callinicos describes such Rawlsian requirements as "wildly Utopian," offers an excuse, and then goes on to say "[n]evertheless, some account is required of the relationship between abstract norms and the historical conditions of their realization" (*Social Theory*, pp. 313–14).

56   C3 1015–16 puts it in a paragraph, in the mode of "to come."

57   I gave an account of this so-called "post-state world" in CPR 371–94.

58   Daniel M. Farrell, "Hobbes and International Relations," in Caws, *Causes*, p. 77.

59   In the discipline of anthropology, this is associated with the work done by Ruth Benedict for the US Defense Department, the result of which was her book, *The Chrysanthemum and the Sword: Patterns of Japanese Culture* (Boston: Houghton Mifflin, 1946).

60   For an idea of the best in the Cultural Studies account of globalization, see *Public Culture* 12.1 (Winter 2000).

61   I cite below the Kogut and Singh Index for Cultural Distance (1988), an important tool for management. It will give a sense of the distance between those whose wrongs are righted and the agents of corporate philanthropy, closely linked to human rights expenditure: "We hypothesize that the more culturally distant the

country of the investing firm from the United States, the more likely the choice to set up a joint venture. Using Hofstede's indices, a composite index was formed based on the deviation along each of the four cultural dimensions (i.e., power distance, uncertainty avoidance, masculinity/femininity, and individualism) of each country from the United States ranking. The deviations were corrected for differences in the variances of each dimension and then arithmetically averaged. Algebraically, we built the following index:

$$CD_j = \sum_{i=1}^{4} \{(I_{ij} - I_{iu})^2 / V_i\} / 4,$$

where I_{ij} stands for the index for the ith cultural dimension and jth country, V_i is the variance of the index of the ith dimension, u indicates the Unites States, and CD_j is the cultural difference of the jth country from the United States" (Bruce Kogut and Harinder Singh, "The Effect of National Culture on the Choice of Entry Mode," *Journal of International Business Studies* 19, 1988, p. 422).

62 Pat Smith and Lynn Roney, *Wow the Dow! The Complete Guide to Teaching Your Kids How to Invest in the Stock Market* (New York: Simon & Schuster, 2000), p. 18. Some other books are Robert T. Kiyosaki with Sharon L. Lechter, *Rich Dad Poor Dad: What the Rich Teach Their Kids About Money – That the Poor and Middle Class Do Not!* (New York: Warner Books, 2000); Gail Karlitz et al., *Growing Money: A Complete Investing Guide for Kids* (New York: Price Stern Sloan, 1999); Diane Mayr, *The Everything Kids' Money Book: From Saving to Spending to Investing – Learn All About Money!* (Holbrook, MA: Adams Media Corp., 2000); Emmanuel Modu and Andrea Walker, *Teenvestor.Com: The Practical Investment Guide for Teens and Their Parents* (Newark, NJ: Gateway, 2000); Willard S. and William S. Stawski, *Kids, Parents & Money: Teaching Personal Finance from Piggy Bank to Prom* (New York: John Wiley, 2000); and Janet Bamford, *Street Wise: A Guide for Teen Investors* (New York: Bloomberg, 2000). This information is taken from my research for "Globalizing Globalization," plenary address at Rethinking Marxism conference, 2000. I invite the reader to update this checklist.

63 Here are passages from one of many undergraduate textbooks. This *is* standard Cultural Studies stuff, but the reminder remains necessary. The banality of these excerpts reminds us not to be absurdly out of touch when a Giddens counsels "antiproductivism."

In a study, Campbell's Soup found that the men who are most likely to shop view themselves as liberated, considerate, achievement-oriented individuals. These are the types of males who do not feel the need to conform to a "macho" image. As a result, a second change has occurred in male purchasing roles: Males are beginning to buy products that at one time might have been dismissed as too feminine – jewelry, skin care products, moisturizers, and cosmetics. In marketing these products, advertisers have had to depict males in a way that is very different from the traditional strong, masculine image of the Marlboro Cowboy or in the typical beer commercial. A new concept of masculinity has emerged – the sensitive male who is as vulnerable in many ways as his female counterpart. As a result, a growing number of advertisers have begun telling males that being sensitive and caring does not conflict with masculinity. Psychoanalytic theory stresses the unconscious nature of consumer motives as determined in childhood by the conflicting demands of the id and the superego. Marketers have applied psychoanalytic theory by using depth and focus group interviews and projective techniques to uncover deep-seated purchasing motives. These applications are known as motivation research.

The broadest environmental factor affecting consumer behavior is *culture*, as reflected by the values and norms society emphasizes. Products and services such as Levi jeans, Coca-Cola, and McDonald's fast-food outlets have come to symbolize the individuality inherent in American values. This is one reason why East Germans quickly accepted Coke after the fall of the Berlin Wall. (Henry Assael, *Consumer Behavior and Marketing Action*, Cincinnati, OH: South-Western College Publishing, 1995, pp. 386, 404, 451)

This is the dominant general global cultural formation, appropriating the emergent – feminism, psychoanalysis, cultural studies, now environmentalism – remember the humble experiment in the Columbia gym case study and take a look at Ruth La Ferla, "Fashionistas, Ecofriendly and All-Natural" (*New York Times*, July 15, 2001). The Derrida–Levinas line, if it were understood as a cultural formation rather than an ethical phenomenology, is an altogether minor enclave compared to this and will show up transmogrified on the dominant register any day now.

64 John P. Clarke, "Going with the (Cash) Flow: Taoism and the New Managerial Wisdom," Britannica.Com, Humanities Web Site (May 2000), and Thomas V. Morris, *If Aristotle Ran General Motors: The New Soul of Business* (New York: Henry Holt and Co., 1997). Examples can be multiplied.

65 Paulo Freire, *Pedagogy of the Oppressed*, tr. Myra Bergman Ramos (New York: Continuum, 1981), pp. 29–31.

66 "Our Voice," Bangkok NGO Declaration (Bangkok: Asian Cultural Forum on Development/ACFOD, 1993), Annex 1, "Selected Government Position during the Final Prepcom," p. 97.

67 A word on the Aboriginal–Untouchable divide. I warn the reader, once again, that this is not the version of an academic historian or anthropologist, but a summary of the narrative on which Indian constitutional sanctions are based. This narrative assumes that there were *adivasi*-s or "original inhabitants" in what we now call "India," when, in the second millennium BC, Indo-European-speaking peoples began to "colonize" that space. These are the "Aboriginals" or "tribals," and there are 67,758,380 of them by the 1991 census. The constitution distinguishes between them and the Hindu Untouchables. The constitution designates them as SCST-s (Scheduled Castes/Scheduled Tribes). Because this distinction between "colonizing Caucasians" (the Indo-European-speaking peoples) and the "Aboriginals" pre-dates the colonial European models by so much, the latter cannot serve us as guides here. In the early days of the Indian case, there was bilingualism and other kinds of assimilation. Without venturing into contested academic territory, it can still be said that they are basically animist, and retain traces of their separate languages.

68 Between my talk in February and this revision, I have told this man, one of my chief allies in the education, land reclaim, and ecological agriculture projects in the area, that I had spoken of the incident abroad. He told me that he had thought very carefully about the incident and it had been a learning experience for him (as indeed for me). One might remember that I have earned their trust by behaving quite differently from either other caste-Hindus or NGO visitors, in a sustained way, over a number of years and that they are as desperate to find a better future for their children, without repercussions, as are migrants.

69 Because these small disenfranchised responsibility-based cultures have not been allowed entry into the progressive legitimation of the colony, they have remained "economies organized by domestic groups and kinship relations" and yet have been re-coded as *voting* citizens of parliamentary democracies without imaginative access to a "public sphere." For them, without the caring pedagogy that I will be outlining, the "distance between poles of reciprocity ... has remained [an anachronistic] social distance," without imaginative access to the commonality of citizenship. The quoted phrases are from Sahlins, *Stone Age*, pp. 41, 191. If this seems too fast, blame

the postcolonial state and please remember (a) that the model here is not Australia, Latin America, Africa: this is a "pre-colonial settler colony"; and (b) that I am not there to study them but to learn from the children how to be their teacher. In the United States too, I can talk about teaching but cannot write for American Studies.

70 I believe it is because Marshal Sahlins intuits this that he defends Marcel Mauss's *Essay on the Gift* against disciplinary criticism of form and/or content although he recognizes that it "is an idiosyncratic venture ..., unjustified moreover by any special study of the Maori or of the philosophers ... invoked along the way." Sahlins is writing about the economic calculus, but in his comments on Mauss, he touches responsibility, only to transform it, via Mauss, into the principle of reason (Sahlins, *Stone Age*, pp. 149, 168–9, 175). As for himself, he ends his book in the mode of a supplemented capitalism "to come": "a primitive theory of exchange value is also necessary, and perhaps possible – without saying it yet exists" (p. 314). This is consonant with my sense that the ethical push for socialism must come from cultural formations defective for capitalism.

71 Justine Burley, ed., *The Genetic Revolution and Human Rights* (Oxford: Oxford University Press, 1999).

72 I am no philosopher, but this is undoubtedly why the later Wittgenstein was interested in children's acquisition of language (Ludwig Wittgenstein, *Philosophical Investigations*, tr. G. E. M. Anscombe, New York: Macmillan, 1972 [1953], §§ 1–32, pp. 200, 208). To mention the part of the mind that dreams would be to muddy the waters with arguments for and against Freud.

73 Derrida explains this phrase in *Rogues*, pp. 85–92.

74 Luce Irigaray, "The Fecundity of the Caress," in Richard A. Cohen, ed., *Face to Face with Levinas* (Albany: SUNY Press, 1986), pp. 231–56.

75 This case has been discussed in Spivak, "The New Subaltern: A Silent Interview," in *Mapping Subaltern Studies and the Postcolonial*, ed. Vinayak Chaturvedi (London: Verso, 2000), pp. 335–6 and in Spivak, "Discussion: An Afterword on the New Subaltern," in Partha Chatterjee and Pradeep Jeganathan, eds., *Community, Gender and Violence: Subaltern Studies XI* (New York: Columbia Univ. Press, 2000), pp. 324–40.

76 I say "supposedly" because the Hindu population of India, 827,578,868 according to the 2001 Census of India, is of course not represented by the poor rural Hindus, although they themselves

think of Hinduism generally as a unified set of codes. (For census data, see http://www.censusindia.net/religiondata/Summary%20 Hindus.pdf.) They are generally prejudiced against SCST-s in their rural poverty, but they are not therefore in the cultural dominant. This is why Raymond Williams, who introduced the powerful instrument of seeing a culture as a dance of archaic-residual-dominant-emergent, proposed it as a solution to the habit of seeing cultures as a "system" rather than a process (Williams, *Marxism and Literature*, Oxford: Oxford Univ. Press, 1977, pp. 121–7). It is interesting that the influential journal *Economic and Political Weekly* has this to say about "[g]rowing democracy": "It requires sustained effort at institution building, transparency in government, effective governance and most importantly the rule of law" (36.23, June 9–15, 2001, p. 2011). Only benefit of the doubt would read the first item as proactive educational effort, which is otherwise not mentioned at all.

77 I hesitate to name these parties because part of my point is precisely that, when no real education is given, the ideational content of a party's platform does not coincide with the held opinions of the rural electorate, who do not hear these ideas except through the opaque high Bengali disquisitions at mass rallies. As it happens, the ruling party in this case is Communist Party of India (Marxist) (CPM) and the opposition parties are Bharatiya Janata Party (BJP/Hindu nationalist) and Trinomul (a splinter of the CPM). To consider this conflict in terms of Communism and fundamentalism would be a complete mistake.

78 Marx, "The Eighteenth Brumaire of Louis Bonaparte," in *Surveys From Exile*, tr. David Fernbach (New York: Vintage, 1973), p. 147; translation modified.

79 Catharine A. MacKinnon, "Crimes-War, Crimes-Peace," in Shute and Hurley, *Human Rights*, p. 84.

80 Carole Pateman, *The Sexual Contract* (Cambridge, UK: Polity Press, 1988), p. x; the next passage quoted is on p. 60. I am not, of course, speaking of the provenance of social contract theories but rather of historical variations on something like actual social contracts.

81 Paine, *Rights*, p. 79.

82 William Sacksteder, "Mutually Acceptable Glory," in Caws, *Causes*, p. 103.

83 These movements must concern themselves with constitutional change (see, for one example among many, here in the Indian

case, Anil Sadgopal, "Centre's Move Places Education at Risk,"
The Hindu, Sept. 26, 2006, p. 10. It is interesting that the unedited
last paragraph of the piece read this way: "Yet, there are those who
pretend that there is nothing like a ruling elite which dominates
policy making. For them, even to raise such a question is to get
caught in a language game, since 'the State is merely an expression of
the mind of the society it serves'," Krishna Kumar, "Ensuring
Elementary Education For All," *The Hindu*, June 27, 2006. [Krishna
Kumar, as the current director of the National Council for
Educational Research and Training in India, at least thinks he represents the point of view of the state.] Such denial of the conflict
of class interests in education must be seen as a design to depo-
liticize the issue. This definitely places education and, therefore,
the entire nation at great risk"). Work such as I am describing
must be a constant supplement to such efforts, as they must be to
any effort to make globalization work through political and economic leaders alone.

84 http://www.un.org/news/Press/docs/1998/19980928.
sgsm6721.html.

85 For an uncritical summary of this cultural formation as universal
history, see Ronald Reagan, "Free Enterprise," Radio Essay (1979),
retrieved from the *New York Times* archives on the Web.

86 We should not forget that Kant fixed the subject of the
Enlightenment as one who could write for posterity and the
whole world *as a scholar* (Immanuel Kant, "An Answer to
the Question: What is Enlightenment?" in James Schmidt, ed., *What
is Enlightenment? Eighteenth-Century Answers and Twentieth-Century
Questions*, Berkeley: Univ. of California Press, 1996, pp. 60–1). As
the reader will see, our effort is to suture a cultural inscription
rather unlike Kant's into the thinking and practice of the public
sphere and an education that will not preserve class apartheid. An
unintended posterity, a world not imagined by him, but imagina-
ble by his philosophical architectonics, as participant in the cos-
mopolitical.

87 Thomas Babington Macaulay, "Minute on Indian Education," in
Speeches by Lord Macaulay with his Minute on Indian Education (Oxford:
Oxford Univ. Press, 1935), p. 349. When Khushwant Singh, an Indian
writer in English, opined in 2000 that you could say "blue sky" a million different ways in English, whereas in Hindi you could only say
"neela asman," I realized the failure of Vidyasagar's experiment.
The problem, then as now, is the one I have already indicated: one

English, the superb and supple, technologically adroit language of the victor; the many languages of the vanquished; restricted permeability. Going down is easy; coming up is hard. The Ford Foundation can run a program called "Crossing Borders." But the literatures in the domestic languages are dying. And even this is a middle-class matter. Let us go back to the rural poor.

88 Iswarchandra Vidyasagar, *Barnaparichaya* (Kolkata: Benimadhab Sheel, n.d.).

89 Binaybhushan Ray, "'Shikkhashar' theke 'Barnaparichaya' – Shomajer Shange Shishu-Patthyer Paribartan," *Akadami Patrika* 6 (May, 1994), pp. 12–62 makes no mention of the experimental pedagogy of the text and the photocopies seem to have been obtained from the India Office Library in London.

90 For self-ethnography, see Rosalind Morris, *In the Place of Origins: Modernity and Its Mediums in Northern Thailand* (Durham, NC: Duke Univ. Press, 2000).

91 The message reads as follows:
Sir, give us a tube well. We will drink water. Give it now. We are thirsty.

---

1. Abani Sabar 2. Kalomoni Sabar 3. Bharat Sabar 4. Shaymoli Sabar
[Serially ordered in Bengali alphabet]

Sabar hamlet
vill: P.O.: Police Station: Manbajar District: Purulia

[name of officer] Kolkata

As I explain elsewhere, Shaymoli is dead of encephalitis, Abani demoralized and back in the hamlet – Bharat, a boy, dropped out to make money by casual labor and perhaps crime. Kalomoni survived in high school, where the teachers "teach" in the old awful way.

92 I have explained this phenomenon in chapter 5.

93 W. E. B. DuBois, "Of Mr. Booker T. Washington and Others," in *The Souls of Black Folk* (New York: Signet, 1995 [1903]), pp. 78–95.

94 Jean Piaget, *The Moral Judgment of Children*, tr. Marjorie Gabain (New York: Free Press, 1965), p. 406. This difference between saying and doing is often honored by the best sayers. Thus Sahlins distinguishes between "a conventional metaphor of exposition" and "a true history of experiment" (Sahlins, *Stone Age*, p. 192).

95   Isaiah Berlin, *The Hedgehog and the Fox: An Essay on Tolstoy's View of History* (New York: Simon & Schuster, 1986 [1953]).

96   This point cannot be developed here. Please see Spivak, "From Haverstock Hill Flat to US Classroom, What's Left of Theory?" in Judith Butler et al., eds., *What's Left of Theory?: New Work on the Politics of Literary Theory* (New York: Routledge, 2000), pp. 1–40; forthcoming in Spivak, *An Aesthetic Education, or, Globalizing the Curriculum?* from Harvard University Press.

97   I have such fear of derision of the detail of my work that I feel obliged to cite a self-defense that I offered at Columbia when I presented a talk whose London version drew forth my invitation to participate in the Amnesty Series at Oxford, where I presented what you are now reading. Please notice this earlier repetition of points made in the current essay. The piece itself was not about Human Rights and the humanities but about what I have learned from the oral formulaic as practiced by the women in Manbhum: "I'm a modernist literary scholar. Acknowledged research methods in my field would be to follow the life-detail of the author or authors beyond the definitive biography, follow through on pertinent items indicated in the correspondence and in interviews, check the relationship between the critical and creative materials, and of course, consult the critical tradition exhaustively. There is no requirement that the method of connecting these details go beyond the simplest cause-effect structure.

"No such research method has been followed in this afternoon's paper.

"My sources of speculation are some women in Manbhum and a man from Birbhum. It occurs to me that an alternative research method could have been followed here. I could have consulted what anthropological and historical literature is available on the Kheriyas and the Dhekaros, the groups to which these people belong. With the latter, it is the very question of belonging that is being negotiated. There is nothing of that in this paper either.

"To tell you the truth, the paper is hopelessly anecdotal. I have tried to encourage myself by saying that the anecdotes have something of the evidentiary contingence of the literary. Depth rather than breadth of evidence? Who knows? I place the facts in place of footnotes: I have been training teachers in Manbhum for the last ten years. My method is simple: to see how the students are learning and not learning, on the basis of these, to give simple practical instructions to the teacher. ...

"Because I work hard to change this state of affairs, because I feed the children a hot meal a day, and because I live with them when I do this work a certain acceptance has come from the men and women on the basis of which a mutual accountability has grown. My justification is this. The examples I offer may seem simple. But it has taken all this work to earn the right to be a person with whom these examples could be produced; and the right to claim a reading that's in the place of library work, detective work, fieldwork.

"For the first few years, talk about this work in progress seemed forbidden, because it was too fragile. Now it seems not only possible, but called for, yet the risk of ridicule or worse, unexamined congratulations loom. Somewhat against my better judgment, then, I will add a word specifically about the work. In the field of subaltern education, the best talk statistics, money, school buildings, teachers, textbooks and supplies. These are fine things. I am focused elsewhere. In the field of training there are, first, some cases of altogether benevolent Eurocentric yet culturalist training. I hesitate to name names because these are, after all, good people. The training provided by the state is generally inferior and formulaic and usually does not trickle down to the level of which I amspeaking. The training provided by activists is generally from above and emphasizes consciousness raising: rights, resistance, nationalism, identity spliced on to literacy and numeracy. My method is to learn from below how to fashion, together, a way of teaching that will put in place reflexes or habits of mind for which the shortcut name is "democracy." Since this is the largest sector of the future electorate, my belief is that without the habit of democracy, no reform will last. To make visible the lines of force here, I offer my first anecdote, by way of preamble." ("Travel and the Nation," Mary Keating Das Lecture, Columbia University, March 2000)

98 For "civilizationism" see Henry Staten, "Tracking the Native Informant: Cultural Translation as the Horizon of Literary Translation," in Sandra Bermann and Michael Wood, eds., *Nation, Language, and the Ethics of Translation* (Princeton: Princeton Univ. Press, 2005) pp. 118–24.

99 For an example of involving the children of exploitation in intense *matha khatano* on the other side, see John Tierney, "Here Come the Alpha Pups," *New York Times Magazine*, Aug. 5, 2001, pp. 38–43.

100 Giddens, *Beyond*, pp. 93–4.

Chapter 2   Responsibility

1 My thanks to Thomas W. Keenan for an astute first reading of this essay, and for insisting that I spell out my surreptitious argument on contamination.

2 Jacques Derrida, "Passions: 'An Oblique Offering'," in David Wood, ed., *Derrida: A Critical Reader* (Cambridge: Blackwell, 1992), p. 9.

3 Spring 2003: I have just been asked to revisit this tired question by the *Boston Globe*, on the occasion of yet another spate of documents expanding upon the irrelevance of "theory": Terry Eagleton, *After Theory* (New York: Basic Books, 2003), Valentine Cunningham, *Reading After Theory* (Oxford: Blackwell, 2002) being the most prominent. Another interminable footnote looms!

4 Derrida, "Passions," p. 15. The following passage is my understanding of pp. 20–2 of the same text.

5 Derrida, "Shibboleth," in Derek Attridge, ed., *Acts of Literature* (New York: Routledge, 1992), p. 373; wording modified.

6 Derrida, *Of Grammatology*, p. 93.

7 For the necessity and impossibility of translation, see Derrida, "Des Tours de Babel," in Joseph F. Graham, ed., *Difference in Translation* (Ithaca: Cornell Univ. Press, 1985), pp. 165–207. In the intervening years, translation theory has grown exponentially.

8 Derrida, "Principle of Reason," pp. 16, 19; emphasis mine, translation modified. For an indication of a distinction between this and Gianni Vattimo's discussion of "setting-to-work" in Heidegger, see my "Psychoanalysis in Left Field; and Field-working: Examples to Fit the Title," in Sonu Shamdasani and Michael Münchow, eds., *Speculations After Freud: Psychoanalysis, Philosophy and Freud* (New York: Routledge, 1994), p. 47. Most philosophical studies of alterity in deconstruction ignore this "activist" or changing-the-world category of the non-philosophical as interpretation's other.

9 Derrida, "Force of Law: The 'Mystical Foundation of Authority'," in Anidjar, ed., *Acts of Religion*, p. 255.

10   Derrida, *Given Time: I. Counterfeit Money*, tr. Peggy Kamuf (Chicago: Univ. of Chicago Press, 1992), pp. ix–x.

11   Derrida says this of justice ("Force of Law," p. 244) and of the gift (not *a* figure, but "the very figure of the impossible – a distinction we cannot elaborate here," *Given Time*, p. 7). Am I right in thinking that every word is susceptible to this sea-change? "But such is the condition of all the words that we will be using here, or all the words given in our language – and this linguistic problem, let us say rather this problem of language before linguistics, will naturally be our obsession here" (*Given Time*, p. 18).

12   For Derrida it surfaces in that cryptic sentence – "I am psychoanalytically irresponsible"– in "Geopsychoanalysis: ... 'and the rest of the world'," *American Imago* 48.2 (1991), pp. 203–4. For Irigaray, see "The Limits of Transference," and "The Poverty of Psychoanalysis," in Margaret Whitford, ed., *The Irigaray Reader* (Oxford: Blackwell, 1991), pp. 105–17, 83–4.

13   Jacques Derrida, *Of Spirit: Heidegger and the Question*, tr. Geoffrey Bennington and Rachel Bowlby (Chicago: Univ. of Chicago Press, 1989); hereafter abbreviated as OS, with page references following. The conference took place at the European Parliament in Strasbourg, May 27–8, 1993.

14   Derrida, "Passions," p. 24. "Responsiveness" in English in the original.

15   Martin Heidegger, *Being and Time*, tr. John Macquarrie and Edward Robinson (New York: Harper, 1962); tr. Joan Stambaugh (Albany: State University of New York Press, 1996).

16   Heidegger, "The Self-Assertion of the German University" and "The Rectorate 1933 / 34: Facts and Thoughts," tr. Karsten Harries, *Review of Metaphysics* 38 (Mar. 1985), pp. 467–502.

17   This statement is shorthand for the position that can be developed from passages such as the following: "No constituted logic nor any rule of a logical order can, therefore, provide a decision or impose its norms upon these prelogical possibilities of logic. ... They are (topologically) alien to it [since the '"structural unconscious" ... is absolutely excluded' by the sort of inspirational academic heroics I describe, this 'metapsychological' notion of the topology of the psyche may be incomprehensible], but not as its ... 'radical' foundation; for the structure of iterability [alteration in every practice, including theoretical utterance] divides and guts such radicality. ... '[T]heory' is compelled to reproduce, to reduplicate in itself the law of its object or its object as law; it must

submit to the norm it purports to analyze" (Derrida, *Limited Inc*, ed. Gerald Graff, Evanston: Northwestern Univ. Press, 1988, pp. 93, [74], 97). Luce Irigaray's formulation, with reference to psychoanalysis, and directed at the upholders of psychoanalysis as theoretical system, is useful for us here: "Will you object that we would be straying into the realm of anything goes? Then you are admitting that you have forgotten that any living body, any unconscious, any psychical economy brings its order to analysis. All you have to do is listen. But an order with the force of an a priori law prevents you" (Irigaray, "Poverty of Psychoanalysis," pp. 83–4).

18   Richard Rorty, "Taking Philosophy Seriously," *New Republic* (Apr. 11, 1988), pp. 31–4.

19   Since many positions against deconstruction are based on hearsay, this is the most common accusation brought against it. In the *New York Times Book Review*, for example, Walter Reich casually remarks that the denial of the Holocaust owes something to "a number of current assumptions, increasingly popular in academia, regarding the indeterminacy of truth ..." ("Erasing the Holocaust," *New York Times Book Review*, July 11, 1993, p. 34).

20   And, if it is "literature," it is where literature also is given over to its other, however the (con)text would limit it. This note is sounded all through Derrida's work. A recent articulation: "Suppose we knew what literature is ... we still could not be sure that it is literary through and through [*de part en part*]. ... Nor could we be sure that this deconstructive structure cannot be found in other texts that we would not dream of considering as literary. I am convinced that the same structure, however paradoxical it may seem, also turns up in scientific and especially juridical utterances, and indeed can be found in the most foundational or institutive of these utterances, thus in the most inventive ones. ... In the suggestion that a deconstruction of metaphysics is impossible 'to the precise extent that it is "literary,"' I suspect there may be more irony than first appears. ... For a deconstructive operation *possibility*, becoming an available set of rule-governed procedures, methods, accessible approaches would rather be the danger" (Derrida, "Invention of the Other," in Attridge, *Acts of Literature*, pp. 327, 328; translation modified. The embedded quotation is from Paul de Man, *Allegories of Reading: Figural Language in Rousseau, Nietzsche, Rilke, and Proust*, New Haven: Yale Univ. Press, 1979, p. 131).

21   Derrida, "Mochlos; or, The Conflict of the Faculties," in Richard Rand, ed., *Logomachia: The Conflict of the Faculties* (Lincoln: Univ.

of Nebraska Press, 1993), p. 11. The next quoted passage is from the same page. This passage is also worth considering because, three pages before this passage, Derrida brings up Heidegger's Rectorate address, offers a short analysis, and remarks: "I cannot explore this path today" (p. 8). I believe the exploration in *Of Spirit* leads him to a different conclusion from the one offered in "Mochlos."

22   In *Lectures on Kant's Political Philosophy* (Chicago: Univ. of Chicago Press, 1982), Hannah Arendt makes the argument that the critique of aesthetic judgment is Kant's unfinished political work." Foucault gives an "ontic" riff to this in his piece on *parrhesia* by thinking "philosophy as an art of life" (Foucault, "*Parrhesia* in the Care of the Self," in *Fearless Speech*, ed. Joseph Pearson, Los Angeles: Semiotext(e), 2001, p. 117). Aesthetic judgment in Kant operates "without concepts" (*Critique of the Power of Judgment*, tr. P. Guyer and E. Matthews, Cambridge: Cambridge Univ. Press, 2000, p. 96). "Mochlos," the essay from which I am quoting is about Kant's "The Conflict of the Faculties." I have discussed the connection between the "subjective universal" in Kant's "Critique of Aesthetic Judgment" and the access to the ethico-political in "Ethics and Politics in Tagore, Coetzee, and Certain Scenes of Teaching," in *Diacritics* 32, 3–4 (Fall–Winter 2002).

23   Derrida, *L'Animal autobiographique: autour de Jacques Derrida*, ed. Marie-Louise Mallet (Paris: Galilée, 1999), pp. 251–301.

24   *The Satapatha-Brāhmana*, tr. Julius Eggeling, Delhi: Motilal Banarsidas, 1972, part 4.

25   *Of Spirit* takes up a question that was first put forward in 1968 ("Ends of Man," in Derrida, *Margins of Philosophy*, tr. Alan Bass, Chicago: Univ. of Chicago Press, 1982): "The 'destruction' of metaphysics or of classical ontology was even directed against humanism... [But, t]he subtlety and equivocality of this gesture [of a return to man], then, are what appear to have authorized all the anthropologistic deformations in the reading of *Sein und Zeit*" (pp. 118, 127). *Of Spirit* makes Heidegger himself also responsible for such a "deformation." Further, "[i]n the thinking and the language of Being, the end of man has been prescribed since always ... in the play of *telos* and death" (p. 134). As we have seen, in *Of Spirit*, death in Heidegger is seen to be without a semantic content. "Are we to understand the eve as the guard mounted around the house or as the awakening to the day that is coming, at whose eve we are? Is there an economy of the eve?" (p. 136). The economy

of the eve is a responsibility that must annul the call even as it
recalls it in a "link without link [*lien sans lien*] of a bind and a non-
bind" (Derrida, *Given Time*, p. 27). And finally, "[i]s not this security [of 'Being is the nearest'] what is trembling today … [and t]his
trembling is played out in the violent relation of the whole of the
West to its other, whether a 'linguistic' relationship …, or ethno-
logical, economic, political, military, relationships, etc. … It is precisely the force and the efficiency of the system that regularly
change the transgressions into 'false exits'" (pp. 133, 134–5). The
thinking of the animal has been much expanded in Derrida's subsequent work as for example, in, "L'animal que donc je suis
(à suivre)."

26 I should perhaps mention that Henry Staten (*Wittgenstein and
Derrida*, Lincoln: Univ. of Nebraska Press, 1984) had said in
conversation that, upon being asked his opinion of my introduction to *Of Grammatology*, Derrida had said that I had over-empha-
sized the "sous rature." This entire discussion might therefore be
marked by a peculiar excess, in its own way a failure and a feature
of responsibility.

27 Sometimes in his early writings, Derrida does sound the tone of
"saving oneself." As in this passage, speaking to the Société
française de philosophie in 1968: "I have attempted to indicate a
way out of this framework via the 'trace,' which is no more an
effect than it has a cause, but which in and of itself, outside its
text, is not sufficient to operate the necessary transgression"
("Différance", *Margins*, p. 12).

28 For a full appreciation of the argument of the book one must
follow carefully Heidegger's curious trajectory regarding the
word "spirit"; its citation, and the valorizing of related words,
painstakingly outlined in it. In this passage an earlier relationship
between *geistig* and *geistlich* is shown to have been altered.

29 Friedrich Nietzsche, *On the Genealogy of Morals and Ecce Homo*, tr.
Walter Kaufmann (New York: Vintage, 1969), p. 23.

30 In "Shibboleth," a "figure" recalls an impossibility, here perhaps
the impossibility of the animal. In a brilliant passage where figure
and trope become synonyms, Derrida recalls Ulysses by using
"polytropy," Homer's first predication of his hero. Derrida's
search for Ulysses, that other Mediterranean given over to troping, is all over his text. For his "schoolmates," the shape of the
word "figure" leads into all the binds and double binds of responsibility ("Shibboleth," *Acts of Literature*, pp. 386–7).

31 Ten years later, at the time of revising this, the person is reconciled with Derrida.

32 For *pharmakon* see Derrida, "Plato's Pharmacy," *Dissemination*,
tr. Barbara Johnson (Chicago: Univ. of Chicago Press, 1981),
pp. 95–117.

33 "Whoever transposes the radical critique of reason into the
domain of rhetoric in order to blunt the paradox of self-referenti-
ality, also dulls the sword of the critique of reason itself,"
Habermas, *Philosophical Discourse*, p. 210. Habermas came around
after working with Derrida. See Giovanna Borradori, *Philosophy in
a Time of Terror: Dialogues with Jürgen Habermas and Jacques Derrida*
(Chicago and London: University of Chicago Press, 2003).

34 For this new politics of reading, see Derrida, "Otobiographies:
The Teaching of Nietzsche and the Politics of the Proper Name,"
in *The Ear of the Other: Otobiography, Transference, Translation*, tr.
Peggy Kamuf and Avital Ronnell (New York: Schocken Books,
1985), pp. 29–32.

35 Sigmund Freud, "Wild Psychoanalysis," *The Standard Edition of the
Complete Psychological Works*, tr. James Strachey et al. (London:
Hogarth Press, 1975), vol. 11, pp. 219–27.

36 Derrida, *De l'esprit: Heidegger et la question* (Paris: Galilée, 1987),
p. 96.

37 Derrida, like Milton, is often a creative literalist of Latin in the
vernacular. Per-verse carries the possible double charge of
"through (its) turning" as well as the more common "by turning
away," "turning in the *wrong* direction."

38 In view of the sentence that follows, it may not be irresponsible to
claim that Derrida is here deeply troubled about Heidegger's letting go of the last vestige of the Enlightenment. Derrida's own
ambiguous attitude to the Enlightenment, which he honors in
Leibniz's formulation of the accountable principle of reason (*principium reddendae rationis*) more than in Kant's formulation of the
public use of reason, is indeed as that which can recall a limit in its
very extensive resource: "Even if the gift" – and I believe responsibility may be one name of the necessary and impossible immediate transformation of the gift into simulacrum – "were never
anything but a simulacrum, one must still *render an account* of the
possibility of this simulacrum and of the desire that impels toward
this simulacrum. And one must also render an account of the
desire to render an account. This cannot be done against or without the *principle of reason (principium reddendae rationis)*, even if

the latter finds there its limit as well as its resource" (Derrida, *Given Time*, p. 31. For the Leibnitz reference, see Derrida, "Principle of Reason," pp. 7 ff). Again, "[n]othing seems to me less outdated than the classical emancipatory ideal. One cannot attempt to disqualify it today, whether crudely or with sophistication, without at least some thoughtlessness and without forming the worst complicities. It is true that it is also necessary to re-elaborate, without renouncing, the concept of emancipation, enfranchisement, or liberation, while taking into account the strange structures we have been describing. But beyond these identified territories of juridico-politicization on the grand geopolitical scale, beyond all self-serving misappropriations and hijackings, beyond all determined and particular reappropriations of international law, other areas must constantly open up that can at first resemble secondary or marginal areas" (Derrida, "Force of Law," p. 258). Derrida's critique of Heidegger, rendered in my irresponsibility for cruder readers, is that he let go of the Enlightenment (which may have opened up to margins) in the name of a spirit that can be traced to a "Europe" that cannot open up to margins. Incidentally, on a more restricted scale, our relationship to capitalism, and Derrida's and my relationship to imperialism, indeed feminism's relationship to both (divided along North–South or postcolonial lines) shares the structure of the relationship between responsibility and the principle of reason.

39 For the reference to the correct password see Derrida, "Shibboleth," pp. 399–409. Speculation opens here through a judgment of Heidegger through the subjects of diaspora and migrancy. Dastur "means" protocol.

40 I take the liberty of referring to my discussion of Freud's *Moses and Monotheism* in "Psychoanalysis in Left Field."

41 For a dismissal of Derrida as conflating philosophy and literature in their disciplinary senses, see Habermas, *Philosophical Discourse*, pp. 185–210.

42 Derrida, "White Mythology: Metaphor in the Text of Philosophy," *Margins*, pp. 207–57.

43 Derrida, *Of Grammatology*, pp. 229–68 and passim.

44 Marx, "The Eighteenth Brumaire of Louis Bonaparte," pp. 143–249.

45 In Derrida, *The Other Heading: Reflections on Today's Europe*, tr. Pascale-Anne Brault and Michael B. Naas (Bloomington: Indiana Univ. Press, 1992), pp. 84–129.

46 Derrida, *Rogues*, pp. 91–2.

47 For a tabulation of the practico-philosophical problems of communication at an international conference, see Derrida, "Signature Event Context," *Margins*, pp. 309–30.

48 This chain of displacements has since then gone forth into the global counter-globalizing movements and the United Nations-backed International Civil Society. I have discussed these developments in CPR 412–21, and in "Righting Wrongs," the first essay in this book.

49 Derrida, "Force of Law," p. 244.

50 It is interesting that Paulo Freire, who worked successfully with church (the World Council of Churches) and state (the Government of Brazil) could assume the achievement of "dialogue," whereas Antonio Gramsci, imprisoned for his thoughts, would not. Gramsci developed a detailed theory of the epistemic interface of subaltern and intellectual which was a double bind of persuasion and coercion.

51 Farhad Mazhar, as quoted in Leonard Sklar, "Drowning in Aid: The World Bank's Bangladesh Action Plan," in *Multinational Monitor* (Apr. 1993), p. 13. The following passage is from p. 8 of the same piece.

52 James K. Boyce, "Birth of a Megaproject: Political Economy of Flood Control in Bangladesh," *Environmental Management* 14.4 (1990), p. 424.

53 See also Derrida, "Eating Well," in Eduardo Cadava et al., eds., *Who Comes After the Subject?* (New York: Routledge, 1991), pp. 96–119.

54 Kant, *Critique of the Power of Judgment*, p. 141; Freud, "Moses and Monotheism," *Standard Edition*, vol. 23, pp. 91, 122, 190n.

55 It is striking how, in neighboring India, where the dominant culture is "polytheist" in its imaginary, the same great rivers are symbolized as mothers/goddesses. One only has to cross the border to feel the weight of the shift. I have gropingly discussed the "polytheist" imaginary in "Response to Jean-Luc Nancy," in Juliet Flower MacCannell, ed., *Thinking Bodies* (Stanford: Stanford Univ. Press, 1994), pp. 32–51, and in "Moving Devi," included in this book.

56 If the story is true in its detail, one is put in mind of the representation of Defoe's "Susan Barton" in J. M. Coetzee's *Foe* (New York: Viking, 1987) discussed as the clumsy interfering benevolence of the "motivated" white woman in Spivak, "Versions of the Margin: J. M. Coetzee's *Foe* Reading Defoe's *Crusoe/Roxana*," in Jonathan

Arac and Barbara Johnson, eds., *The Consequences of Theory: Selected Papers of the English Institute, 1987–8* (Baltimore: Johns Hopkins Univ. Press, 1990), pp. 154–80.

57 Boyce, "Birth of a Megaproject," p. 421.
58 For a list of donors, see *Bangladesh Action Plan for Flood Control: Achievements and Outlook: An Update* (World Bank, Nov. 1992), p. 14. The agonizing over the role of the high embankments or levees over the Mississippi in the US flood disaster of 1993 will make the issue clear to US readers. "The peak flow of the Ganges-Brahmaputra confluences in the Bengal delta is more than double that of the lower Mississippi" (Boyce, "Birth of a Megaproject," p. 424).
59 Derrida, *Given Time*, pp. 6–32.
60 A rough explanation of this process is offered in "Cultural Talks in the Hot Peace: Revisiting the 'Global Village,'" in Pheng Cheah and Bruce Robbins, eds., *Cosmopolitics: Thinking and Feeling Beyond the Nation* (Minneapolis: Univ. of Minnesota Press, 1998), pp. 329–448. In the case of India and China at least, comprador and alternative economic sector status have changed to assent.
61 The classic explanatory and informative texts here are still Cheryl Payer, *The World Bank: A Critical Analysis* (New York: Monthly Review, 1982) and Payer, *The Debt Trap: The IMF and the Third World* (New York: Monthly Review, 1974). See also Joseph E. Stiglitz, *Globalization and Its Discontents* (New York: W. W. Norton, 2002).
62 A point made by Dr. Syed Hashemi, Professor of Economics at Jahangirnagar University, at the conference. See also, Sklar, "Drowning," p. 8: " ... [T]he true beneficiaries of the plan will be foreign consultants and contractors who will collect hundreds of millions of dollars in fees, the cost of which will be added to Bangladesh's already crushing foreign debt."
63 Derrida, *Given Time*, p. 30.
64 Point made at the conference by Dr. Mohiuddin Farooque, Secretary General of Bangladesh Environmental Lawyers' Association. I keep the present tense to keep the conference as text being read.
65 Derrida, "Force of Law," p. 244.
66 For detail, see Shapan Adnan and Abu M. Sufiyan, *State of the FAP: Contradictions between Plan Objectives and Plan Implementation* (Dhaka: Research and Advisory Services, 1993).
67 Spivak, "Limits and Openings of Marx in Derrida," *Outside in the Teaching Machine* (New York, Routledge, 1993), pp. 97–120.

68   "Most World Bank disbursements flow right back again out of
      borrower countries in the form of procurement contracts, and
      the lion's share of these contracts go to the ten richest industri-
      alized nations" (Bruce Rich, Attorney for the Washington,
      DC-based Environmental Defense Fund, quoted in Sklar,
      "Drowning," p. 13).
69   See, e.g., Jane Bennett, *Unthinking Faith and Enlightenment: Nature
      and the State in a Post-Hegelian Era* (New York: NYU Press, 1987),
      and Bill McKibben, *The End of Nature* (New York: Random House,
      1989). I thank Thomas W. Keenan for these suggestions.
70   All correspondence is available in the dossier of the conference.
71   Crystal L. Bartolovich, "Boundary Disputes: Surveying, Agrarian
      Capital and English Renaissance Texts" (Diss., Emory University,
      1993).
72   One or two conferences do not constitute evidence, but even one
      conference provides a counterexample to statements such as "it
      was precisely insofar as Heidegger remained faithful to certain
      precepts of 'Western thought' that he was *prevented* from identify-
      ing wholesale with the 'racial-biological thinking' of the National
      Socialists: a party whose doctrines and deeds represented … *the
      very negation of that tradition"* (Richard Wolin, " 'L'Affaire Derrida':
      Another Exchange," *New York Review of Books* 11.6, Mar. 25, 1993,
      p. 66). As we have seen, Derrida values the monitory virtue of the
      Enlightenment and the accountable principle of reason. It is the
      unreasonable confidence in the European tradition that he warns
      against. In July 1992 I attended a conference on Global Civilization
      and Local Cultures in Darmstadt, Germany. The country was
      ablaze with violent xenophobia. The conference did not once
      mention this, but spent three luxurious days on the assumption
      that Civilization was the Enlightenment (Habermas today), the
      theoretical champions of the local (read fragment) were the "post-
      modernists," and the good local color could be discovered by
      enlightened cultural relativism toward exotic practices. This is
      what is meant by Nazism (xenophobia today) growing up in the
      shelter of the big trees in the European forest (confusedly) called
      culture.
73   I am grateful to Muhammad Ghulam Mustafa Dulal for provid-
      ing these details of quiet change in connection with a flood-man-
      agement project with "compartments" controlled by locks. I
      cannot of course claim that such changes have taken place all
      over Bangladesh.

74   Marx, *Grundrisse: Foundations of the Critique of Political Economy*, tr.
     Martin Nicolaus (New York: Vintage, 1973), p. 471; translation
     modified.
75   In the intervening years, "permanent parabasis" as a figure of
     political practice has invaded my thought. It is there in *An Aesthetic
     Education*, forthcoming from Harvard, and the debt has been
     acknowledged, with a textual reading, in "Learning from de Man:
     Looking Back," *boundary 2* 32.3 (Fall 2005), pp. 21–35.
76   These points were presented by Mushrefa Mishu, President of
     the Bangladesh Student Unity Forum, at the conference. I hope
     the reader will forgive a long quotation, inserted into this already
     too-long chapter, to illustrate the relay from Imperialism to
     Development and the continuity of subaltern insurgency, a per-
     manent parabasis: "By the mid-eighteenth century, the Bengalis
     had extensively engineered the delta, both to protect against
     floods and to ensure that the silt-bearing river-waters could ferti-
     lize and irrigate fields. The first Britons to travel across the delta
     reported seeing thousands of kilometres of canals and embank-
     ments. ... What they never realised, says Willcocks [the imperial
     water engineer who first made sense of the structures in a report
     published in 1930] was that the primary purpose of the canals was
     to irrigate and fertilise the land of the delta. ... The British over-
     saw the gradual destruction of the ancient feudal system under
     which landlords forced peasants to maintain the dykes and clear
     the canals. ... As the canals silted up, they began to overflow and
     became, for the British, 'a menace to the country.' Inspectors were
     appalled to see that the peasant farmers continued to cut holes in
     the canal banks during the flood season. Ignorant of the fact that
     the breaches fertilised fields, they banned this practice. For many
     years, there were running battles between gangs of peasants who
     set out each night to cut holes in the canals, and the British police,
     who tried to stop them. ... Willcocks concluded with proposals for
     the restoration of the ancient works, in order to 'bring in again the
     health and wealth which central [the larger part of today's
     Bangladesh flood-plain] and west Bengal once enjoyed.' ... The
     ancient works took many years to construct. They were built, more-
     over, in small steps, bending to the will of the rivers at each stage. It
     was a training, rather than a taming, of the rivers. The Bangladeshi
     authorities and their foreign advisers today show neither the patience
     nor the contrition to adopt such an approach. They want to mould
     the rivers to their design" (Fred Pearce, *The Dammed: Rivers, Dams,*

and the Coming World Water Crisis, London: Bodley Head, 1992, pp. 243–5). The peasants and fishers are still cutting embankments.

77 If the French *revenant* provides one sort of link with the entire chain on *venir* in Derrida's work to the extent that the subterranean neologism *é-venir* occupies the place of the presenting of the present, the English provides its own kind of commentary by clandestinely making visible Heidegger's kinship with Christian metaphysics: the holy ghost.

78 Derrida, *Specters of Marx: The State of the Debt, the Work of Mourning and the New International*, tr. Peggy Kamuf (New York: Routledge, 1994).

79 I borrow this term from Vandana Shiva, *Monocultures of the Mind: Perspectives on Biodiversity and Biotechnology* (London: Zed, 1993).

80 Andrew Steer, "All-in-One Note," June 5, 1993.

81 Derrida, *Given Time*, pp. 31, 32–3. The embedded quotation is from Baudelaire, "Counterfeit Money."

82 Derrida, *Other Heading*, pp. 76–80.

83 I have tried to show an extreme case of this, where a woman tried to "speak" insurgency against a regulative psychobiography by inscribing her body in death, and at a deferred time; and yet was not able to secure a response, from upwardly-mobile women of her own family, at two generations' removed (CPR 306–11).

84 Derrida, *The Post Card: From Socrates to Freud and Beyond*, tr. Alan Bass (Chicago: Univ. of Chicago Press, 1987), p. 123.

85 Spivak, "Acting Bits/Identity Talk," *Critical Inquiry* 18.4 (Summer 1992), p. 778.

86 See, for example, an otherwise excellent piece by Peter Custers, "Banking on a Flood-Free Future? Flood Mismanagement in Bangladesh," *Ecologist* 22.5 (Sept.–Oct. 1992), pp. 244, 246.

87 Boyce, "Birth of a Megaproject," p. 419.

88 M. Aminul Islam, "Agricultural Adjustments to Flooding in Bangladesh: A Preliminary Report," *National Geographical Journal of India* 26.1–2 (Mar.–June 1980), p. 50.

Chapter 3   1994: Will Postcolonialism Travel?

1 Cited in Ira Katznelson, *Desolation and Enlightenment: Political Knowledge After Total War, Totalitarianism, and the Holocaust* (New York: Columbia Univ. Press, 2003), pp. 82–3. Nicole Rizzuto, "Reading Sarah Kofman's Testimony to Les Anneés Noires in *Rue*

Ordener, Rue Labat," *Contemporary French and Francophone Studies* 10.1 (Jan. 2006), pp. 5–14.

2 President Kagema's remarks about the case-description "genocide" not bringing closure were uttered at the World Leaders' Forum, Columbia University, September 15, 2005. For resistance to "refugee"-ship and its ramifications, see Nina Bernstein, "Refugee Groups Reaching Out to Victims of Hurricane," *New York Times*, Sept. 18, 2005 (from the Web).

3 "During the 1990s, the entities opposing the opening of the border between Armenia and Turkey included the Armenian Diaspora, nationalist groups in both Armenia and Turkey and most importantly Azerbaijan" (Asbed Kotchikian, "Border Politics: The Geopolitical Implications of Opening the Turkish-Armenian Border," Armenian International Policy Research Group (AIPRG), 3rd International Conference, World Bank, Washington, DC, January 15–16, 2005). The entire essay is worth reading to see evidence of a good deal of practical goodwill on both sides. I selected the papers from this particular meeting – the most recent at the time of writing – to look at economic data apart from the cultural politics of postcoloniality and genocide. One must obviously keep track of such accounts and "read" them as the years go by. The vanishing present remains the most important locus of work such as mine.

4 *Armenian Forum* 1 (Spring 1998), pp. 19–36. Hereafter cited in text as KK with page references following.

5 Svante E. Cornell, *Small Nations and Great Powers: A Study of Ethnopolitical Conflict in the Caucasus* (Richmond, Surrey: Curzon, 2001), pp. 366, 367. Hereafter cited in text as SN, with page references following.

6 Karl Marx, *Early Writings*, tr. Rodney Livingstone (New York: Vintage, 1975), p. 281 and passim.

7 Ephrain Nimai, *Marxism and Nationalism: Theoretical Origins of A Political Crisis* (London: Photo Press 1991) contains a good account of the discussion between Lenin and Rosa Luxemburg upon this issue. The work of the Subaltern Studies group as a whole should be consulted for references. In the general context, the following books can be the start of a vast inquiry: Erica Benner, *Really Existing Nationalisms: A Post-Communist View from Marx and Engels* (New York: Clarendon Press, 1995); Joan Cocks, *Passion and Paradox: Intellectuals Confront the National Question* (Princeton: Princeton Univ. Press, 2002); Ali A. Mazrui, *Power, Politics and the*

African Condition (Trenton, NJ: Africa World Press, 2003). See also the essays by Aijaz Ahmad and Spivak in *Nation and Imagination*, ed. Meenakshi Mukherjee (forthcoming).

8   Marx, *Grundrisse*, pp. 471–9.

9   C1 125. Marx carefully distinguishes between Britain and Germany in the "Postface" to the second edition (pp. 95–8).

10   For a trenchant statement see Perry Anderson, *In the Tracks of Historical Materialism* (New York: Columbia Univ. Press, 1983).

11   Marx, *Surveys From Exile*, p. 150. The Hegelian passage is to be found in *Philosophy of Right*, tr. T. M. Knox (Oxford: Oxford University Press, 1967 [1975]), pp. 11–12.

12   Although these were "unevenly pre-capitalist," being harnessed by international commercial capital (Britain, France, Germany), the controlling example, with Victorian England as the determining Marxist set, is always British India! Lenin's lucid analysis of the connection between imperialism and finance capital does not investigate the Ottoman theatre, and of necessity keeps the historico-political sphere out of the discussion (V. I. Lenin, *Imperialism: The Highest Stage of Capitalism*, New York: International Publishers, 1939).

As for subaltern access to a thinking of the nation, over a decade of fieldwork in India has made it abundantly clear to me that, in spite of India's climb up the development ladder, hundreds of people at the ground level (and more if the pattern were extended) have no idea that they live in "India" or "Bharat," or indeed what such a place is. I do not wish to generalize from limited experience, but I cannot imagine that the case is different in the larger states of Africa and Asia, just as such ignorance cannot be imagined in Palestine and, perhaps, Bangladesh. In such cases, the metropolitan migrant's testimony cannot be taken at face value. Before I had started my fieldwork, I would not have been able to imagine the spread of such unknowing. This was a blank in my thinking of Armenia, but I now know that this small "nation" came to collective thinking some centuries ago, perhaps because of ethnicization by the surrounding peoples. How much does Christianization play a part in it? I quote here, not academic scholarship, but a book written in the spirit of my imagining "Asia," Armenia imagining its antiquity, as imagined by the first modern Greek ambassador to modern Armenia, clearly a man of considerable general culture ("his assignment there was viewed as a golden opportunity for Greece to rebuild 'an alliance as old as history,'" said the York University press release for his book launch), imagining Greece and Asia Minor. I will quote two extended passages to give a sense of Armenia as "proto-European," a self-representation that creeps into the post-colonial imaginary, as the recently established Armenian National Movement (November 1989) would demonstrate. There is nothing destructive here, as there is in Hindu "Aryanism" in India. But the analogy, creeping Aryanism in postcoloniality, a field ripe for the demonization of a monolithic Islam, would hold. That topic would take us way out of this conversation.

Here let me point out how Rohinton Mistry, the Asian-Canadian novelist, has recently dramatized this more European than European versus more Persian than the Persians dilemma on the part of the Indian Parsees, also a beleaguered "superior" minority, to which he belongs by extraction: one of his characters, Yezad, yearns to be "a little Englishman of a type that even England did not have." He has now "returned to Parsi ideals and principles with a vengeance. He is now a Persian of a type that Persia may never have had" (John Sutherland, "King Lear in Bombay," *New York Times Book Review*, Oct. 13, 2002, p. 7).

Now here is the Greek Ambassador to Armenia, first on the subject of ancient Christian Armenian solidarity, and secondly on the imagination of Armenia as partner in a pre-Christian Hellenic Europe before Europe. One: "according to tradition the apostles Bartholomew and Thaddeus were the first to preach the gospel to Armenia. It was Saint Gregory the Illuminator, however, who brought Christianity to Armenia in earnest in 301. He was of Parthian origin ..." (Leonidas Chrysanthropoulos, *Caucasus Chronicles: Nation-Building and Diplomacy in Armenia, 1993–1994*, Princeton: Gomidas Institute, 2002, p. 87). I confess my scholarship is confined to the *Encyclopædia Britannica*, the lot of the familiar essayist at large, away from home turf. Yet, since the oppression and distancing of the groups among whom my fieldwork was undertaken – the Indian "Aboriginals," victims from the very first waves of Indo-European colonization, millennia ago, I have been plotting the activities of "colonial subjects" in the ancient world in "Righting Wrongs," the first essay in this book. By such reckoning, Gregory, who fled the heathen invasion of Parthia, who was educated in the Greek culture of Caesarea, who Christianized Armenia, and established Christianity as the world's first state religion, would qualify as a colonial subject. "The liturgy was performed first in Greek, then in Syriac, until 404, when the scribe Mesrop Mashtots invented the Armenian alphabet. ... The Armenian Church, like the Greek Orthodox Church, played and continues to play an instrumental role in preserving and promoting the Armenian language, religion, traditions, and consequently national identity among Armenians, especially when they have been living under conditions of oppression or in the diaspora" (pp. 87, 88).

Two: a glimpse of Armenia as a reminder of pre-Christian Greece – Europe before Europe: "Armenia in antiquity had adopted the Greek drachma, which at that time was being used throughout the civilized world. In Armenian they called it the dram. [The first President of Armenia] was seriously contemplating introducing a national currency that would be called the dram. I gave him my blessing, adding that once Greece joined the European Monetary System and adopted the Euro as its national currency, Armenia would be the only country in the world that would continue to carry, throughout history, the name of the drachma" (p. 116).

These are moving narratives. But they do not fit the postcolonial stereotypes. It might also be mentioned that the "High level of dollarization of the Armenian economy and population's low level of trust in the national currency and in the banking sector in general has created a favorable situation in which the businesses and population prefer to use US dollars, instead of drams for making payments in large transactions. For official reporting the parties usually use smaller contract amounts, which allows them to limit their tax liabilities by underreporting the real value of the contract and in the official accounting. The state authorities are not able to capture this type of economic transactions because it is impossible to measure the amount of informally agreed contracts' values denominated in US dollars" (Bagrat Tunyan, "The Shadow Economy of Armenia: Size, Causes and Consequences," AIPRG 3rd International Conference, 2005, http://pdc.ceu.hu/archive/00002657/01/WP0502.pdf). Passing from the imposed ruble to the chosen dollar does not allow for the postcolonial moment.

13 At the Peace of Westphalia, the two victorious nations, France and Sweden, exacted right of voice for nation-states from the Holy Roman Empire. For the opinion that it was not as significant a rupture as is usually assumed, see Stephen D. Krasner,

"Westphalia and All That," in Judith Goldstein and Robert O. Keohane, eds., *Ideas and Foreign Policy* (Ithaca: Cornell Univ. Press, 1993), pp. 235–64.

14 Nora Dudwick, "The Pen and the Sword: Intellectuals, Nationalism and Violence in Armenia and Azerbaijan," unpublished manuscript.

15 Richard G. Hovannisian, "Intervention and Shades of Altruism During the Armenian Genocide," in Richard G. Hovannisian, ed., *The Armenian Genocide: History, Politics, Ethics* (New York: St Martin's Press, 1992), p. 180. It is not my intention to deny the importance of the name "genocide," only if we remember that it is a legal entity that brings with it a mediated satisfaction. As Etienne Balibar has advised in another context, although the law requires definitions, the citizen unpacks them (Etienne Balibar, "Dissonances within Laïcité," *Constellations* 11.3 (2004), pp. 356–7). This is the lesson of the old African-American women, refusing to receive aid by being legally named "refugees". This is the lesson of President Kagame of Rwanda, wondering aloud about the problems that remain after the solution offered by the legally unifying name of "genocide".

16 Marc Nichanian, "On the Archive I. Shame," forthcoming in Spivak, ed., *What Is It to Read?: Reading With Jacques Derrida*.

17 Fact Sheet, Bureau of European and Eurasian affairs, Washington, DC, Sept. 11, 2002, http://www.state.gov/p/eur/ris/fs/13502.htm.

18 The ethno-cultural conflict of "Europe" and "Asia" is an old story in this region. Goenawan Mohamad captures it in "At the Border Where Ali Dies (and Ka Asks Questions)" (*Prince Klaus Fund Journal* 12 (Apr. '06), pp. 7–30, although I should perhaps have produced a more nuanced reading of "Kurban Said"'s 1937 *Ali and Nino* (tr. Jenia Graman, New York: Random House, 1970), a novel of Azerbaijan; and the woman in question is not Armenian, as Mohamad claims, but Georgian.

19 I am here stepping on territory thoroughly covered by Wittgenstein and his interpreters, not to mention Saussure and his interpreters. See, for examples, G. E. M. Anscombe, "A Theory of Language?" in Irving Block, ed., *Perspectives on the Philosophy of Wittgenstein* (Cambridge: MIT Press, 1983), pp. 148–58; and Cora Diamond, "Throwing Away the Ladder: How to Read the Tractatus," in *The Realistic Spirit* (Cambridge: MIT Press, 1991). I am grateful to Candace Vogler for suggesting these pieces.

20   For more on these connections see Thomas Trautman, *Aryans and British India* (Berkeley: Univ. of California Press, 1997).

21   Mahmood Mamdani, *Citizen and Subject: Contemporary Africa and the Legacy of Late Colonialism* (Princeton: Princeton Univ. Press, 1996).

22   Romila Thapar, "The Perennial Aryans," Lecture at Columbia University, September 30, 1993. I have discussed this with respect to Hegel in CPR 37–58.

23   Jack Gallagher, "The Decline, Revival and Fall of the British Empire," in Anil Seal, ed., *The Decline, Revival and Fall of the British Empire* (New York: Cambridge Univ. Press, 1982); David Washbrook, *The Emergence of Provincial Politics: The Madras Presidency, 1870–1920* (Cambridge and New York: Cambridge Univ. Press, 1976); Christopher Bayly, *Indian Society and the Making of the British Empire* (Cambridge and New York: Cambridge Univ. Press, 1988).

24   On the role of dates, see Derrida, "Shibboleth," pp. 387 ff.

25   Marx's most elaborate account of this is in "The Eighteenth Brumaire." For the mole, see *Surveys from Exite* p. 237.

26   Following Derrida's lead in *Glas*, tr. John P. Leavy, Jr and Richard Rand (Lincoln: Univ. of Nebraska Press, 1986), p. 207, I refer the reader to Charles Ritter, for a modern scientific consolidation of this theme.

27   For the Judeo-Christian complicity, see "Faith and Knowledge," in Anidjar, ed., *Acts of Religion*, pp. 42–101.

28   Edward W. Said, *Orientalism* (New York: Pantheon, 1978).

29   Levon Chorbajian et al., eds., *The Caucasian Knot: The History and Geo-Politics of Nagorno-Karabagh* (Atlantic Highlands, NJ: Pluto Press, 1994), pp. 112, 118, 109.

30   Spivak, "Harlem," *Social Text* 81 (Dec. 2004), pp. 113–39.

31   Geoffrey Wheatcroft, "The Other Side of Globalism," *New York Times Book Review*, Sept. 8, 2002, p. 5.

32   Spivak, "Terror: A Speech After 9/11," *boundary 2* 31.2 (2004), pp. 81–111, now part of work in progress on the secular university. The embedded citation is from *The Economist*, June 1, 2002, p. 11.

33   Zbigniew Brezczinski, "Confronting Anti-American Grievances," *New York Times Week in Review*, Sept. 1, 2002, p. 9. In India the connection with Israel was perceived strongly by the Hindu nationalists, as a group of us pointed out in "Vasudhaiva Kutumbakam," a well-researched piece we were unaccountably unable to place. At the same time, the Rashtriya Swayamsevak Sangh, the militant

arm of the Hindu Right, glorifies Hitler. For connections between Zionism and the Third Reich, see Lenni Brenner, *Zionism in the Age of the Dictators: A Reappraisal* (London: Croom Helm, 1983).

34 Christopher J. Walker, *Armenia: The Survival of a Nation* (London: Croom Helm, 1980), p. 217.

35 Nora Dudwick, "The Cultural Construction of Political Violence in Armenia and Azerbaijan," *Problems of Post-Communism* 42.4 (1995), pp. 18–23.

36 Heather S. Gregg, "Divided They Conquer: The Success of Armenian Ethnic Lobbies in the United States," Inter-University Committee on International Migration, Rosemarie Rogers Working Paper No.13. The paper gives a good idea of the consolidating institutions of the Armenian diaspora, in Washington and elsewhere.

37 One example among many: During the Spanish Civil War (1936–9), Francisco "Franco's nationalists were just as keen to claim a Christian heritage – even as they took the country with a largely North African, Muslim army. * (* This situation led to a number of absurd rhetorical contradictions. For example, at the Feast of the Assumption in Seville on August 15, 1936, the religious invective of one monarchist poet named José Maria Péman was forceful enough to obscure his view of the Moroccan soldiers in Franco's Army of Africa, which was at that very moment battling its way toward Madrid. 'Twenty centuries of Christian civilization are at our backs,' he intoned, even describing the war being fought with North African troops as 'a new war of independence, ... a new expulsion of the Moors!')," Brent Edwards, "How to Read a Diaspora," in Spivak, ed., *Reading With Jacques Derrida* (forthcoming).

38 In Turkey, novelist and intellectual Orhan Pamuk is currently on trial because he has acknowledged the Armenian genocide. Emrah Efe Çakmak, the editor of the Turkish journal *Cogito*, has just requested an interview discussing the genocide from an acknowledging point of view. This reflects a general radical trend that would question the stereotype.

39 Aaron H. Sherinian, "'Marketing' Assistance Programs to the Diaspora: The US Embassy, Yerevan Experience," AIPRG 3rd International Conference, 2005, p. 1. Information regarding the US Government assistance programs in Armenia may be found on the US Embassy Yerevan official Web site at www.usa.am/ assistance.

40   Gregg, "Divided They Conquer."

41   See, e.g., SN 369, 377.

42   The very Orhan Pamuk who acknowledges Armenian genocide identifies also with the grand Ottoman past and with Atatürkian Euro-modernity (*Istanbul*, tr. Maureen Freely, New York: Knopf, 2005). There is nothing on the other side of "the Asian shore," as in Homer (see p. 210). Except this one sentence: "[I]t is not enough to say that Istanbul is much richer than Delhi or Sao Paulo. (If you go to the poor neighborhoods, the cities and the forms poverty takes are in fact all too similar.) The difference lies in the fact that in Istanbul the remains of a glorious past civilization are everywhere visible" (p. 101). I hope, of course, not to be a nationalist. The fact that Delhi, among Indian cities, is not strikingly poor (much greater poverty in Mumbai or Kolkata), or that there are easily visible ruins of earlier capitals on the same site, the earliest going back to the beginnings of the last millennium, or yet that Edward Lutyens's grand colonial Delhi is as "Westernized" – Pamuk's favorite word – as you could hope for, does not necessarily trouble me. Perhaps the analogy with Sao Paulo does not work either. I just mind that such texts cannot foster a pluralized Asian *synoikismos*, a word used by Edward Soja to mean the creation of economic and ecological interdependencies whose cohabitation in space is rendered purposeful (Edward W. Soja, *Postmetropolis: Critical Studies of Cities and Regions*, Oxford: Blackwell, 2000, p. 12). Pamuk's novel *Snow* (tr. Maureen Freely, New York: Knopf, 2004) shows the epistemic divide between this Turkey and the more susceptible hinterland. Paradoxically, this too is a scenario not readily reducible to a postcolonial narrativization.

43   I have sharpened the difference between postcolonial and postimperial in "Supplementing Third Space," keynote lecture, Seminar on Third Space, Malmö-Lund (Sweden), November 30, 2002.

44   This account leans heavily on Mesrob J. Seth, *Armenians in India* (Kolkata: M. J. Seth, 1937). Part of the pro-British tone of the book may well be due to the fact that it was written in the heyday of British India. But that may also be symptomatic of what I am describing here.

45   Ranajit Guha et al., eds., *Subaltern Studies* (Delhi: Oxford Univ. Press, 1982–), vols. 1–4 until 1987.

46   Francis Rolt, *The Last Armenian* (London: Hamilton, 1987). I am grateful to Shapan Adnan for mentioning this book to me.

47   Walker, *Armenia*, pp. 179–81.

48   This is a shorthand summary of a Foucauldian trajectory: force-fields are unmotivated and sub-individual. The "simple [Foucault's word would be "rarefied"] and contentless" face-to-face clusters in them are activated to give what I, an old Marxist, can only call "ideological" content. Power in the value form.

49   The academic subdivision of labor makes itself felt in general theories of *Indian* colonial discourse and feminism as well. See CPR 199–244.

50   For the Lenin letter see Walker, *Armenia*, pp. 328–9. Incidentally, this letter, "To the comrades communists of Azerbaijan, Georgia, Armenia, Daghestan, and the Mountaineer Republic," may well provide the answer to Kassabian and Kazanjian's query. Given the miserable patterns of migration in that period, and the originarily diasporic character of the Armenians, the US move did not seem to correspond with the lot of political refugees. It seemed rather a new home and thus a metropolitan postcolonial discourse did not develop. For the full text of the letter, see Lenin's *Collected Works*, tr. Yuri Sdobnikov (Moscow: Progress Publishers, 1965 [1975]), vol. 32, pp. 316–18.

51   Lady Mary Wortley Montagu, *The Turkish Embassy Letters* (London: Virago, 1994).

52   See Mark von Hagen, "Empires, Borderlands, and Diasporas: Eurasia as Anti-Paradigm for the Post-Soviet Era," *American Historical Review* 109.2 (Apr. 2004), pp. 445–68.

53   On Armenian matters, I am always grateful to my friend Khachig Tölölyan for his overview of problems. Errors are of course my own.

54   Chorbajian, *Caucasian Knot*, p. 10.

55   Richard Giragosian, "Toward a New Concept of Armenian National Security," paper presented at AIPRG 3rd Annual International Conference, 2005.

56   Fiona Hill, "'Russia's Tinderbox': Conflict in the North Caucasus and its Implications for the Future of the Russian Federation" (Harvard Univ.: Strengthening Democratic Institutions Project, 1995), p. 4.

57   For "mochlos," see Derrida, "Mochlos," pp. 1–34).

58   Victor-Yves Ghebali, "The OSCE's Istanbul Charter for European Security," *NATO Review* 48.1 (Spring–Summer 2000), pp. 23–6. In 2004, some in Israel want the country to enter NATO. "Uzi Arad, a former Israeli intelligence official who heads the Institute for Policy and Strategy, says 'The Euro-Atlantic community is Israel's

natural habitat.' ... In his efforts, he has been joined by former American and European officials who helped manage the two expansions of NATO since the Soviet collapse and draft NATO's Partnership for Peace, which has countries like Georgia and Azerbaijan prettying themselves up for possible membership. One former American official, Ronald Asmus, who is now with the German Marshall Fund, said he has wondered why NATO, which extends through Turkey and is fighting in Afghanistan, was seeking partnership with Georgia and not Israel. 'Israel is already a Western democracy that shares our values and interests in a part of the world that is becoming central to NATO,' he said. 'So why is Israel off limits?'" (Steven Erlanger, "A Modest Proposal: Israel Joining NATO," *New York Times*, Dec. 19, 2004). But then, the next move: "Russia, for example, has withdrawn its support for an observation mission on its dangerous southern border with Georgia. The mission, run by the Organization for Security and Cooperation in Europe with American help, has been credited with curbing the movements of Chechen separatists. But in New York last Thursday, Russia's Minister of Defense, Sergei B. Ivanov, said the presence of American forces in Georgia and in Central Asia was 'a very sensitive issue for us.' Russia has countered with a military buildup of its own in the region. Not too long ago, Russia seemed to value American respect. Mr Putin is a proud leader of a proud nation that still considers itself a balance, if not a rival, to the world's only superpower" (Steven Lee Myers, "You Go Your Way, and Let Us Go Ours, *New York Times*, Jan. 16, 2005). I will stop here, but the moves will continue.

59   For an astute analysis of the interpretation of Azerbaijan within the stereotype of "Islam," see Farideh Heyat, *Azeri Women in Transition: Women in Soviet and post-Soviet Azerbaijan* (London: Routledge Curzon, 2002). For a representation of the Muslim/Christian binary, consider the following statement, included on the Nagorno-Karabakh Web page: "I will continue the struggle on the political arena to have justice toward Nagorno Karabakh succeed. We, Europeans, should be grateful to the Karabakh people for their defense of the frontier of Christian faith and freedom, and I will do my best to persuade the international community to recognize the Karabakh people's victory.' (Baroness Caroline Cox, Vice-Speaker of the House of Lords, Parliament of Great Britain, http://www.nkr.am/eng/news/). In the case of the Taliban and Saddam Hussein, we have seen that expediency soon gives way to

a more Judeo-Christian script. If in 2004, Israel wants to enter NATO, the Ukraine wants to enter the European Union.

60   Giragosian, "Iran and the Caucasus: Armenian-Iranian Relations," Center for Strategic and International Studies, Feb. 14, 2005, http://www.ArmenianDiaspora.com.

61   Hannah Arendt, "The Decline of the Nation-State and the End of the Rights of Man," in Arendt, *Origins of Totalitarianism* (New York: Harcourt, 1976 [1966]), pp. 267–302.

62   Obrad Savić and Dušan I. Bjelić, eds., *Balkan as Metaphor: Between Globalization and Fragmentation* (Cambridge: MIT Press, 2002). This is reflected in our inability to contextualize Slavoj Žižek's exhortation for universalism or Sartre's hagiography of Frantz Fanon. It is folly to think that an unmarked universalism can be produced in politics or philosophy. According to Marx, even Hegel, the great universalizer, was not capable of this! The vanity of human wishes.

63   "The Armenia Lobby," *Washington Post*, Editorial, Aug. 1, 1996 (Autumn, 4.3). It is interesting that two parties whose political positions are rather different are united in the lobby of their shared interest in Armenia. They are the Armenian National Committee, sympathetic to the old leftist Dashnak party, and the Armenian Assembly of America, more recent and liberal-right in its tendencies.

64   Smadar Lavie, *The Poetics of Military Occupation: Mzeina Allegories of Bedouin Identity Under Israeli and Egyptian Rule* (Berkeley: Univ. of California Press, 1990). The two quoted passages are from pp. 340 and 311 respectively.

65   Herman Melville, in his *Benito Cereno* (1855), had represented the victorious slaves representing themselves as enslaved as a strategy, raising this thematic of auto-ethnicization into a superb political fiction.

66   See Spivak, "Examples to Fit the Title," in *American Imago* 51.2 (Summer 1994), pp. 161–96, especially the section entitled "Migrants," for the consequences of the displacement of the colonial subject into the Eurocentric immigrant.

67   Gilles Deleuze and Felix Guattari, *Anti-Oedipus: Capitalism and Schizophrenia*, tr. Robert Hurley et al. (Minneapolis: Univ. of Minnesota Press, 1983), p. 10 and passim.

68   Here one might keep Foucault's suggestion of the double focus in mind (*History of Sexuality*, tr. Robert Hurley, New York: Pantheon,

1978, pp. 100–2). See also Arturo Escobar, "Imagining a Post-Development Era? Critical Thought, Development and Social Movements," *Social Text* 31/32 (1992), pp. 20–56. We remind ourselves of the sentence from Nigel Harris quoted on p. 12 in this book.

69   The reference here is to C3, "The Trinity Formula," pp. 953–71, where Marx questions the felicitousness of "capital-profit/land-ground rent/labor wages" as a "trinity formula applicable to all space at all times." The governors of the globe are, in effect, the permanent members of the UN Security Council.

70   For an interesting discussion of the time of the nation for minorities, see Homi K. Bhabha, *Nation and Narration* (New York: Routledge, 1990), pp. 308–11.

71   Consider the brilliant staging of the contrast between the Indian and *ladino* woman in terms of make up in Elisabeth Burgos-Debray, ed., *I, Rigoberta Menchu: An Indian Woman in Guatemala*, tr. Ann Wright (London: Verso, 1983), p. 210. The master text of race rather than gender making itself up as the enemy sees it in order to secure victory remains Herman Melville's *Benito Cereno*. The grandeur of that text is that in the main narrative the reader focalizes *as* the enemy and thus the final matter of the narrative becomes politically active without advancing a position.

72   Stina Katchadourian, *Efronia: An Armenian Love Story* (Boston: Northeastern Univ. Press, 1993).

73   The book was sent to me by an officer of the press with a request that I write an Introduction to the next volume in the series, written in "Indian"! (letter available upon request). Given the twenty-odd languages of India, my unpopular position in multiculturalist euphoria was consolidated, I fear. I was at the moment reading *It Does Not Die* by Maitreyi Devi (Chicago: Univ. of Chicago Press, 1994). The author's vehement denial of any race or religion lines in a strikingly similar love story gives us a sense of the very differentiation in the texts of imperialism that is my topic here. Let me put it in telegraphese: Classic-case-scenario + more-similar-to-than-different-from the British in India vs. conflictual-coexistence-acknowledging-difference-with the common Ottoman, within the lines of great waves of genocide, involving Europe in its range in Armenia.

74   Sara Cohan, "The World Was Silent," *Teaching Tolerance* 22 (Fall 2002), pp. 50–6.

75   And this just in. Please note the sly put-downs, which I have
     emphasized, rather different from the pieties of tolerance at
     home. Armenia is now on the map, not of Asia, but of a quaintly
     out of the way place US tourists can visit:

     "If you're thinking of spending your next vacation in Armenia – *and,
     really, who isn't?* – you'll be happy to know that this former Soviet
     republic now has its first boutique hotel chain." *This may be a sign that
     Armenia is truly "in," or that boutique hotels are officially "out."*
          The owners of the Tufenkian Heritage Hotels (www.tufenkian-
     heritage.com) are hoping their three new properties will lure tourists
     to Armenia's mountainous countryside, set between the Black and
     Caspian Seas. Each hotel features Tufenkian carpets, handmade by
     Armenian weavers, as well as local cuisine.
          At Avan Dzoraget, a 34-room hotel in Lori (on the main road to
     Tbilisi), there is an indoor pool, a spa and a gym. At Avan Marak Tsapatagh,
     on Lake Sevan – a popular lakeside resort town with outdoor sports – the
     lodge is completely constructed of Armenian stone. Avan Villa, a
     14-room hotel 10 minutes from the city of Yerevan, however, sounds the
     most stylish, with Frette linens and rooms with traditional Armenian
     fireplaces – the kind used to make lavash bread. But the Web site descrip-
     tion also proudly mentions that all Villa *rooms have "hot and cold water
     24 hours a day" – normally not a big selling point for the average boutique hotel"*
     (Jennifer Conlin, "Boutique Hotels Arrive in Armenia: Will Tourists
     Follow?" *New York Times*, Feb. 4, 2007, from the Web; emphasis mine).

76   This is a modified version of the last words of Virginia Woolf's
     A Room of One's Own (New York: Harper, 1989), p. 114. This cita-
     tion also connects *Other Asias* to my *Death of a Discipline* (New
     York: Columbia Univ. Press, 2003), where Woolf's prescient read-
     ing of the value of mere economic growth and personal inde-
     pendence is offered on pp. 41–53.

77   Tani Barlow, "Women in Re-regionalization," unpublished manu-
     script, 2003.

78   As of October 2004, the Association for Progressive Communi-
     cations (APC) has announced the launch of a new Africa ICT
     Policy Monitor Web site. With the second World Summit of the
     Information Society to be held in Tunis in 2005, this Web site is
     deemed particularly important and appropriate at this time.
     Collecting indispensable documentation since 2001, the new look
     Africa Monitor has a new design and structure to make it even
     easier for African civil society to find the materials they need to
     get in order to be involved in ICT policy lobbying.

79   The role of USAID in "reconstructing" areas first laid waste by US
      military intervention are too many in the second Bush regime to
      recount here, since this area has not yet transformed ethnic con-
      flict into a US war zone, precisely because of the logic of the
      Great Game. In this area, the US wants to be that other warlike
      thing: a peacekeeper, promoting the establishment of a Central
      European Peacekeeping Battalion or CENTRASBAT (SN 380).
      It is therefore not altogether irrelevant to notice the multitudi-
      nous irregularities, especially misreporting of results, that are
      now being reported about USAID in Iraq, a more sensitive area
      under greater scrutiny. James Glanz, "Audit Finds US Hid Actual
      Cost of Iraq Projects," *New York Times*, July 30, 2006, late edn (East
      Coast), xl.1.

80   T. T. Sreekumar, "State, Civil Society and Development E-topia:
      Information Communication Technologies and the Making of
      a Rural Network Society in India," PhD Dissertation, Division
      of Social Science, Hong Kong University of Science and
      Technology, Hong Kong (2004), provides valuable documenta-
      tion and analysis of the debate in the Indian case. Steve Woolgar,
      Virtual Society? Technology, Cyberbole, Reality (Oxford: Oxford
      Univ. Press, 2002), a book whose research was undertaken
      largely in Britain, convinces us of the gap between promise
      (they have coined "cyberbole" on the model of "hyperbole")
      and performance. The essays in the book emphasize the impor-
      tance of context. The final essay says something rather interest-
      ing: "the hype and rhetoric surrounding ICT is an important
      part of the technology itself. The fact that the rhetoric then
      comes adrift against 'actual' social relations is beside the point:
      it has already provided a measure of sorts for them" (Marilyn
      Strathern, "Abstraction and Decontextualization: An Anthro-
      pological Comment," pp. 310–11).

81   Audrey N. Selian, "The Use of Information and Communication
      Technologies (ICTs) as Tools for Institutional Transformation in
      Armenia," submitted for AIPRG 3rd International Conference,
      2005, p. 7. The subsequent quotations from this article are from
      pp. 3, 12, 6, 19. The organicist metaphor that concludes the pas-
      sage is problematic, of course. Let us rewrite it as not allowing
      the development of a democratic hybridity.

82   One source of such research would be Charles L. Briggs, *Learning
      How to Ask: A Sociolinguistic Appraisal of the Role of the Interview in
      Social Science* (New York: Cambridge Univ. Press), 1986.

83 Asghik Minasyan, "Targeting State Social Assistance to the Most Needy: The Armenian Experience," AIPRG 3rd International Conference,2005,http://www.armpolicyresearch.org.Information about the World Bank's Poverty Reduction Strategy is readily available on the Web. Gohar Minasyan and Aghassi Mkrtchyan show conclusively that "continuous high economic growth, including growth in the agricultural sector [agri-business, $\frac{1}{3}$ GDP], failed to reduce rural poverty" ("Factors behind Persistent Rural Poverty in Armenia," AIPRG 3rd International Conference, http://www.armpolicyresearch.org/Publications/Working Papers/pdf/WP0508.pdf. All quotations in this footnote are from this source). Indeed, they write that "[t]he elasticity of poverty reduction in respect to growth [in general] has been one of the lowest in developing countries." The authors also point at the unreliability of statistics, the unavailability of household information and the like. It is not too much to say that the subaltern is not speaking when we assert that there is an inalienable line between economic growth and poverty reduction. My entire argument about democracy and the largest sector of the electorate also applies here. It remains an interesting fact that, as a result perhaps of the detritus of the soviet welfare structure, "state benefits" remain one of the two most important "survival tool[s] for rural households." For the general argument the classic discussion is to be found in Jean Dreze and Amartya Sen's "Economic Growth and Public Support," in *Hunger and Public Action* (Oxford: Clarendon Press, 1989), pp. 179–203. See especially the distinction therein between growth-mediated and support-mediated strategies, and the related analysis.

84 The last few sentences are taken from Spivak, "Harlem," p. 124.

85 It would need too much preparation to launch the necessary argument here. International civil society, abundantly accessible to the metropolitan diasporic, often connects with different versions of locally benevolent feudality, which has no interest in the labor-intensive work that transforms subalternity through well-planned and executed pedagogy. Antonio Gramsci, "The Study of Philosophy" (*Selections from the Prison Notebooks*, ed. and tr. Quentin Hoare and Geoffrey Nowell Smith, New York: International Publishers, 1971, pp. 323–77) is pertinent here.

86 Thomas de Waal, "Crossing the Line – Reflections on the Nagorny Karabakh Peace Process," http://www.reliefweb.int/rw/rwb.nsf/db900sid/ACOS-64CF4M?OpenDocument.

87 Giragosian, "Armenian National Security."
88 Harvard's Kennedy School of Government produces a stream of such documentation. See, for one example among many, Hill, "Russia's "Tinderbox". Indeed, a sentence such as the following, mentioning Azerbaijan, shows that North Caucasus bleeds into South Caucasus by way of the Azerbaijan–Armenia conflict: "The North Caucasus is a tinderbox where a conflict in one republic has the potential to spark a regional conflagration that will spread beyond its borders into the rest of the Russian Federation, and will invite the involvement of Georgia, Azerbaijan, Turkey and Iran and their North Caucasus diasporas" (p. 4).
89 The excellent theoretical and empirical work of Petya Kabakchieva, based on, but not confined to, postcommunist Eastern Europe, is to be consulted here.
90 In "Rationality" (in *Philosophy and the Human Sciences*, Cambridge: Cambridge Univ. Press, 1985), Charles Taylor describes this as logical consistency. For rationality, leading to "theoretical cultures" in the heritage of Plato, he has a higher claim and uses it to show that "one culture can surely lay claim to a higher, or fuller, or more effective rationality, if it is in a position to achieve a more perspicuous order than another. It seems to me that a claim of this kind can be made by theoretical cultures against atheoretical ones" (p. 150).

This alarming essay needs to be unpacked more carefully than I can do here. All I can point out is that it shares a common goal with his object of criticism Peter Winch ("Understanding a Primitive Society," in *American Philosophical Quarterly* 1.4, Oct. 1964), and indeed with Peter Winch's object of criticism, E. E. Evans-Pritchard, *Witchcraft, Oracles and Magic among the Azande* (Oxford: Oxford Univ. Press, 1937): "how to make intelligible in our terms institutions belonging to a primitive culture" (Winch, p. 315).

As I pointed out in chapter 1, I am interested in "setting-to-work," not merely academic transcoding, "making intelligible." I am interested in "the task of recoding the ritual-to-order habits of disenfranchised systems with the ritual-to-order habits of parliamentary democracy, with a teaching corps whose idea of education is unfortunately produced by a terrible system." Speaking more broadly, it is an interest in how the non-scientists, the non-philosophers, the non-political-scientists of the world can share the basic consistencies of a reasonable polity: the public sphere.

Not every Westerner uses the arcana of "modern science" "rationally," after all.

Pierre Bourdieu started off the mother lode of anthropologizing Europe (*Distinction: A Social Critique of the Judgment of Taste*, tr. Richard Nice, Cambridge: Harvard Univ. Press, 1984) with this presupposition. Its flip side is to realize that we do not *touch* the "non-European" other *only* anthropologically, however benevolent, however culturalist. The trend that third-worldizes the colored metropolitan diasporic in order to "empower" themselves (grabbing power for the metropolitan viewpoint, as if it were only the academic lefties, whose hearts are good, and the desperate underclass, whose circumstances are bad) reproduces Charles Taylor's line.

Reading Zillah Eisenstein's "What's In a Name?: Seeing Feminism, Universalism, and Modernity," excerpted from her forthcoming book *Against Empire, Feminisms, Racism and Fictions of "The" West* (Zed Press) I went back in time to the eighties, when Taylor's piece was written. Politically correct, narcissistic in the name of "experience" ("I identified as a socialist feminist to distinguish myself from the mainstreamed liberal movement. Then came the revolutions of '89 and eastern European women's indictment of the misuses of feminism by so-called socialist states. Socialist feminist no longer felt like an effective identity. I started to just say I was a feminist. But then I also felt that anti-racism needed to be specified if feminism were to not be assumed to be white and western. Given the new excesses of global capital I am tempted to start using socialist alongside anti-racist again"), but of course an ally for those of us whose commitment to socialism does not swing on this week's flavor.

The rhetoric of the piece is a repetition automatism of "needs to be done" and its variants. The declared stance is obsessively non-Eurocentric. Who is the appropriately placed agent of these doings in the logic consistent with this rhetoric? Go figure. If asked the question, Eisenstein would no doubt produce a list of diversified figures and organizations. I remain mindful of Barbara Herrnstein Smith's wise caution: "Accordingly, I suggest that, insofar as we see ourselves as intellectually responsible scholars and teachers, we ... expose the straw-herring 'claims' and 'theses' as what they are, and take on the task of actually engaging actually existing ideas, relativistic and other. That means engaging them capaciously, in their extended textual

forms, concept by concept, analysis by analysis, argument by
argument, example by example" ("Conclusion," *Scandalous
Knowledge: Science, Truth, and the Human*, forthcoming from
Edinburgh University Press).

For me, the mere reason that can run the state, keeping it clear
of nationalism and fascism, is the commitment to consistency
shared by us all. The claim to a "better reason" that only Europe
has is as dangerous as it is powerful.

91   In *De vulgari eloquentia* (Marianne Shapiro, *De Vulgari Eloquentia,
Dante's Book of Exile*, Lincoln: Univ. of Nebraska Press, 1990), a
source-text of rationalist European humanism, Dante is ideologi-
cally compelled to misrepresent Biblical evidence to assert that
Adam spoke first!

92   See David Rohde and Carlotta Gall, "The US Has a Favorite in
Afghanistan. That's a Problem," *New York Times*, Sept. 26, 2004.
The presidential candidacy of Massouda Jalal is being so
claimed as a result of US intervention that it is impossible to
know her political position. Anticipating the next chapter, I
keep thinking of Anahid, the powerful woman on the Afghan
left in the early twentieth century. That same week, the *New
York Times Sunday Magazine* carried an article on former US
diasporics in Iraq ("Iraq's Disappearing Election"). To correspond to an era when Anahid was possible, I offer a returning
diasporic's memory of her Iraqi hometown in 1991: "Basra,
my home, used to be a modern port city. After I came back,
almost all the women were covered" (Elizabeth Rubin, "Fern
Holland's War," *New York Times*, Sept. 19, 2004). A single day's
newspaper does not constitute "truth." It is a starting point.
This is a longstanding problem with Americanization. I have
elsewhere cited Gramsci's insight that African-Americans
would be used to Americanize Africa (CPR 376). In 1887, there
were no Hawaiian diasporics in the continental United States.
The US officially declared Euro-Americans resident in the
kingdom legal voters electing candidates for both the houses
in the Hawaiian kingdom. This provision is to be found in
Articles 59 and 62 of the so-called "Bayonet Constitution" of
1877. This is clearly an earlier link in the chain of displacements that brings us to the use of diasporics in contemporary
geopolitics. In 1887, when territorial imperialism was still an
alternative, the "Bayonet Constitution" was a prelude to annex-
ation. Today the use of diasporics contributes variously to

"democratization" on the way to capitalist globalization and the dismantling of the state apparatus.

93   "Corruption in Armenia: Analyzing the 'Weak State' Syndrome from an Economic Perspective" (private e-mail, Jan. 2002). For an introduction to the state of the Southern Caucasus, Giragosian's Web site is an interesting place to start. He is himself a diasporic, of course. In this particular piece, which shows the folly of a nostalgic nationalism at this juncture, the writers call for a strengthening of the state through good governance. We are aware that this has to be accompanied by a persistent critique, for governance heralds governmentality. That is where subaltern (read electoral) education, in the house of the subject, is crucial. I discuss the relationship between subject and agent in this text and elsewhere. The authors also point at a commonly encountered fact that economic growth does not necessarily lead to social justice (read redistribution). And finally, they lay to rest a glib argument from the depoliticized right and left alike, that immigrants sending money home is a point in favor of migration: "Private Diasporan inflows, although providing basic but crucial subsistence support to families, when failing to be utilized by the country's banks or capital markets, do not result in sustainable growth." See Spivak, "Subaltern Historiography," *In Other Worlds* (New York: Routledge, 1998), pp. 197–221.

94   Michael Moore, *Fahrenheit 9/11* (documentary, USA, 2004).

95   Marine Adamyanm "Integrated Approaches to Well-Being and Quality of Life Improvement," AIPRG 3rd International Conference, 2005.

96   "Making Poverty History in 2006," Editorial, *New York Times*, Jan. 1, 2006, p. WK 7.

97   A. L. Becker, *Beyond Translation: Essays Toward a Modern Philology* (Ann Arbor: Univ. of Michigan Press, 1995), p. 12.

98   See Spivak, "Scattered Speculations on the Subaltern and the Popular," *Postcolonial Studies* 8.4 (2005), pp. 475–86.

99   Soviet information from the United Nations Economic and Social Commission for Asia and the Pacific Web page. Nagorno-Karabakh information from the appropriate line on their homepage. Hilda Grigorian, "Human Trafficking in the Republic of Armenia," AIPRG 3rd International Conference, 2005, http://www.armpolicyresearch.org. The next quoted passage is from the same source.

100   Archives of the Refugee Studies Centre, University of Oxford.

Chapter 4   1996: Foucault and Najibullah

1   I wrote this piece when the Taliban came into power in Afghanistan. I have not updated this after September 11, 2001. My reading of that is developing into a piece on the secular university. There is a naïveté to the piece, as if the reader would not be well-acquainted with a place called Afghanistan, suddenly a news blip, only to sink into oblivion again. I have not revised the tone, although here and there I have added a detail.

2   Michel Foucault, *Discipline and Punish: The Birth of the Prison*, tr. Alan Sheridan (New York: Pantheon, 1977); hereafter cited in text as DP, page references following.

3   DP 314 n. 1. The consequences of applying something like this narrative to all the children of the world reveal themselves in the interested manipulation of "child labor" today and are discussed in CPR 415 n. 133.

4   I have just had the benefit of listening to this in a concentrated form at the Conference on "Economics for an Imperfect World" (Columbia University, October 24–5, 2003); the session was on "Managing Globalization for Poverty Reduction" and the participants were Jeffrey Sachs, George Soros, Eisuke Sakakibara, Jagdish Bhagwati, Juan Somavia, and Joseph Stiglitz.

5   Cecil Rhodes, letter to W. T. Stead, August 19, 1891, in W. T. Stead, ed., *The Last Will and Testament of Cecil John Rhodes: With elucidatory notes to which are added some chapters describing the political and religious ideas of the testator* (London: Review of Reviews Office, 1902), pp. 58, 98.

6   Direct mail "Census" distributed to potential party members, 2003.

7   See "Foreword", n. 15.

8   Rudyard Kipling, *Kim* (New York: Penguin, 1987); references to the Great Game begin on p. 195.

9   Michel de Certeau, *The Capture of Speech and Other Political Writings*, tr. Tom Conley (Minneapolis: Univ. of Minnesota Press, 1997), pp. 3–4.

10   Samir Amin, *Unequal Development: An Essay on the Social Formations of Peripheral Capitalism*, tr. Brian Pearce (New York: Monthly Review Press, 1976). This is the largely implicit presupposition of the entire book.

11   Title of a piece by Robert D. Kaplan (*Atlantic Monthly*, Feb. 1994, pp. 44–76). In the intervening years, Kaplan has consolidated his argument, such as it is, into a full-fledged justification for US

imperialism, in *Warrior Politics: Why Leadership Demands a Pagan Ethos* (New York: Random House, 2002). Indeed, in the wake of the destruction of the World Trade Center towers, other books justifying US imperialism have started to appear. See, e.g., Max Boot, *The Savage Wars of Peace: Small Wars and the Rise of American Power* (New York: Basic Books, 2002).

12 De Certeau, *Capture*, p. 20.

13 See especially chapter II, Sultan Mahomed Khan, ed., *The Life of Abdur Rahman: Amir of Afghanistan G.C.B., G.C.S.I* (Karachi: Oxford Univ. Press, 1980), vol. 2, pp. 14–48. The argument from the *pharmakon* runs through this book.

14 Muhammad Mahfuz Ali, *The Truth about Russia and England: From a Native's Point of View* (Lucknow: London Press, 1886), p. 51. "Besides, the oriental mind" – we read in the next paragraph – "does not much appreciate a friendship which is based on high principles and noble intentions – a friendship which is always insisting on dealing in a straightforward and honest way with all questions, political or otherwise. For instance, the Ameer could never perhaps understand how it would be consistent with real friendship on the part of the British Government to help him *only on condition* that he never entertained any aggressive aims towards his neighbours," p. 51. I should like to detect irony in this passage but that may be wishful thinking. It is a pity that neither the British Library nor the National Archives in India, nor yet the libraries at Aligarh University and Jamia Milia Islamia could yield the original.

15 Etienne Balibar, "Globalization/Civilization" in Jean-François Chevrier, ed., *Politics, Poetics: Documenta X, The Book* (Ostfildern-Ruit, Germany: Cantz, 1997), pp. 774–99.

16 Toda, Gey this brings at least two things to mind. First, that the imprisoned members of the Taliban being held at Guantanamo Bay could not be given Prisoner of War status as stipulated by the Geneva Convention because they wore no uniform and could not be recognized as soldiers (Ann Slaughter, "Tougher than Terror," in *The American Prospect*, Jan. 28, 2002, pp. 22–7). And, second, of John Walker Lyndh and his successful masquerade and subsequent trial as "the American Taliban." Both these items are rupture as well as repetition.

17 Khan, *Life of Abdur Rahman*, vol. 2, pp. 32–5. Although the authorship of this volume is disputed, details such as this seem

credible. The historical containedness of nationalist colonialism is too outrageous an idea to be readily accepted. Consider, however, the general hybridity of the "Afghan." "The city of Kabul was also [in addition to the countryside] diversified in population. Of its 40,700 inhabitants (in 1876), 103,050 were detribalised Kabulis, 12,000 Tajiks, 9,000 Pashtuns (Durranis, Ghilzays, and Safays), 4,000 Hindus, 3,000 Kashmiris, 3,000 Parachas [people of obscure origin!] and 100 Armenians" (M. Hasan Kakar, *Government and Society in Afghanistan: The Reign of Amir 'Abd al-Rahman Khan*, Austin: Univ. of Texas Press, 1979, p. 14). Step back a century and you are into the hybrid Imaginary of the European: "… the true Afghans, in the limited sense of the term, are a race of Jewish or Arab[!] extraction. More or less mixed up with them are Pathans, of Indian descent, Ghilzais, who are identified with the Turk tribe of Kalagi, the Aryan Tajiks, the Mongolian Hazaras, and an assortment of other races … Afghana, it is said was Solomon's Commander-in-Chief" (Stephen Wheeler, *The Ameer Abdur Rahman*, New York: Frederick Warne, 1895, pp. 21–2).

18 As I have suggested since "Can the Subaltern Speak?" (1982), Foucault has always ignored imperialism as part of the constructive dynamics of his theorizing. This is why there is no notice taken in his suggestions for international nongovernmental humanitarianism that white folks energizing native radical groups replicate the structure of the robust benevolent imperialist traditions of schools, hospitals, etc. (see Thomas W. Keenan, *Fables of Responsibility*, Stanford: Stanford Univ. Press, 1997, pp. 134–74).

19 Barnett Rubin, *The Fragmentation of Afghanistan: State Formation and Collapse in the International System* (New Haven: Yale Univ. Press, 1995), p. 57. The next quoted passage is from p. 55.

20 Kipling, *Kim*, p. 311.

21 Rem Koolhas, *Conversations with Students* (New York: Princeton Architectural Press, 1996), p. 47.

22 Gregory J. Massell, *The Surrogate Proletariat: Moslem Women and Revolutionary Strategies in Soviet Central Asia, 1919–1929* (Princeton: Princeton Univ. Press, 1974), pp. xxii–xxiii.

23 Diego Cordovez and Selig S. Harrison, *Out of Afghanistan: The Inside Story of the Soviet Withdrawal* (New York: Oxford Univ. Press, 1995), p. 31.

24 *The Life of Abdur Rahman*, vol. 2, pp. 67, 198.
25 For a careful and largely sympathetic analysis of Amanullah's reforms, see Leon B. Poullada, *Reform and Revolution in Afghanistan: King Amanullah's Failure to Modernize a Tribal Society* (Ithaca: Cornell Univ. Press, 1973).
26 Polly Toynbee, "Behind the Burqa," *Guardian*, Sept. 28, 2001.
27 Claude Lévi-Strauss, *Structural Anthropology*, tr. Claire Jacobson and Brooke Grundfest Schoepf (Garden City, NY: Anchor, 1967).
28 Mohammad Hashim Kamali, *Law in Afghanistan: A Study of the Constitutions, Matrimonial Law and the Judiciary* (Leiden: E. J. Brill, 1985), pp. 1, vii.
29 *The United Nations and the Advancement of Women: 1945–1995* (New York: United Nations, 1995), p. 180.
30 Thomas L. Friedman, "The Least Bad Option," *New York Times*, Oct. 12, 2003. This rational liberatory pose seems dangerous if one glances at the fantasmatic degradation of women reflected in the pinups in the quarters of soldiers certainly staged as representative though diverse in background (American diversity!) by *Time International* ("War Ages a Roguish Son," and "A Soldier's Life," pp. 42–3, 37, Dec. 29, 2003–Jan. 5, 2004).
31 Spivak, "Ghostwriting," *Diacritics* 25 (Summer 1995), pp. 65–84. See also Djebar, "Forbidden Gaze, Severed Sound," in Marjolijn de Jager, tr., *Women of Algiers in Their Apartment* (Charlottesville: Univ. of Virginia Press, 1992), pp. 133–54 and *Les Blancs de l'Algérie* (Paris: Albin Michel, 1995).
32 Melanie Klein, *Love, Guilt and Reparation* (New York: Macmillan, 1975), p. 191.
33 Indeed, my childhood images of the Afghan, who lived 1,500 miles to the west, were altogether benign; from Tagore's short story "Kabuliwala," later made into a film by Satyajit Ray, and Syed Mujtaba Ali's *Deshe Bideshe*, in *Rachanabali*, vol. 10 (Kolkata: Mitra o Ghosh, 1385 [Bengali date]), an urbane account of Russo-Afghan diplomatic, intellectual, and cultural life at the time of Amanullah's deposition.
34 Mahfuz Ali, *The Truth*, p. 29. As a cultural stereotype that reflects upon Russia's subsequent use of Marxism, the entire passage is worth quoting. It is also interesting that, looking for examples of early Communism, Marx at 26 could not do better than German Coffee Houses (Karl Marx, "Economic and Philosophical Manuscripts," in Rodney Livingstone and Gregor Benton, tr., *Early Writings*, New York: Vintage Books, 1975, p. 364), just as Foucault's

example of modernism is Baudelaire as dandy (Foucault, "What is Enlightenment?" tr. Catherine Porter, in Paul Rabinow, ed., *The Foucault Reader*, New York: Pantheon, 1984, pp. 32–50).

35 Dinesh Mohan, "Rules of Academia," *Seminar* 434 (Oct. 1995), p. 23. This is one of hundreds of such passages that one might have selected. A recent influential entry is Deepak Lal, *In Praise of Empires: Globalization and Order* (New York, Palgrave, 2004).

36 Jacques Derrida, "Fors: The Anglish Words of Nicolas Abraham and Maria Torok," *The Verbarium of the Wolf-Man*, tr. Nicholas Rand (Minneapolis: Univ. of Minnesota Press, 1986), pp. xi–xlviii. In my current work, I am speculating upon the terrible possibility that suicide bombing is undertaken in extremis in the hope of undoing the division between mourning and execution – another sort of impersonal half-mourning.

37 Melanie Klein, "Mourning and Its Relation to Manic-Depressive States," *Love, Guilt and Reparation*, pp. 344–69.

38 This section is a reworking of *Thinking Academic Freedom in Gendered Post-coloniality* (Cape Town: University of Cape Town, 1992), pp. 16–17.

39 Ama Ata Aidoo writes a wisdom poem with comparable sentiments in *Our Sister Killjoy: Reflections of a Squint-Eyed Susan* (New York: Longman, 1977), pp. 86–7.

40 Farhad Mazhar, "The Corpse-Keeper of Revolt," in *Ebadatnama 2* (Dhaka: Prabartana, 1989), p. 36. Translation mine.

41 I can hear liberal and wise US readers recounting what a bad Najib he was and how bad the Soviet regime was et cetera. I can agree (or disagree) with all of that and still work with the figure who, at last ditch, was working on a translation as a remedy! A fellow-translator, and a figure: "Lenz" to my Celan (see Derrida, "Shibboleth," in *Acts of Literature*, pp. 370–413). Henri Bréaud's 1921 novel *Vitriol de Lune* (Paris: Albin Michel), with Damien as its hero, does not touch the thematic of cultural mourning or funeral rites at all.

42 Assia Djebar, *Fantasia: An Algerian Cavalcade*, tr. Dorothy S. Blair (New York: Quartet, 1985), p. 157; translation modified. This theme is continued in the depiction of the Algerian War of 1957–62 in a film named after the prison Barberousse. The women active in the War were so vocal in their objection, that the director Bouabdallah invited them to participate in a documentary where they recount their participation and their critique: *Barberousse mes soeurs*. I am grateful to Dr. Nadia Aït-Sahalia for showing me a

private video of the film. These are examples from South Asia and Mediterranean Africa, two major theaters of nineteenth-century imperialism. Of sub-Saharan Africa, Wole Soyinka has used the metaphor of "the open sore" (Wole Soyinka, *The Open Sore of a Continent: A Personal Narrative of the Nigerian Crisis*, New York: Oxford Univ. Press, 1996). His bitter and brilliant book takes no notice of women at all. Yet it is well-known that most sub-Saharan African cultures had a more active "traditional" role for women than a normative Euro-US narrative of feminism would allow. Ifi Amadiume, *Male Daughters, Female Husbands: Gender and Sex in African Society* (Atlantic Highlands, NJ: Zed Books, 1987) tells part of the story. Buchi Emecheta, *The Rape of Shavi* (New York: G. Braziller, 1985) instantiates it in fiction. For South Africa, my best example is J. M. Coetzee's *Disgrace* (New York: Viking, 2000), which stages a critique of the Enlightenment as a critique of heteronormativity.

43 For a description of this see Leerom Medovoi et al., "Can the Subaltern Vote?" *Socialist Review* 20.3 (July–Sept. 1990), pp. 133–49.

44 Michael Ignatieff, "Nation-Building Lite" (*New York Times Magazine*, July 28, 2002, pp. 26–34). It seems utterly amazing to me that Ignatieff calls positions against imperialism merely "politically correct": Gandhi, Nehru, Fanon, Toussaint l'Ouverture, Nelson Mandela, José Martí simply "p.c."! Ignatieff has elaborated upon the theme of imperial America once again in the pages of the *New York Times Magazine* ("The Burden," Jan. 5, 2003, pp. 22–30), and finally, as indicated in "Why Are We in Iraq? (And Liberia? And Afghanistan?)" (*New York Times*, Sept. 7, 2003, p. 38).

45 See Spivak, "Feudalism and Democracy: A True Story," *Economic and Political Weekly* (forthcoming).

46 These words from de Certeau are quoted on p. 20. The protocol of de Certeau's book strains toward an opening into "responsibility," as, I will argue below, does Mahmood Mamdani's. De Certeau, albeit in his language of binary oppositions, gives a rare description of the script our educational philosophy desperately presupposes and tries to be haunted by, as a "passive belonging": "On the one hand, practices, or traditional ways of doing things that belong to the group, are henceforth deployed in the network of different givens that another order imposes; on the other hand, *collective fragments of memory* constitute, whether consciously or unconsciously, the roots or the 'fixed points' by which a collective irreducibility is engraved in individual members. The first might

designate the 'active' traits of a belonging, while the latter are 'passive,' if these two terms are understood as styles of production and forms of inscription" (p. 161). Yet he too, like Mamdani, cannot get beyond the language of "collective *rights*" as "capable of balancing the economy that, in the name of individual rights, exposes the entire social reality to the great universal light of the market and of the administration" (p. 157). This may be because, like Benedict Anderson, de Certeau too cannot enter pre-coloniality as a terrain of subjectship; and like Balibar, his resistant history begins with the migrant as minority: "He or she [translator's silent politically correct modification] is the exemplary figure imposed by modernity" (p. 133). I quote my sullen marginal note: "*yr.* mod.ty." The imposed "other order" in the longer passage is the metropolitan state in migrancy, not imperialism in the colony. It must be admitted that Derrida tries to drag responsibility into collectivity in the opening pages of the mysterious section entitled "*tout autre est tout autre*" (every other is altogether other) in the *Gift of Death* (tr. David Wills, Chicago: Univ. of Chicago Press, 1995, pp. 82–115). And he asks the question of woman there. As I have pointed out elsewhere, he prudently leaves the question open. You see how much is at stake in the subaltern girl-child.

47   Paulo Freire, *Pedagogy of the Oppressed*, tr. Myra Bergman Ramos (New York: Continuum, 2000 [1968]).

48   M. Hasan Kakar, *Afghanistan: A Study of International Political Developments, 1880–1896* (Kabul: Kabul University, 1971), pp. 291–4. All the quotations are from these pages. I am grateful to Hauman Sarshar for walking me through the text and to Hamid Dabashi for enriching my reading with etymological advice.

49   For the irreducible performative-constative ruse see, as always, Derrida, "Declarations of Independence," tr. Tom Keenan and Tom Pepper, *New Political Science* 15 (Summer 1986), pp. 7–15.

50   In this 800 year old proto-nationalist tract, Dante theorizes the emergence of a curial Italian which relates to Latin as the colloquial to the grammatical.

51   Kakar, *Afghanistan*, p. ii.

52   How is *haq* being used, for example, by the fifteenth-century Indian mystic Kabir? I discuss it in the context of the draft Afghan Constitution.

53   At the other extreme, Barnett Rubin cites this as an example of the Amir as imam (*Fragmentation*, p. 50).

54 The English word "sovereign" has performed this sort of occlusion elsewhere as well. Witness the situation of the Treaty of Waitangi, signed in 1840 by representatives of the British Crown and Maori chiefs, that inaugurated modern New Zealand. Where English says "sovereign," Maori says "Rangatira," a word more aligned to something like governance. It is no surprise that Giorgio Agamben's account of sovereignty does not comment on this particular double-edged-ness of the word. I feel that the word can be classed with "supplement" (see Derrida, *Of Grammatology*, pp. 141–64). In *Rogues*, Derrida consolidates his earlier discussions of sovereignty and points at the impossibility of pure sovereignty, because, being self-sufficient, it cannot move. It cannot save itself, because it is auto-immune. This powerful opening cannot be discussed here.

55 Read too quickly, this remark would generate accusations of nativism, essentialism, cultural conservatism, even sympathy with fundamentalism. Yet on August 23, 1997, the day I wrote the words, New York 1 News reported approvingly on two children's programs. One, called "Passing On," trained them in Caribbean dance steps. The other, where they got T-shirts, took them to the floor of the New York Stock Exchange. This too is children's education: relegating "tradition" to "culture" and a past museumized into a dynamic present being played out on the subject's involvement with the Stock Exchange. We are trying to undo this pattern. For, to graft the indeterminacy of rights-and-responsibility on to capitalism, persistently, would be the real trick of the socialist movement. The welfare state is not just the public use of reason and the rule of law. It can only work through an accountability that is the necessary but impossible translation of the time perhaps gifted to the subject. A secular access to this is through the empowered imagination. The rapaciousness of the generally imaginatively decrepit USA today teaches us that lesson.

56 "Most modern Afro-Asia is free, and the overwhelming majority of these nations had been overseas colonies of European nations. Many of their problems, therefore, have been inherited as legacies of empire. ... An important exception to the above processes is Afghanistan, which, although never actually a colony of an European power, did find itself an unwilling and unwitting pawn in the nineteenth century power struggles between Czarist Russia and Victorian England" (Louis Dupree, "Foreword," in Kakar, *Afghanistan*, p. 1). At this point, Dupree could simply write that

Afghanistan was "a hodge-podge of tribal and ethnic units moving toward the creation of a modern nation-state, a process continuing today." Our faithful Mahfuz Ali showed greater prescience in 1885 and recommended partition between Russia and Britain: "From the European standard, such a partition would perhaps be looked upon as a rare blessing. The verdict would, not improbably, go forth that, a petty State, in a miserable corner of the earth, which could not justify its existence by acquiring civilization on its own account, was improved off its face by two great civilized powers, bent on eradicating barbarism from such dreary, inhospitable regions" (Ali, *Truth*, p. 56). Najibullah was hoping to ward off such verdicts, a century later. The second volume of Abd-ur Rahman's *Life* was probably composed by his Indian secretary. For a comparable set of opinions from a colonial subject who was obliged to contain his racism, the book makes interesting reading. Most biographers conjecture that it was as a result of the contents of this volume that Abd-ur Rahman's heir Nasirullah banished the secretary from Afghanistan.

57 To see the contradictory presuppositions generated by these historical ironies, consider the peculiar loyalties of David Prosser, *Out of Afghanistan* (Montreal: Eden Press, 1987).

58 Réda Bensmaïa, "The Phantom Mediators: Reflections on the Nature of Violence in Algeria," *Diacritics* 27.2 (1997), pp. 85–97. Let us assume for a moment, with Michel de Certeau, that communication can be successful, and attend to his words about mediators, far from phantom: "We should like to associate these mediator/intermediaries with shifters who can identify information that can be memorized in its general form, who retain it, and then retransmit it in a particularized translation that is set into a specific situation according to the requirements of the interlocutor, the circumstances, and the context of the transmission. In this sense, these cultural intermediaries are first of all *translators* who decode and recode fragments of knowledge, link them, transform them by generalization, convey them from one case to another through analogy or extrapolation, treat every conjuncture of events by comparison with a preceding experience, and, in accord with their own style, shape a juridical logic of the general and the particular, of norms, and of qualities of action and time" (de Certeau, *Capture*, p. 117). The metropolitan migrant mediator at least translates as a ghost, in an archaic metaphor, as a translation of the fleshed body, as, perhaps, that which can also be metaphorized

as the "original," shared by ghost and person, that which makes the ghost *this* ghost. By contrast, the translations in the "buffer state," as we have noticed in the case of the English translation of the proclamation of the Muhammadzay "[e]ras[es] the past by mobilizing it in the service of the ideology that it is supposed to confirm [and therefore] also ... negat[es] the alterity of others or of the future" (ibid., p. 45). This can only lead to counter-translations, attempted by individuals like Amanullah or Najibullah, that must needs be cut off. There is no mediation here.

59   Frank A. Martin, *Under the Absolute Amir* (New York: Harper, 1907).

60   Compare the working of this animal-machine to the reckoning (*Zurechnungsfähig*) approach of mere reason, "which by nature finds moral working-through [*Bearbeitung*] vexing" (Kant, "Mere Reason," p. 95). Derrida has found a similar problem in Jean-Luc Nancy's typographical negotiations to solve a problem which should be named "aporia" (Derrida, *Rogues*, pp. 50–3). By contrast, Mao's problem was to bring about subaltern (and elite) epistemic re-coding by rational imposition – mere reason without moral working-through in another form.

61   Cordovez and Harrison, *Out of Afghanistan*, p. 374.

62   Rubin, *Fragmentation*, p. 76.

63   Khan, *Life of Abdur Rahman*, vol. 2, p. 43.

64   This is the general argument of Kaplan, "Coming Anarchy."

65   It is only when, through collision with an alien discursive formation, subalternity brings itself into crisis and thus creates insurgency, that we can begin to track it. This is the lesson of the Subaltern Studies collective. I can understand the Sioux ghost dance religion of 1890–1 by this logic (James Mooney, *The Ghost-Dance Religion and the Sioux Outbreak of 1890*, Lincoln: Univ. of Nebraska Press, 1991 [1896]).

66   Habermas's notion of constitutional patriotism is not feasible without massive systemic change in the global South. Habermas pays no attention to globalization.

67   Marx, "Economic and Philosophical Manuscripts," pp. 327 ff.

68   In order not to be inaccessible to the general reader, I suggest in a footnote that, in the field of responsibility, economy and ecology can at best be each other's *différance*, in the way that I have described in "Supplementing Marxism," in Bernd Magnus and Stephen Cullenberg, eds., *Whither Marxism?* (New York: Routledge),

pp. 109–19. This *différance* is a disclosure in erasure of the call of the radically other, one of whose transcendental figurations is what we call Nature.

69   "There are at least four main categories of threats to security, namely: *military, economic, social,* and *ecological threats*" (*Conceptual Framework: Encyclopedia of Life Support Systems*, Whitstable: Oyster Press, 1997, p. 13). Kaplan, "Coming Anarchy," pp. 54–60. As Kaplan writes sentences such as: "It is time to understand 'the environment' for what it is: *the* national security issue of the twenty-first century" (p. 58), he seems unaware that the environment has been a chief global issue for a few decades now.

70   Farhad Mazhar has produced figures to show that, if traditional seeds are cultivated in an optimal way, the results are more than competitive with genetically engineered high-yield seeds, supported by chemical fertilizers (unpublished Research Report available upon request), even on a large scale, though not, of course, as large as super-state subsidized agri-business.

71   *Aajkal*, Nov. 16, 2004, p. 5.

72   See my discussion of Bruce Ackerman's interpretation of US constitutionality in the first part of Spivak, "Scattered Speculations on the Question of Culture Studies," in *Outside in the Teaching Machine*, pp. 258–62. Am I doing more than reminding us that when someone like Frank Chikane rightly remarks about Black Consciousness, as I do here about academic freedom, that it is "a means to ... the end ... that we'd move into a non-racial type of society where there would be justice," the justice meant is a task rather than an event (Raymond Suttner and Jeremy Cronin, *Thirty Years of the Freedom Charter*, Johannesburg: Ravan Press, 1986, p. 236.)

73   Marx knew that a contentless concept was simply a way to make things measurable and therefore defined the value-form as "without content" (C1 90). It would be interesting to compute to what extent guaranteed abstract freedoms are instruments of social measurement.

74   I am grateful to Nargis Nusraty for help with the Dari text.

75   Any extended reading of the document will also have to take into consideration the opposite case, where Dari set phrases are literally translated into absurdities. *Haq wa adālatra bartebok* – an approximation would be the juridical and the ethical – becomes "judicial justice and righteousness." *Din-e-mukadma* – approximately spiritual jurisprudence – becomes "provisions of the sacred religion," and, "of Islam" must of course be added. A bit like "in

the Christian God we trust." The most farcical is the rendering of *kasoi wa doyra* – approximately case and session – into "case or sphere," taking the literal meaning of *doyra* as a round thing. And so on ...

76   The word "qawm" is at least as complex as the word "nation." Here is a use of the word in fifteenth-century India: *sadhanma chhatees kaum* (transcription of the Hindi spelling, which lacks the Arabic guttural "q") *hai* (Hazariprasad Dwivedi, *Kabir*, New Delhi: Rajkamal, 1990 [1941], p. 179). Of spiritual effort, there are 36 "kinds." To comment on the genealogy of "kind" (*qawm*) here would be to launch a book. Kabir is probably using it to critique the notion of caste. But ethnicity seems absurd.

77   See the revised version of "Can the Subaltern Speak?" in CPR 267–8.

78   Bessie Head, *A Question of Power* (London: Heinemann, 1974).

Chapter 5   Megacity

1   Conversation between Robert Reich and David Bennahum on "Into the Matrix," http://www.reach.com/matrix/meme2-02.html.

2   Spivak, "Planetarity," in *Death of a Discipline* (New York: Columbia Univ. Press, 2003), pp. 71–102.

3   Saskia Sassen, "On Economic Citizenship," in *Losing Control? Sovereignty in an Age of Globalization* (New York: Columbia Univ. Press, 1996), pp. 31–58.

4   See Spivak, "Feudalism and Democracy."

5   "Beyond the Vision," *Economic and Political Weekly* 34.46–7 (Nov. 20–6, 1999), pp. 3247–8.

6   Ibid., p. 3247. The next quoted passage is from the same page.

7   Derrida, *Post Card*.

8   Sassen, "The Global City: Destabilizing Borders/Producing New Subjects," lecture delivered at Princeton University, conference on Comparative Literature in Transnational Times, Thursday, March 23, 2000.

9   Vandana Shiva, *Stolen Harvest: The Hijacking of the Global Food Supply* (Cambridge: South End, 2000).

10 Kevin Lynch, *Good City Form* (Cambridge: MIT Press, 1981), p. 385.

11 Spivak, "Planetarity." For internal threats to such efforts, see note 4.

12 Deutsche, *Evictions: Art and Spatial Politics* (Cambridge: MIT Press, 1996).

13 Bernard Stamler, "Artists Stake Out a New Patch of Turf," *New York Times*, Apr. 9, 2000, p. CY 4. Razorfish, an Internet company, pushed Isa Catto's studio into the Garment District. Gentrification may push them out with the hardcore industrials, who sometimes operate class exploitation, old style. The resistant opinion was offered in a telephone conversation by the sculptor Toland Grinnell, one of the artists featured in the piece. In 2004, the Museum of Modern Art returned to its lavish new quarters in Manhattan. P.S. 1 continues as alternative space.

14 *Kolkata 300: Plan for Metropolitan Development 1990–2015* (Kolkata: CMDA, 1990). I am not qualified to judge such planning texts. But it does seem that the entire document, coming out of the state of West Bengal rather than the nation-state India, is devoted to projected infrastructural changes, accompanied by real-space practice and land use, that has rather little to do with the city as instrument for virtualization nexuses.

15 I am not suggesting that living in Kolkata is "empowering," or that the rural or urban poor in Kolkata "are happy." Such misunderstandings seem particularly rife in Britain (Gary Day, "Muffling the Voice of the Other," *Times Higher Education Supplement*, Aug. 6, 1999, p. 23; Chetan Bhatt, "Primordial Being: Enlightenment, Schopenhauer and the Indian Subject of Postcolonial Theory," *Radical Philosophy* 100, Mar.–Apr. 2000, p. 38). I quote Shyamal Bagchee's perceptive words: "Spivak reads ... from an Indian perspective – which is one of many Indian perspectives available – and she speaks of the possibilities of a transnational literacy – not a postnational one. (We may recall how, even in the centennial year of Canada's confederation, Northrop Frye called this the world's first postnational society; and closer to our time Frank Davey has elaborated on that unhappy fate in his examination of recent Canadian fiction.) Spivak's critique of globalization comes untroubled by any deep fear about the disappearance of the world's nations, at least outside of the West – and it is precisely in the belief that a newer, non-coercive relationship of states can emerge, does she posit her notion of transnationality. I think she manages to see the West/First World/America as the Other, a

dim possibility for most of us living in the gradually homogeniz-
ing West – a fate which we in turn project, in faintly imperialistic
wistfulness, on the rest of the world. Postnationalism, Spivak
forcefully declares, is 'Northern radical chic'" (Shyamal Bagchee,
review of *A Critique of Postcolonial Reason,* in *Literary Research/
Recherche littéraire* 16.32, Fall–Winter/automne-hiver, 1999, p. 337).

16   http://www.nypn.org/htm/resources/janice-perlman.html.

Chapter 6   Moving Devi

1   *parallax* 1 (Nov. 1995), pp. 1–31; "Cultural Talks in the Hot Peace:
Revisiting the 'Global Village'," in Cheah and Robbins, eds.,
Cosmopolitics.

2   "Terror: A Speech After 9/11," *boundary 2,* 31.2 (2004), pp. 81–111.

3   I thank Jean Franco and Val Daniel for reading early versions of
this chapter. I thank Maitreyi Chandra for her understanding and
her help with library work. I thank Jessica Forbes and Blythe Frank
for their support.

4   "In Response: Looking Back, Looking Forward," in Rosalind
Morris, ed., *Can the Subaltern Speak? The History of an Idea* (forthcoming from Columbia University Press).

5   "Moving Devi," in Vidya Dehejia, ed., *Devi: The Great Goddess*
(Washington, DC: Smithsonian Institute, 1999), pp. 181–200.

6   It is this "mistake" that is reflected in the phrase "subaltern
nations" in Michael Hardt and Antonio Negri, *Empire* (Cambridge:
Harvard Univ. Press, 2000), the only consideration of non-Europe
in that monumental book.

7   The relationship between the metropolitan Hindu minority and
the overwhelming Hindu majority in India is reflected in another
way. From this essay one cannot surmise my horror at the violence against Indian Muslims and Christians perpetrated in the
name of Hinduism with the tacit participation of the machinery
of the state. Indeed, a largely unintended consequence of the kind
of cultural celebration mounted by exhibitions as magnificent as
the one at the Smithsonian is to lend sympathy and support for
such nationalist religious violence.

8   C. Mackenzie Brown, *The Triumph of the Goddess: The Canonical
Models and Theological Visions of Devi-Bhāgavata Purāna* (Albany:
State Univ. of New York Press, 1990), p. ix. It is still appropriate to
make such statements in a disciplinary textbook. For a somewhat

more scholarly register, see Thomas B. Coburn, *Devi-Māhātmya: The Crystallization of the Goddess Tradition* (Delhi: Motilal Banarsidass, 1984). No academic could be against disciplinarization. We are interested in what is left out when the discipline consolidates. These remains cannot become disciplinary authority as "experience." They can only interrupt knowledge to indicate its vulnerability and to signal pathways for the imagination, as dangerous as they are challenging. An inventory without traces.

9   In 1999 I read "[w]hat thus turns out to be interrupted, ... in the first moment of hospitality is nothing less than the figure ... of truth as revelation" (Derrida, *Adieu: To Emmanuel Levinas*, tr. Pascale-Anne Brault and Michael Naas, Stanford Univ. Press, 1999, pp. 52–3). Is there something like a relationship between the interruption of the production of disciplinary knowledge by "cultural responsibility" – to each goddess as guest, if you like – and that more austere, messianic insistence? Can the ethical subtend such quotidian common sense?

10   This story is repeated in all histories of Hinduism, often between the lines. For a sober and learned account see Sukumari Bhattacharji, *The Indian Theogony: A Comparative Study of Indian Mythology From the Vedas to the Puranas*, American Edition (London: Cambridge Univ. Press, 1988).

11   Biju Matthew et al., "Vasudhaiva Kutumbakam: The Internet Hindu." As I have already indicated I am a bit bemused as to why this was found unpublishable by both *Subaltern Studies* and *Diasporas*.

12   Williams, *Marxism*, pp. 128–35.

13   The argument about Marx is in Derrida, *Specters*, pp. 95–176. In making this move, Derrida draws upon Kierkegaardian-Levinasian thought, which is best explained in *Adieu*, pp. 70–8. In what follows in my text, the reader is asked to keep in mind that the two-ness of the Peoples of the Book is not the two-ness of the *dvaita*, although there is something like a relationship between them, perhaps. Derrida's work here relates, willy-nilly, to Jewish particularism and its vicissitudes, Levinas and Heidegger, if you like, and as such can take on board the figure of "a structure of feeling," not necessarily connected to an intending subject although, as Levinas at least would argue, it is indistinguishable from intentionality as such: "hospitality opens as intentionality" (Derrida, *Adieu*, p. 48).

14   This is how I think Derrida and Williams together. This is inappropriate, according to some, because Williams thinks only in

terms of an intending subject. I think "structure of feeling" can be
thought of as a tiny narrateme without violence to Williams's
system. It is of course (im)possible to think anything without the
trace of an intending subject. That argument would take us too
far afield. In so far, however, as "structure of feeling" is thought as
a structure, it need not entail the *philosophical* presupposition of
an intending subject, although the contamination of the philosophical by the trace of the empirical cannot be too strenuously
disavowed. It seems to me, therefore, altogether possible to use
Williams's bold methodological suggestion in a deconstructive
way. I speak of feeling in thinking as a way of knowing. *Pouvoir-
savoir* – the ability to know – is delivered by means of that structure, perhaps.

15 This is the first line of Rainer Maria Rilke's *Duino Elegies* (1923). It
means "every angel is terrible." Literally, "each one angel is terrible."

16 Mahasweta Devi, "Statue," in *Old Women*, tr. Spivak (Kolkata:
Seagull, 1999), p. 67.

17 Max Müller called this "henotheism" in the nineteenth century
(Friedrich Max Mueller, *Lectures on the Origin and Growth of
Religion*, London: Longmans, 1882, pp. 260–98).

18 Derrida, "The Law of Genre," *Glyph* 7 (1980), p. 206.

19 De Man, *Allegories of Reading*, p. 301. I have altered two words. I
invite the reader to ponder the changes.

20 Freud, "Moses and Monotheism," *Standard Edition*, vol. 23,
pp. 83, 93.

21 This is not necessarily "feminist." It can even be a limit to feminism within permissible narratives. Indeed, this is the problem
with Levinas's apparent privileging of the feminine. The best
treatment of the question of woman in Levinas is Luce Irigaray,
"Questions to Emmanuel Levinas: On the Divinity of Love,"
Robert Bernasconi and Simon Critchley, eds., *Re-Reading Levinas*
(Bloomington: Indiana Univ. Press, 1991), pp. 109–18. The general
insight about permissible narratives is part of Melanie Klein's
legacy, not necessarily connected to feminism.

22 The task here is to transfer Gauri Viswanathan's extraordinary
argument about "the resistances of converts to the erasure of
their subjectivity" (*Outside the Fold: Conversion, Modernity, and
Belief*, Princeton: Princeton Univ. Press, 1998, p. 17), *mutatis
mutandis*, to a pre-colonial setting. My friend Farhad Mazhar, who
introduced me to "responsibility" in Lalan Shah, tells me that I am
more interesting in my analysis of *bhakti* in Bengali conversation.

I had not sensed that as I wrote for a US audience. I am obliged to acknowledge that the "felt discourse" in Bengali will not translate, and would irritate the specialists even further.

23 For the sheer multiplicity of the *rasa*s, see Venkatarama Raghavan, *The Number of Rasa-s* (Madras: Adyar Library, 1975).

24 Lalan's use of *bhakti* puts me in mind of something I touched upon in the previous chapter. Derrida has always been a courageous critic of the state of Israel and has often attempted to be hospitable to Islam, the youngest of the Abrahamic religions. For us, the striking thing is the history of Islam's imaginative embrace of – hospitality toward if you like – grassroots tribal animist and polytheist traditions. Sufi is its millennial marker and Bengali rural Islam one of its most moving examples. If Bimal Krishna Matilal was my tutor in reading Hinduism, Farhad Mazhar, as I mention in the previous footnote, has introduced me to these hospitable texts, this counter-theological music. To call Lalan a Sufi is to give him the wrong name for the sake of general accessibility. Mazhar gives an account of Lalan's views on Sufism which I have been unable to trace.

25 In "From Haverstock Hill Flat to US Classroom, What's Left of Theory?" for instance, I have suggested this as a description of actually existing counter-globalist struggles in the Southern hemisphere (in Butler et al., *What's Left of Theory?* p. 31).

26 Parita Mukta, *Upholding the Common Life: The Community of Mirabai* (Delhi: Oxford Univ. Press, 1994) is indispensable for an understanding of women's *bhakti* in India today.

27 Achintya Kumar Deb, *The Bhakti Movement in Orissa: A Comprehensive History* (Kolkata: Kalyani Devi, 1984), pp. 122–200.

28 Ibid., p. 199. "Gora" (golden) is also a sobriquet of Chaitanya. Fault of karma could also mean just simply "fault." Edward C. Dimock, *The Place of the Hidden Moon: Erotic Mysticism in the Vaisnava-Sahajiya Cult of Bengal* (Chicago: Univ. of Chicago Press, second edn, 1989) is deservedly the text most consulted internationally. I have mostly consulted "Hindu" scholarship for the problem of negotiating the *dvaita* structure of feeling-thinking for uneven scholarly recoding, always negotiating with that unreliable autobiographical element, that "structure of feeling" that spells responsibility.

29 I say "emphasis" rather than "shift" because most of the members of the museum-going group also participate in an academic-institutional acculturation since childhood; which comes to the fore in the United States.

30   G. W. F. Hegel, *Aesthetics: Lectures on Fine Arts*, tr. T. M. Knox (Oxford: Clarendon Press, 1975), vol. 1, p. 340.

31   For the distinction between "story" and "fabula," see Mieke Bal, *Introduction to the Theory of Narrative*, tr. Christine van Boheemen (Toronto: Univ. of Toronto Press, 1985), p. 5.

32   Bhattacharji, *Theogony*, p. 158.

33   Woolf, *A Room of One's Own*, pp. 4–5.

34   Bhattacharji, *Legends of Devi* (Kolkata: Orient Longmans, 1996), pp. 46–7.

35   *Kālikāpurāna* 17.16, in B. N. Shastri, ed., *The Kālikāpurāna* (Delhi: Nag Publishers, 1991), part I, p. 179.

36   *Devibhāgavatapurāna* 7.30.37, in Panchanan Tarkaratna, ed., *Devibhāgavatam* (Kolkata: Nabobharat, 1981), p. 696.

37   *Devi* 7.30.45–6, p. 696; *Kālikā* 18.41–3, p. 194.

38   There is a large body of female-authored collective oral tradition and some written work which remains peripheral to the authoritative voice of these Puranas. Navaneeta Dev Sen has written two ethereal texts around this fact for the reader of Bengali (Navaneeta Dev Sen, *Sita Theke Shuru*, Kolkata: Ananda Publishers, 1996, pp. 13–78; and *Bama-Bodhini*, Kolkata: Deb Sahitya Kutir, 1997).

39   *Devi* 7.30.85, p. 698.

40   For "poetic function," see Roman Jakobson, "Closing Statement: Linguistics and Poetics," in Thomas A. Sebeok, ed., *Style in Language* (Cambridge: MIT Press, 1960), p. 358.

41   For "archaic," see Williams, *Marxism*, p. 122.

42   For a stateside account of this "passing off," see Matthew et al., "Vasudhaiva."

43   The list is available in English in Thomas B. Coburn's good translation, *Encountering the Goddess: A Translation of the Devi-Māhātmya and a Study of Its Interpretation* (Albany: SUNY Press, 1991), pp. 53–4.

44   Alexander Garcia Düttmann, "On Translatability," *qui parle* 8.1 (Fall–Winter 1994), p. 36.

45   Freud, "The Uncanny," *Standard Edition*, vol. 17, pp. 244–5. A discussion of this in terms of modern fiction is to be found in Spivak, *Death of a Discipline*, pp. 78–81.

46   On "focalization," see Bal, *Narrative*, pp. 100–14, and Shlomith Rimmon-Kenan, *Narrative Fiction: Contemporary Poetics* (New York: Routledge, 1983), pp. 71–85.

47   Subroto Kumar Mukhopadhyay, *Cult of Goddess Sitala in Bengal* (Kolkata: KLM, 1994), p. 50.

48 Derrida, *Politics*, p. 69; translation modified. It is not a good idea to describe a phenomenon as an unmediated example of deconstructive discourse. But this old historically uncertain settler colony – India – requires from me a bolder and more "mistaken" descriptive gesture than the more visibly violent examples of Australia or South Africa. I feel this even more strongly today having witnessed a *Manasā-puja* in an Aboriginal household yesterday.

49 Shambhunath Gangopadhyay, *Madhyayuger Dharmabhavana o Bangla Sahitya* (Kolkata: Sanskrita Pustak, 1994), p. 27; translation mine. I have tried to keep to the sense of *tal* in "error" as mistake and wandering. I have also tried to keep to the polysemous relationship between teacher and student – whether the teacher can only speak to students who are deaf, whether when the teacher says this the student is deaf, and the like.

50 Prankrishna Pal and Bijoykumar Pal, eds., *Meyeder Brotokatha* (Kolkata: Annapurna Library, n.d.).

51 Jacques Lacan, "The Splendor of Antigone," in *The Ethics of Psychoanalysis*, tr. Dennis Potter (New York: Norton, 1992), pp. 243–83.

52 Sanat Kumar Mitra, *Folk Life and Lore in Bengal* (Kolkata: G. A. E. Publisher, 1981), p. 9.

53 Brown, *Triumph*, p. ix.

54 I have put together two popular reference sources here. One is of course the dictionary. The other is Bimla Churn Law, *Historical Geography of Ancient India* (Delhi: Ess Ess Publications, 1976).

55 Bhattacharji, *Theogony*, p. 159.

56 Freud, *Standard Edition*, vol. 21, pp. 152–7.

57 Both the earlier Sudhir Kakar and the earlier V. S. Naipaul, coming from quite different politics but applying a "real" Freudian standard, had concluded that Indian men do not pass Narcissus (Sudhir Kakar, *The Inner World: A Psycho-analytic Study of Childhood and Society in India*, New York: Oxford Univ. Press, 1981, especially pp. 154–211; and V. S. Naipaul, *India: A Wounded Civilization*, New York: Vintage Books, 1978). They changed their minds through varieties of cultural conservatism from which approaches such as mine are to be distinguished.

58 Lacan's geometrics of the gaze pre-comprehend the Oedipus and cannot be significantly helpful here.

59 Nirode Mazumdar, *Song for Kali: A Cycle of Images and Songs*, tr. Gayatri Chakravorty Spivak (Kolkata: Seagull, 2000).

60   N. N. Bhattacharya, *History of the Tantric Religion* (New Delhi: Manohar, 1982), p. 283.

61   Not all *tantra* is *vāmāchāri* or sex-practicing *tantra*. See Swami Lokeswarananda, ed., *Studies on the Tantras* (Kolkata: Ramakrishna Mission Inst. of Culture, 1989). Nirode Mazumdar's use of the *yantra* points toward *vāmāchār*.

62   N. N. Bhattacharya, *History*, p. 333.

63   *Song for Kali*, p. 52; translation modified to reflect the philosophical vocabulary mingled by Sen with simple Bengali. W. S. Merwin has translated the line in the following way: "Look at all this. It's the bitch's tricks. / She plays the hidden game right out in the open. / She sets against qualities / No qualities / And she breaks the lumps with the lumps" (unpublished ms).

64   N. N. Bhattacharya, *History*, p. 370.

65   See Aijaz Ahmad and Gayatri Spivak, "Feudalism and Democracy."

66   In *Devoted to the Goddess: The Life and Work of Ramprasad* (Albany: SUNY Press, 1998), Malcolm McLean confuses the limning of desire and the use of metaphorology with the author's practice. It is like calling someone a psychoanalyst because s/he uses psychoanalytic imagery with conviction. In my estimation, Ramproshad's use of the available topos of the rhetorical question is somewhat overemphasized by McLean as genuine characterological astonishment at the contradictory "personality" of Kali.

67   Surendramohan Bhattacharya, *Brihat Adi o Asal Bagalamukhi Tantram* (Kolkata: Benimadhab Seal's Library, n.d.), p. 81.

68   B. Bhattacharya, *The World of Tantra* (New Delhi: Munshiram Manoharlal, 1988), pp. 357–70.

69   Parita Mukta gives a fine account of these practices in *Upholding*, pp. 41–2. The woman-as-procuress is active in the trafficking of women today. Here too, the *quality* of children's education is of crucial importance (Spivak, Jury Statement, *Casting Curious Shadows in the Dark*: The South Asia Court of Women on the Violence of Trafficking and HIV/AIDS, Asian Women's Human Rights Council: Report on Crimes Against Women, Aug. 13, 2003, Bangalore: 2003, pp. 101–2).

70   The possibility of this resistance is already inscribed in the socius. The opening lines of the second chapter of *Manusmriti* (the laws of Manu) are one famous engagement of it: "[now] understand intrinsically [*nibōdhata*] the constant [*nitya*] sustaining principles or code [*dharma*], assent to which is [already] a knowing-tendency of the heart [*hridayena abhi-anu-jnāta*]. Although it is

not commendable to be predicated by desire alone [kāmātma], there is no such thing as being desireless. To accede to (knowledgeability or) the vedas and to act (knowledgeably, or) according to the vedas [I put the alternative there because Manusmriti invariably inserts that heart-tendency clause] is desirable [kāmya]" (Panchanan Tarkaratna, ed., Manusamhitā, Kolkata: Samskrita Pustaka Bhandar, 1993, p. 19; translation mine). Commentators have worried about the heart-tendency clause, that would seemingly make the distinction between the proper name Veda (the ancient texts of knowledge) and the simple verb form "know(s)" as in the Brāhmanas (ya evam veda = "who knows thus" (Monier Monier-Williams, A Sanskrit-English Dictionary, Delhi: Motilal Banarsidass, 1993, p. 963) or vedāhametat = "I know this." Perhaps Manusmriti attempts what all lawgivers do: to equate desire with law. The commentators close this off. Kullukabhatta (fl. mid-fourteenth century), arguably the best-known commentator on the laws, glosses the invagination of desire (access to vedas contained in human desire) by breaking it into a binary opposition: srutisca dvibidha – vaidiki tāntriki ca (Manusamhitā, p. 19). Heard or orally transmitted wisdom (the most sacred kind) is of two kinds (as in dispositions) – vedic and tāntric. Since sruti could literally also take the meaning of hearing or rumor, there is the possibility that Kulluka, using Sanskrit as an active language, is also making a distinction between sacred knowledge (veda) and profane oral dissemination (tantra). It is only by reversing this already available distinction and then displacing it that tantra in the narrow sense discloses the possibility of resistance and begins to efface it by institutionalizing it, at one go. And the instrument of effacement is the relative autonomy of the baseline institution: gendering. The Devi is caught in it. Michel Foucault lays out the possibility of describing this sort of thing in History of Sexuality, vol. 1, pp. 94–7. There is no guarantee, of course, that that is how it "really happens."

71   Jacques Derrida represents comparable (though not identical) masculine contortion effects on his own part, in order to accede to his dying mother, in "Circumfessions," in Geoffrey Bennington, Jacques Derrida (Chicago: Univ. of Chicago Press, 1993). In the more "vedic" mode, it is also Derrida who warns us that, if we set a practical course on intractable "new philosophies," we risk falling into the opposite of the new. Yet one cannot quite ignore the call to sapere aude (dare to know). This see-saw is, I believe, the dynamic of Derrida, Politics, pp. 75–7.

72 Mukundaram Chakrabarti, *Chandimangal*, ed. Sukumar Sen (Kolkata: Sahitya Akademi, 1986).

73 Williams, *Marxism*, p. 127.

74 Ibid., pp. 195–6. For a fuller list, see Somnath Mukhopadhyay, *Candi in Art and Iconography* (Delhi: Agam Kala, 1984), pp. 102–4. How would Derrida figure this economic use of *bodol* – qualitative exchange in barter – in his consideration of the Arabic original in Massignon (Derrida, "Hostipitality," in *Acts of Religion*, pp. 356–420)?

75 See Sanjay Subrahmanyam, ed., *Money and the Market in India 1100–1700* (Delhi: Oxford Univ. Press, 1994), for a sense of the turbulence of the scene.

76 Chaudhuri, *Asia Before Europe: Economy and Civilisation of the Indian Ocean from the Rise of Islam to 1750* (New York: Cambridge Univ. Press, 1990).

77 Satyendranath Datta, "Amra," in *Kabbo-Sanchayan* (Kolkata: M. C. Sarkar & Sons, n.d.), p. 32.

78 Roland Barthes, "Introduction to the Structural Analysis of Narrative," in Stephen Heath, ed., *Image/Music/Text* (New York: Hill & Wang, 1977), p. 104.

79 Or indeed the parabolic impulse of the ten principal Upanisads, an altogether separate stream in the service of the *advaita* as such. Romila Thapar has connected this to the movement in India from lineage to state.

80 PIO (= Person of Indian Origin) is a category devised by the Ministry of Home Affairs of the Government of India in 1999, for granting certain visa privileges.

81 See Sen, "Introduction," *Chandimangal*, pp. 20–4.

82 Ibid. For the immediately contemporary situation vis-à-vis the global "rural," see George Monbiot, "The African Gene," *Guardian*, London, June 4, 1998, p. 22; and Bob Herbert, "At What Cost?" *New York Times*, June 7, 1998.

83 The phrase "willing suspension of disbelief" is from one of the great texts of English literary criticism that generations of disciplinary students of English are invited to internalize (Samuel Taylor Coleridge, *Biographia Literaria*, New York: Dutton, 1960, pp. 168–9).

84 Derrida, " 'This Strange Institution Called Literature'," in *Acts of Literature*, p. 49.

85 Kant, *Critique of the Power of Judgment*, p. 111.

86 Wordsworth does speak of producing good cultural *habits* in *Lyrical Ballads and Other Poems*, ed. James Butler and Karen Green (Ithaca: Cornell Univ. Press, 1992), p. 745.

87 One of the women interviewed is not even conventionally "decrepit." I hope to comment on her extraordinary remarks about her chosen life in a more appropriate context.

88 I am thinking also of Sivani Chakravorty (1913–2003) who, a month before her death, in a shaking hand, cites in her journal a poem of Radha addressing Death as the image of her dark lover. What is it to cite in extremis? That, I have argued, is the essence of *bhakti*, divided-toward-the-other. Ms Chakravorty, institutionally educated in Bengali literature, quotes a modern version of the subaltern song, by Rabindranath Tagore; and she keeps her distance: "for me now it is as if dear Death you're like my Shyam." I have argued elsewhere that her generation of women was the implied reader of a significant section of Tagore's fiction and poetry (Spivak, "Burden of English," in Carol Breckenridge and Peter van der Veer, eds., *Orientalism and the Postcolonial Predicament: Perspectives on South Asia*, Philadelphia: Univ. of Pennsylvania Press, 1993), pp. 137–8.

89 Jeffrey J. Kripal has read this act, and indeed Ramakrishna's life as a *bhakta*, as *tāntric* practice. For the former, see Kripal, *Kālī's Child: The Mystical and the Erotic in the Life and Teachings of Ramakrishna* (Chicago: Univ. of Chicago Press, 1995), pp. 133–6. Unfortunately the book is so full of cultural and linguistic mistranslations that the general premise cannot be taken seriously.

90 I have not been able to grasp the simple poetry of the Bengali, where the abstract nouns are implied rather than stated.

Chapter 7 Our Asias

1 This piece was delivered to a Hong Kong audience. I have not altered the attendant enunciative pattern.

2 *Iliad* 2. 461.

3 See George Kimble, *Geography in the Middle Ages* (London: Methuen, 1938) and Natalin Lozovsky, *"The Earth is Our Book": Geographical Knowledge in the Latin West ca. 400–1000* (Ann Arbor: Univ. of Michigan Press, 2000), pp. 53–5, 70–7, 80–3, 95, 105–9, 112, 134–7.

4 J. B. Hartley and David Woodward, eds., *Cartography in the Traditional East and Southeast Asian Societies* (Chicago: Univ. of Chicago Press, 1994).

5   Andre Gunder Frank, *ReOrient: Global Economy in the Asian Age* (Berkeley: Univ. of California Press, 1998). The problem with arguments such as Frank's is that, in seeking to prove that there is nothing but world-systems continuity and that the argument from capitalism is Eurocentric, they throw the baby out with the bathwater. As enlightened Europeans, they want to give Asians back their history of economic dominance, implicitly underplaying the difference between culture and economy. In doing so, they emphasize commerce and credit and ignore the emergence of the working class. I am certainly against privileging organized labor as last instance. But all specificities of Asian (unorganized) labor, including its expansion into feminist economics, can only be played out over against that rational narrative. History is not just a repetition of cycles. Putting economy over against the state, as Jeffrey Garten can write: "However they [CEOS] behave, their influence will be at least as important as that of national governments and international institutions – probably more so" (*The Mind of the CEO,* New York: Basic Books, 2001, p. 7). Frank would simply admonish – it was always so. Our stake is with a future whose potential for change is in its undecidability, although, of course, there can be "no future without repetition."

6   Chaudhuri, *Asia Before Europe,* p. 23.

7   Orhan Pamuk, *Istanbul: Memories and the City,* tr. Maureen Freely (New York: Knopf, 2005) and *Snow.*

8   Martin Jacques, "Life and Death at the Bottom of the Race Pile," *South China Morning Post,* Tuesday, Mar. 6, 2001, p. 18.

9   Spivak, "Aesthetic Encounters," Keynote Address, Conference on Aesthetic Encounter, University of Kuwait, March 17, 2001. The pointblank refusal of the library at a reputable Hong Kong University to subscribe to the long-established and much-respected and consulted Indian journal *Economic and Political Weekly,* although the library possesses multivolume sets on Early Greek Philosophy and medieval Europe which I was often the first one to check out, is yet another example among many.

10   Aristotle already sets the stereotypes: "The nations inhabiting the cold places and those of Europe are full of spirit but somewhat deficient in intelligence and skill, so that they continue comparatively free, but lacking in political organization and capacity to rule their neighbors. The peoples of Asia on the other hand are intelligent and skillful in temperament, but lack spirit, so that they are in continuous subjection and slavery. But the Greek race

participates in both characters, … for it is both spirited and intelligent; hence it continues to be free and to have very good political institutions, and to be capable of ruling all mankind if it attains constitutional unity" (*Politics*, tr. H. Rackham, Cambridge: Harvard Univ. Press, 1932, pp. 197–9). Once Greece is recoded as the origin of Europe, we are on our way, establishing stereotypes that are legitimized and relegitimized by reversals and counter-reversals.

11   For these connections, especially with Yemen, see Engeng Ho, *The Graves of Tarim: Genealogy and Mobility Across the Indian Ocean* (Berkeley: Univ. of California Press, 2006). For the Indian Ocean rim, see of course Chaudhuri, *Asia Before Europe*.

12   Felicia R. Lee, "Filipino Rap Debates City Life, Pro and Con," *New York Times*, Sunday, Apr. 15, 2001, sec. 14, p. 1.

13   Macaulay, "Minute on Indian Education," p. 349.

14   Ghosh, *The Glass Palace* (New York: Random House, 2001), p. 446.

15   For a more detailed consideration see Spivak, "Deconstruction and Cultural Studies," pp. 14–43.

16   Unpublished lectures in the Shomburg Museum, New York.

17   Marina Carter, *Voices From Indenture* (London: Leicester University Press, 1996), p. 232.

18   I have coupled the two together to make a comparable though not identical point in the last chapter of *Death of a Discipline*.

19   Philip Foner, "Introduction," in Elinor Randall, tr., *On Art and Literature: Critical Essays by José Martí* (New York: Monthly Review Press, 1982), p. 24.

20   Jeffrey Belnap and Raúl Fernández, "Introduction," *José Martí's "Our America"* (Durham: Duke Univ. Press, 1998). The passage quoted below is from p. 6. The essays in the collection, especially those by Rosaura Sanchez and Donald Pease, redress the balance, pointing at the historical difference rather than effacing it by appropriation.

21   A reference to the general spirit of Hermann Levin Goldschmidt, *Frage des Mitmenschen und des Mitvolkes: 1951–1992* (Zurich: Nyffeler, 1992).

22   Colleen Lye, *America's Asia: Racial Form and American Literature 1893–1945* (Princeton: Princeton University Press, 2004).

23   Spivak, *Imperatives*, p. 2.

24   Sigmund Freud, *Standard Edition*, vol. 17, p. 245.

25   For Freud's disclaimers along these lines, see "Moses and Monotheism," *Standard Edition*, vol. 23, p. 27 n. 2, and p. 105.

26   Ferdinand de Saussure, *Course in General Linguistics,* tr. Roy Harris (LaSalle, IL: Open Court, 1986), pp. 67–9, 130–2.

27   Freud, *Standard Edition,* vol. 17, p. 221.

28   This is not the contrast between totalism and pluralism that Schmuel Eisenstadt discusses. That discussion describes a competition in the field of knowing: "By totalistic I mean that there is in these movements the potential to claim that they have [the] only legitimate answer" (Eisenstadt, unpublished transcript of lecture delivered at Hong Kong University of Science and Technology, n.d., p. 17). What I am pointing at is a contrast between the desire for the singular as a guarantee of my specificity on the one hand, and the recognition of the constitutive loss of the originary in the plural – a problem in the field of being: Who am I rather than What do I know? It should be mentioned that a certain pluralization of "Our America" beyond the binary is implicit in the disposition of Pablo Neruda's *Canto General,* tr. Jack Schmitt (Berkeley: Univ. of California Press, 1991); as in Pedro Mir, "Countersong to Walt Whitman," in Jonathan Cohen and Donald D. Walsh, tr., *Countersong to Walt Whitman and Other Poems* (Washington, DC: Azul, 1993), pp. 47–99. Yet a unified predication of a "Latin" America over against the United States is geopolitically possible in a way inaccessible to Asia, for which an antonym is impossible to find.

29   Penny Marie von Eschen has provided documentation on African-American pan-Africanism in *Race Against Empire: Black Americans and Anticolonialism, 1937–1957* (Ithaca: Cornell Univ. Press, 1996). An important period text is Alain Locke, "The Legacy of the Ancestral Arts," in Locke, ed., *The New Negro* (New York: Atheneum, 1968 [1925]), pp. 254–67. Richard B. Moore signals others in "Africa-Conscious Harlem," in John Henrik Clarke, ed., *Harlem, USA* (New York: Collier, 1971 [1964]), pp. 37–56.

30   For a discussion of the distinction between the Afro-Caribbean diaspora and Africa, see Spivak, "The Staging of Time in Maryse Condé's *Heremakhonon*".

31   Spivak, "Teaching for the Times," in Anne McClintock et al., eds., *Dangerous Liaisons: Gender, Nation, and Postcolonial Perspectives* (Minneapolis: Univ. of Minnesota press, 1997), pp. 468–90.

32   W. E. B. DuBois, *The Souls of Black Folk* (New York: Signet, 1995 [1903]); the passages quoted are from pp. 30 and 37.

33   Tony Cade Bambara, "My Man Bovanne," in *Gorilla My Love* (Vintage: 1992 [1960]), pp. 1–10.

34 DuBois, "The Negro Mind Reaches Out," in Locke, ed., *The New Negro*, pp. 385–414.

35 José Saldívar, *The Dialectics of Our America: Genealogy, Cultural Critique, and Literary History* (Durham: Duke Univ. Press, 1991); see also Colleen Lye, *America's Asia*, and William Peterson, "Success Story: Japanese American Style," *New York Times Magazine*, Jan. 9, 1966, pp. 20–1, 33–43. "Success story of one minority group in US," *US News and World* Report, Dec. 29, 1966, pp. 73–7.

36 Robert Hayden, "Preface to the Atheneum Edition," in Locke, ed., *The New Negro*, p. xii.

37 *Loving v. Virginia* 388 US 1 (1967).

38 March 20, 2001, Columbia Law School, Asian American Jurisprudence Panel. This material is not for citation.

39 Leti Volpp, "Feminism Versus Multiculturalism," *Columbia Law Review* 101.5 (June 2001), pp. 186–7.

40 Immanuel Wallerstein et al., *Open the Social Sciences: Report of the Gulbenkian Commission on the Restructuring of the Social Sciences* (Stanford: Stanford Univ. Press, 1996). It is a brave book, but altogether too abstract. The history is altogether European. The rationale is an encounter with Cultural Studies, feminism, multiculturalism. The description of these phenomena is vague and short (pp. 66–9). The spectrum of power is plotted between the United States and Africa. Asia is hardly mentioned. And structural change is by implication seen as isomorphic with epistemic change. It is interesting that the epigraph to chapter 3: "What Kind of Social Science Shall We Build Now?" is taken from that bible of the Third Way, Anthony Giddens's *Beyond Left and Right* (p. 70). For discussions of the report, see Amiya Bagchi, review, *Indian Economic Review* 32.1 (Jan.–June, 1997), pp. 117–18; and T. T. Sreekumar, "Reaping the Whirlwind?: Reflections on the Gulbenkian Commission Report," in *Review of Development and Change* 4.1 (Jan.–June, 1999), p. 154.

41 Kazuko Watanabe informs me of the consequence for UN feminism of the fact that "[i]ncluded in [the] membership [of the Financial Action Task Force, for example] are the G-7 [including Japan] and the European Union, Hong Kong, New Zealand, Australia, Singapore, Switzerland, and Turkey." This has more to do with geopolitics than with feminism.

42 Mark Landler, "In Hong Kong, Scholars Keep Safe Distance from Trouble," *New York Times*, Apr. 22, 2001, late ed. final: Foreign Desk 11. I am grateful to Avi Matalon for bringing this to my attention.

43   Michael Ondaatje, *Anil's Ghost* (New York: Knopf, 2000). The quoted passage is on p. 156.

44   Qadri Ismail, "A Flippant Gesture Toward Sri Lanka: A Review of Michael Ondaatje's *Anil's Ghost*," *Pravada* 6.9 (2000), p. 28.

45   See a comparable point about *A Room of One's Own* and the Gandhi–Irwin Pact in Spivak, *Death of a Discipline*, pp. 32–54.

46   *Seminar* 487 (Mar. 2000) gives a good idea of India's connection to East and Southeast Asia for the lay reader.

47   "Progress is Made Toward Free Trade Pacts Linking Asian Regions," *New York Times*, Sept. 5, 2004, p. 15.

48   Garten, *Mind of the CEO*, pp. 223, 281, 68–9, 82, 181.

49   John P. Clarke, "Going with the (Cash) Flow: Taoism and the New Managerial Wisdom," first published *Britannica.com*, Dec. 4, 2000, in *Research on Anarchism*, July 27, 2002, http://melior.univ-montp3.fr/ra_forum/en/clark_j/taoism_managers.html; Tom Morris, *If Aristotle Ran General Motors* (New York: Henry Holt, 1997).

50   Charles Tilly, "How Empires End," in Karen Barkey and Mark von Hagen, eds., *After Empire: Multiethnic Societies and Nation-Building; the Soviet Union and the Russian, Ottoman, and Habsburg Empires* (New York: Westview Press, 1997), p. 2.

51   See Frank, *ReOrient*, pp. 117–23 for a spirited case for the importance of Central Asia.

52   For a layperson's starting point on the historical and cultural diversity of Chinese Islam, see Dru C. Gladney, "Making Muslims in China: Education, Islamicization and Representation," in Gerard Postiglione, ed., *China's National Minority Education: Culture, State, Schooling and Development* (New York: Falmer Press, 1999), pp. 55–87.

53   Nothing can condone the use of living human beings to destroy symbols of destructive exploitation. I am a New Yorker, my heart breaks at the violation of my City's integrity. What I ask is a task for the imagination. Is it possible to imagine that much of the global South outside the upwardly mobile classes perceives the United States as an arrogant bully that does not think of others as quite human (whether objects of benevolence or malevolence) and this produces a dehumanizing effect?

54   See for example Francesco Bonami, "The Electronic Bottle: Dreaming of Global Art and Geographic Innocence," in *Trade Routes: History and Geography*, Second Johannesburg Biennale, 1997, Exhibition Catalogue, pp. 13–15. Francesco Bonami is the US editor of *Flash Art*.

55 Ranajit Guha, *A Rule of Property for Bengal: An Essay on the Idea of Permanent Settlement* (Paris: Mouton, 1963).

56 Hamid Dabashi, *The Untimely Thoughts of 'Ayn Al-Qudat Al-Hamadhani* (Richmond, Surrey: Curzon Press, 1999), p. 109.

57 See n. 59, ch. 3.

58 Somini Sengupta, "For Iraqi Girls, Changing Land Narrows Lives," *New York Times*, June 27, 2004.

59 Maryse Condé, "Unheard Voice: Suzanne Césaire and the Construction of a Caribbean Identity," in Adele S. Newson and Linda Strong-Leek, eds., *Winds of Change: The Transforming Voices of Caribbean Women Writers and Scholars* (New York: Peter Lange, 1998), p. 65. I have been privileged to celebrate the 150th anniversary of the arrival of the first Indian indentured labor on the island of Guadeloupe and have been able to write on this project of unity: "*Une expansion de l'âme,*" unpublished keynote.

60 See my gentle criticism of Radha Hegde and Raka Shome on "power-study cultural studies is better" in "Postcolonial Scholarship: Of Productions and Directions," *Communications Theory* 12.3 (Aug. 2002), pp. 271–86.

61 See Rorty, *Objectivity, Relativism and Truth: Philosophical Papers* (Cambridge: Cambridge Univ. Press, 1991) and *Essays on Heidegger and Others: Philosophical Papers* (Cambridge: Cambridge Univ. Press, 1991) for the most powerful example of this effort.

62 Jean Franco, "Indecent Exposure?: feminismo en la época del neo-liberalismo," Keynote Address, Conference on Women and Literature, Bel Horizonte (Brazil), August 24, 2001.

63 Frank, *ReOrient*, p. 226.

64 "Frame Resonance" is a concept in contemporary sociology. I first encountered it in John Burdick, *Blessed Anástacia: Women, Race, and Popular Christianity in Brazil* (New York: Routledge, 1998), p. 9. I contrasted it to musical resonance, resonance in detail.

65 *Collected Poems of W. B. Yeats* (London: Macmillan, 1965).

66 Kwame Anthony Appiah, "The Case for Contamination," *New York Times*, Jan. 1, 2006, from the Web.

67 Spivak, "Thinking Academic Freedom in Gendered Post-Coloniality," cited from Joan Vincent, ed., *The Anthropology of Politics*, p. 458. The passage quoted is specifically about academic freedom but applies upstream.

68 Spivak, "Scattered Speculations on the Subaltern and the Popular."

69 The most accessible may be "Culture," *Theory, Culture & Society* 23.1–2, (Feb.–Apr. 2006), pp. 359–60.

Index